# DEMOCRACY AND ITS CRITICS

# ROBERT A. DAHL

◆◆◆◆◆◆◆◆◆◆◆◆◆

# DEMOCRACY
## AND ITS CRITICS

◆◆◆◆◆◆◆◆◆◆◆◆◆

Yale University Press
New Haven and London

Set in Times Roman type by The Composing Room of Michigan, Inc. Printed in the United States of America.

*Library of Congress Cataloging-in-Publication Data*
Dahl, Robert Alan, 1915–
   Democracy and its critics / Robert A. Dahl.
      p.  cm.
   Bibliography: p.
   Includes index.
   ISBN 0-300-04409-7 (cloth)
      0-300-04938-2 (pbk.)
   1. Democracy.  I. Title.
JC423.D2478  1989
321.8—dc19                               89-5375
                                            CIP

The paper in this book meets the guidelines for permanence and durability of the Committee on Production Guidelines for Book Longevity of the Council on Library Resources.

10     9     8     7

# CONTENTS
✦✦✦✦✦✦✦✦

# ACKNOWLEDGMENTS
◆◆◆◆◆◆◆◆◆◆◆◆◆◆◆◆◆

This book has been in the works for many years. Perhaps, without my quite knowing it, it has been under way since I began teaching an undergraduate course called "Democracy and Its Critics" some years ago. I later gave it separately as a seminar for graduate students. I wish I had dreamed up the title, but I did not. A course with that title had been taught at Yale for some time before I took it over. The late Professor Louis Hartz also had given a course with a somewhat similar title at Harvard. Perhaps it was Hartz's course that B. F. Skinner had in mind when he had Frazier, the chief guardian in his undemocratic republic, Walden Two, remark:

> "I think you had better give the reader the whole story," Frazier said. "After all, you must realize that some fool professor is going to assign your book as outside reading in a course in political science. 'The Critics of Democracy'—something like that. You'd better be explicit." (Skinner 1948, 263)

However that may be, in much of what I have written in the last decade I was deliberately working out problems I intended to discuss in this book. Consequently, wherever I felt that a passage from one of my previously published pieces was pretty much what I wanted to say here, I shamelessly reappropriated it, though rarely without some revision. With only a few exceptions, however, I have not cited my own publications but instead I have listed in the appendix my earlier works from which passages in this text have been adapted.

My obligations are so enormous that I can explicitly mention only a few. It will be obvious to the reader that my greatest debt, and my most long-lasting one, is to the extraordinary thinkers from Socrates onward who have engaged in the everlasting debates about democracy. Without them, this book would not and could not exist.

Not many years after my first encounters with Socrates and his successors, I began to incur another long-standing debt—to my students, both undergraduates and graduate students, from freshmen to advanced Ph.D. candidates. They have stimulated me to think afresh about old problems, compelled me to deepen and clarify my ideas, and by no means infrequently have provided me with new insights. As I have already suggested, it was in my graduate and undergraduate seminars and lectures that I first began in a systematic way to shape the argument of this book.

My specific obligations to colleagues who have read and commented on some part of one draft or another are extensive. While indicating them here is scant recognition for their contributions, to acknowledge each more fully would burst the limits of an already long book. My thanks, then, to Bruce Ackerman, David Braybrooke, David Cameron, James Fishkin, Jeffrey Isaac, Joseph LaPalombara, Charles E. Lindblom, David Lumsdaine, Jane Mansbridge, Barry Nalebuff, J. Roland Pennock, Susan Rose-Ackerman, James Scott, Rogers Smith, Steven Smith, Alan Ware, and Robert Waste.

Although I offer the usual caveat exempting those I have named from responsibility for the final product, honesty requires me to insist that their comments and criticisms resulted not only in my making significant changes but also, I feel certain, in my writing a better book.

In addition, research by Michael Coppedge and Wolfgang Reinecke contributed greatly to chapters 16 and 17.

Finally, I am happy once again to acknowledge the superb editing by Marian Ash at the Yale University Press.

# INTRODUCTION
◆◆◆◆◆◆◆◆◆◆◆◆◆

From ancient times some people have conceived of a political system in which the members regard one another as political equals, are collectively sovereign, and possess all the capacities, resources, and institutions they need in order to govern themselves. This idea, and practices embodying it, appeared in the first half of the fifth century B.C. among the Greeks, who though few in number and occupying but a tiny fragment of the world's surface exerted an exceptional influence in world history. It was the Greeks, and most conspicuously the Athenians, who brought about what I want to call the first democratic transformation: from the idea and practice of rule by the few to the idea and practice of rule by the many. To the Greeks the only thinkable site of democracy was, of course, the city-state.

That extraordinary conception of rule by the many all but vanished for long periods of time; and only a minority of the world's people have ever sought and successfully managed to adapt political reality in some significant measure to its demanding requirements. Yet that early vision has never wholly lost its ability to charm the political imagination and foster hopes that the vision of an ideal but nonetheless attainable polity might be more fully realized in actual experience.

At about the same time that the idea of rule by the many was transforming political life in Athens and other Greek city-states, it also took root in the city-state of Rome. It is of the utmost relevance to our understanding of democracy that the pattern of the political institutions of the Roman Republic continued to reflect the original mold of the small city-state long after Romans had burst through the bounds of their city to begin their conquest of the Italian peninsula and eventually much of Europe and the Mediterranean. A thousand years after the republican government was superseded by Caesar and Augustus, popular government reappeared among the city-states of medieval and Renaissance Italy.

But the city-state was made obsolete by the nation-state, and in a second demo-

*1*

cratic transformation the idea of democracy was transferred from the city-state to the much larger scale of the nation-state. This transformation led to a radically new set of political institutions. It is this new complex of institutions that taken together we commonly refer to as "democracy."

Is a third transformation now within reach? Even if it is, ought we to make an effort to achieve it? These questions guide the discussion in this book. To answer them we need to understand not only why democracy is desirable but also what its limits and its possibilities are. If we overestimate the limits we shall fail to try, and if we underestimate them we shall probably try—and fail. One could easily fish out innumerable historical examples of both.

Today, the idea of democracy is universally popular. Most regimes stake out some sort of claim to the title of "democracy"; and those that do not often insist that their particular instance of nondemocratic rule is a necessary stage along the road to ultimate "democracy." In our times, even dictators appear to believe that an indispensable ingredient for their legitimacy is a dash or two of the language of democracy.

It may seem perverse that this historically unprecedented global expansion in the acceptability of democratic ideas might not be altogether welcome to an advocate of democracy. Yet a term that means anything means nothing. And so it has become with "democracy," which nowadays is not so much a term of restricted and specific meaning as a vague endorsement of a popular idea.

An important cause of the confusion over what democracy means in our present world is that it has developed over several thousand years and stems from a variety of sources. What we understand by democracy is not what an Athenian in the time of Pericles would have understood by it. Greek, Roman, medieval, and Renaissance notions intermingle with those of later centuries to produce a jumble of theory and practices that are often deeply inconsistent.

What is more, a close look at democratic ideas and practices is bound to reveal a considerable number of problems for which no definitive solution seems to exist. The very notion of democracy has always provided a field day for critics. Critics are roughly of three kinds: those fundamentally opposed to democracy because, like Plato, they believe that while it may be possible it is inherently undesirable; those fundamentally opposed to democracy because, like Robert Michels, they believe that, while it might be desirable if it were possible, in actuality it is inherently impossible; and those sympathetic to democracy and wishing to maintain it but nonetheless critical of it in some important regard. The first two might be called adversarial critics, the third sympathetic critics.

My aim in this book is to set out an interpretation of democratic theory and practice, including the limits and possibilities of democracy, that is relevant to the kind of world in which we live or are likely to live in the foreseeable future. But I believe that no interpretation of this kind can be satisfactory unless it deals fairly with the major problems posed by both the adversarial and sympathetic critics of democracy.

◆

What the critics often focus on are problems that advocates of democracy tend to neglect, or worse, to conceal. What might loosely be called democratic theory—a term about which I shall have something more to say in a moment—depends on assumptions and premises that uncritical advocates have shied away from exploring, or in some cases even openly acknowledging. These half-hidden premises, unexplored assumptions, and unacknowledged antecedents form a vaguely perceived shadow theory that forever dogs the footsteps of explicit, public theories of democracy.

By way of illustration, and to anticipate the argument ahead of us, let me mention a few of the key problems concealed in the explicit theories that make up part of the shadow theory of democracy. Many of these problems were present at the creation. Take, for example, the elementary idea of "rule by the people." To designate their new conception of political life and the practices it gave rise to in many city-states, toward the middle of the fifth century B.C. Greeks began to use the word *demokratia*. Although the root meaning of that term is simple enough, even self-evident—*demos*, people, and *kratia*, rule or authority, thus "rule by the people"—the very roots themselves raise urgent questions: who ought to comprise "the people" and what does it mean for them "to rule"?

What properly constitutes "the people" is doubly ambiguous and has frequently been a source of controversy. The first ambiguity is in the notion of "a people": what constitutes "a people" for purposes of democratic government? The Greeks took it for granted that the Athenians, the Corinthians, the Spartans, and the residents of the other numerous Greek city-states each constituted "a people" that was entitled to its own political autonomy. By contrast, although the ancient Greeks saw themselves—the Hellenes—as a distinct people with their own language and history, they did not regard themselves as "a people" in the political sense of a group of persons who, rightly considered, should govern themselves in a single democratic unit. Greek democracy was not, in fact, *Greek* democracy; it was Athenian, or Corinthian, or whatever. Although the city-state mentality may seem quaintly parochial today, the same issue is still with us. Why should Americans constitute "a people" and their neighbors the Canadians and the Mexicans separate peoples? Why should there be a political boundary between, say, Norway and Sweden, or Belgium and Holland, or French-speaking Swiss and French-speaking French? Or put the question another way: are people in local communities within a nation-state entitled to a measure of self-government? If so, what persons, on what matters? No doubt questions like these transcend "democratic theory." But that is precisely my point. Advocates of democracy—including political philosophers—characteristically presuppose that "a people" already exists. Its existence is assumed as a fact, a creation of history. Yet the facticity of the fact is questionable. It is often questioned—as it was in the United States in 1861, when the issue was settled not by consent or consensus but by violence.

The assumption that "a people" exists, and the further presuppositions of that assumption, thus become a part of the shadow theory of democracy.

The second ambiguity is nested in the first. Within "a people" only a limited subset of persons is entitled to participate in governing. These constitute *the* people in another sense. More properly, they are the citizens or citizen body, or as I shall often say here, the *demos*. Who ought to be a member of the demos? This question has always been troublesome to advocates of democracy. Democratic advocates, including as we shall see in chapter 9 many of its most celebrated theorists like John Locke and Jean Jacques Rousseau, have often proposed an explicit public theory of the demos that is remarkably discordant with their half-hidden, or sometimes wholly concealed, assumptions, which lurk unacknowledged in the shadow theory, from where, however, they are plucked by the external critics of democracy to be displayed as witnesses to the alleged self-contradictions in the democratic idea.

Again, historical experience lends concreteness to the abstract question of the demos. As we shall see in the next chapter, even at the height of Athenian democracy the demos never included more than a small minority of the adult population of Athens.[1] Although Athenian democracy may have been extreme in its exclusivity, it was in no sense unique. From classical Greece to modern times some persons have invariably been excluded as unqualified, and until this century, when women gained the suffrage, the number of persons excluded has exceeded— sometimes as in Athens by a wide margin—the number included. Such was the case in the first modern "democracy," the United States, which excluded not only women and, of course, children, but most blacks and native Americans as well.

While the exclusions are invariably said to be justified on the ground that the demos includes everyone *qualified* to participate in ruling, the hidden assumption dispatched to the shadow theory of democracy is that only some people are competent to rule. But the adversarial critics of democracy gleefully expose this hidden assumption and convert it into an explicit argument in the antidemocratic theory of guardianship. The idea of guardianship, which is probably the most beguiling vision ever created by the adversaries of democracy, not only was espoused by Plato in democratic Athens but has appeared throughout the world in a variety of disparate forms, of which Confucianism and Leninism, different as they are, have influenced by far the greatest number of people. The adversarial critics compel us to scrutinize in the full light of day the assumptions about political competence hidden in the shadow theory.

Another assumption that usually reposes unnoticed in the shadow theory (except when critics of democracy, both adversarial and sympathetic, force it into the open) is the question of scale. Just as the Greeks took for granted that the proper scale of democracy, or for that matter any decent political system, was necessarily extremely small—a few tens of thousands of people—so since the late eighteenth century advocates of democracy have generally assumed that the natural locus of democracy is the nation-state or, more generally, the country. In adopting this assumption, what often goes unacknowledged is how profoundly the historic shift in scale, from city-state to nation-state, has transformed the limits and possibilities of democracy. The transformation is so profound that if a fifth-century Athenian citizen were suddenly to appear in our midst he (being a citizen of Athens, it would necessarily be he, not she) would probably find what we call democracy unrecognizable, unattractive, and undemocratic. To an Athenian of Pericles' day, what we regard as democracy would probably not look like democracy at all, mainly because of the consequences for political life and political institutions of the shift in scale from the small, more intimate, and more participatory city-state to the gigantic, more impersonal, and more indirect governments of today.

One consequence of the change in the scale of democracy is to magnify the already significant utopianism of the democratic ideal. The public theory of democracy tends to assume that today's large-scale democracy can retain all the advantages of large scale and still possess the virtues and possibilities of small-scale democracy. And the public theory tends to neglect the limits of both. Thus the problem of scale is mainly relegated to the shadow theory.

A final illustration. Considered as an actually existing or real-world entity, democracy has been variously conceived of as a distinctive set of political institutions and practices, a particular body of rights, a social and economic order, a system that ensures certain desirable results, or a unique process of making collective and binding decisions. The central conception I adopt in this book is the last. As we shall see, this way of thinking about democracy—as the *democratic process*—by no means excludes the others and in fact has strong implications for the others. Yet any conception of democracy as a process will and I believe should cause concern. Critics, not only the adversaries but those who are sympathetic to "rule by the people," contend that a process of collective decision-making, no matter how "democratic," cannot be justified unless it produces—or at least tends to produce—desirable results. These critics thus cast the familiar problem of process versus substance in the setting of democratic ideas and practices. Although the problem itself has become fairly prominent in discussions of democratic theory, proposed solutions to it (and nonsolutions) usually depend on assumptions in the shadow theory.

The issues I have mentioned—we shall encounter others as we proceed—are I hope sufficient to illustrate my point. To develop a satisfactory theory of democracy will require us to excavate the assumptions in the shadow theory, subject them to critical examination, and try to recast the theory of democracy into a reasonably coherent whole. In identifying and exploring the assumptions on which to build a coherent democratic theory, the arguments of critics of democracy, both adversarial and sympathetic, are invaluable.

◆

The two millennia since the idea and institutions of democracy were explicitly developed by the Greeks have added enormously to what is relevant to democratic theory and practice. Yet the use of the term "democratic theory" to designate a particular field of inquiry, analysis, empirical description, and theorizing is fairly recent, and what a "democratic theory" might reasonably include remains unclear.

At the outset we confront the fact that in both ordinary and philosophical language democracy may properly be used to refer both to an ideal and to actual regimes that fall considerably short of the ideal. The dual meaning is often confusing. In addition, if democracy is both an ideal and an attainable actuality, how are we to judge when an actual regime is sufficiently proximate to the ideal that we can properly regard it as a democracy? The problem is not merely a trivial one of word usage, though it is also that. It is a problem of deciding on a reasonable threshold. In short, how can we reasonably judge that a regime, system, or process is democratic, as against, say, oligarchic, aristocratic, meritocratic, or whatever? Evidently we need indicators that can be reasonably applied to the world of actual political systems. In building and using indicators of democracy we necessarily move from the language and orientation of justification and evaluation—in the jargon of contemporary political science, normative theory—toward more empirical discourse. Can both the normative and the empirical aspects of democracy be combined in a single theoretical perspective? As this book will show, I believe they can, but the task is a wide-ranging one.

I like to think of democratic theory as if it were like a very large three-dimensional web. Much too large to take in at a single glance, the web is constructed of interconnected strands of differing elasticities. While a few parts of the web are composed of rigidly connected strands (that is, strictly deductive arguments), other parts are more loosely held together, and some connections are very tenuous indeed. Like one well-known model of the universe, the web appears to be finite but unbounded. As a result, when you make your way along a strand of argument, you do not come to a definite edge that marks a distinct and conclusive limit to the unbounded universe of democratic theory. Follow out an argument to what you think might be the end, and you find yourself pursuing yet another strand. And so on, indefinitely I fear.

Table 1 is a crude mapping of some of the important aspects of democratic theory. As with a finite but unbounded web, one could well start anywhere, but why not begin at the northwest corner? Here the argument is more explicitly philosophical, as it would be, for example, in efforts to set out the grounds on which a belief in democracy would be justified. The argument here is also less critical, more sympathetic with democratic values. If we were now to proceed directly eastward, we would find the argument taking on a more and more empirical tone. For example, after pausing at (3) to examine the criteria that distinguish a fully democratic process from other processes for making decisions, we might move back to (2) in order to consider the characteristics of an association for which the democratic process would be a desirable, even the most desirable, form of government. Presumably states would qualify. Would economic enterprises? Universities? And what about the family? Or the military? Or government bureaucracies? If democracy is not appropriate for some of these, why not, and what does their exemption imply about the limits of the democratic idea?

Venturing still further eastward to (4) we might begin to explore the institutions

Table 1. *Some Aspects of a Theory about the Democratic Process (Domain: Associations that satisfy the requirements of (2) below)*

The argument is more explicitly philosophical: assertions as to values, epistemology, "human nature," etc. → The argument is more explicitly empirical

| (1) | (2) | (3) | (4) | (5) |
|---|---|---|---|---|
| **Less critical** | | | | |
| Philosophical grounds (justifications) for the assumptions of (2) | Characteristics of an association sufficient to require the democratic process (3) | Criteria specifying a fully democratic process | Institutions required in order to satisfy (3) at the levels historically achieved by certain concrete associations | Conditions that facilitate[a] the development and persistence of (4) |
| | | | 4.1. Very small demos<br>4.2. Small demos<br>4.3. Large demos<br>4.31. . . . .<br>4.321. . . . .<br>4.32. Variations in the institutions of polyarchy | 5.1. . . . .<br>5.2. . . . .<br>5.3. Conditions that facilitate the institutions of polyarchy<br>5.31. Effects of variations in conditions |
| **More critical** | | | | |
| (6) | (7) | | (8) | (9) |
| Other valid grounds and criteria, not (1) and (2) | Critique and evaluation<br>7.1. The extent to which the institutions of (4) fail to meet the ideal criteria of (3)——e.g., incomplete democratization 7.2. Defects by other criteria (6) | | Institutions that would be required to meet deficiencies specified under (7): e.g., for further democratization of polyarchy | Conditions that would facilitate (8) |

[a]Deliberately ambiguous: may mean necessary to, sufficient for, or increase (significantly) probability of . . . .

that the democratic process would require in order to operate. An assembly of citizens? A representative legislature? Evidently the institutions required would vary depending on circumstances, particularly the scale of the society. Still further eastward on our journey, at (5) we could investigate the conditions that would facilitate the development, and the continuing existence, of the institutions that are necessary to a democratic order.

You may have noticed that by now we seem to have moved into a part of democratic theory where we intend our inquiry to be almost entirely empirical, and it may look like a long distance back to the philosophical northwest corner where we started. Yet none of the terrain we have explored lies outside the bounds of democratic theory.

To complicate matters further, at this point we might want to explore the historical origins of democratic institutions and of the conditions that make these institutions possible. Here our flat, two-dimensional map might be better represented as three-dimensional, as a cube, perhaps, with time—history—as the third dimension. Notice, though, that insofar as historical experience is necessary to an explanation, we still remain within the domain of democratic theory—empirical theory, if you like, but surely a part of the finite but unbounded web of democratic theory.

Suppose we move in another direction. Advocates of democracy sometimes appear to believe that the values of democracy constitute the complete universe of value: if you could have a perfect democracy, they imply, then you would have a perfect political order, maybe even a perfect society. But this is surely too restricted a vision. Democracy is only a part, though an important part, of the universe of values, goods, or desirable ends. By proceeding toward (6) in the southwest corner we could begin to explore some of these other values—efficiency or distributive justice, for example. You might suppose our exploration has now moved us right off the map of democratic theory; yet these other goods or values could give us grounds for criticizing even a perfect democracy, if it failed to achieve these substantive ends. We are, therefore, still on the map, still moving along the boundless web of democratic theory.

Perhaps I can now leave further explorations of the map to the reader. Our brief tour will have sufficiently shown, I think, that democratic theory is not only a large enterprise—normative, empirical, philosophical, sympathetic, critical, historical, utopianistic, all at once—but complexly interconnected. The complex interconnections mean that we cannot construct a satisfactory democratic theory by starting off from an impregnable base and marching straight down the road to our conclusions. Although strictly deductive arguments have a place in democratic theory, their place is necessarily a small one, and they are embedded in crucial assumptions with which strictly deductive argument does not concern itself and probably cannot handle successfully. Consequently, I will not often use a favorite word of deductive theory—"rational"—nor ever indulge myself in its favorite assumption of perfect rationality. However, I shall often say that it is "reasonable" to believe so and so, and I try to show why it is reasonable. Whether it is so, the reader will have to judge.

As I explore one part of the complex, interconnected web of democratic theory in this book, I shall have to ignore the other parts momentarily, though I may nod in their direction to acknowledge that they await our exploration in due time. In the path I have chosen, however, there is a certain logic, or at least, if I may say so, a reasonableness. While what I set out here is in no sense a strictly deductive theory, the argument is cumulative, and the later chapters depend heavily on the argument of the earlier chapters.

# PART ONE

◆◆◆◆◆◆◆◆

# THE SOURCES OF
# MODERN DEMOCRACY

# Chapter 1

◆◆◆◆◆◆◆◆

# The First Transformation:
# To the Democratic City-State

During the first half of the fifth century B.C., a transformation took place in political ideas and institutions among Greeks and Romans that was comparable in historical importance to the invention of the wheel or the discovery of the New World. The change reflected a new understanding of the world and its possibilities.

At its simplest, what happened was that several city-states, which from time out of mind had been governed by various undemocratic rulers, whether aristocrats, oligarchs, monarchs, or tyrants, were transformed into systems in which a substantial number of free, adult males were entitled as citizens to participate directly in governing. Out of this experience and the ideas associated with it came a new vision of a possible political system, one in which a sovereign people is not only entitled to govern itself but possesses all the resources and institutions necessary to do so. This vision remains at the core of modern democratic ideas and continues to shape democratic institutions and practices.

But modern democratic ideas and institutions consist of far more than this simple vision. And since the theory and practices of modern democracy have resulted not only from the legacy of popular government in ancient city-states but also from other historical experiences, both evolutionary and revolutionary, they are an amalgam of elements that do not fully cohere. As a result contemporary democratic theory and practice exhibit inconsistencies and contradictions that sometimes result in deep problems.

To help us understand how the amalgam we call "democracy" came about, I am going to describe four of its most important sources. In doing so, I shall also indicate some problems that will require attention in later chapters.

These four sources are classical Greece; a republican tradition derived more from Rome and the Italian city-states of the Middle Ages and Renaissance than from the democratic city-states of Greece; the idea and institutions of representative government; and the logic of political equality. The first is the subject of this chapter.

## A GREEK PERSPECTIVE

Although the practices of modern democracy bear only a weak resemblance to the political institutions of classical Greece, our ideas, as I suggested in the introduction, have been powerfully influenced by the Greeks, particularly the Athenians. That Greek democratic ideas have been more influential than their institutions is ironic, since what we know of their ideas comes less from the writings or speeches of democratic advocates, of which only fragments survive, than from their critics.[1] These range from mild adversaries like Aristotle, who disliked the power that he thought the expansion of democracy necessarily gave the poor, to Plato, an outright opponent who condemned democracy as rule by the unfit and advocated instead a perennially appealing system of government by the best qualified.[2]

Because we have no Greek equivalent in democratic theory to Locke's *Second Treatise* or Rousseau's *Social Contract*, one cannot provide chapter and verse on Greek democratic ideas. That *demokratia* involved equality in some way was not in doubt. But exactly what sorts of equality? Before the word "democracy" gained currency, Athenians had already referred to certain kinds of equality as desirable characteristics of their political system: equality of all citizens in the right to speak in the governing assembly (*isegoria*) and equality before the law (*isonomia*) (Sealey 1976, 158). These terms remained in use and evidently were often assumed to be characteristics of "democracy." But during the first half of the fifth century when "the people" (the *demos*) steadily gained acceptance as the sole legitimate authority in *ruling*, the word "democracy"—rule by the people—also seems to have gained ground as the most appropriate name for the new system.

While much of the character of Greek democratic ideas and practices remains unknown and may forever elude us, historians have uncovered enough evidence to allow a reasonable reconstruction of the views an Athenian democrat might have advanced in the late fifth century B.C.—in, say, 400 B.C. This convenient date is a little more than a century after the reforms of Cleisthenes had inaugurated the transition to democracy in Athens, a decade after the restoration of democracy following its overthrow in 411, four years after the brief, cruel, and oppressive rule of the Thirty Tyrants had been replaced by democracy, and one year before the trial and death of Socrates.

A democrat, being Greek, would have adopted certain assumptions that appear to have been widely shared among Greeks who thought about the nature of political life and, in particular, about the polis—shared even by antidemocrats like Plato or moderate critics like Aristotle. We might therefore imagine our Athenian strolling through the Agora with a friend to whom he is expounding his views.

### The Nature of the Polis[3]

We know, of course (our Athenian is saying), that only in association with others can we hope to become fully human or, certainly, to realize our qualities of excellence as human beings. The most important association within which each of us lives, grows, and matures is, naturally, our city—the polis. And so it is with everyone, for it is our nature to be social beings. Although I have once or twice heard someone say—perhaps only in order to provoke a discussion—that a good man might exist outside the polis, it is self-evident that without sharing the life of the polis no person could ever develop or exercise the virtues and qualities that distinguish men from beasts.

Yet a good man requires not just a polis but a good polis. Nothing is more important in judging the quality of a city than the qualities of excellence it fosters in its citizens. It goes without saying that a good city is one that produces good citizens, promotes their happiness, and encourages them to act rightly. It is our good fortune that these ends are harmonious; for the virtuous man will be a happy man, and no one, I think, can be truly happy unless he is also virtuous.

So it is also with justice. Virtue, justice, and happiness are not enemies but companions. Since justice is what tends to promote the common interest, a good polis must also be just; and therefore it must aim at developing citizens who seek the common good. For one who merely pursues his own interest cannot be a good citizen: a good citizen is one who in public matters aims always at the common good. I know that in saying so I appear to raise an impossible standard, one we often fail to meet in Athens as in all other cities. Yet there can be no better meaning of virtue in a citizen than this: that in public matters he looks always to the good of the polis.

Because one aim of the city is to produce good citizens, we cannot leave their training to chance or only to their families. Our life in the polis is an education, and life in our city must so form us that we aspire inwardly toward the common good of all. Thus our outward actions will reflect our inner natures. Civic virtues must also be strengthened by virtues in the constitution and laws of the city and by a social order that makes justice attainable. For excellence would be impossible if one had to act wrongly in order to be a good citizen, or if in order to act rightly one had to be a bad citizen.

I think then that in the best polis, citizens are at once virtuous, just, and happy. And because each seeks the good of all, and the city is not divided into smaller cities of rich and poor, or of different gods, all citizens can live together in harmony.

I do not mean that everything I am saying is true of Athens or any other actual city. Instead, I mean it as a model we observe with the eye of our mind when we praise our city for its virtues or criticize it for its faults.

What I have been saying is of course no more than we all believe. Even young Plato would not disagree. To be sure, I have sometimes heard him talk cleverly, claiming to represent Socrates, about how silly it is to expect ordinary people to rule wisely and how much better Athens would be if it were governed by wise philosophers—such as he fancies himself, I suppose. Yet I think even one who despises democracy as he does would agree with me so far. It is what I am now going to say that he would quarrel with, joined, I do not doubt, by some of the others who forever criticize democracy for its shortcomings, such as Aristophanes and, needless to say, all those Athenians who gave their support to the Thirty Tyrants.

## The Nature of Democracy

The polis we democrats strive to attain (our Athenian democrat might continue) must first of all be a good polis; and to be a good polis it must possess the qualities I have just described, as we all believe. But to be the best polis it must also be, like Athens, a democratic polis.

Now in order for citizens to strive for the common good, in a democratic polis, we need not all be alike, or have no interests of our own, or dedicate our lives only to the polis. For what is a polis if it is not a place where citizens may live a full life and not be subject at every waking moment to the call of civic duties? That is the way of the Spartans. It is not ours. A city has a need for shoemakers and shipmakers, carpenters and sculptors, farmers who tend their olive groves in the countryside and physicians who tend their patients in the city. Each citizen may aim at some things that are not the aim of others. The good of one of us, then, need not be exactly the same as the good of another.

Yet our differences must never be so great that we cannot agree on what is best for the city, that is, what is best for all and not merely for some. That is why, like any good polis, a democratic polis must not be split into two cities, a city of the rich and a city of the poor, each city looking to its own good. Not long ago I heard Plato speak of this danger, and though he is no friend of our Athenian democracy, on this, at least, we agree. For such a city will be cursed by conflict, and civil strife will overwhelm the public good. Perhaps it was because two cities had been growing within Athens, and the wealthier few came to hate the city governed by the many who were poor—or so the wealthy thought them to be—that the city of the more wealthy invited the rule of the Thirty Tyrants.

A democracy must also be of modest size, not only so that all citizens can meet together in the assembly and thus act as rulers of the city, but also in order that all citizens may know one another. To seek the good of all, citizens must be able to apprehend the good of each and thus be capable of understanding the common good that each shares with the others. But how could citizens come to understand all they have in common if their city were so large and their demos so numerous that they could never know one another or see their city whole? The Persian empire is an abomination, not merely because it is a despotism but because, being so huge that it dwarfs every person within its limits, it can never be anything other than a despotism.

Even Athens, I fear, has grown too large. It is said that our demos now comprises some forty thousand citizens.[4] How can we know one another when we are so many? Citizens who neglect the meetings of the Assembly, as many now do, fail in their duties as citizens. Yet if every citizen were ever to attend the Assembly, we would be too numerous. Our meeting place on the hill of Pnyx would not hold us all, and if it could, out of forty thousand none could speak except a few orators, yet what orator possesses so stentorian a voice as to be heard by so many?

Like an athlete who in growing fat loses his swiftness and agility and can no longer participate in the games, the enormity of our demos is ill-suited for democracy.

For how can a city be a democracy unless all its citizens can assemble often in order to exercise their sovereign rule over the affairs of the city? I have heard some Athenian citizens complain that it is an excessive burden to trudge up Pnyx hill forty times a year, as we are expected to do, starting our meeting in the early morning and staying often until darkness falls, especially when some of us must make our way here from the distant parts of Attica the night before and make our way back to our farms the night after. Yet I do not see how we could get our business done with fewer meetings, and sometimes even so we need extraordinary sessions.

But it is not only through the Assembly that we in Athens rule over our city. We also take our turn in administering the work of the city—in the Council, which prepares the agenda of the Assembly, in our citizen juries, in the almost countless boards of magistrates. For us, democracy is not simply making important decisions and laws in the Assembly, it is also serving in office.

So a polis would not truly be a polis, and it could never be a democratic polis, unless both its citizen body and its territory were no larger than ours—and better yet that it be not quite so large. I well know the danger: that we are vulnerable to defeat in war by a large state. I do not mean other city-states like Sparta, but monstrous empires like Persia. Well, that risk we must run, and as the Persians well know, in alliance with other Greeks we have been their match and more.

Although we may need allies in times of war, even then we do not forgo our independence. Some say that we and our allies might form a permanent league, in which we could choose fellow citizens to represent us in some kind of council that would decide on matters of war and peace. But I do not understand how we could yield authority over us to such a council and still remain a democracy or even a true polis. For we should no longer be able to exercise sovereign power, in our own assembly, over our own city.

Thirty years ago my father was among those who attended the funeral of those who had fallen in the war with Sparta, and there he heard Pericles, who was chosen to give the eulogy for the dead heroes. So often did he later tell me what Pericles had said on that day that even now it is as if I myself had been there.

Our constitution, Pericles said, does not copy the laws of neighboring states; we are rather a pattern to others than imitators ourselves. Its administration favors the many instead of the few; this is why it is called a democracy. If we look to the laws, they afford equal justice to all in their private differences; if to social standing, advancement in public life depends on reputation for ability, class considerations not being allowed to interfere with merit; nor again does poverty bar the way, for if a man is able to serve the state, he is not hindered by the obscurity of his condition. The freedom we enjoy in our government extends also to our ordinary life. Far from exercising a jealous surveillance over each other, we do not feel called upon to be angry with our neighbor for doing what he likes or even to indulge in those injurious looks that cannot fail to be offensive. But all this ease in our private relations does not make us lawless as citizens. Our chief safeguard against lawlessness is our respect for the laws, particularly those protecting the injured, whether they are actually on the statute book or belong to that code which, although unwritten, yet cannot be broken without acknowledged disgrace.

Our public men, Pericles said, have, besides politics, their private affairs to attend to, and our ordinary citizens, though occupied with the pursuits of industry, are still fair judges of public matters. Instead of looking on discussion as a stumbling block in the way of action, we think it an indispensable preliminary to any wise action at all.

In short, said Pericles, as a city we are the school of Hellas (Thucydides 1951, 104–06).

## The Vision in Summary

The democratic ideal described by our hypothetical Athenian is a political vision so lofty and charming that a modern democrat can hardly fail to be attracted by it. In the Greek vision of democracy, the citizen is a whole person for whom politics is a natural social activity not sharply separated from the rest of life, and for whom the government and the state—or rather, the polis—are not remote and alien entities distant from oneself. Rather, political life is only an extension of, and harmonious with, oneself. Values are not fragmented but coherent: for happiness is united with virtue, virtue with justice, and justice with happiness.

Nonetheless, two things must be said about this view of democracy. First, as a vision of an ideal order it should not be mistaken for the reality of Greek political life, as it sometimes is. As befits a eulogy for the fallen dead in a great war, even Pericles' famous funeral oration was, like Lincoln's Gettysburg Address on a similar occasion, an idealized portrait. I shall say something about the reality in a moment. Second, one cannot judge the relevance of that vision for the modern (or postmodern) world unless one understands how radically different it is from democratic ideas and practices as they have developed since the eighteenth century.

In the Greek view, as we have just seen, a democratic order would have to satisfy at least six requirements:

1. Citizens must be sufficiently harmonious in their interests so that they can share, and act upon, a strong sense of a general good that is not in marked contradiction to their personal aims or interests.

2. From this first requirement, a second follows: they must be highly homogeneous with respect to characteristics that would otherwise tend to produce political conflict and sharp disagreements over the public good. In this view, no state could hope to be a good polis if its citizens were greatly unequal in their economic resources and the amount of leisure time available to them, or if they adhered to different religions or spoke different languages or differed significantly in their education or, certainly, if they were of differing races, cultures, or (as we say today) ethnic groups.

3. The citizen body must be quite small, ideally even smaller than the forty to fifty thousand of Periclean Athens. The small size of the demos was necessary for

three reasons: It would help to avoid the heterogeneity and hence the disharmony that would result from extending the boundaries and thereby including, like Persia, people of diverse languages, religions, history, and ethnicity, with almost nothing in common. It was necessary also in order for citizens to acquire the knowledge of their city and of their fellow citizens, from observation, experience, and discussion, that would enable them to understand the common good and to distinguish it from their private or personal interests. Finally, the small size was essential if citizens were to assemble in order to serve as the sovereign rulers of the city.

4. Fourthly, then, citizens must be able to assemble and directly decide on the laws and decisions of policy. So deeply held was this view that the Greeks found it difficult to conceive of representative government, much less to accept it as a legitimate alternative to direct democracy. To be sure, from time to time leagues or confederacies of city-states were created. But genuinely federal systems with representative governments failed to develop, in part, it seems, because the idea of representation could not compete successfully with the profound belief in the desirability and legitimacy of direct governments with primary assemblies.[5]

5. Citizen participation was not limited, however, to the meetings of the Assembly. It also included actively participating in the administration of the city. It has been estimated that in Athens over one thousand offices had to be filled—a few by election but most by lot—and nearly all these offices were for one-year terms and could be occupied only once in a lifetime. Even with the relatively "large" demos of Athens, every citizen was almost certain to occupy some office for a year, and a large number would become members of the highly important Council of Five Hundred, which determined the agenda for the Assembly.[6]

6. Finally, the city-state must, ideally at least, remain fully autonomous. Leagues, confederacies, and alliances might sometimes be necessary for defense or war, but they must not be allowed to preempt the ultimate autonomy of the city-state and the sovereignty of the assembly within that state. In principle, then, each city must be self-sufficient, not only politically but also economically and militarily. Indeed, it must possess all the conditions required for a good life. But to avoid too heavy a dependence on foreign trade, a good life would necessarily be a frugal life. In this way, democracy was linked to the virtues of frugality, not to affluence.

Each of these requirements stands in stark contradiction to the realities of every modern democracy located in a nation-state or country rather than a city-state: Instead of the tiny demos and territory presupposed in the Greek view, a country—even a small country—comprises a gigantic body of citizens spread over a territory vast by Greek standards. As a consequence, citizens are a more heterogeneous body than the Greeks thought desirable. In many countries, in fact, they are extraordinarily diverse: in religion, education, culture, ethnic group, race, language, and economic position. These diversities inevitably disrupt the harmony envisioned in the Greek ideal; political conflict, not harmony, is the hallmark of the modern democratic state. And of course the citizens are far too numerous to assemble: As everyone knows, not only at the national level but usually also at regional, provincial, state, and municipal levels, representative government, not direct democracy, prevails. Nor do citizens, on the whole, occupy the administrative offices, which nowadays are typically in the hands of full-time professionals who make a career of public administration. Finally, in all democratic countries it is taken for granted that units of government small enough to permit something like the participation envisioned in the Greek ideal cannot be autonomous but must, on the contrary, be subordinate elements in the larger system; and far from controlling their own agenda, citizens in these small units at best exercise control over a narrow range of matters whose limits are set by the larger system.

So profound are the differences, then, that if our hypothetical Athenian citizens were somehow to appear in our midst, he would surely contend that a modern democracy is not, after all, a democracy. However that may be, confronted by a radically different world that offers a radically different set of limits and possibilities, we are entitled to wonder how much if any of the Greek vision of democracy is relevant to our times or a conceivable future. I shall touch upon this question in later chapters.

### LIMITS

It is reasonable to conclude, as many have, that government, politics, and political life in Athens and very likely in numerous other democratic city-states as well were, at least when viewed from a democratic perspective, greatly superior to the innumerable nondemocratic regimes under which most people have lived throughout recorded history. Even if the democratic city-states of classical antiquity were but tiny islands in the vast sea of human experience, they nonetheless demonstrated that human capacities far exceed the sorry standards displayed in the dismal performance of most political systems.

Yet we should not allow that impressive achievement to blind us to its limits. Without much doubt there were the usual gaps between the ideal and the reality of political life that all too human qualities invariably cause. What *was* that reality? The answer, alas, is that to a great extent we do not know and probably never shall know. Only shards of evidence exist.[7] These provide information mainly about Athens, which was only one, though far and away the most important, of several hundred democratic city-states. Because classical scholars, like physical anthropologists who recreate a whole primate from the fragment of a jawbone, are compelled to reconstruct Greek democracy from very scanty evidence, their interpretations and evaluations are necessarily highly subjective.

Yet there is ample evidence for concluding that the political life of the Greeks, as of other peoples then and later, was markedly inferior to political ideals. It would scarcely be necessary to make this point if it were not for the influence of the view of some classical historians that in his unswerving devotion to the public good the Athenian citizen set a standard for all time.[8]

So far as one can make out from the fragmentary evidence, politics in Athens as in other cities was a tough, hard game in which issues were often subordinated to personal ambitions. Although political parties in the modern sense did not exist, factions based on ties of family and friendship evidently played a powerful role. The supposedly superior claims of the common good yielded in practice to the stronger claims of family and friends.[9] Factional leaders were not above using the process of ostracism by a vote in the assembly in order to banish their opponents for ten years.[10] Outright betrayal of the state by political leaders was not unknown, as in the famous case of Alcibiades (Thucydides 1951, 353–92).

Although (in Athens, at least) citizen participation in public administration was exceptionally high by any standard, it is impossible to determine the general level of political interest and concern among citizens or the extent to which participation varied among the different strata. There are grounds for believing that only a rather small minority of citizens attended the meetings of the Assembly.[11] How representative of the entire demos this minority was, it is impossible to say. Doubtless leaders would try to ensure that their supporters turned out, and Assembly meetings may often have been largely attended by such followings. Since in much of the fifth century these followings consisted of coalitions of groups based on ties of kinship and friendship, the assemblies would probably not have tended to include poorer and less well connected citizens.[12] In all likelihood, most of the speeches in the Assembly were made by a relatively small number of leaders—men of established reputations, excellent as orators, who were acknowledged leaders of the demos and therefore entitled to a hearing.[13]

It would be a mistake, then, to assume that in the democratic city-states, Greeks were significantly less concerned with their private interests and more actively devoted to the public good than are citizens in modern democratic countries. Conceivably they may have been, but the conclusion is not warranted by the evidence.

However, it is not the merely human failings exhibited in political life that seem important to me but rather the limits that were inherent in the theory and practice of Greek democracy itself—limits that, to the continuing discomfiture of writers who uphold Greek democracy as establishing the proper standards for all time, modern democratic theory and practice had to break out of. Although one might object that to appraise Greek democracy by standards other than those relevant in its own time is inappropriate, the fact is that we cannot determine how relevant that experience is to our own time except by using standards appropriate to us.

From a contemporary democratic perspective, one crucially important limit on Greek democracy, in both theory and practice, was that citizenship was highly *exclusive* rather than *inclusive* as modern democracy has become. To be sure, Greek democracy was more inclusive than other regimes of the time; and democrats who saw their regime in comparative terms no doubt believed it, rightly, to be relatively inclusive, a judgment they would have expressed in the already commonplace division of regimes into rule by the one, the few, and the many. Nonetheless, in practice a demos of "the many" excluded many. Yet so far as one can tell, Greek democrats did not see the exclusiveness of their democracies as a grave defect. Indeed, insofar as they saw the alternatives as rule by one or the few, democrats may literally not have seen how many persons were in fact excluded from "the many."

In both theory and practice, Greek democracy was exclusive in two senses: internally and externally. Within the city-state, a large part of the adult population was denied full citizenship: the right to participate in political life, whether by attending meetings of the sovereign assembly or by serving in public offices. Because the population of Athens is a highly conjectural matter, percentage estimates are unreliable and vary wildly. But not only were women excluded (as of course they continued to be in all democracies until the twentieth century), but also long-term resident aliens (*metics*) and slaves. Since the requirement for Athenian citizenship from 451 onward was that both parents must be Athenian citizens themselves, citizenship was for all practical purposes a hereditary privilege based on primordial ties of kinship (though full citizenship was a privilege inheritable only by males). Consequently no metic or his descendants could become citizens, despite the fact that many metic families lived in Athens for generations and contributed greatly to its economic and intellectual life during the fifth and fourth centuries (Fine, 1983, 434). Although metics were without the rights of citizens and in addition were also prohibited, in Athens at least, from owning land or a house, they had many of the duties of citizens (435).[14] They engaged in social, economic, and cultural life as artisans, traders, and intellectuals, possessed rights protected in the law courts, were sometimes wealthy, and evidently enjoyed a certain standing.

Not so the slaves, who were not only denied all rights of citizenship but were denied all legal rights whatsoever. Legally slaves were no more than the property of their owners, wholly without legal rights. The extent and depth of slavery in classical Greece is a subject of profound dispute (cf. Finley 1980 and Ste. Croix 1981), but the democratic city-states were in some substantial sense slave societies. Where even poor citizens had some protection against abuse by virtue of their rights as citizens, and where metics had some protection from mistreatment by their freedom to move elsewhere, slaves were defenseless. Although some slaves became freedmen through manumission by their masters, in Greece (unlike Rome) they became metics, not citizens.[15]

Greek democracy was also, as we have seen, exclusive rather than inclusive *externally*. Indeed, among *Greeks* democracy did not exist: It existed, and in the views of Greeks could only exist, among members of the same polis. So deeply held was this view that it fatally weakened attempts to unite various cities in larger entities.

That democracy was exclusive rather than inclusive among the Greeks was not unrelated to a second important limit in their theory and practice: They did not acknowledge the existence of *universal* claims to freedom, equality, or rights, whether political rights or, more broadly, human rights. Freedom was an attribute of membership—not membership in the human species but membership (that is, citizenship) in a particular city.[16] "The Greek concept of 'freedom' did not extend beyond the community itself: freedom for one's own members implied neither legal (civil) freedom for all others resident within the community nor political freedom for members of other communities over whom one had power" (Finley 1972, 53). Even in a democratic polis, "freedom meant the rule of law and participation in the decision-making process, not the possession of inalienable rights" (78).[17]

Thirdly, then, as a consequence of the first two limits, Greek democracy was inherently limited to small-scale systems. Although the small scale of Greek democracy provided some extraordinary advantages, particularly for participation, many of the advantages of a large-scale political system were beyond its reach. Because the Greeks had no democratic means of extending the rule of law beyond the small compass of the city-state, in their external relations the city-states existed in a Hobbesian state of nature where not law but violence was the natural order of things. They found it difficult to unite even against external aggression. Despite their military prowess on land and sea, which enabled them to fend off the numerically superior forces of the Persians, they could combine their forces for defensive purposes only feebly and temporarily. Consequently the Greeks were finally united not by themselves but by their conquerors, the Macedonians and the Romans.

Two millennia later, after the focus of primordial loyalties and political order had been transferred to the far larger scale of the nation-state, the limitation of democracy to small-scale systems was seen as an irremediable defect. The theory and practice of democracy had to burst the narrow bounds of the polis. And while the vision of the Greeks was not wholly lost to democratic thought, it was replaced by a new vision of a vaster democracy extended now to the giant compass of the nation-state.

# Chapter 2

♦♦♦♦♦♦♦♦

# Toward the Second Transformation: Republicanism, Representation, and the Logic of Equality

Despite the extraordinary influence of classical Greece on the development of democracy, modern democratic ideas and institutions have also been shaped by many other factors, of which three are particularly important: a republican tradition, the development of representative governments, and certain conclusions that tend to follow from a belief in political equality.

## THE REPUBLICAN TRADITION

By the republican tradition I mean a body of thought, far from systematic or coherent, that traces its origins less to the democratic ideas and practices of classical Greece described in the last chapter than to the most notable critic of Greek democracy: Aristotle. Moreover, as an embodiment of its political ideals republicanism looks not so much to Athens as to its enemy, Sparta, and even more to Rome and Venice. Grounded in Aristotle, shaped by the centuries-long experiences of republican Rome and the Republic of Venice, interpreted in varying and even conflicting ways during the late Renaissance by Florentine writers like Francesco Guicciardini and Niccolò Machiavelli, the republican tradition was reformulated, reshaped, and reinterpreted in seventeenth- and eighteenth-century England and America. If, during this process, some of the important themes in classical republicanism lost their centrality or were rejected outright, others retained their vitality.[1]

Although the republican tradition diverged from Greek democratic thought, and in some respects was antithetical to it, republicanism nevertheless shared several of its assumptions. To begin with, republicanism adopted the view, common in Greek political thought (whether democratic or antidemocratic) that man is by nature a social and political animal; to fulfill their potentialities, human beings must live together in a political association; a good man must also be a good citizen; a good polity is an association constituted by good citizens; a good citizen possesses the quality of civic virtue; virtue is the predisposition to seek the good of all in public matters; a good polity, therefore, is one that not only reflects but also promotes the virtue of its citizens.

More specifically, like Greek democrats republicans also held that the best polity is one in which citizens are in important respects equal: in their equality before the law, for example, and in the absence of a relation of dependency between one citizen and another, such as exists among masters and servants. Republican doctrine insisted further that no political system could be legitimate, desirable, or good if it excluded the people from participating in ruling.

Despite these similarities however, republicanism was more than a simple reaffirmation of the ideals and practices of Greek democracy. Like Aristotle, in some crucial respects it offered an alternative to democracy as understood by many Greeks. While republican doctrine laid great stress on the fundamental importance of civic virtue, it laid equal or greater stress on the fragility of virtue, the danger that a people or its leaders would become corrupt, and thus the likelihood that civic virtue would so far decay into corruption that a republic would become impossible. In the republican view, a major threat to civic virtue is generated by factions and political conflicts. These in turn tend to result from an all but universal characteristic of civil society: "The people" is not a perfectly homogeneous body with identical interests; it is normally divided into an aristocratic or oligarchic element and a democratic or popular component—the few and the many—each with somewhat different interests. Following Aristotle, one might also add a third component to the few and the many: a monocratic or monarchical element, a leader who might seek to enhance his own position, status, and power. The task of republicans, then, is to design a constitution that reflects and somehow balances the interests of the one, the few, and the many by providing for a mixed government of democracy, aristocracy, and monarchy so constituted that all three components will finally concur in the good of all.

The most obvious constitutional model was of course republican Rome with its system of consuls, Senate, and tribunes of the people. (Rome also furnished the obvious example of the decay and corruption of civic virtue: The rise of civil conflict and the transformation of the republic into Imperial Rome demonstrated how even a great republic could be destroyed.) In the eighteenth century another obvious example was added to the Roman model: the British constitution, which with its marvelously contrived arrangement of monarchy, Lords, and Commons appeared to some republican theorists—notably Baron de Montesquieu—the very epitome of a perfectly balanced system of government.

Thanks to events in Britain and America, the eighteenth century also saw the development of a strain of radical republicanism that was in some respects at odds with the older tradition. If the older view might be called aristocratic republicanism, the newer was more emphatic—and increasingly so—in its emphasis on the fundamental importance of the democratic component in the constitution of a republic. The more aristocratic or conservative strain of republicanism is to be found in Aristotle, in Guicciardini and the *ottimati* of Renaissance Florence, and in

America in John Adams; the more democratic strain in Machiavelli, in the radical Whigs of the eighteenth century, and in Thomas Jefferson.

In the aristocratic republican view, even though the people, the many, ought to have an important role in government, because they are more to be feared than trusted their role ought to be a limited one. To aristocratic republicans, perhaps the most difficult constitutional problem is to create a structure that will sufficiently restrain the impulses of the many. The proper function of the people is not to rule, as they did in Athens, but rather to choose leaders competent to perform the demanding function of governing over the entire polity. To be sure, since leaders are obligated to govern in the interests of the community as a whole, and the people are naturally an important element of the community, properly qualified leaders would govern in the interests of the people; but they would not rule exclusively in the interests of that single element, important as it necessarily must be. For, accepting the essential legitimacy of the interests of the few and the many, to aristocratic republicans the public good requires a balancing of these interests.

In the emergent democratic republicanism of the eighteenth century, by contrast, the element most to be feared is not the many but the few, not the people but the aristocratic and oligarchic elements. Indeed, the confidence of republicans in the prospects of good government rests in the qualities of the people. What is more, the public good does *not* consist in balancing the interests of the people with the interests of the few: the public good *is* nothing more or less than the welfare of the people. The constitutional task, therefore, is to design a system that will somehow overcome the inevitable tendency toward the preponderance of the few or the single despot and his hangers-on.

While aristocratic and democratic republicans agree that concentration of power is always dangerous and must always be avoided, their solutions to that problem diverge. Aristocratic or conservative republicans continue to emphasize the solution of a mixed government that balances the interests of the one, the few, and the many, and thus seek to reflect those interests in the monarchy, the aristocratic upper chamber, and the lower house for the commons. To democratic republicans, however, the idea of representing different interests in different institutions is increasingly more dubious and unacceptable. The difficulties in the older theory of mixed government become particularly evident in America. In the absence of an hereditary aristocracy, who are the specially worthy few? Presumably they comprise a "natural aristocracy," an idea dear even to democratic republicans like Jefferson. But how are the natural aristocrats to be identified? And how is it possible to ensure that they will be chosen to perform their proper role in governing? For example, should they be permitted to choose their own kind to compose an upper house of the legislature, where they would constitute a functional equivalent in a democratic republic to the House of Lords in Britain? As the framers of the American Constitution discovered in 1787, the problem is for all practical purposes without solution. In a democratic republic, the framers concluded, the interests of "the few" do not entitle them to their own second chamber. And it would be even less acceptable to protect a "monarchical interest" by locating it in the executive. For surely the chief magistrate of a republic can scarcely be counted legitimately as a separate and special interest in the community.

Because of the intractability of solutions to the problem of designing a mixed government for a democratic republic, republicans, though by no means always perfectly clear on the matter, in effect replaced the ancient idea of mixed government with the newer idea, made famous by Montesquieu, of a constitutional and institutional separation of powers into the three main branches: legislative, executive, and judicial. It became an axiom of republican theory that the concentration of these three kinds of power in a single center was the very essence of tyranny and that they must therefore be located in separate institutions, each serving as a check on the others (Montesquieu [1748] 1961, bk. 11, chap. 6; Hamilton, Jay, and Madison, no. 47). Although the notion of balancing conflicting interests by no means disappeared (it was, for example, central to James Madison's view), the constitutional task was to ensure a proper balance among the three main functions or "powers" of government.

Like Greek democratic theory and practice, the republican tradition passed on to later advocates of democracy some unresolved problems. Of these, four were closely interrelated. First, as democratic republicans in the eighteenth century began to discern, the concept of interest or interests in orthodox republicanism was much too simple. Even if some societies were once stratified into the interests of the one, the few, and the many, that was no longer the case. How then were interests in more complex systems best understood, and, if need be, represented or "balanced"?

Second, how could a republic be designed to handle the conflicts that a diversity of interests seemed to make inevitable? After all, despite all the high-flown talk about civic virtue and balance of interests, in practice conflict was a pronounced, one might say normal, aspect of political life in earlier republics. Were political parties, which appeared in rudimentary and rather durable form in eighteenth-century Britain, somehow to be banished from public life in order to ensure public tranquility? If so, how—without destroying the essentials of republican government itself?

Third, if republican government depends on the virtue of its citizens, and if virtue consists in dedication to the public good (rather than one's own interests or those of some particular part of the "public"), then is a republic really possible, particularly in large and heterogeneous societies like those of Britain, France, and America? The orthodox republican answer was simple: republics could exist only in small states (Montesquieu 1961, bk. 8, chap. 16). But if so, then the republican tradition was irrelevant to the great task to which democratic republicans were firmly committed: democratizing the large nation-states of the modern world.

Fourth, then, could republican theory—and democratic ideas more generally—be applied on the scale of the nation-state? Just as with Greek democratic ideas and institutions, so with the republican tradition the attempt to adapt democratic republicanism to the requirements of large-scale societies required a far-reaching transformation. As democratic republicans discovered in the course of the eighteenth century, a part of the answer to the problem of scale was to be found in institutions that hitherto had little place in democratic or republican theory, and not much in practice: the institutions of representative government.

## REPRESENTATIVE GOVERNMENT

As we have seen, the Greeks rejected the notion that a large-scale political system could be desirable and never created a stable system of representative government. Nor did the Romans, despite the ever increasing expansion of the republic in both territory and citizens (Larsen 1955, 159–60). No matter how far from Rome a citizen might be, the only democratic institutions open to him were the assemblies held in Rome for electing magistrates and passing laws. Yet how could a Roman be a good citizen if, for all practical purposes, he could not attend the assemblies in Rome and therefore could not fully participate in public life? As more and more citizens lived at too great a distance for them easily to make the journey to Rome, the assemblies were gradually transformed (in fact if never in theory) into "representative" bodies; but, to use a later expression, for most citizens representation was "virtual" rather than actual, and it was badly though somewhat haphazardly biased in favor of those who could manage to attend.[2] (For details, see Taylor 1961, 50–75; Taylor 1966, 64–70.) Nor was representation a concern of the republican theorists of Renaissance Italy, who largely ignored the problem of how a citizen in a large republic like Rome could participate effectively, and in a realistic sense equally, with his fellow citizens. In any case they left the problem unsolved.

Thus from classical Greece to the seventeenth century, the possibility that a legislature might properly consist not of the entire body of citizens but of their elected representatives remained mainly outside the theory and practice of democratic or republican government—difficult as this fact may be for a contemporary democrat to understand.

An important break from the prevailing orthodoxy occurred, however, during the English Civil War, when the Puritans were compelled in their search for a republican alternative to monarchy to raise many of the most fundamental questions of democratic (or republican) theory and practice. In the course of elaborating their demands for a broader franchise and a government responsive to a broad electorate, the Levellers in particular foreshadowed the future development of the democratic idea, including the legitimacy—indeed the necessity—for representation. Yet the complete assimilation of representation into the theory and practice of democracy was still more than a century away. Even Locke, who expressed the view in the *Second Treatise* that the consent of the majority (specifically to taxes) might be given "either by themselves or their representatives chosen by them" (chap. XI, para. 140, p. 380), had little to say about representation and its place in democratic or republican theory.[3] And Rousseau's insistence in the *Social Contract* that representation was impermissible (bk. 3, chap. 15) was perfectly in line with the traditional view.

In actual practice, representation was not invented by democrats but developed instead as a medieval institution of monarchical and aristocratic government.[4] (See, for example, Mansfield 1968.) Its beginnings are to be found, notably in England and Sweden, in the assemblies summoned by monarchs, or sometimes the nobles themselves, to deal with important matters of state: revenues, wars, royal succession, and the like. In the typical pattern, those summoned were drawn from and were intended to represent the various estates, with the representatives from each estate meeting separately. Over time, the estates diminished to two, lords and commoners, who were of course represented in separate houses (an arrangement, as we just saw, that created a problem for eighteenth-century radical Whigs, who found it difficult to explain why a second chamber was necessary in a democratic republic).

In the eighteenth century, writers began to see what the Levellers had seen earlier, that by joining the democratic idea of rule by the people to the non-democratic practice of representation, democracy could take on a wholly new form and dimension. In *The Spirit of the Laws* (1748) Montesquieu wrote admiringly of the English constitution and declared that, since it was impossible in a large state for the people to meet as a legislative body, they must choose representatives to do what they could not do themselves. Although as I just mentioned Rousseau subsequently rejected this view in the *Social Contract*, his flat rejection in that work was inconsistent with both his earlier and later writings, where he accepted representation as legitimate (Fralin 1978, 75–76, 181). Within a few generations of Montesquieu and Rousseau, representation was widely accepted by democrats and republicans as a solution that eliminated the ancient limits on the size of democratic states and transformed democracy from a doctrine suitable only for small and rapidly vanishing city-states to one applicable to the large nation-states of the modern age.

To those steeped in the older tradition, the union of representation and democracy sometimes seemed a marvelous and epochal invention. Thus by the early nineteenth century, a French writer much admired by Jefferson, Destutt de Tracy, insisted that both Rousseau and Montesquieu were obsolete: "Representation, or representative government, may be considered as a new invention, unknown in Montesquieu's time . . . Representative democracy . . . is democracy rendered practicable for a long time and over a great extent of territory" (De Tracy 1811, 19). In 1820 James Mill proclaimed "the system of representation" as "the grand discovery of modern times" in which "the solution of all difficulties, both speculative and practical, will perhaps be found" (Sabine 1964, 695). Within a few years, what De Tracy, James Mill, and James Madison had correctly seen as a revolutionary transformation of democracy was taken for granted: it was obvious and unarguable that democracy must be representative.[5]

The transformation of democratic theory and practice that resulted from its union with representation has had profound consequences. Although we shall consider these more fully in later chapters, it may be helpful to mention several of them here. The most important consequence, as everyone was aware, was that popular government need no longer be confined to small states but could now be extended almost indefinitely to include vast numbers of persons. Thus the idea of democracy, which might have perished with the disappearance of city-states, became relevant to the modern world of nation-states. Within the far larger domain of the nation-state, new conceptions of personal rights, individual freedom, and personal autonomy could flourish. Moreover, important problems that could never be solved within the narrow limits of the city-state—and these grew ever more numerous as interdependence increased—might be dealt with more effectively by a government capable of making laws and regulations over a far larger territory. To this extent, the capacity of citizens to govern themselves was greatly enhanced.

Yet the change in democracy resulting from its union with representation created its own problems. An entirely new and highly complex constellation of political institutions, which we are only beginning to understand, superseded the sovereign assembly that was central to the ancient conception of democracy. These institutions of representative democracy removed government so far from the direct reach of the demos that one could reasonably wonder, as some critics have, whether the new system was entitled to call itself by the venerable name of democracy. Further, the older idea of monistic democracy, in which autonomous political associations were thought to be unnecessary and illegitimate, was transformed into a pluralist political system in which autonomous associations were held to be not only legitimate but actually necessary to democracy on a large scale. On the large scale of the nation-state, a diversity of interests and interest groups came into existence. And these diverse groups were by no means an unmixed blessing. Where in the older view factionalism and conflict were believed to be destructive, political conflict came to be regarded as a normal, inevitable, even desirable part of a democratic order. Consequently the ancient belief that citizens both could and should pursue the public good rather than their private ends became more difficult to sustain, and even impossible, as "the public good" fragmented into individual and group interests.

Thus a conflict was created, one still with us to which we must return in later chapters, between the theory and practice of representative democracy and earlier conceptions of democratic and republican government that were never wholly lost.

## THE LOGIC OF POLITICAL EQUALITY

Modern democratic governments have not been created by philosophers or historians familiar with Greek democracy, the republican tradition, or the concept of representation. Whatever independent influence ideas like these may have had, and however complex the interplay of ideas and action may be, we know that democratic theories are not self-fulfilling.

It is obvious, however, that the emergence and persistence of a democratic government among a group of people depends in some way on their *beliefs*. Thus if a substantial majority, or possibly even a substantial minority, were opposed to the idea of democracy and preferred an alternative—rule by a monarch or an aristocracy, say—then such a group would be most unlikely to govern itself democratically. Conversely, among a group whose members believe that they are all about equally well qualified to participate in the decisions of the group, the chances are relatively high that they will govern themselves through some sort of democratic process. How such a belief might come about among the members of a group I am not prepared to say. In some times and places, however, three circumstances occur that favor beliefs in the democratic process. Certain persons constitute a fairly well-defined group or association. The group is, or its members believe it will become, relatively independent of control by outsiders. Finally, the members of the group perceive themselves as about equally qualified to govern, at least in a rough and ready sort of fashion. This final aspect of their beliefs might be more specifically and a bit more abstractly described as follows. The members believe that no single member, and no minority of members, is so definitely better qualified to rule that the one or the few should be permitted to rule over the entire association. They believe, on the contrary, that all the members of the association are adequately qualified to participate on an equal footing with the others in the process of governing the association.

I am going to call this idea the Strong Principle of Equality.[6] In chapters 6 and 7 I shall show how the Strong Principle might reasonably be justified. The important point here is that *if* the members believe that the Strong Principle is valid, then they are likely to hold certain further beliefs that tend to follow from this principle. These further beliefs have to do with the kind of government within the association that would be consistent with the Strong Principle. As we shall see in chapter 8, only a democratic government would be fully consistent. I do not mean to imply that most people are highly logical in political matters. But working out the gross implications of the Strong Principle is well within the reach of ordinary human beings, as a wealth of human experience testifies. For repeatedly throughout human history groups of people have seen the implications and attempted to bring about a political order that would be more or less consistent with the principle.

These historical experiences reveal two important features of the Strong Principle. First, belief in something like the principle, and the development of at least a rude democratic process, have often come about among people who had little or no acquaintance with Greek democracy or the republican tradition or the eighteenth-century discovery of representation. Unnumbered tribal associations developed rude forms of democracy without any knowledge of these Western ideas. The local trade clubs (or unions) that appeared in England in the eighteenth century adopted practices of simple, direct democracy, which later developed into representative systems—all without benefit of theoretical knowledge.[7] And after all, in 500 B.C. the Greeks themselves had no known precedents to draw on. At about the same time, the Romans were beginning the transition from kingship to an aristocratic republic, independent of Greek influence. Later, the further democratization of the republic came about primarily because the plebes (and their leaders) insisted that they were sufficiently qualified to participate and acted to bring about their inclusion, that is, they insisted in effect that the Strong Principle applied to plebes as well as patricians. The origins of the Viking Ting, a judicial-legislative assembly of freemen, are lost in time but clearly were independent of external influences. The creation of the Althing in Iceland in 930 and the development of a quasi-democratic constitutional system unique in Europe for its time were offshoots of Norwegian Viking settlers who, it is safe to say, knew nothing of Greek democracy, Roman republicanism, or political theory or philosophy in a formal sense. What they did know, or believe, is that they were essentially equal in their qualifications for participating in government. So, too, with the democracies in the Alpine communities that took the first steps toward the formation of the Swiss Confederation. It is doubtful that in overthrowing the monarchy and creating a republic, the seventeenth-century English Puritans, Levellers, and Commonwealthmen were nearly as much influenced by Greece, Rome, or the republican tradition—though of course they were familiar with and made use of the institution of representation—as they were by their Christian beliefs, according to which all men were not only equal in the eyes of God but equally qualified to understand the word of God, to participate in church government, and by extension to govern the Commonwealth.[8] In 1646, Richard Overton, a Leveller, wrote in a tract entitled *An Arrow Against All Tyrants*:

> For by natural birth all men are equal . . . and as we are delivered of God by the hand of nature into this world, every one with a natural innate freedom and propriety . . . even so we are to live, every one equally . . . to enjoy his birthright and privilege, even all whereof God by nature hath made him free. . . Every man by nature being a king, priest, prophet, in his own natural circuit and compass, whereof no second may partake but by deputation, commission, and free consent from him whose right it is (Woodhouse 1938, 69).

It was ideas like these that the Puritans took with them when they fled to the New World.

These and other historical experiences reveal another important point about the Strong Principle: It need not necessarily be applied very broadly. On the contrary, more often than not it has been interpreted in a highly exclusive way. As we saw, the male citizens of Athens did not believe that the Strong Principle applied to the majority of adults in Athens—women, metics, and slaves. In Venice, so much admired by republican theorists from Guicciardini to Rousseau, the nobles extended the principle only to themselves, a tiny minority of the Venetian population. In fact, because the Strong Principle does not specify its own scope, its implications are as powerful for aristocrats as for commoners. The principle could equally well apply to a democracy with universal suffrage and to aristocratic institutions like the House of Lords or the College of Cardinals.

Thus whenever members of a group or association come to believe that the Strong Principle pretty much applies *to themselves*, then the imperatives of logic and practical knowledge will strongly tend to lead them to the adoption of a more or less democratic process *among themselves*. We might describe the "democracy" that results as democratic with respect to its own demos, but not necessarily democratic with respect to all persons subject to the collective decisions of the demos.

Once again, we encounter a problem that was not satisfactorily solved by any of the important sources of democratic theory and practice described in this chapter. Even if all persons who are adequately qualified to participate in making collective decisions ought rightfully to be included in the demos, and the demos ought to make collective decisions by means of a democratic process, what persons *are* adequately qualified and therefore ought to be included in the demos? As we shall discover, just as democracy in its origins did not provide a conclusive answer to this question, so too the major justifications that have been offered for modern democracy fail to answer it satisfactorily. Clearly, then, one of our first tasks, which we undertake in chapter 9, is to find a satisfactory answer.

# PART TWO

◆◆◆◆◆◆◆◆

# ADVERSARIAL CRITICS

# Chapter 3

◆◆◆◆◆◆◆

# Anarchism

Two kinds of objections to democracy are so fundamental that unless they can be satisfactorily met any further exploration of the democratic idea would be futile. Though radically different, these objections come from the advocates of anarchism, which I am going to consider in this chapter, and the advocates of guardianship, which I shall consider in the next two chapters.

One could imagine a society consisting only of purely voluntary associations, a society without a state. This is the vision of anarchism, and the anarchist ideal has probably existed in some form as long as states have existed.

The philosophical theory of anarchism holds that because states are coercive and because coercion is intrinsically bad, states are inherently evil; and further that states could be—and as an unnecessary evil should be—eliminated by replacing them with voluntary associations. Because democracy might well be the most desirable process for governing these associations, it might also be the prevalent form of government in an anarchist society. But in the anarchist view democracy cannot redeem a state. For even if coercion were the product of a perfectly democratic process, coercion would remain, as it must, an intrinsic (and avoidable) evil; thus even a state governed by a democratic process is evil. Being evil, a democratic state, like every state, lacks any justifiable claim to our loyalty, our support, or our obligation to obey its laws.

This in simplified form is the essential argument of anarchism. Although the argument is widely and often unthinkingly dismissed as foolish or unreasonable, it merits serious consideration, because it focuses attention on a central problem in the democratic idea. Advocates of the democratic process have always meant it to be applied to the state. Yet to apply democracy to the state necessarily implicates democracy in coercion. But if coercion is intrinsically bad, as most people would agree it is, can the democratic process somehow make it good?

## THE ARGUMENT

Although I have just presented a summary version of the anarchist argument, an anarchist might object that I have misrepresented anarchist ideas. The difficulty is that anarchism is an even less coherent body of thought than democracy, which, as we have seen, is hardly a model of philosophical coherence and consistency. Not only have anarchists presented a great diversity of views but they have often displayed a looseness of thought that defies systematic analysis, almost as if they were opposed even to the coercive force of logical reasoning. William Godwin, P. A. Kropotkin, Mikhail Bakunin, Pierre-Joseph Proudhon, Emma Goldman, and others have all advanced anarchist views—sometimes as with Bakunin and Goldman with more passion than logic, sometimes as with Kropotkin and Proudhon with admirable clarity and coherence and yet markedly divergent prescriptions. Or, to take a recent example, the American political philosopher Robert Paul Wolff has written a small, deductively reasoned essay that is exceptional in the rigor of its defense of anarchism (Wolff 1976). However, he presents a justification (which we examine below) that is rather outside the mainstream of anarchist thought. The many different visions of anarchist society are by no means compatible. Thus while some anarchists have advocated complete individualism, and a few have proposed a kind of anarcho-capitalism, many have advocated a comprehensive communism. While many have opposed the market, some like Proudhon have incorporated markets into a system of contractual relations without a state.[1]

Despite this diversity, one finds some common threads in anarchist thought. Its most distinctive idea is of course suggested by the name itself: *an + archos*, or ruler-less. As I have said, anarchists tend to agree that a state, being coercive, is undesirable and therefore should—and what is more, could—be replaced *entirely* by voluntary associations based on continuing consent. The "entirely" is what distinguishes the true anarchist (in the sense in which I use the term here) from others, like Robert Nozick, who draw close to anarchism but shrink from totally abolishing the state and would therefore retain it in some minimal form (Nozick 1974).

Opposition to the existence of a state also distinguishes anarchism from civil disobedience or a principled refusal to obey a law. Although the two are sometimes confused, the question (1) is it rational or reasonable to consent to a state? is clearly different from the question (2) if I consent to a state, must I always obey it? Since to anarchists the answer to the first is no, the second is irrelevant. But others, who say yes to the first, might still reasonably say no to the second, as we shall see.

Although no canonical statement exists, from the wide array of anarchist thought one can construct a reasoned argument consisting of four assumptions and five conclusions. Challenged by a democrat, an anarchist familiar with the theory of anarchism might argue as follows.

## Four Assumptions

CONCERNING OBEDIENCE TO A BAD STATE

DEMO: I have sometimes heard you claim to be the true advocate of democratic ideas. Yet you attack democrats like me when we contend that the most important place for democracy is in governing the state.

ANARCH: Yes, of course. You can no more turn a state into a good state by making it democratic than you can turn a rotten fish into a fresh fish by putting a fancy sauce on it.

DEMO: If I may say so, dear friend, your metaphor stinks. You seem to believe that a state is inherently bad. Yet we could not live a decent life without a state.

ANARCH: I think that when you hear my argument, you may approve of my metaphor after all. I feel quite sure that you share my premises, and if so I don't really see how how you can disagree with my conclusions.

DEMO: Let us see.

ANARCH: My first assumption is that *no one is obligated to support or obey a bad state*.

What gives power to this assumption is that far from being unique to anarchism, it lies at the common core of general belief in the Western world today. Although support for the assumption has had a long and complex history in Western thought, in modern times it has gained wide acceptance, as you will surely agree.

DEMO: I wouldn't deny that. The wide acceptance you speak of was initiated in the West, though, not by anarchists but mainly by Christians.

ANARCH: Exactly! The strength of our argument is that it rests on premises that most of us accept. Consider the role of Christianity in helping to make our case for us. Christians have been compelled (often literally) to answer the question: What ought I to do if the rules laid down by the state conflict with those laid down for me by God or my conscience? I don't want to go into the history of Christian responses to this question, which is vast and complex, but it is worth recalling that whereas in the thirteenth century Aquinas had insisted that in some circumstances a Christian had not only a right but a duty to resist tyranny, in the sixteenth century Luther contended that Christians must obey even an unjust government. Yet the religious conflicts of the sixteenth and seventeenth century that Luther triggered off made it impossible for all Christians to yield obedience to the commands of the state without violating their beliefs as Catholics or Protestants. As a consequence, Christian thought veered back toward a restatement of the position of Aquinas, sometimes in even blunter language.

By the eighteenth century, the belief gained ground that if constitutions and man-made laws were to be legitimate and acceptable, they must not violate the "higher laws" prescribed by nature and by natural rights. The American and French revolutions both helped to lend legitimacy to the idea that people possess a natural right to overthrow an oppressive state. Thus by the time anarchism was recast in a modern setting in the nineteenth century, belief in the moral right to revolt against a bad regime was widely shared, certainly by most liberals and democrats. In the twentieth century the systematic terror, brutality, and oppression of totalitarian regimes converted what once might have been an arguable proposition into an almost uncontested assumption. Democrats, liberals, conservatives, radicals, revolutionaries, Christians, Jews, Muslims, atheists, and agnostics all agree with us that no person has an obligation to support or obey an evil state.

### CONCERNING THE NATURE OF STATES

DEMO: The point is, however, that a democratic state is not an evil state.

ANARCH: Please don't rush to your conclusions until you have heard the rest of my argument. My second assumption is that *all states are coercive.*

Here too we anarchists adopt a widely shared assumption. Today, in fact, coercion is generally thought to be an essential characteristic in the very definition of what we mean by a state. For among the crucial characteristics that distinguish a state from other associations is its capacity to impose, or at any rate to regulate the imposition of, severe and even violent sanctions on persons within its boundaries who violate its rules or laws: sanctions which, even if not sufficient to coerce everyone who might otherwise choose not to comply with a law, are applied coercively to punish those who disobey and are apprehended and convicted.[2]

DEMO: I would hardly contest so elementary a proposition. Like any state, a democratic state would use coercion to enforce democratically enacted laws, if that should turn out to be necessary.

### CONCERNING THE EVIL OF COERCION

ANARCH: I'm pleased that we agree so far, and I'm quite sure you'll agree with my next assumption as well. This is simply that *coercion is intrinsically bad.*

Once again, we anarchists adopt an assumption that few persons who give much thought to the matter would wish to dispute. I imagine that you and I can distinguish things that we judge to be *intrinsically* good or evil (things we believe are good or bad in themselves) from things that may be *extrinsically* or *instrumentally* good or bad in some circumstances. Surely most of us would judge coercion to be intrinsically bad.

DEMO: But something might be intrinsically bad and yet instrumentally justifiable.

ANARCH: You mean that the end justifies the means?

DEMO: I see where your argument is leading, and I warn you that I will come back to that distinction between what is intrinsically good or bad and what may be instrumentally justified as essential to a good purpose.

ANARCH: Let me stay with the intrinsic evil of coercion for a moment. Coercion typically means compelling someone to obey a demand by using a credible threat of serious physical or emotional harm to those who refuse. To make the threat credible, ordinarily it must be carried out against a significant number of those who do refuse. Insofar as the threat of coercion succeeds, and people are compelled to obey laws they oppose, the persons coerced are deprived of their freedom—not least, their freedom of self-determination—and they may suffer irreparable harm in many other ways as well. If the threat fails to deter, and the person who disobeys is punished, the punishment usually results in acute physical suffering, in the form of imprisonment or worse. To argue that consequences like these are good *in themselves*, or even neutral, would be remarkably perverse. If we could achieve our ends without the use of coercion and punishment, would not most of us gladly choose to dispense with these means? That we would do so is perhaps the best proof of the intrinsic undesirability of coercion.

DEMO: I'm not going to quarrel with your third assumption. On the contrary, we democrats have argued that one reason why a *state* ought to be democratic is precisely because a state is not a purely voluntary association. Because it does possess the capacity for coercion a state is potentially dangerous. To ensure that the state's enormous potential for coercion is used for the public good and not for public harm, it is infinitely more important that the state be democratic than that any private or nonstate association be so.

CONCERNING ALTERNATIVES

ANARCH: Here's where we part company. While my previous assumptions are the common currency of modern thought, my fourth is obviously not: *A society without a state is a feasible alternative to a society with a state.*

DEMO: Your fourth assumption is absolutely essential. Without it anarchism would simply present a philosophical problem for which it had no solution.

ANARCH: I agree, of course. It is this last assumption, together with the first of the conclusions I now want to urge on you, that gives substance to the anarchist vision of a society in which autonomous individuals and strictly voluntary associations perform all the activities needed for a good life. We anarchists oppose all forms of hierarchy and coercion, not simply in the state but in every kind of association.

## Five Conclusions

DEMO: I mean to challenge the validity of your fourth assumption. But first I want to hear the rest of your argument.

ANARCH. I can't speak for other anarchists. No one can. But I believe that it is from premises like these (perhaps more often implied than stated) that we anarchists tend to draw certain conclusions. I'm going to put my conclusions in a more schematic form than most anarchists would find acceptable, and I'll even strip my argument of the passionate sense of injustice, outrage, and humanity that adds such power to much anarchist writing. Let me swiftly summarize some propositions with which most anarchists would agree.

Because all states are necessarily coercive, all states are necessarily bad.

Because all states are necessarily bad, no one has an obligation to obey or support any state.

Because all states are bad, because no one has an obligation to obey or support any state, and because a society without a state is a feasible alternative, all states ought to be abolished.

It follows that even a democratic process cannot be justified if it merely provides procedures, like majority rule, for doing what it is inherently wrong to do: allow some persons to coerce others. A democratic state is still a state, still coercive, and still bad.

Because the requirement of unanimity would prevent coercion, associations might be justified if their decisions were to require unanimity. Therefore a democratic process would be justified if it were to require unanimity. But since a unanimity requirement would guarantee that no one could ever be coerced, an association in which decisions were made by unanimity would not be a state.

## WOLFF'S DEFENSE OF ANARCHISM

Robert Paul Wolff's defense of anarchism is not greatly at odds with the argument presented by the fictional Anarch of the preceding dialogue, but because it takes a different tack and is besides exceptionally compact and lucid, it is well worth special attention. His argument may be summarized as follows.[3]

### The State

The distinctive characteristic of the state is supreme authority. Authority is the right to command and the right to be obeyed.

Authority in this sense must be distinguished from power—the ability to compel compliance through the use or threat of force. So too, obedience to authority (in this sense) must be distinguished from complying with a command because of the fear of consequences for disobedience, prudence, the expectation of beneficent effects, or even recognition of the force of an argument or the rightness of a prescription. Authority is a matter of the *right* to command, and the correlative obligation to obey the person who issues the command. It is a matter of doing what he tells you to do *because he tells you to do it*.

In its prescriptive (rather than descriptive sense), the state is a group of persons who have the *right* to exercise supreme authority within a territory. And to obey the authority of a state (in the prescriptive sense) means doing what the officials of the state tell you to do simply and solely *because they tell you to do it*.

### Responsibility and Moral Autonomy

Adult human beings are (a) metaphysically free, or possess free will, in that in some sense they are capable of choosing how they shall act, and (b) possess the capacity to reason. Consequently they are responsible for their actions. Taking responsibility involves determining what one ought to do, which requires gaining knowledge, reflecting on motives, predicting outcomes, criticizing principles, and so forth.

Since a responsible person arrives at moral decisions that he expresses to himself in the form of imperatives, we may say he gives laws to himself, or is self-legislating (or self-determining). In short, he is *autonomous*.

The autonomous man is not subject to the will of another. He may do what another tells him, but not *because* he has been told to do it.

Responsibility and autonomy are different in this crucial respect: Autonomy can be forfeited but responsibility cannot. Since responsibility is a consequence of man's capacity for choice, human beings cannot give up or forfeit responsibility for their actions. They can, however, refuse to acknowledge or take responsibility for their actions. Consequently, inasmuch as moral autonomy is simply the condition of taking full responsibility for one's actions, it follows that men can forfeit their autonomy at will. That is, one can decide to obey the commands of another without making any attempt to determine for oneself whether what is commanded is good or wise.

There are many forms and degrees of forfeiture of autonomy. Nevertheless, so long as we recognize responsibility for our actions and acknowledge the power of reason within us, we must acknowledge as well the continuing obligation to make ourselves the authors of such commands as we may obey.

### Autonomy Versus the State

The defining mark of the state is authority, the right to rule. The primary obligation of man is autonomy, the refusal to be ruled. Therefore there can be no resolution of the conflict between the autonomy of the individual and the putative authority of the state.

If all men have a continuing obligation to achieve the highest degree of autonomy possible, then there would appear to be no state whose subjects have a moral obligation to obey its commands. Hence philosophical anarchism would seem to be the only reasonable political belief for an enlightened person.

## A CRITIQUE OF ANARCHISM

Like the idea of democracy in early classical Greece and again in the seventeenth and eighteenth centuries in Europe and America, anarchism presents a novel vision of human possibilities, a society in which the major institution of organized coercion has disappeared. It would be easy and convenient to dismiss that vision as utterly impractical if it were not for the familiar fact that the revolutionary ideas of the impractical visionaries of one epoch sometimes become the orthodoxy of the next. Democrats in particular should need no reminding that democracy has often been dismissed by its critics as a hopelessly unrealistic absurdity. In fact, little more than two centuries ago most democrats would themselves have said—and many did say—that to apply democracy to the nation-state was impossible.

Yet despite our imperfect capacity for predicting human change, in appraising anarchism we cannot avoid judgments about human tendencies and possibilities. In particular, the anarchist vision invites four questions:

Even if coercion is intrinsically bad, can the use of coercion be reasonably justified in some circumstances?
Even if so, is it reasonable to establish a state?
Even if so, are we always obliged to support the existence of a state?
And even assuming we live in a good or satisfactory state, should we always obey its laws?

Although, strictly speaking, one could decide to accept or reject anarchism without answering the last two questions, confronting them helps to round out our consideration of the problems anarchism poses for democratic theory and practice.

## On the Justifiability of Coercion

As I have already said, the two most crucial parts of the anarchist vision are the assumption that an alternative to the state exists and the conclusion that all states are necessarily bad because they are coercive. Let me consider these in reverse order.

Is coercion, even though intrinsically bad, sometimes justified? The answer depends upon both moral and empirical judgments. Although as is often the case these are somewhat interdependent, we can roughly distinguish two different sets of judgments.

First, we need to judge how likely it is that coercion would occur *even without a state*, that is, if people existed in what political philosophers in the seventeenth and eighteenth centuries who confronted this very question liked to call a "state of nature." Suppose, for example, that people in a state of nature find that one of the persons in their vicinity is a wrongdoer who simply will not refrain from doing serious harm to others. Despite the best efforts of his associates, neither reason, argument, persuasion, public opinion, nor the final sanction of social ostracism dissuades him from doing harm. His associates finally conclude that he will persist in harming others unless he is forcibly restrained or threatened with severe harm (that is, coerced). In the extreme case, such a recalcitrant wrongdoer might use weapons to appropriate another's goods, commit rape, enslave another person, engage in torture, and so on. Now if recalcitrant wrongdoers were to exist in a society without a state, then a dilemma would arise for all those who believe that coercion must not be permitted because it is intrinsically bad: whether or not the wrongdoers were coercively restrained, coercion would be employed—either by the wrongdoers or by those who restrained them.

The dilemma would become even sharper if several recalcitrant wrongdoers were to accumulate enough resources to enable them, by judicious use of rewards and punishments, to gain control over others. Thus a small gang of wrongdoers might come to dominate certain associates. By first dominating a few, they might then gain power over more, until finally they subjected the entire society to their rule. In effect, the wrongdoers would have employed coercion to create a state—a gangster state, if you will.[4]

Anarchists contend that if states did not exist coercion would soon disappear or decline to a tolerable level. Obviously this empirical judgment is crucial to the validity of their argument. If they are mistaken, if instead coercion would very likely persist even without a state, and if the most distinctive feature of anarchism—eradicating the state—is justified as a means to avoid coercion, then their dilemma is without a solution and the case for anarchism is, to say the least, profoundly weakened. Conversely, if anarchists are mistaken about the likelihood of coercion in the absence of a state, then the case for trying to create a good or satisfactory state in order to restrict and regulate coercion is considerably strengthened. If one were to conclude that on balance the gains from creating a state are likely to exceed the costs, then from a utilitarian perspective it would be reasonable to opt for a state.

The second kind of judgment we need to make is therefore essentially a moral one. Though not everyone will evaluate coercion from a utilitarian perspective, if one concludes that coercion would be very likely to exist even in the absence of a state, one is then obliged to ask whether and in what circumstances it might be justifiable to use coercion. Even anarchists disagree about the answer. According to some, like Bakunin, coercive violence is justified and necessary in the supreme cause of overthrowing the state. But other anarchists, like Leo Tolstoy, believe that coercion and violence are never justified; in this view, the only consistent position for an anarchist is to adhere strictly to a doctrine of nonviolence (Carter 1978).

The difficulty with the first view is that if coercion is justified as a means for overthrowing the state, then it follows obviously that coercion must be justifiable provided it is used for sufficiently good or important purposes. But if so, then surely coercion might be justified in restraining recalcitrant wrongdoers, particularly if their aim was to create a gangster state. Moreover, if the reason for overthrowing the state is not only to abolish coercion but also to achieve other ends like freedom, equality, security, and justice—as most anarchists have believed—then might not coercion be justified if it were employed to achieve greater freedom, equality, security, or justice? In short, if the objection to coercion as a means is not absolute but contingent on consequences, might one not justifiably seek to create a democratic state and support its existence in order to maximize freedom and justice, minimize unregulated private coercion, and prevent a gangster state from developing?

The alternative position, according to which violence and coercion are absolutely forbidden for any purpose, is heir to at least two difficulties. First, if coercion is likely in any case to be employed by wrongdoers, then the position is self-contradictory. For one must either allow it to occur, and in so doing permit the wrongdoer to coerce others or permit coercion to be used in order to prevent wrongdoers from engaging in coercion. But a moral position that is so self-contradictory that it leaves one without guidance for the most elementary choices is indefensible. Second, why is avoiding coercion a supreme end that dominates all other ends? What makes noncoercion superior to justice, equality, freedom, security, happiness, and other values? If any of these ends are superior to noncoercion, then would not coercion be justified if it were the sole means in some situations for achieving the superior value? Alternatively, if one believes that the world of values is not dominated by a single absolute end but is, in William James's phrase, a pluralistic universe, then one must make judgments about trade-offs between coercion and other values.

## On the Need for a State

A moment ago I suggested that one might opt for creating a state on the ground that, given the likelihood of some coercion persisting even in the absence of a state, the advantages of regulating coercion through a state might outweigh the disadvantages. One might argue, however, that the advantages would *not* necessarily outweigh the disadvantages and that, even if occasional violence and coercion existed, a stateless society consisting exclusively of voluntary associations would on the whole be preferable to the compulsions of a state. Many anarchists believe that sociopathic behavior is not inevitable but is created because people are socialized into behaving in conformity with the requirements of states and the socioeconomic systems they uphold, Consequently, they insist, once states are eliminated and decent social and economic arrangements are introduced, shaming, public reprimands, shunning, and ostracism would reduce wrongdoing to tolerable levels. Thus on balance a stateless society would be better than a society with a state.

It is true that human beings have sometimes achieved a tolerable existence, perhaps even a highly satisfactory life, without a state. Judging from ethnographic descriptions, many preliterate tribes may have done so. By means of an astounding and highly humane adaptation to a harsh and dangerous environment, the Inuit (Eskimo) in northern Canada evidently existed for many centuries—until a few generations ago—without a state. Typically they lived in tiny groups of a dozen or so families united by multiple bonds of kinship, culture, religion, myth, and common fate. Transgressions of important rules were met with shame, ridicule, gossip, and occasionally ostracism. Although individual violence may have been rare, it did occur. Yet the social bonds of the Inuit and their use of social sanctions brought about a high degree of conformity with the basic rules and norms, and relations among them appear to have been far more orderly and peaceful than societies with states have ever managed to achieve.

Yet while some romantic anarchists may imagine our returning to the tiny autonomous groups of some preliterate societies, short of a cataclysm that no sane person wants, a return to the infancy of the species looks to be impossible or, if not impossible, highly undesirable. Since I want to return to this theme in chapter 13, where we shall confront the problem of scale and the nation-state, let me simply mention three reasons. First, the world is already too densely populated to provide much space for autonomy; the Inuit, after all, were few in number and inhabited a gigantic area thought by others to be an uninhabitable wasteland. Second, a multiplicity of interdependencies cannot be snapped apart without enormous costs that few people would accept.

Third, virtually the entire globe is now already occupied by states. Throughout recorded history, small autonomous groups of people have been extraordinarily vulnerable to conquest and absorption by larger states, a phenomenon that continues to the present day. Thus either the return to a life of small autonomous stateless groups would have to occur almost simultaneously throughout the world or some states would continue to exist with their exceptional capacity and propensity for conquest and absorption. If anarchism requires the first, then anarchism must be set aside as at best an appealing fantasy. If it does not, then it must show why states would permit any small, independent group to exist anywhere on earth, with the possible exception of a few of the most remote and forbidding places on the globe where almost no one, and probably few advocates of anarchism, would care to live.

In sum, the following judgments seem reasonable:

1. In the absence of a state, highly undesirable forms of coercion would probably persist.
2. In a stateless society, some associates might in any case acquire sufficient resources to create a highly oppressive state.
3. A degree of social control sufficient to avoid the creation of a state appears to require that an association be highly autonomous, very small, and united by multiple bonds.
4. Creating such associations on a significant scale in the world today appears to be either impossible or highly undesirable.

These judgments support the conclusion that *it would be better to try to create a satisfactory state than try to exist in a society without a state*.

## OBJECTIONS TO WOLFF'S ARGUMENT

Though Wolff's argument departs from the mainstream of anarchist thought, it nonetheless encounters similar difficulties. Let me mention five deficiencies in his argument.[5]

1. In Wolff's schema the contradiction between moral autonomy and the state exists *by definition*. Thus his search for a solution is doomed to failure from the outset simply because, given the problem as he poses it, logically there can be no solution. But as a consequence of his definition of authority, his argument cuts a far broader swath than he may have intended. For on his showing it is not only a state that is incompatible with moral autonomy: so is authority of any kind. By defining authority as a right to command a mindless, unreflective, robotic obedience, Wolff is logically confronted by a choice between a world of robots subject to authority, on the one hand, and, on the other, a world of human beings subject to no authority whatsoever but responsibly exercising their moral autonomy.

2. Consequently Wolff fails, as he must, in his attempt to show that authority and autonomy could be reconciled in a state governed by unanimous direct democracy.

Under unanimous direct democracy, every member of the society wills freely every law which is actually passed. Hence, he is only confronted as a citizen with laws to which he has consented. Since a man who is constrained only by the dictates of his own will is autonomous, it follows that under the directions of unanimous direct democracy, men can harmonize the duty of autonomy with the commands of authority. (23)

But the "authority" here is not the "authority" of his earlier definition: doing what someone tells you to do *because he tells you to do it*. Either the will one is obeying is nothing other than one's own will, in which case no exercise of authority occurs or one is subject to the authority of one's fellows, and one obeys simply because one's fellows tell one to obey, in which case one fails to act autonomously. Although Wolff struggles to escape this dilemma, he simply cannot succeed, for he has already blocked off all possible escape routes.[6] Wolff finally rejects the solution of unanimous direct democracy as unworkable except under highly improbable conditions. He is left, then, with no feasible solution. But he fails to see that unanimous direct democracy, even if were feasible, would not be a solution to the problem as he has posed it.

3. If it really were true that authority and the state are fundamentally incompatible with autonomy, then why not sacrifice some moral autonomy? Wolff presents autonomy as an absolute value to which all other ends should give way. But why should happiness, justice, personal freedom, equality, security and all other values yield to the supreme value of autonomy? Is autonomy good in itself, or is it good, at least in some measure, to the extent that it is exercised in a responsible choice of good ends? But if authority and a state prove to be necessary means to maximizing these ends, then might one not responsibly exercise one's autonomy in choosing to create the best possible state? Wolff does not seriously consider this possibility, because he has defined it away from the outset.

4. But by defining away that possibility, Wolff poses a false problem. Does anyone seriously argue that authority or a state require mindless obedience?

Moral action always occurs within limits, many of which—probably most of which—are beyond the actor's control. Like absolute and unlimited freedom, unlimited autonomy is impossible. This Wolff recognizes. Moral autonomy is not a constant but a variable; it is not all or nothing, either 0 or 1, but a property or good that one might, so to speak, seek to maximize within reasonable limits. For example, one may reasonably forfeit some autonomy to one's doctor on matters of health. "From the example of the doctor, it is obvious that there are at least some situations in which it is reasonable to give up one's autonomy" (15).[7] But might not the absence of a state be precisely such a situation, one in which it is reasonable to give up some autonomy? But if it were the case that within the limits set by the circumstances in which I exist, I can *maximize* my autonomy by choosing to create and support a state, then would it not be perfectly reasonable to do so? Indeed, would these not be circumstances in which as a responsible human being I *ought* to do so?

5. Clearly then, if I am to act responsibly I must confront the alternatives available to me and make a judgment as to the conditions under which I might

maximize my moral autonomy or, if you like, the conditions that will minimize the limits on my capacity for exercising moral autonomy. Given human experience, I may reasonably conclude that in a stateless society the limits on my moral autonomy, as well as on my capacity for achieving other ends, would be far greater than they would in a democratic state. Among other reasons, I might be subjected to the arbitrary will of others, recalcitrant wrongdoers not open to dissuasion by me or any associates sympathetic with my plight. If I concluded that the actions of others in a stateless society would reduce my autonomy more than a democratic state, then insofar as I believe moral autonomy to be desirable I could reasonably and responsibly decide to opt for a democratic state.[8]

In attempting to build the edifice of anarchism on the foundations of responsibility and moral autonomy, Wolff is ultimately self-contradictory. For it is perfectly reasonable to conclude that except in extraordinary circumstances that are rarely attainable in our world, if we wish to maximize autonomy our only reasonable and responsible choice is to seek the best possible state. If a democratic state is the best possible state (as probably few anarchists would deny), then the most responsible way of exercising our moral autonomy is to opt for a democratic state.

## ON OBEDIENCE

Where an anarchist might have us reject any state, even a democratic state, as worse than no state, some opponents of anarchism would ask us to accept any state, even an authoritarian state, as far better than no state at all. In rejecting the first position, however, a democrat need not adopt the second. The democratic claim is only that it is better to choose a democratic state than any other state, or no state. That democratic claim leaves open how one who lives under the rule of a nondemocratic state ought to act. Decisions would require one to judge alternatives against prudence, principles, and probabilities. But the principle that no one is obligated to support or obey a bad state would clearly apply.

In choosing to support a democratic state as the best alternative, does one logically choose also to obey its laws? Presumably one might choose a democratic state from purely prudential or opportunistic considerations, without intending ever to obey any of its laws except when it was prudent or convenient to do so. But it would be highly unreasonable to choose a democratic state without accepting any obligation whatsoever to obey its laws. For the existence of the democratic process presupposes not only a body of rights, both legal and moral, but also a correlative body of duties, that is, obligations to uphold the rights. It would be logically contradictory to choose to be governed by a democratic process and refuse to support the essential requirements of the democratic process. Since we shall return to this question in chapter 10, I shall not pursue it further here.

But is one morally bound to obey *every* law passed by the democratic process? I do not believe that in choosing the democratic process, and by implication its essential requirements, I am thereby bound to obey every law properly enacted by means of that process. In a diverse society in which I find myself in a minority on some issues, a majority (even a qualified majority) might enact a law requiring me to do or refrain from doing something that violated my most profound moral commitments. I would then be faced by a conflict among my obligations. To act responsibly, I would need to consider the alternatives and their consequences and weigh as best I could the consequences of obeying or disobeying, including the effects on respect for law. Although the problem of civil disobedience is complex and requires more attention than I am prepared to give it here, in a situation of this kind it might well be reasonable for me to choose to disobey the law.[9]

In sum: If I have the opportunity to choose, and believing that a democratic state is superior both to no state and to any other state I choose to support a state governed by means of the democratic process, I do not thereby choose to turn myself into an obedient robot. I may accept the moral "authority" and moral "legitimacy" of a democratic state and yet in no sense forfeit my obligation to act responsibly when a law is enacted that seriously violates my moral standards. And sometimes responsibility may require me to disobey a law, even one enacted by the democratic process.

♦

Although the anarchist critique of democracy is unconvincing, it is important to recognize its strengths. As we saw, several of its assumptions are widely shared, among others by advocates of democracy. Moreover, in portraying the possibility of society without a state, anarchism reminds us that, as a form of social control, coercion by law is marginal in most societies most of the time and in democratic orders always. The anarchist critique calls attention to important and often half-concealed implications of democratic theory and practice. Applied to the government of a state, the democratic process may reduce but cannot by itself completely exorcise the coerciveness of the state. Unless unanimity prevails, democracy in the state may, and in practice generally does, require coercion of those who would otherwise disobey. The anarchist critique also reminds us that it is difficult and quite possibly in practice impossible to govern with the consent of all. For true consent would have to be continuous—of the living now subject to the laws, not the dead who enacted them. For a reasonable and responsible person will always treat consent not as absolute and irrevocable but as contingent. Yet no state, past or existing, fully achieves continuing consent.

Thus what the anarchist critique tells us is that all states have been, are, and perhaps always will be imperfect. The best states exist not in the universe of Plato's perfect forms but in the universe of the best attainable. And anarchism offers a criterion for evaluating states in the universe of the best attainable states. In arguing that all states are equally and absolutely bad, anarchism is not so much a *political* philosophy as a *moral* doctrine which holds that societies may be judged relatively good or bad according to the extent to which they maximize consent and minimize coercion. At the limit, then, in a perfect society coercion would cease to exist and decisions would always have the consent of all.

And is this not also part of the democratic vision? Yet in a dialogue with a thoughtful anarchist, a democrat might also add something like this:

If it is your view that coercion would not exist in a perfect or ideal society, I can't disagree. But we don't live in a perfect society, and we aren't likely to. We're likely instead to go on living in an imperfect world inhabited by imperfect human beings, that is, human beings. Therefore, unless and until your society comes into existence, the best possible society would have the best possible state. In my view, the best possible state would be one that would minimize coercion and maximize consent, within limits set by historical conditions and the pursuit of other values, including happiness, freedom, and justice. Judged by ends like these, the best state, I believe, would be a democratic state.

# Chapter 4
◆◆◆◆◆◆◆◆
# Guardianship

A perennial alternative to democracy is government by guardians. In this view, the notion that ordinary people can be counted on to understand and defend their own interests—much less the interests of the larger society—is preposterous. Ordinary people, these critics insist, are clearly not qualified to govern themselves. The assumption by democrats that ordinary people are qualified, they say, ought to be replaced by the opposing proposition that rulership should be entrusted to a minority of persons who are specially qualified to govern by reason of their superior knowledge and virtue.

Most beautifully and enduringly presented by Plato in *The Republic*,[1] the idea of guardianship has exerted a powerful pull throughout human history. Although a rudimentary democracy may well have existed for millennia among our ancestral hunter-gatherers, in recorded history hierarchy[2] is older than democracy. Both as an idea and as a practice, throughout recorded history hierarchy has been the rule, democracy the exception. Even in the later twentieth century, when lip service is all but universally given to the legitimacy of "rule by the people," only a minority of the countries of the world, and only a minority of the people of the world, are governed by regimes that might qualify as "democracies" in a modern sense. In practice, then, hierarchy is democracy's most formidable rival; and because the claim of guardianship is a standard justification for hierarchical rule, as an idea guardianship is democracy's most formidable rival.

One further point. Although the idea of guardianship is often used in its most vulgar form as a rationalization for corrupt, brutal, and inept authoritarian regimes of all kinds, the argument for it does not collapse simply because it has been badly abused. When we apply the same harsh test to democratic ideas, they too are often found wanting in practice. For both democracy and hierarchy, their worst failures are relevant to a judgment about these two alternatives. But so too are the more successful instances of each, as well as the relative feasibility and desirability of the ideal standards of democracy and guardianship.

*52*

## VISIONS OF GUARDIANSHIP

The idea of guardianship has appealed to a great variety of political thinkers and leaders in many different guises and in many different parts of the world over most of recorded history. If Plato provides the most familiar example, the practical ideal of Confucius, who was born more than a century before Plato, has had far more profound influence over many more people and persists to the present day, deeply embedded in the cultures of several countries, including China, where it offers a vigorous though not always overt competition to Marxism and Leninism for political consciousness. To mention Karl Marx and Nikolai Lenin is to remind us of another, perhaps more surprising version of guardianship: Lenin's doctrine of the vanguard party with its special knowledge of the laws of history and, as a consequence, its special, indeed its unique, claim to rule. Finally, there is a more obscure instance, one without much influence on the world but interesting because it reveals something of the variety of forms the appeal of guardianship may take. I have in mind the utopia sketched by the illustrious psychologist B. F. Skinner in *Walden Two*.

To Plato, political knowledge constituted the royal science, the supreme art: "No other art or science will have a prior or better right than in the royal science to care for human society and to rule over men in general" (*Statesman*, in *Dialogues* II, Jowett, trans., para. 276, p. 303). The essence of the art and science of politics is, of course, knowledge of the good of the community, the polis. Just as all men are not of equal excellence as physicians or pilots, so some are superior in their knowledge of the political art. And just as excellence as a physician or a pilot requires training, so too men and women must be carefully selected and rigorously trained in order to achieve excellence in the art and science of politics. The guardians must not only, like true philosophers, be completely devoted to the search for truth and, like true philosophers, discern more clearly than all others what is best for the community, but they must also be wholly dedicated to achieving that end and therefore must possess no interests of their own inconsistent with the good of the polis. Thus they would unite the truth seeking and knowledge of the true philosopher with the dedication of a true king or a true aristocracy—if such could exist—to the good of the community over which they rule.

Obviously rule by philosopher-kings would be unlikely to come about by chance. To create such a republic and the class of guardians to rule over it would require exceptional care, including, certainly, much attention to the selection and education of the guardians. Yet if such a republic were to come into existence, its citizens, recognizing the excellence of the rulers and their unswerving commitment to the good of the community, would give to it their support and loyalty. In this sense, in the language not of Plato but of modern democratic ideas, we could say that the government of the guardians would enjoy the consent of the governed.

To leap forward more than two thousand years to the ideas of Lenin is to move into a world, and a view of the world, so different from Plato's that it may seem to be stretching commonalities beyond the breaking point. Even if the Leninist incarnation of that idea were to disappear, I believe that the idea would—and surely will—reappear in a new incarnation, one that could be far more attractive to people who reject its embodiment in Leninism.

Lenin originally formulated his view, in the essay *What Is To Be Done?*, as an argument for a new kind of revolutionary party. This argument could be and was transposed, however, to the postrevolutionary society the party was instrumental in bringing about. It was then more fully developed in the work of the Hungarian philosopher and literary critic George Lukács and can be found even in more recent work, like that of the Mexican Marxist Adolfo Sánchez Vázquez (Sánchez Vázquez 1977). A synthesis of their views would be something like the following: The working class occupies a unique historical position, for its liberation necessarily means the inauguration of a society without class divisions based on the ownership or nonownership of the means of production. In a classless society (in this sense) where the means of production are socially owned and controlled, everyone will be relieved of the burden of economic exploitation and oppression and will enjoy a degree of freedom and opportunities for personal development beyond all previous historical possibility. However, it would be wholly unrealistic to think that a working class shaped by exploitation, oppression, and the dominant culture of capitalism could sufficiently understand its own needs, interests, and potentialities, and the strategies its liberation would require, to bring about, unaided, a revolutionary transformation of capitalism to socialism and the later stage of communism in which the state itself, and with it all forms of collective coercion, will have disappeared. What is needed, then, is a dedicated, incorruptible, and organized group of revolutionaries, a vanguard, who possess the knowledge and the commitment necessary to that task. These revolutionaries would need knowledge of the laws of historical development. That knowledge is to be found in the only body of scientific understanding capable of unlocking the door to liberation: the science of Marxism, now, in virtue of this new insight, the science of Marxism-Leninism. Like Plato's guardians, the members of the vanguard party must be carefully recruited, trained, and selected for their dedication to the goal of achieving the liberation of the working class (and thereby humanity itself) and expert in their knowledge of Marxism-Leninism. Since the historical transition may be long and arduous, the leadership of these guardians of the proletariat may well be necessary for some time even after the revolutionary overthrow of the capitalist state. But as with Plato's guardians, the guiding role of the party would have the consent—if not express, at least implied—of the working class itself and thus of the overwhelming majority of people.

With B. F. Skinner we turn from contemplative philosophy and revolutionary action to a distinguished modern psychologist renowned for his contributions to learning theory and behavioral psychology, a man with deep faith in rigorous empirical science. In his vision, so far as we can make it out from *Walden Two* and *Beyond Freedom and Dignity*, the guardian's knowledge is the modern psychologist's science of behavior. The philosopher-king is replaced by the psychologist-king who, like his predecessor in Plato's *Republic*, possesses the scientific knowledge that is necessary and sufficient, for the fulfillment of human potential. Once a group of human beings had experienced the beneficent rule of such a guardian, they would cease their foolish, vain, and self-defeating efforts to govern themselves, give up the illusions of democracy, and willingly—even enthusiastically—consent to the gentle and enlightened rule of the psychologist-king.

Despite their enormous differences, what is striking about these three visions is how much they have in common. Each in its own way poses an alternative to democracy and challenges the assumption that people are competent to govern themselves.

While no single interpretation can do justice to the variations among the many different visions of guardianship, it is possible to construct an account that I think fully captures the essentials of the argument. In a discussion with a modern democrat, a contemporary advocate of guardianship might make a case along the following lines.

## THREE SHARED ASSUMPTIONS

ARISTOS: You're badly mistaken if you think that you and I begin from diametrically opposed assumptions. Not at all. To begin with, like you and everyone else who is not a philosophical anarchist, I assume that the good or welfare of citizens requires that they be subject to some binding collective decisions, or laws. In some cases, at least, laws will have to be enforced by a state. In short, we advocates of guardianship agree with you democrats on the need for a state.

In the second place, I'm quite willing to accept an assumption that I presume democrats like you believe is important to your case for democracy: that the interests of all human beings ought to be given equal consideration. Perhaps some who defend guardianship would reject this principle. I presume Plato would have. You will remember his proposal in *The Republic* for a "noble fiction"—or, to call it rightly, a lie—intended to make the rulers acceptable to other citizens. The gullible citizens of his republic were to be persuaded that the god who fashioned people in the earth mixed gold in the nature of those who were to be capable of ruling, silver in the auxiliaries, and bronze in farmers and other workers. Utter nonsense! No Athenian of his time would have been convinced by such rubbish. If the case for guardianship were to depend on such absurdities, I would be the first to reject it. But I see no reason why I can't accept the idea of equal consideration as a basic moral axiom, just as you do. In fact, what I want to argue is that only a body of highly qualified people —guardians, if you like—can reasonably be counted on to possess both the knowledge and virtue needed to serve the good of everyone subject to the laws.

DEMO: I'm beginning to see where your path will veer away from mine.

ARISTO: Before I show you why you really ought to join me on that path, I want to call your attention to still another assumption we both share. Though this may surprise you, you really *do* agree with me that the process of governing the state ought to be restricted to those who are qualified to govern. I know most democrats recoil from such an idea. You fear that by openly admitting to this assumption you'll give the game away at the start to those of us who support guardianship. Certainly in your democratic theory, philosophy, and argument this dangerous premise is rarely made explicit, precisely because it is so dangerous to your case. Yet I don't believe that any important political philosopher in the democratic tradition—Locke, Rousseau, Jeremy Bentham, James Mill, for example—has ever rejected it, though perhaps only John Stuart Mill made it fully explicit.[3] You know as well as I that your great advocates of democracy have always considered that a substantial proportion of persons are just unqualified to participate in governing. To make my point, I could remind you of the way your democratic predecessors denied full citizenship to women, slaves, the unpropertied, the illiterate, and others. Because these people were excluded, their interests were neglected or, worse, terribly abused even though they comprised a majority of the adult population in some of the early democracies you so much admire. However, since that shameful part of the history of democratic ideas and practices is now behind us, I'll just agree to let us pass it by, as a part of the shabby history of democratic theory and practice.

I'll make my point instead with children. In all democratic countries, children are still excluded from full citizenship, as they always have been. Why? Because every grown-up knows that children are not qualified to govern. Surely you agree. Children are denied the rights of full citizenship simply and solely because they are unqualified. Their exclusion demonstrates conclusively that democratic theory and practice share with the theory and practice of guardianship the assumption that governing must be restricted to those who are qualified to govern.[4]

So the issue between us, my good friend, is the answer to the question posed by Plato: who *are* the best qualified to govern? Will the interests of ordinary folk best be protected by themselves, acting so far as they may be able through the democratic process, or by a body of meritorious leaders who possess exceptional knowledge and virtue?

## GUARDIANSHIP AND MERITOCRACY

DEMO: I object strenuously to your implication that the democratic process necessarily excludes expertise. Whatever may have been true in classical Greece, in modern democracies expert knowledge is enormously important in policymaking. In fact, no sensible democrat believes that citizens, or for that matter their representatives, should administer every blessed law and rule of government. Even Rousseau wrote that democracy in this narrow and absurd sense has never existed and never will exist. And today we are a very long way from Rousseau's vision (at least his vision in the *Social Contract*) of all the citizens assembling together and adopting the laws, governing themselves without representatives. As everyone knows, in modern democratic countries most laws and policies aren't adopted by town meetings, plebiscites, referenda, or other forms of direct democracy. Policies don't even flow directly out of elections. Instead, proposals are filtered through specialized committees in legislative bodies and through executive and administrative agencies, which are often staffed by highly qualified people of exceptional expertise. In fact, expertise is so important that our systems of government have sometimes been called a mixture of democracy and meritocracy.

ARISTOS: I would question just how effectively the elected leaders actually control the bureaucracies. Though bureaucrats generally lack the qualities necessary for true guardianship, I think they do often exercise a kind of de facto rulership that manages to escape popular and parliamentary controls. However, to consider that issue would distract us from the major questions. So here again, in order to get on with my argument for guardianship, let's pretend that your description of how democracies make use of expertise is roughly accurate.

What I mean by guardianship is not just democracy cum meritocracy. Perhaps it would help to avoid confusion if you will let me make a distinction between what I mean by guardianship and what you just called meritocracy. Meritocracy, which is a pretty recent term, usually refers, as you suggested, to a body of officials selected exclusively by merit and competition but who are at least nominally subordinate to others—a cabinet, prime minister, president, legislature, and the like. Meritocracy in this sense might in principle be perfectly consistent with your idea of the democratic process, provided only that the authorities who control the bureaucracies are themselves subject to the democratic process. The experts in the bureaucracies, then, might be conceived of as indirect agents of the demos, just as the elected representatives might be seen as direct agents. I think this interpretation is a rather farfetched account of the real world, but once again let's assume it as a sort of theoretical model. "Meritocracy" then could refer to a bureaucracy based on merit that operates within a democratic regime, under the full control of elected leaders. But a meritocracy in this sense isn't at all what I mean by guardianship. Guardianship isn't a mere modification of a democratic regime; it's an alternative to democracy, a fundamentally different *kind* of regime. By guardianship I mean a regime in which the state is governed by meritorious rulers who consist of a minority of adults, quite likely a very small minority, *and who are not subject to the democratic process*. That's why I prefer to call the rulers by Plato's more evocative term "guardians."

## THE QUALIFICATIONS OF THE QUALIFIED

DEMO: I suppose the difference between us will now turn on what you mean by "qualified."

ARISTOS: No, I think we may agree on what we *mean* by "qualified." Where we're going to disagree is on *who* is qualified. You'll probably agree with me that in order to be qualified to govern—to be politically competent—people should possess three qualities. People who govern should have an adequate understanding of the proper ends, goals, or objectives that the government should strive to reach. Let me call this the quality of *moral understanding* or *moral capacity*. You exclude children from the demos because they lack the moral capacity to govern: they don't know what the government should do even to protect their own interests as children. In the same way, if ordinary people don't understand their own interests, you would have to concede that like children they are morally unqualified to govern themselves.

DEMO: But in my judgment most people understand their own interests better than your guardians are likely to!

ARISTO: A base and baseless dogma. But if you'll allow me, I'd like to proceed. Even if ordinary people adequately understood their own interests, they would still not be fully qualified to govern. Since it would be utterly useless if people knew the right ends—whether their own interests or some other good—but failed to act to achieve them, those who govern should also possess a strong disposition actually to seek good ends. It's not enough to know what is best, or, like most modern philosophers and other academics, merely to talk about it. To be qualified to govern, rulers—whether guardians or the demos—must actively attempt to bring it about. This quality or disposition I like to call by an old name: *virtue*. When moral understanding and virtue are combined in the same person, they make for *morally competent* rulers. But even moral competence is not sufficient: we all know what the road to Hell is paved with. Rulers should also know the best, most efficient, and most appropriate means to achieve desirable ends. In short, they ought to possess adequate *technical* or *instrumental knowledge*.[5]

No single one of these qualities, or even any pair, would be enough. All three are necessary. To be properly qualified to govern, I say, one should be both morally competent and instrumentally competent. In combination, then, the three qualities define *political competence*. I can't help thinking that you really agree with me about the need for political competence as a requirement for ruling, no matter whether the rulers are my guardians or your demos.

DEMO: Not so fast! If I accept the assumptions so far, haven't I already conceded your case for guardianship?

ARISTOS: That may be so. But on what grounds can you reasonably reject the premises? Would you or anyone else argue that people who definitely lack political competence—children, for example—are nevertheless entitled to participate fully in governing this country? You democrats simply must confront the elementary implications of the undeniable fact that you choose deliberately to exclude children from the demos. If we agree that children aren't qualified to govern, even though they may someday become qualified, then no matter how uncomfortable it may be to acknowledge it, you have already accepted the premise that people who are definitely unqualified should not be permitted to participate fully in governing.

DEMO: You make too much of the example of children. After all, they're a unique category. As you just mentioned, they are in the earlier stages of the process of becoming adults. As adults they'll be qualified when they come of age.

ARISTOS: Now you move too fast! Once you accept a boundary that excludes certain persons, you are obliged to justify drawing the boundary there rather than somewhere else. The exact location of the boundary surely isn't self-evident, even among democrats. For example, would you want your demos to include persons who suffer from such severe mental retardation or insanity that they are legally judged to be incompetent to protect their own fundamental interests and are therefore placed under the control of a legal guardian, a paternalistic authority equivalent to a parent? And what about persons convicted of felonies? Shouldn't they be deprived of the right to vote on the ground that they have shown themselves to be morally incompetent?

Isn't the crucial issue the question of where to draw the boundary between political competence and incompetence? The answer to that by those of us who advocate guardianship, from Plato to the present day, is that the average person is plainly not qualified to govern. The Strong Principle of Equality that I've heard you assert, which claims that adults are all about equally well qualified to govern, is just as absurd as Plato's royal lie. Surely a definitely better-qualified minority of adults could be found, or if need be they could be created by education. And surely this minority, the potential guardians, ought to rule.

DEMO: Not just temporarily or transitionally but indefinitely?

ARISTOS: Nothing lasts forever, least of all political regimes. Even Plato assumed that his republic would be subject to inevitable decay, dissolution, and ultimate transformation into a different kind of regime. Some people who invoke the idea of guardianship to justify a specific regime would say that their hierarchical system is intended only to be transitional.[6] However, the argument for a transitional, though possibly quite long lasting, guardianship is in substance very similar to the defense of guardianship as an ideal and more enduring regime.

DEMO: Isn't it about time that you finally reveal to me just what that argument is?

ARISTOS: I first wanted to make sure that you understood my assumptions. I would now like to indicate the main lines of the argument. My reasons for contending that guardianship is superior to democracy are both negative and positive. My negative argument is that ordinary people lack the necessary qualifications for ruling. My positive argument is that a minority who possess superior knowledge and virtue—an elite, a "vanguard," an aristocracy in the original and etymological meaning—can be discovered and created. Unlike the great majority of people, this qualified minority would possess both the moral and the instrumental competence needed to justify a claim to govern.

## MORAL COMPETENCE

DEMO: I doubt whether you can sustain either the negative or the positive part of your argument. I believe just the opposite is true: An adequate level of moral competence is widely distributed among human beings, and in any case no distinctively superior moral elite can be identified or safely entrusted with the power to rule over the rest. I think Jefferson and the philosophers of the Scottish Enlightenment were correct in holding that most human beings possess a fundamental sense of right and wrong that is not significantly stronger in some groups than in others. If anything, ordinary folk may often have a clearer judgment on elementary moral issues than their supposed superiors. Jefferson once wrote: "State a moral case to a ploughman and a professor. The former will decide it as well and often better than the latter because he has not been led astray by artificial rules" (quoted in Wills 1978, 203). More recently John Rawls has rested his whole system of justice on the assumption that human beings are fundamentally equal as moral persons, that is, in their capacity for arriving at a reasonable conception of what is just (Rawls 1971, 505ff.). These judgments about human beings seem sound to me. Put aside the stray case of the person who is definitely impaired, and every adult of ordinary intelligence is capable of making adequate moral judgments.

ARISTOS: Aren't you greatly exaggerating the moral capacity of the average person? To begin with, many people seem to lack much understanding of their *own* basic needs, interests, or good, whichever you prefer. Isn't it a fact that very few people bother to reflect very deeply, if at all, as to what would constitute a good life? Are many people given to much introspection? Do many of us ever manage to obtain anything beyond a rather superficial understanding of ourselves? "Know thyself," said the Delphic oracle. Socrates gave his life to doing so. But few of us live with such devotion to that purpose. Take one telling example. The Jewish prophets, Christ, the ancient Hindu texts, Buddha, even so modern a philosopher as Bertrand Russell, all have deplored the utter futility of searching for happiness through the endless gratification of desire, particularly through the acquisition and consumption of things. Yet haven't Americans made the consumption of a never ending and forever increasing stream of material goods a principal objective of our lives and organized our society toward that end? And doesn't most of the rest of the world nowadays, whether Hindu, Buddhist, Jewish, Christian, or Marxist, rush headlong toward the same goal? Or consider this: for three centuries the Americans avidly collaborated in the destruction of their natural environment, indifferent in the main to its importance to their well-being. Only a little introspection might have revealed to a great many people how costly, in the long run, that indifference would be. Yet only a few people were enlightened enough to foresee the consequences.

I could multiply the examples. So could you. Well, then, can you deny that a great many people—not children, mind you, but adults—are unable or unwilling to do whatever may be necessary to acquire an elementary understanding of their own needs, their own interests, their own good? If they don't even understand their own interests, aren't they, like children, incompetent to govern themselves?

And if they are incompetent to govern themselves, surely they are even less competent to govern others. Don't most people find it difficult, perhaps even impossible, to take the good of others—very many others, anyway—into account in making decisions? Their deficiency is partly in knowledge, partly in virtue. It is, heaven knows, often difficult in a world as complex as ours to know enough to judge accurately where your own interests lie. But it's infinitely more daunting to acquire an adequate understanding of the good of other people in your society. The problem is even more acute in modern democratic countries because our fellow countrymen are so numerous that none of us can possibly know more than a small fraction of them. Consequently we have to make judgments about the good of people we don't know personally and can know about only indirectly. In social science-ese, the information costs in trying to acquire an understanding of the interests of all our fellow citizens are far too high for most of us to bear. I think it's downright inhuman to expect very many of us to do so.

Even more to the point, most people seem unwilling to give the interests of a stranger, or anyone unknown to them, anything like an equal weight in comparison with their own. This willingness to neglect the interests of people who are distant from you is particularly strong if their interests conflict with your own, your family's, your friends', or those of other people in your immediate circle. Yet even in a small country, like Denmark, say, and all the more so in a country as large as the United States, most other people are far outside your own intimate circle of family and friends or the broader circle of your acquaintances. In this sense, most of us are egoists, not altruists. But egoism is inconsistent with the need for virtue as a qualification for ruling. A moment ago, I said I agreed with you about a principle of equal consideration. What I'm now saying, though, is that few people are actually willing to act on that principle. In political life most of us lack the quality I've called virtue: we just aren't very strongly predisposed to act in behalf of the general good. That's why individual and group interests usually prevail over general interests in democratic countries.

So the question is this: If both knowledge and virtue are required for moral competence, and moral competence is required for political competence, are we really justified in believing that very many people are politically competent? And if they aren't, can they be qualified to govern? The clear answer seems to be no.

DEMO: Even if I were prepared to grant all that you say (and I'm not) I still wouldn't conclude that guardianship would be better than democracy unless you could show me that your proposed guardians, whoever they may be, would definitely possess both the knowledge and the virtue that you contend most people lack. As to that, I am profoundly skeptical.

## INSTRUMENTAL COMPETENCE

ARISTOS: Anyone who professes to believe that people are about equally well qualified to govern can't be much of a skeptic. But maybe I can overcome your doubts with some further observations. Consider technical knowledge for a moment. If it's problematic, to say the least, whether very many people possess the moral qualifications for ruling, their lack of technical competence seems to me undeniable. Today, most questions of public policy involve highly technical issues. I'm thinking partly about questions of obvious technicality like nuclear weapons and strategies, nuclear waste disposal, the regulation of recombinant DNA research, the desirability of a manned space program; I could go on and on with examples. But I also mean matters much closer to everyday life: health care and delivery, social security, unemployment, inflation, tax reform, crime, welfare programs . . .

We who aren't experts on these matters could deal with them more intelligently if the experts agreed on technical solutions, or, failing that, if we could judge the comparative expertise of the experts. But experts don't agree, and we don't know how to evaluate the qualifications of the experts.

DEMO: But isn't that a fatal flaw in your argument? If the best-qualified experts disagree, why should we make them guardians? Incidentally, how would your guardians settle their disagreements—by majority rule?

ARISTOS: A nice debating point. But you mustn't assume that expert technicians are qualified to be guardians. Most of them probably aren't. The guardians would have to be carefully trained and carefully selected for their special qualities of knowledge and virtue. Plato devotes an extraordinary amount of attention in *The Republic* to the education of the guardians, and every serious advocate of guardianship since then has done likewise. Unlike the haphazard process of selecting leaders in your democratic system, recruiting and educating the future guardians is a central element in the idea of guardianship.

DEMO: But how would you go about that? Your solution gets more and more demanding. It's not for nothing that Plato's *Republic* is generally dismissed as a utopia.

## THE NEED FOR SPECIALIZATION

ARISTOS: I don't think it's useful to draw up detailed blueprints, as utopian writers like to do. Your democratic systems weren't built from utopian blueprints. They were built by applying general principles and ideas to concrete historical situations. The guardians would of course be experts of a certain kind. They would be experts in the art of governing. They would be specialists whose specialization would give them superiority as rulers in comparison not only with ordinary people but also with other kinds of experts: economists, physicists, engineers, and so on. As Plato argued, the deficiencies in the moral and instrumental competence of ordinary people can be overcome only by specializing to a degree that most people can hardly be expected to do. We don't have to accept his myth about the origins of his guardians in order to accept the advantages they would possess from specializing in the art and science of governing. Even if you believe that most persons are potentially capable of acquiring the qualifications desirable for ruling—a possibility I don't necessarily reject—they lack the time to do so. After all, a society needs many different kinds of activities. Ruling is only one specialized activity among a great many. We also need plumbers, carpenters, machinists, doctors, teachers, physicists, mathematicians, painters, dancers. . . . In a modern society we require thousands and thousands of other specialists in infinitely greater variety than Plato could ever have imagined. Acquiring the skills necessary for these tasks and then performing them makes it impossible for very many people to spend the time they would need to gain the moral and instrumental competence for ruling. And that of course includes most experts.

It isn't easy to learn the art and science of ruling. In a world as complex as ours, governing is extraordinarily difficult. I think it's probably easier to become an excellent mathematician than an excellent ruler. Certainly there are more good mathematicians than good rulers. To suppose that many people have the capacity to acquire and use well lots of different specialized skills is merely romantic. How many true polymaths have you ever known? One or two, maybe? Would you entrust yourself to a physician who was also attempting seriously to be a ballet dancer, an opera singer, an architect, an accountant, and a stockbroker?

So I would answer your question in this way: In a well-ordered society, just as some persons would receive the rigorous training and meritocratic selection essential to the art and science of the physician, so also others would be rigorously trained and selected to function well as rulers. Because rulership is so crucial—it has never been more so than today—nothing could be of greater importance than the education of our rulers, whether they are to be ordinary citizens in your democracy or specialized leaders in my system of guardianship.

## HISTORICAL EXPERIENCE

DEMO: I must say, despite your disavowal of any intention to portray a utopia, like Plato you do begin to sound more and more utopian. Imperfect as they are, democracies really do exist. The idea of guardianship might be fine as a utopian fancy, but applying it to the real world is something else again. Can you give me any reason for thinking that your ideal of guardianship has any practical relevance? If your idea of guardianship is represented by the Soviet Union, Argentina during the period of military rule, North or South Korea, or dozens of other examples I could suggest, I'll take even a mediocre democracy any day.

ARISTOS: I admit that the ideal has often been badly misused to justify an evil or incompetent authoritarian regime. Even the most vicious and oppressive monarchies, oligarchies, and dictatorships have tried to present themselves as the true guardians of the collective interest. In this century, fascism, nazism, Leninism, Stalinism, Maoism, military regimes in Argentina, Brazil, Chile, Uruguay, and many other countries—all have tried to legitimize their rule by claiming that the leaders possess superior knowledge of the general good and are genuinely dedicated to bringing it about. It's no wonder that you democrats find it so easy to discredit the idea of guardianship that you never have to meet the argument for it. Yet you won't deny that all political ideals have been greatly abused. It would be a mistake to reject an ideal because you judge its possibilities only by the worst case. Would you want to judge democracy only by its failures or by the shabby and corrupt regimes that sometimes claim the mantle of democracy?

DEMO: I agree that we ought also to consider the best cases. But are there any good examples of guardianship?

ARISTOS: I was hoping you'd ask. A most impressive case is the Republic of Venice. It endured, though of course not unchanged, for about eight centuries. For sheer endurance that's worthy of the *Guinness Book of World Records*. It not only endured. As regimes go in the history of mankind, it has to be counted as exceptionally successful. I don't deny that it had its faults. But on the whole it provided peace and prosperity to its citizens, had an excellent legal system, possessed an elaborate, carefully constructed, and closely observed constitution, was a center dazzling in its creativity in the arts, architecture, town planning, and music, suffered comparatively little from outbreaks of popular discontent, and appears by and large to have enjoyed widespread acceptance by the Venetian people. Yet from about 1300 onward it was legally governed by about 2 percent of its population—less than two thousand citizens. Although its rulers weren't selected and trained in the rigorous fashion prescribed in *The Republic*, every male member of the aristocratic families entitled to participate in the government would have known from infancy that to participate in governing Venice was to be his privilege and responsibility. The constitutional system was carefully constructed to ensure that the officials, and particularly the doge, would not act from self-interested motives of personal or family aggrandizement but to secure the broader interests of the republic.

I could cite other examples, too, such as the Republic of Florence under the Medici in the fifteenth century, or even China during the periods of stability and prosperity under the rule of an emperor and a bureaucracy greatly influenced by Confucian ideas of meritocratic rule.

So you would be mistaken if you were to say that the ideal of guardianship is impossible of fulfillment in at least a reasonably satisfactory approximation, which is the most we can ask of political ideals.

DEMOS: I don't think your historical examples are relevant to today's world.

◆

ARISTOS: Well, I've tried to help you to see another vision than democracy. Mine is a vision of a well-qualified minority, whom I call the guardians, experts in the art and science of governing, who rule over the rest, governing in the best interests of all, fully respecting the principle of equal consideration, indeed perhaps upholding it far better than would the people if they were to govern themselves. Paradoxically, then, at its best such a system might actually rest on the consent of all. In this way, a system of guardianship might attain one of the most important ends of both anarchism and democracy—but by very different means.

DEMOS: I admit that it is a powerful vision. It has always been the strongest competitor to the democratic vision and remains so today, when so many non-democratic regimes—left, right, revolutionary, conservative, traditional—justify themselves by appealing to it for legitimacy. If democracy were to decline and perhaps even to disappear from human history in the centuries to come, I think its place would be taken by hierarchical regimes claiming to be legitimate because they were governed by guardians of virtue and knowledge.

# Chapter 5

♦♦♦♦♦♦♦♦

# A Critique of
# Guardianship

Lofty as guardianship may appear as an ideal, its extraordinary demands on the knowledge and virtue of the guardians are all but impossible to satisfy in practice. Despite the example of the Republic of Venice and a few others that an advocate might offer as proof that guardianship is a genuine historical possibility, it cannot be reasonably defended, I think, as superior to democracy either as an ideal or as a feasible system in practice.

Much of the persuasiveness of the idea stems from its negative view of the moral and intellectual competence of ordinary people. But even if this view were accepted (in later chapters I shall offer reasons for rejecting it), it does not follow that potential guardians of definitely superior knowledge and virtue exist, or could be created, and could be trusted to rule in behalf of the public good. However one might appraise the negative arguments, the positive arguments for guardianship do not withstand critical scrutiny.

## KNOWLEDGE

Plato, as I have said, believed that his guardians would possess knowledge of the "royal science" of government. Much as later advocates may differ philosophically from Plato, they have agreed with him in asserting that the particular class of guardians they have in mind would be uniquely qualified to rule by virtue of their superior knowledge of a special set of truths—moral, philosophical, historical, psychological, or other. Like Plato, they have also assumed, explicitly or implicitly, that these truths are "objective" and knowledge of them constitutes a "science."

What is not always sufficiently noted is that this kind of justification for guardianship consists of two logically independent propositions.[1] First, knowledge of the public good and the best means to achieve it is a "science" composed of objectively valid and validated truths, as the laws of physics or (in a very different

65

way on most accounts) mathematical proofs are usually thought to be "objective." Second, this knowledge can be acquired only by a minority of adults, quite likely a very small minority. You will notice, however, that even if the first proposition were true, the second might be false. Yet if *either* proposition is wrong, then the argument falls. For example, suppose we were convinced that moral knowledge does consist of objectively valid assertions. Even so, might it not be possible for most adults, given adequate education, to acquire sufficient knowledge of those truths to justify their participating in governing themselves? Plato himself failed to explain convincingly why his "royal science" could be learned only by a minority.[2] Later advocates of guardianship have also often neglected to show why their "science" of ruling would be accessible only to a minority. But unless we are satisfied that this is so, then the argument for guardianship is unconvincing.

The main burden of the argument, however, is usually placed on the first proposition. When advocates of guardianship contend that a "science of ruling" exists, composed of rationally unquestionable and objectively determined truths, some depict these essential truths primarily or exclusively as *moral* propositions, while others portray them as *empirical* propositions comparable to the laws of physics, chemistry, biology, and so on. And sometimes, though less commonly, the science of ruling is presumed to be a combination of objective truths of both kinds, moral and empirical. None of these claims, however, can be supported.

### Moral Knowledge

As to *moral* propositions, few moral philosophers, and probably not many thoughtful and educated people, now believe that we can arrive at absolute, intersubjectively valid, and "objectively true" moral judgments, in the same sense that we understand propositions in the natural sciences and mathematics to be "objectively true."[3] Although some moral philosophers would make such a claim, they have conspicuously failed to demonstrate the absolute and objective status of any specific moral judgments they may be prepared to assert. Instead, their "objective moral truths" invariably prove to be highly debatable; their pretense of intersubjective validity cannot be upheld; and their claim to the possession of objective truths comparable to those of the natural sciences or pure logic and mathematics fails.[4]

This terrain is too well worn to need further exploration here, but perhaps a simple comparison may be useful. If moral knowledge were really comparable in objectivity to mathematics or the physical sciences, then the intersubjective validity of this knowledge could surely be demonstrated to us in ways as convincing as those that satisfy us that many propositions in mathematics or the physical sciences are "objectively true." We would probably be convinced that moral knowledge is "objective" if we could be shown that, as in mathematics or the natural sciences, experts on the subject employ well-defined, replicable procedures which they agree are appropriate for judging the validity of their assertions; further, that those who use the appropriate procedures converge toward agreement on the truth of certain laws or general propositions; finally, that the "laws" on which they agree constitute a significant, nontrivial body of propositions—in the case of moral knowledge, moral laws that definitely limit the domain of our moral choices. Yet with moral claims, these indicators of objectivity are notoriously lacking.

To say that moral inquiry does not lead to the discovery of objective and absolute moral laws does not compel us to rush to the other extreme: that moral discourse is utterly "subjective," arbitrary, a mere matter of taste, a domain without appeal to reason or experience. Between the two extremes lie a number of alternatives that provide a place for argument drawing on human reason and human experience (Fishkin 1984). As must be evident from the nature of this book, even if we cannot justify democracy by demonstrating that it can be derived from "objectively true" moral absolutes, we can, I believe, justify it on grounds that satisfactorily withstand tests of reason and experience.

It might be said, then, that even though the guardians could not really possess knowledge of a "science of ruling," their moral judgments would nonetheless be so superior to those of ordinary people that they should be entrusted with rulership. But to concede that the guardians do not understand an objective "science of ruling," while not necessarily fatal to the idea, vastly increases the practical problems of identifying and appointing the guardians and removing those who prove to be unfit. Before turning to these problems, however, we need to consider a different kind of "science" that is said to justify a system of guardianship—not by Plato's guardians, to be sure, but by others who claim to possess knowledge of a science of ruling.

## Instrumental Knowledge

To govern properly, one might contend, does not require moral knowledge. Therefore my criticisms of claims to such knowledge are irrelevant. For what governing requires is only instrumental knowledge, that is, a correct understanding of the most efficient means for achieving widely or even universally accepted ends like human happiness or well-being. Instrumental knowledge, the argument might continue, is primarily, perhaps exclusively, *empirical* knowledge about mankind, society, nature, human and social behavior, tendencies, laws, processes, structures, and the like. In principle, then, the instrumental knowledge necessary to govern well could be a science like other empirical sciences.

Some such view is meant to support claims that guardians should be drawn from the ranks of scientists, engineers, technicians, experts in public administration, experienced civil servants, or others who are presumed to possess specialized empirical knowledge. In the psychologist B. F. Skinner's utopia, Walden Two, the guardians would be, naturally, behavioral scientists (specifically Skinnerians, it seems). With Leninists, the guardians during the transition to true democracy are to be those who uniquely understand the laws of history and economics, and who, it turns out, are exclusively Marxist-Leninists. Natural scientists are predisposed to assume that policymakers would be far better qualified if only they followed the methods of natural science. (For a recent example, see the editorial by Daniel E. Koshland, Jr. in *Science*, 25 October 1985, 391.) Engineers would prefer . . .

engineers. And so on. The underlying assumption is that the task of deciding on the best public policies depends essentially on empirical knowledge; if so, then the necessary knowledge is, or could be, an empirical science, theoretical or practical.

As an example, take decisions about American nuclear weapons strategies. These, it might be argued, are in essence purely instrumental, because virtually everyone in the United States agrees on the primacy of certain ends: survival of the human species, survival of a civilized world, survival of the United States as we know it, and so on. The difficult questions, then, are not about ends; they concern means. But the choice of means (the argument runs) is strictly instrumental, not moral; the question is how best to achieve the ends that everyone agrees on. The knowledge required for these decisions is therefore technical, scientific, instrumental, empirical. Because this knowledge is extraordinary complex, and much of it unavoidably secret, it is inherently far beyond the reach of ordinary citizens. Consequently, decisions about nuclear strategy should not be made by public opinion or through democratic processes; they should be made by experts who have special knowledge of nuclear weapons strategies. Sadly for democracy, these experts are necessarily a small minority of American citizens.

Plausible as the argument might appear, it is fundamentally mistaken. To begin with, to suppose that decisions about nuclear weapons are purely instrumental and devoid of crucial and highly controversial moral questions is a profound misunderstanding. Consider some of the issues: Is nuclear war morally justifiable? If not, is a strategy of deterrence permissible? If so, in what circumstances, if any, should nuclear weapons be used? What targets are morally permissible? For example, should cities and other population centers be targeted? If not, how would it be possible to destroy an opponent's command and control centers, much less industry, transportation, and other economic centers, or even military forces? Finally, in what circumstances short of "victory" would it be best to end a nuclear war—in the extreme case, to accept defeat as preferable to annihilation?

Clearly, decisions about matters like these are not merely instrumental. They also involve moral choices, some of which are extraordinarily difficult and perplexing. Although for decades strategic decisions were made with little attention to their moral presuppositions either by key decisionmakers (Bracken 1983, 239) or the general public, a pastoral letter of American Catholic bishops in 1983 brought many of the moral issues to public attention ("The Challenge of Peace," 1983). Subsequently, others undertook to explore the moral dimension of strategic decisions from other, sometimes conflicting, perspectives (e.g., Russett 1984; MacLean 1986). Whatever one's judgment on the moral issues may be, the fact that strategic decisions do depend on moral judgments completely undermines the assumption that they are purely instrumental and could be made wisely on purely empirical, scientific, or technical considerations.

Nor are strategic decisions unique. Decisions about crucial public policies rarely, if ever, require knowledge only of the technically most efficient means to ends that can be taken as given because they are self-evidently right or universally accepted. Because "scientific" knowledge about the empirical world cannot be a sufficient qualification for ruling, pure empirical "science" is not and cannot be enough to constitute a "royal science" of ruling.

## Experts as Policymakers

It is surely true, however, that, although moral judgments are always necessary to intelligent decisions, as they obviously are in decisions about nuclear forces, they are never sufficient. One must also make judgments about the empirical world—how it operates, what feasible alternatives it allows, the probable consequences of each, and so on. At least some of these judgments require specialized knowledge of a sort we cannot reasonably expect most people to possess: instrumental knowledge. If nuclear weapons policy is perhaps unrepresentative in the extreme difficulty of its moral choices, it is less atypical in its requirements for technical knowledge. Though decisions about nuclear weapons do pose technical questions, these may be no more demanding than technical questions related to many other complex issues.

Because both moral understanding and instrumental knowledge are always necessary for policy judgments, neither alone can ever be sufficient. It is precisely here that any argument for rule by a purely technocratic elite must fail. As in the case of nuclear forces, technocrats are no more qualified than others to make the essential moral judgments. They may be less so. For technocrats suffer from at least three other defects that are probably irremediable in a world where knowledge is as complex as it is in ours. In the first place, the specialization required in order to acquire a high degree of expert knowledge is today inherently limiting: one becomes a specialist in *something*, that is, in *one* thing, and by necessity remains ignorant of other things.

Second, Plato's royal science simply does not exist, and therefore its practitioners cannot exist. Thus, *pace* Plato, there is no single art or science that can satisfactorily demonstrate a claim to unite in itself the moral and instrumental understanding required for intelligent policymaking in today's world. Perhaps a few philosophers, social scientists, or even natural scientists might make such an extravagant claim for their own specialty. But a simple test would, I believe, quickly expose the weakness of any such claims: let those who assert such claims be subjected to examination by experts in each area, and let us be the judges of their performance.

The third weakness of technocrats as policymakers is that, on a great many questions of policy, instrumental judgments depend on assumptions that are not strictly technical, scientific, or even very rigorous. Often these assumptions reflect a kind of ontological judgment: the world is like *this*, not *that*, it tends to work *this* way, not *that* way. With nuclear weapons, for example, ordinary people, as Bracken points out (1983, 50), are likely to believe in Murphy's famous law: If things can go wrong, they probably will. Although supported by a great deal of experience (in fact probably as well supported by experience as most generalizations in the social sciences), Murphy's law is of course not a well-validated empirical law in the strict sense. It is a commonsense judgment about a tendency of things, an ontological view about the nature of the world.

Because of these defects in specialized knowledge, experts often utterly fail to comprehend how the real world may stubbornly refuse to play by their rules.[5] Although the gaffes of specialists in nuclear weapons planning tend to be hidden from public view and may never be known until it is too late, enough is known to indicate that specialists in nuclear weapons are no exception to the general experience.

Thus the decision to increase the destructive power of launchers by adding multiple, independently targeted re-entry vehicles (MIRVs) carrying nuclear warheads is now understood to have been a mistake. The Russians naturally undertook to deploy MIRVs on their launchers, and the problem of arms control became even more difficult. Much later, the Pentagon proposed that perhaps the launchers armed with MIRVs should be replaced on both sides by smaller launchers, each carrying a single warhead, thus making verification easier. Yet at the time the MIRV decision was made, many critics, arguing from a commonsense point of view—and a certain ontological judgment about the way the world works—contended that what has happened would surely happen. Nor is one's confidence in the implicit assumptions of decisionmakers much strengthened by knowing that as late as 1982 the North American Aerospace Defense Command (NORAD) warning center lacked a reliable emergency power supply. Somehow that simple problem had "just slipped through the cracks" (Bracken 1983, 113).

Experience with nuclear weapons decisions thus lends additional support to the conclusion of common sense that technocrats ought to be not rulers but ruled over. This conclusion is summed up in Georges Clemenceau's famous aphorism that war is too important to be left to the generals, a principle amply justified by the slaughter that highly trained general staffs managed to bring about during the First World War. Human experience, codified in Clemenceau's comment and Murphy's law, provides little ground for counting on experts to possess the wisdom to rule that is promised by the theory of guardianship.[6]

## KNOWLEDGE: THE GENERAL GOOD

The case for guardianship sometimes depends on assumptions about the composition of the general good (or the public good, the collective good, the general interest, and so on) and how knowledge of what composes the general good may be acquired.

To clarify the issue, I want to make a simplifying assumption. Let us assume that an adult person is more likely, as a general rule, to understand his or her personal interests better than another person. In chapter 7 I shall explain why it seems to me prudent to adopt such an assumption for making collective decisions. In order to get on with the argument here, however, I want now to presuppose that we have already accepted it. We assume, then, that unlike children adults do not, in general, need paternalistic guardians to make decisions on their behalf. If the general good were composed only of individual interests, and if we could also agree on a satisfactory principle for aggregating individual interests—a majority principle, perhaps—then just as paternalism would be unnecessary and undesirable in private life, so too guardianship would be unnecessary and undesirable in public life. To reach the best possible collective decision about the general good we would need only to ensure that everyone had an adequate opportunity to express a choice among the alternatives (say, by casting a vote) and that the process of arriving at the collective decision followed a rule for aggregating these individual choices into a public choice (say, by a majority principle).

But if the general good consists of something *more* than an aggregation of personal interests, then to achieve it will require more than this. To bring about the general good will then require an understanding of the respects in which the general good differs from a combination of individual interests. If it is also true (as Aristo insisted in the last chapter) that most people are mainly concerned with their own individual interests, then most people could hardly be counted on to understand, much less to act in behalf of, the general good. In these circumstances might it not be prudent to entrust the task of deciding on the general good to persons specially trained to understand what the general good consists of (and, of course, strongly predisposed to bring it about)? In short, would we not arrive by a different route at the conclusion that the best rulers would be guardians who possess both knowledge and virtue?

What would the guardians' special knowledge of the general good consist of? Obviously that depends on what is meant by the general good. To explore that matter fully would require a lengthy quest into a tangled thicket of linguistic and conceptual snares, shadowy concepts, and false paths. We shall work our way through some of these in later chapters. But a briefer exploration may do for the moment.

Before undertaking that foray, however, it is important to remind ourselves that the obstacles to providing a conclusive rational basis for moral judgments, which I mentioned a moment ago, still remain. Rationally justifying a judgment about the good of a collectivity is no easier than rationally justifying a judgment about the good of an individual. If anything, it is even more difficult. Once again, in saying that moral judgments are problematical I do not mean to say that the search for rational justification is futile. As I suggested earlier, assertions about what is best for an individual, a group, a country, or humankind can be much more than mere arbitrary and mindless expressions of taste; moral judgments need not be "purely subjective." In judging the validity of statements about the general good we can and should employ reason and experience. Nonetheless, no assertion that "the public good definitely consists of such and such" can be shown to be "objectively true" in the same sense that many statements in mathematics, logic, or the natural sciences are understood to be "objectively true." Even if we were to conclude, then, that the public good is different from an aggregation of individual goods, no set of putative guardians could reasonably sustain the claim that they possessed a "science of ruling" consisting of "objectively true" knowledge of the public good.

Still, if we believe the general good is more than an aggregation of individual interests, might we not be more inclined to conclude that in order to understand it one must possess an expertise that most people cannot reasonably be expected to possess? Evidently we need to know whether the general good differs from an aggregation of individual interests, if so how, and whether, insofar as differences exist, the case for guardianship is strengthened.

## The Public Good: Organic or Person-Centered?

From antiquity a ghostly presence has haunted the discussion of the general good. This is the phantom created by organismic interpretations of collective entities.

When we speak of the good of a person, we understand (more or less) what we mean by a person. But when we speak of the good of some collective entity, what sort of thing is that entity? Concretely, of course, the collectivity might be a polis, city, community, nation, country, state, or whatever. But is a city comparable to a person, and if so in what ways? A collectivity such as a city is sometimes referred to as if it were equivalent to a living organism; thus a city may be likened to a person. From ancient times organic metaphors have been applied to political collectivities. But how we are supposed to interpret the metaphor is not always clear. In *The Republic*, for example, Socrates often speaks of "the city as a whole" as if it were a kind of holistic entity like a person; he also turns the metaphor around to assert that "the individual is like the city."[7] Organism as metaphor is one thing; it is quite another to consider a political collectivity to be an organism. Should we seriously regard both cities and persons as members, so to speak, of the class of living organisms?

An organic metaphor is obviously meant to suggest a special way of thinking about the general good. One interpretation of an organic metaphor might be this:

*Just as the good of a person is something more than the "good" of any specific part of the person, so too the good of a collectivity is more than the good of its parts; the good of a city is more than the good of its citizens; the general good therefore cannot be reduced ultimately to the good of the persons composing the collectivity.*

Since some writers who employ *organic* metaphors would probably reject this interpretation, to distinguish it I shall call it an *organismic* view of the general good.

An alternative to the organismic view might be called *the human-centered ground for collective decisions*:

*The general good of a city or a nation can always be decomposed into what is good for the persons in the community or nation or who are affected by it. The general good is not something different from the interests or the good of the persons who compose the collectivity or are affected by it.*

Unlike the organismic view, given this assumption we are never allowed to smuggle into the general good anything more than the goods of persons, of human beings.

The organismic view is sometimes thought to be superior to the human-centered view in two ways: because it recognizes that a system, particularly a living system, cannot always be reduced to the sum of its parts; and because it therefore allows for values like order, community, and justice that cannot be accounted for in the human-centered view. But both criticisms reflect a misunderstanding of the human-centered assumption.

## Communities as Systems, not Aggregates

The human-centered postulate does *not* presuppose "methodological individualism," the doctrine that social phenomena must be explained only by referring to facts about individuals.[8] Since systems consist not only of parts but also of relationships among the parts, the properties of a system cannot always be reduced to the properties of the units in a system. Because a community is not simply an aggregate of individual persons but consists also of the relations among them and among the various subsystems, it follows that the characteristics of a community are not reducible to individual characteristics.[9]

That a collectivity may have properties that are not reducible to properties of individual persons is not, however, the issue. If we believe that some property of a human system—justice, let us say, or political equality—is valuable, does the value of that quality arise because it benefits the system, quite apart from any value it may have for the people in the system? Or is the property valuable instead because it benefits the people who compose the system? What one might mean by the first is obscure. Attempts to clarify it would, I think, invariably founder on the shoals of a simple question: Why should we human beings value a human system above and beyond the value it has for us? If we reject organismic views, a human-centered view will still enable us to appreciate the values that human beings derive from life in a community, or communities. We can see why this is so by considering some possible community values.

## Private Interests and Collective Interests

The human-centered assumption does not in any way minimize the importance of values that depend on membership in a group or a community: altruism, love, friendship, fellowship, fraternity, participation, justice, order, security, loyalty, and so on.

To be sure, models and theories of society and behavior that emphasize individualism and minimize the importance of community ties or collective interests are human centered. However, a human-centered view does not imply egoism or individualism either as fact or value. Surely it is true that membership in a community is a good for almost everyone, if not indeed for everyone. But if so, then this good or interest must be included among the goods or interests of everyone, or nearly everyone. A person's interests may be, and usually are, broader than merely one's *private* or *self-regarding* interests. That is why, in defining the human-centered view, I chose the word "person" rather than "individual"; for I want to emphasize the whole person, including all the social aspects of the person. If the expression "human interests" is meant to include all of one's interests as a person, as a human being, then "human interests" include membership in a community, nowadays in many communities and collectivities. But the value of community memberships accrues to the persons who compose a community and not to some ghostly organic entity that incurs harm or benefits *independent of the people in it*.

Thus while the organic metaphor may have its utility as a way of emphasizing the interdependence of human beings and the values of human intercourse and association, an organic (as distinct from organismic) conception of human sociability implies nothing that is not fully consistent with the human-centered ground for collective decisions.[10] If on the other hand organic language is meant to imply an organismic conception of the general good, then it seems to me plainly mistaken and adds nothing but befuddlement.

If we accept the human-centered view, then, to understand the general good of a collectivity requires knowledge of the interests of persons, and nothing more. The claim that rulers ought to possess knowledge about a special kind of general good that consists of something different from a combination of the interests of those who compose the collectivity, or are affected by its policies, cannot be sustained.

## Collective Decisions: The Problem of Composition

It is one thing to say that the general good is composed only of personal goods. But it is quite another to say exactly *how* the general good ought to be composed from personal goods. To compose the general good from personal goods, we need a satisfactory principle, a rule of some sort for decisions.[11] Yet if recent discussions have shown anything, it is that all rules for arriving at collective decisions are defective in some circumstances. Since democracy would be hard to justify if it could not employ fair procedures for making collective decisions, the defects of the majority principle and other democratic decision rules are often chalked up against democracy; the implication might seem to be that an alternative to democracy ought therefore to be sought.

In chapter 10, I shall take up the question of majority rule and its alternatives. The relevant point here is that the argument for guardianship no less than that for democracy presupposes that collective decisions are sometimes highly desirable. Unless guardians were always unanimous, they too would need decision rules. If your guardians disagree among themselves, Demo asked Aristo, how will they decide—by majority rule? Demo's question cannot be brushed aside as a flippant triviality. Although advocates of guardianship tend to be conspicuously silent about disagreements among the guardians, to believe that disagreements would not happen defies all human experience. If disagreements were to occur, as surely they would, and if the guardians' decisions were not to be merely arbitrary, then they would require decision rules to settle their disagreements. It follows that, if the problem of finding fair decision rules is a serious one for the democratic process, it is no less serious for any alternative process for making collective decisions, including guardianship.

## RISK, UNCERTAINTY, AND TRADE-OFFS

The defense of guardianship often presupposes that moral and scientific knowledge, and thus political judgments, can be based on rational certainty. Thus, in comparison with the judgments of ordinary people, which reflect all the uncertainties of mere opinion, the guardians can acquire knowledge of what is best for the community that approaches something like rational certainty. Yet any assumption of this kind neglects an inherent characteristic of judgments about most important issues of policy: They must be based on assessments of *risk, uncertainty*, and *trade-offs*. Recent analyses of decisionmaking have brought to light this new and fatal flaw in the argument for guardianship that older philosophical defense and criticism were not equipped to discern.

Policy decisions are almost always risky at best, in the sense that they require a choice between alternatives the consequences of which are only probable. If the consequences were certain, some of the anguish of decisionmaking would vanish. But what is so dismaying is the terrible riskiness of the outcomes. Suppose one faces the following situation. An unusual and virulent form of influenza has appeared in Asia, and it is expected to reach the United States. Unless a program is adopted to attack it, the disease will kill 600 people. Two alternative programs have been proposed. If one is adopted, 200 people will be saved. If the other is adopted, there is a one-third probability that 600 people will be saved, and a two-thirds probability that no one will be saved. So which program should be adopted?

There is no unambiguously right answer to this question. Moreover, the answers people give to questions like these seem to depend on the way the alternatives are presented. It has been found experimentally that, when the alternatives are formulated in the way I just presented them, most people will choose the first alternative. Yet, with a different—though logically identical—formulation, most people will choose the second! Moreover, this reversal "is as common among sophisticated respondents as among naive ones." In the face of risks or choices, people commonly make logically inconsistent judgments, and the performance of experts, it appears, is not better than that of ordinary people.[12]

However, the problem of rational choice is made even more difficult because (unlike the example just given) ordinarily the probabilities themselves are unknown. The outcomes are not merely risky in the sense that we can assign a definite probability to each, as we can when we toss properly made dice. The outcomes are genuinely uncertain in the sense that we can at best only guess at probabilities over a large, vague range. Though we are playing with loaded dice, we have no way of knowing in advance how the dice are loaded.

At the same time, virtually all important policy decisions require judgments about the relative desirability of trade-offs between different values: equality versus liberty, high wages versus international competitiveness, savings versus consumption, short-run gains versus long-run gains, and so on.

Ordinarily, policy judgments require an assessment of *both* uncertainties *and* trade-offs. In these instances, the superior competence of experts diminishes to the vanishing point. Suppose, for example, that we could choose between two nuclear strategies. One carries a substantial chance that nuclear war can be indefinitely avoided; but, if it does occur, virtually the entire population of the United States will be wiped out. The other strategy stands considerably less chance of avoiding war, but a war is likely to cause fewer deaths—perhaps around a quarter of the U.S. population. Clearly there are not, nor can there be, "expert" answers to problems like these.

## VIRTUE

It is then highly doubtful that the guardians would possess the *knowledge*, whether moral, instrumental, or practical, they would need to justify their entitlement to rule. But even superior knowledge would not be enough. Could we trust our putative guardians to *seek* the general good rather than merely their own? Would they possess the requisite virtue?

An advocate of guardianship might answer that guardians would be no more likely to abuse their authority than officials to whom authority is delegated in democratic systems. But the theory of guardianship does not propose that we *delegate* authority to rulers. The authority of the rulers would not be *delegated* at all. In effect, the authority to rule would be permanently *alienated*, not delegated; the people could not legally or constitutionally, or I suppose rationally or morally, recover authority whenever they might conclude that it had become desirable to do so. Their only recourse would be revolution.

Not only would the guardians be free of popular controls, however defective these are at times in democratic orders. Presumably they would not hold democratic values. Indeed, the guardians would have only contempt for public *opinion* as not true *knowledge*.

Having mentioned Clemenceau's aphorism and Murphy's law, perhaps I should add two others. The third, which is perhaps even better known, and equally well if not better supported by human experience, is Lord Acton's assertion that power tends to corrupt, and absolute power corrupts absolutely. The fourth is John Stuart Mill's:

> The rights and interests of every or any person are only secure from being disregarded when the person interested is himself able, and habitually disposed, to stand up for them. . . . Human beings are only secure from evil at the hands of others in proportion as they have the power of being, and are, self-*protecting* (Mill [1861] 1958, 43).

The generalizations of Mill and Acton, like those of Clemenceau and the apocryphal Murphy, are of course not really "laws" in the hard-edged sense. They are, rather, practical judgments, prudential rules, informed conclusions about the ways of the world. But if they are roughly correct descriptions of the world, as I believe they are, then the vision of true guardianship makes inhuman demands on the guardians.

## HISTORICAL EXPERIENCE

This judgment is buttressed, I think, by recent historical experience. The conditions that made the Republic of Venice possible no longer exist and are unlikely to reappear in this century or the next. In our age we have witnessed a new historical phenomenon, which we have called totalitarianism. While the novel and extreme characteristics of those regimes have often been exaggerated, they have greatly sharpened our awareness of the vast potentialities for misrule contained in modern society. For human society possesses a potential for centralized domination beyond all previous limits. Throughout the world, authoritarian regimes varying greatly in structure, ideology, and performance have all laid claim to legitimacy as the true and only guardians of the general good. Their record justifies at least three conclusions.

First, the essential truth in Acton's melancholy aphorism has been reaffirmed. Second, we observe in these systems a strong propensity for blunder, because the power of the rulers leads to a tendency for information to be distorted by those who report to them and by the unchecked eccentricities of the rulers themselves. Third, none has developed a satisfactory way of identifying, recruiting, and educating the guardians for their responsibilities or for removing guardians at the highest level who are unsatisfactory. Thus these regimes lack, and conspicuously lack, rulers who possess the virtue and the knowledge—moral, instrumental, and practical—required to justify their power as guardians.

At the same time, democratic theory and practice have undergone fundamental alterations in order to cope with modern problems of knowledge, information, understanding, and the utilization of experts. Although Plato and other critics have often attacked democracy as a regime of rule by raw, unmediated, uninformed public opinion, this is an interpretation presented by the enemies of democracy, not its friends. Even among advocates of direct democracy, all but the most simpleminded have supposed that decisions in the assembly would take place only after education, open inquiry, discussion, and other forms of civic instruction have clarified the issues. Modern democracies, with their elaborate systems of representation, delegation, committee specialization, and administrative expertise, have enormously increased the amount and quality of information and understanding brought to bear on decisions. It is foolish, and irrelevant, to contrast an idealized portrait of rule by a wise and virtuous elite with a mobocracy disguised as democracy, as Plato did and many enemies of democracy have done since his time.

## WHY PHILOSOPHERS SHOULD NOT BE KINGS AND VICE VERSA

With all its defects, the argument for guardianship renders an important service to political thought by insisting on knowledge and virtue as essential qualities of rulership in a good polity. For democratic theory and practice to deprecate the importance of these would be perilous to the future of both.

Prudence and practical wisdom nonetheless counsel us to reject as illusory the hope that the best possible regime cannot be attained "unless philosophers rule as kings in the cities, or those whom we now call kings and rulers genuinely and adequately study philosophy, until, that is, political power and philosophy coalesce, and the various natures of those who now pursue the one to the exclusion of the other are forcibly debarred from doing so" (*Plato's Republic*, Grube, trans., para. 473d, p. 133).

For the two activities exclude one another. I do not mean that rulers cannot have a somewhat "philosophic" cast of mind, as some have had. But to have a philosophic cast of mind is one thing; to be a philosopher is another. By philosopher I do not mean the word in its present-day professional sense, as one who teaches in an academic department of philosophy, writes in journals of philosophy, and so on. I mean it in the sense of Socrates and Plato, as one engaged in a passionate search for truth, enlightenment, and understanding, particularly about justice and human good.[13] Rulers are unlikely to have much interest in such a search, and few would find the results comforting. Nor can philosophers in Plato's sense have much desire to rule, for ruling would impede their search for truth, as they well know. Plato himself knew this. Hence some scholars have argued that *The Republic* must be ironic: Plato means for us to understand why the fictitious republic he portrays is impossible. However that may be, in his famous metaphor of the cave he tells us that one who leaves the cave, with its images flickering on the wall from the light of a distant fire, and sees what is real and true under the full light of the sun will be reluctant to return to the cave. Yet the world of politics is in the cave, where truth is never wholly accessible.

Prudence and practical wisdom will argue against the vision of guardianship on yet other grounds. An imperfect democracy is a misfortune for its people, but an imperfect authoritarian regime is an abomination. If prudence counsels a "maximin" strategy—that is, choose the alternative that is the best of the worst outcomes—then the experience of the twentieth century argues powerfully against the idea of guardianship.

But if instead we choose a "maximax" strategy, it will also lead us to endorse democracy rather than guardianship. For in its ideal outcomes, democracy is better. In an ideal system of guardianship, only the guardians can exercise one of the most fundamental of all freedoms, the freedom to participate in the making of the laws that will be binding on oneself and one's community. But in an ideal democracy, the whole people enjoys that freedom.

It is true that a democratic regime runs the risk that the people will make mistakes. But the risk of mistake exists in all regimes in the real world, and the worst blunders of this century have been made by leaders in nondemocratic regimes. Moreover, the opportunity to make mistakes is an opportunity to learn. Just as we reject paternalism in individual decisions, because it prevents the development of our moral capacities, so too we should reject guardianship in public affairs, because it will stunt the development of the moral capacities of an entire people. At its best, only the democratic vision can offer the hope, which guardianship can never do, that by engaging in governing themselves, all people, and not merely a few, may learn to act as morally responsible human beings.

# PART THREE

◆◆◆◆◆◆◆◆◆◆◆

# A THEORY OF THE DEMOCRATIC PROCESS

# Chapter 6

◆◆◆◆◆◆◆◆

# Justifications: The Idea
# of Equal Intrinsic Worth

To show that the arguments for anarchism and guardianship are unsatisfactory is far from showing that democracy is the best alternative. On what grounds can a belief in the democratic process be rationally justified, or if "rationally" seems too demanding, at least reasonably justified?

To answer this question we begin with the asssumption that in order to live together in an association, the members of the association will need a process for making decisions about the association's principles, rules, laws, policies, conduct, and so on. The members are expected to conform to these decisions: the decisions are *binding*. Because association decisions like these are different in important ways from individual choices and decisions, we can call them *governmental* or *binding collective* decisions.

To live together in an association, then, people need a *process* for arriving at governmental decisions: a political process. If I may oversimplify the alternatives, one solution might be a hierarchical process: certain leaders would make the decisions. Ideally, perhaps, these leaders would be a relatively small group who to an extraordinary degree possessed qualities of knowledge and virtue. This ideal solution is, of course, a government by guardians. The alternative that I now turn to, however, is a democratic process for governing. In chapter 8 I am going to present a set of criteria that distinguish the democratic process not only from guardianship but from other alternatives as well. Meanwhile, we can get along adequately with the notion of democracy as "rule by the people," or, to narrow down the idea a bit more, as rule by a demos, a citizen body consisting of members who are considered equals for purposes of arriving at governmental decisions.

## DEMOCRACY AS TENDING TO PRODUCE THE BEST
## FEASIBLE SYSTEM TAKEN ALL AROUND

Many attempts to justify democracy refer to democratic systems that pretty closely approximate their ideal. Yet ideal political systems, and ideal states in

*83*

particular, have never existed, do not exist, and almost surely never will exist. I want therefore to mention a justification for democracy that, although much too loose and nonphilosophical to convince political theorists and philosophers, may have far wider appeal than more philosophical arguments. In fact, I should not be surprised if it were the unstated conviction of many democratic theorists and the unphilosophic ground of their enterprise.

This is simply that, when the idea of democracy is actively adopted by a people, it tends to produce the best feasible political system, or at any rate the best state, taken all around. In this view, many of the philosophical justifications offered for democracy may be true. But they speak to political ideals rather than directly to human experience. A hardheaded look at human experience, historical and contemporary, shows that among political societies that have actually existed, or now exist, those that most nearly satisfy the criteria of the democratic idea are, taken all around, better than the rest. This does not mean that actual "democracies" are or ever have been highly democratic, measured against the exacting criteria of democratic ideals. But as a consequence of meeting those criteria more fully than other regimes, and also of the political culture that the idea and practices of democracy generate, on the whole they are, with all their imperfections, more desirable than any feasible nondemocratic alternative.

How are we to judge the validity of a claim like this? We cannot reasonably decide whether democracy is justified until we have compared it with its alternatives. Is democracy superior, for example, to a system of guardianship like that envisioned by Plato in *The Republic*? To make such a comparison we would not only need to understand a great deal about democracy, both as an ideal and as a feasible reality; we would also need to understand the alternative, both as an ideal and as a feasible reality. In making such comparisons, however, we must avoid comparing ideal oranges with actual apples, a procedure nicely designed to show that actual apples are inferior to ideal oranges. Although comparisons are often made, explicitly or implicitly, between the ideal performance of one kind of regime and the actual performance of another, it is hard to know what to make of them. It seems more appropriate to compare the democratic ideal with the ideal of guardianship and the actuality of democracy in practice with the actuality of hierarchical regimes in practice. But clearly this is a major undertaking. To complete it will take much of this book. Consequently, the argument in this chapter and the next must be read as contingent on the arguments of the chapters that follow.

## THE IDEA OF INTRINSIC EQUALITY

An obvious objection to the claim that the best feasible system tends to exist when a people actively adopts the idea of democracy is that the argument is meaningless unless we know what is meant by "best." By what criteria are we to appraise the worth of democracy whether as an ideal or as an actuality?

I believe that virtually all attempts to answer a question like this ultimately fall back, even if only by implication, on an assumption so fundamental that it is presupposed in most moral argument. This is what might be called the idea of intrinsic equality.

A version of this idea is contained in a well-known passage in Locke's *Second Treatise of Government*:

> Though I have said above . . . *That all Men by Nature are equal*, I cannot be supposed to understand all sorts of *Equality*: *Age* or *Virtue* may give Men a just Precedency: *Excellency of Parts and Merit* may place others above the Common Level: Birth may subject some, and *Alliance* or *Benefits* others, to pay an Observance to those to whom Nature, Gratitude or other Respects may have made it due; and yet all this consists with the *Equality*, which all Men are in, in respect of Jurisdiction or Dominion one over another, which was the *Equality* I there spoke of, as proper to the Business in hand, being that *equal Right* that every Man hath, *to his Natural Freedom*, without being subjected to the Will or Authority of any other Man. (Locke [1689/90] 1970, chap. 6, para. 54, p. 322)

Locke was ascribing to men a kind of *intrinsic equality* that while clearly irrelevant to many situations should definitely be decisive for certain purposes, specifically for purposes of government. Though Locke casts his version in a special form, he shares with many others a fundamental belief that at least on matters requiring collective decisions "all Men" (or all persons?) are, or ought to be considered, equal in some important sense. I am going to call this underlying notion the Idea of Intrinsic Equality.

In what respects are persons intrinsically equal, and what requirements, if any, does their equality impose on a process for making collective decisions? It is easier to say what intrinsic equality does *not* mean, as Locke does, than to say more precisely what it does mean. To Locke intrinsic equality evidently means that no one is naturally entitled to subject another to his (or, certainly, to her) will or authority. It follows that "no one can be . . . subjected to the Political Power of another without his own *Consent*" (chap. 8, para. 95, p. 348).[1] To some, however, intrinsic equality means that all human beings are of equal intrinsic worth, or, put the other way around, that no person is intrinsically superior to another.[2] To John Rawls, who finds the idea that human beings are of equal intrinsic worth excessively vague and elastic, their intrinsic equality consists rather of the capacity for having a conception of their good and acquiring a sense of justice.[3] To others, intrinsic equality means that the good or interests of each person must be given equal consideration; this is the well-known Principle of Equal Consideration of Interests (e.g., Benn 1967, 61ff.).

How these various interpretations of intrinsic equality are related, and whether all finally depend on the idea of intrinsic worth, are unsettled questions that need not detain us here.[4]

Yet democracy might, like Plato's republic, be little more than a philosophical fantasy were it not for the persistent and widespread influence of the belief that human beings are intrinsically equal in a fundamental way—or at any rate some substantial group of human beings are. Historically, the idea of intrinsic equality gained much of its strength, particularly in Europe and the English-speaking countries, from the common doctrine of Judaism and Christianity (shared also by Islam) that we are equally God's children. Indeed it was exactly on this belief that Locke grounded his assertion of the natural equality of all persons in a state of nature.

Even when moral reasoning is intended to stand independent of its religious origins, as it commonly has been in recent centuries, the Idea of Intrinsic Equality is nevertheless usually taken for granted. Thus we have Bentham's dictum, "everybody to count for one, nobody for more than one," which John Stuart Mill asserted "might be written under the principle of utility as an explanatory commentary" (Mill [1863] 1962, 319).[5] What Bentham meant, and what all utilitarians assume as a premise, is that no matter who Jones and Smith may be, and no matter how the ultimate standard of goodness may be described (whether happiness, pleasure, satisfaction, well-being, or utility), Jones's happiness (or whatever) must be counted in exactly the same units as Smith's. We ought not to measure Jones's happiness in shrunken units because he is an illiterate farm laborer and Smith's in larger units because he is an artist of exquisitely refined tastes. Even when J. S. Mill contended that some pleasures are better than others, he continued to assume the axiom, for to Mill as to Bentham the relative value of an object or activity depended on its contribution to the pleasure or happiness of the recipient, not on the intrinsic and peculiar worth of the recipient.[6]

Utilitarianism is vulnerable in many ways, of course, and it has always been subjected to heavy attack, particularly by those who try to demonstrate a right course of action, duty, obligation, or right that is not justified solely by its utilitarian consequences. But these philosophers, from Kant to Rawls, usually also adopt a premise of intrinsic equality.

The persistence and generality of the assumption of intrinsic equality in systematic moral reasoning could be attributed to the existence of a norm so deeply entrenched in all Western cultures that we cannot reject it without denying our cultural heritage and thereby denying who we are. But a ground for adopting it that appeals less to history and culture and more to its reasonableness is the difficulty of presenting a rational justification for any alternative to it. To be sure, the idea can be rejected without self-contradiction.[7] But to reject it is to assert, in effect, that some people ought to be regarded and treated as *intrinsically* privileged quite independent of any social contribution they may make. To justify such a claim is a formidable task that no one, to my knowledge, has accomplished.

Still, the question persists: What does intrinsic equality actually mean? The aspect that seems to me most relevant to the democratic process is expressed in the Principle of Equal Consideration of Interests. Yet what that principle requires is far from evident. Let me try to clarify it both by filling in some additional meaning and then, following Locke, by saying what it does *not* mean.

To begin with, the principle implies that during a process of collective decision-making, the interests of every person who is subject to the decision must (within the limits of feasibility) be accurately interpreted and made known. Obviously, without this step, the interests of each "subject" could not be considered, much less given equal consideration. Yet the principle does not imply that the "subject" whose interests must be considered should also be the "interpreter." Nor need the "interpreter" necessarily be the decisionmaker.

Suppose the subjects are Able, Baker, and Carr, but Dawson is the best possible interpreter of their interests, while decisions are best made by Eccles, who is required to give equal consideration to the interests of Able, Baker, and Carr. The principle would require not only that (1) Dawson accurately interprets and expresses the interests of Able, Baker, and Carr; (2) Eccles fully understands Dawson's interpretation, and (3) Eccles makes the decision, after having fully considered and taken into account the interests of each, as interpreted by Dawson. But additionally (4) in deciding, Eccles gives "equal consideration" to the interests of each. What this means is that Eccles treats Able, Baker, and Carr as equally entitled to having their interests served, with no one having an intrinsically privileged claim. Suppose Able's interest is best served by choosing X, Baker's by Y, and Carr's by Z. The principle prohibits Eccles from choosing Z, say, on the ground that Carr's claim to Z is intrinsically superior (for whatever reasons) to Able's claim to X or Baker's to Y. Eccles must search for a decision that is *neutral* with respect to Able, Baker, and Carr.[8]

### Two Weaknesses in the Idea of Intrinsic Equality

Standing alone, however, the Idea of Intrinsic Equality is not robust enough to justify much in the way of conclusions—and certainly not democracy. It is weak in at least two ways. In the first place, whatever limits it may set on inequalities are extremely broad. It does not mean, for example, that we are all entitled to equal shares, whether in votes, civil rights, medical care, or anything else. While it would rule out some allocations, it would allow an immense range. If my neighbor has defective kidneys and needs dialysis in order to survive, equal shares would require that both of us, or neither of us, would be entitled to it, which of course would be nonsensical.

We can see the limits of the principle more clearly with the aid of Douglas Rae's "grammar of equality" (Rae 1981). In some situations, Eccles's best solution might be to award amounts that would provide each person with "goods" of *equal value to each person*. What is of "equal value to each person" might be determined by considering each person's needs, wants, satisfactions, ends, or whatever. This is "person-regarding equality." However, while intrinsic equality might seem always to require person-regarding equality, sometimes Eccles might reasonably choose to award Able, Baker, and Carr equal lots, bundles, or quotas of "goods." This is lot-regarding equality. Ordinarily equality of lots will violate person-regarding equality, and conversely.

The Idea of Intrinsic Equality also leaves open other deeply troublesome questions that Dawson the interpreter and Eccles the decisionmaker will have to answer. What ought Dawson the interpreter to take as Able, Baker, and Carr's "interests"—their own preferences, for example, their wants, their needs, or some other basis of substantive good? Nor does the principle tell Eccles the decisionmaker whether to award each person the appropriate goods *directly* or try instead to ensure that Able, Baker, and Carr all have equal *opportunities* to attain the appropriate substantive goods. Suppose Eccles concludes that the interests of Able, Baker, and Carr would be best served by providing them with equal opportunities. Does their intrinsic equality require Eccles to award each of them the identical means or instruments for attaining their interests, such as twelve years of essentially identical schooling? Or instead should Eccles try to ensure that Able, Baker, and Carr all have an equal *probability* of attaining their ends, for example by special (and more costly) education for Able, who is intellectually gifted in certain ways, and for Baker, who is culturally handicapped?

The second weakness is a consequence of the first. As I have already said, nothing in the assumption of intrinsic equality implies that Able, Baker, and Carr are the best judges of their own good or interests. Suppose it were true that a few people like Eccles not only understood much better than the others what constitutes their individual and common good, and how best to bring it about, but could be fully trusted to do so. Then it would be perfectly consistent with the Idea of Intrinsic Equality to conclude that these persons of superior knowledge and virtue, like Eccles, should rule over all the others. Even more: if the good of each person is entitled to equal consideration, and if a superior group of guardians could best ensure equal consideration, then it follows that guardianship would definitely be desirable, and democracy just as definitely would be undesirable.

In the next chapter, therefore, I shall introduce a second—and equally familiar—principle, which I call the Presumption of Personal Autonomy. Joined with the Idea of Intrinsic Equality, it helps to provide a sturdy foundation for democratic beliefs.

Before turning to personal autonomy, however, it is important to see what further content we can give to the term "interests." Advocates of democracy have generally interpreted the most fundamental "interests" or "good" of human beings in three ways. It is in the interests of human beings that they have opportunities to achieve maximum feasible freedom, to develop fully their capacities and potentialities as human beings, and to attain satisfaction of all the other interests they themselves judge important, within limits of feasibility and fairness to others. Democracy, it can be argued, is an essential means to these fundamental interests, even though it may be far from a sufficient condition for achieving them.

## DEMOCRACY AS INSTRUMENTAL TO MAXIMUM FEASIBLE FREEDOM

Since the seventeenth century, advocates of democracy have strongly stressed its relation to freedom. From this perspective, democracy is instrumental to freedom in three ways.

### General Freedom

It has long been recognized by both advocates and opponents of democracy that it is linked to freedom in a way different from that of any other kind of regime. Because certain rights, liberties, and opportunities are essential to the democratic process itself, as long as that process exists then these rights, freedoms, and opportunities must necessarily also exist. These include rights to free expression, political organization, opposition, fair and free elections, and so on. Consequently the minimal range of political freedom in a democratic system inherently comprises a fairly broad range of important rights.[9] But these fundamental political rights are unlikely to exist in isolation. The political culture required to support the existence of a democratic order—what Tocqueville called the *manners* of a people, "namely, the moral and intellectual characteristics of social man taken collectively" (1840, 2:379)—tends to emphasize the value of personal rights, freedoms, and opportunities. Thus not only as an ideal but in actual practice, the democratic process is surrounded by a penumbra of personal freedom.

As a result of the rights inherently required for the democratic process, together with a political culture and a broader domain of personal freedom associated with that process, democracy tends to provide a more extensive domain of personal freedom than any other kind of regime can promise.

### Freedom of Self-Determination

However, democracy is uniquely related to freedom in still another way: It expands to maximum feasible limits the opportunity for persons to live under laws of their own choosing. The essence of the argument might be summarized as follows: To govern oneself, to obey laws that one has chosen for oneself, to be *self-determining*, is a desirable end. Yet human beings cannot attain this end by living in isolation. To enjoy satisfactory lives, they must live in association with others. But to live in association with others necessarily requires that they must sometimes obey collective decisions that are binding on all members of the association. The problem, then, is to discover a way by which the members of an association may make decisions binding on all and still govern themselves. Because democracy maximizes the opportunities for self-determination among the members of an association, it is the best solution.

The most celebrated exposition of this argument is to be found in the *Social Contract*; indeed in that work Rousseau explicitly set out to "find a form of association that defends and protects the person and goods of each associate with all the common force, and by means of which each one, uniting with all, nevertheless obeys only himself and remains as free as before" (Rousseau [1762], 1978, bk. 1, chap. 6, p. 53).

The justification for democracy as maximizing the freedom of self-determination has also been endorsed by all those, from Locke onward, who have believed that governments ought to be based on the consent of the governed. For no other form of government can go so far, at least in principle, to ensure that the structure and processes of government itself and the laws it enacts and enforces depend in a significant way on the genuine consent of the governed. For in a democracy, and only in a democracy, are decisions as to the constitution and laws decided by a majority. By contrast all the feasible alternatives to democracy would permit a minority to decide these vital issues.

This claim might be, and often has been, contested on three grounds. First, even if democracy ensures in principle that these questions will be decided by a majority, the losing minority will not necessarily be governed by laws of its own choosing. While a member of a majority may "obey only himself and remains as free as before," a member of the minority may be compelled to obey a law imposed by others—the majority—and to that extent is less free than they. Rousseau sought to get around this difficulty by proposing that the original social compact would require unanimous agreement, but "except for this primitive contract, the vote of the majority always obligates all the others" (bk. 4, chap. 3, p. 110). His argument, however, is too weak and undeveloped to be convincing. Unfortunately, Rousseau is not alone, for the justification of majority rule has remained a perplexing problem, one I shall turn to in chapter 10. But that problem need not detain us here, for if the only nondemocratic alternatives to majority rule all presuppose some form of minority rule, then the claim that democracy will maximize the opportunities for freedom by self-determination is still valid, since under any nondemocratic alternative the number of members enjoying the freedom of governing themselves would necessarily be smaller than in a democracy.

However, this restatement of the claim now leaves it open to a second objection: If a political association based on majority rule extends the freedom of self-determination more broadly than one based on government by a minority, then the larger the majority required, the more broadly the freedom of self-determination would be extended. In principle, then, unanimity would be the best principle of all. In this view, the unanimity principle, which Rousseau (like Locke) restricted to a mythical "original contract," would be superior to the majority principle for adopting not only the original compact but also for all subsequent laws. Since a unanimity requirement would ensure that no law could be enacted without the assent of every member, one might suppose that it would also ensure freedom of self-determination to every member. Unfortunately for this happy result, however, the unanimity principle has its own grave disadvantages, which will be explored in later chapters, where it will be seen that unanimity is neither feasible nor desirable as a general rule for collective decisions. But we do not need to anticipate that discussion here. For we need only note that *if* unanimity were a desirable and feasible decision rule for the democratic process, then the justification for democracy as maximizing freedom through self-determination would not be in any way vitiated: democracy would then maximize freedom through unanimity rather than through the majority principle.

Yet a third objection still remains: When we postulate a democratic political society, whether governed according to the majority principle or the unanimity principle, we evidently have in mind an ideal system. But as I have said, actually existing political systems, including democratic systems, do not measure up to their ideals. And it is sometimes argued that actual "democracies" fall so far short of the ideal that in practice minorities rule over majorities and the vaunted freedom of self-determination proclaimed as an ideal is effectively denied to a majority of people. The defects of actual "democracies" as measured against the ideal are so well-known and so serious that one cannot simply reject criticisms like this as implausible. At the same time, however, the task of appraising actual "democracies" is enormously difficult, whether we compare them against non-democratic regimes or their own ideal standards. This task awaits later chapters. Yet most critics who raise the objection I have just described would probably contend that what is wrong with actual "democracies" is the fact that they fail to meet democratic standards. Obviously an objection along these lines need not deny, and probably is not ordinarily intended to deny, that if democracy were to meet its own standards, it would expand the freedom of self-determination more broadly than any feasible alternative to it.

## Moral Autonomy

One might agree to all that has been said so far and yet object to the implicit assumption that the freedom to govern oneself under laws of one's own choosing is a desirable goal. Probably few critics would actually challenge the assumption, and most would take it for granted. Yet the question needs asking: Why is this form of freedom desirable?

An important part of the answer is to be found in the other justifications for democracy that we are about to explore. To live under laws of one's own choosing, and thus to participate in the process of choosing those laws, facilitates the personal development of citizens as moral and social beings and enables citizens to protect and advance their most fundamental rights, interests, and concerns.

There is, however, a deeper reason for valuing the freedom to govern oneself, a reason having less to do than these with its usefulness as an instrument to other ends. This is the value of moral autonomy itself. By a morally autonomous person I mean one who decides on his moral principles, and the decisions that significantly depend on them, following a process of reflection, deliberation, scrutiny, and consideration. To be morally autonomous *is* to be self-governing in the domain of morally relevant choices (cf. Kuflik, 1984, 272).

This is hardly the place to discuss the disputes over the meaning of moral autonomy.[10] Nor shall I say much about the reasons why moral autonomy should be respected.[11] In the end, I believe, the reasons for respecting moral autonomy sift down to one's belief that it is a quality without which human beings cease to be fully human and in the total absence of which they would not be human at all.[12] In short, if it is desirable that human beings be moral beings, as I feel certain no reader of this book will deny, then their moral autonomy must be respected.

To limit one's opportunity to live under the laws of one's own choosing is to limit the scope of moral autonomy. Because the democratic process maximizes the feasible scope of self-determination for those who are subject to collective decisions, so it also maximally respects the moral autonomy of all who are subject to its laws.

## DEMOCRACY AS INSTRUMENTAL TO HUMAN DEVELOPMENT

That the character of a regime and the qualities of its people are somehow related has been a commonplace of political philosophy since the Greeks. In his

*Considerations on Representative Government*, John Stuart Mill echoed this ancient view:

> The first element of good government . . . being the virtue and intelligence of the human beings composing the community, the most important point of excellence which any form of government can possess is to promote the virtue and intelligence of the people themselves. The first question in respect to any political institutions is how far they tend to foster in the members of the community the various desirable qualities, moral and intellectual. (Mill [1861] 1958, 25)

But there has not been much agreement as to the precise nature of the relation between regimes and human character, or even the direction of causation. Nonetheless, it has been argued on behalf of democracy that it tends more than other regimes to enhance certain desirable qualities among its citizens.

In Mill's view, by providing opportunities for all to participate actively in political life, democracy fosters, as no other kind of regime can, qualities of independence, self-reliance, and public-spiritedness (53–55). The argument that political participation fosters desirable personal and social qualities in democratic citizens has often been advanced since Mill's time, particularly by advocates of participatory democracy (cf. Pateman 1970, 43; Barber 1984, 153).

Although attractive and plausible, as a justification for democracy the argument suffers from a grave difficulty: It depends entirely on what is after all an *empirical* hypothesis asserting a relation betwen the characteristics of a regime and the qualities of its people. To determine the relation between regime and personal qualities is a formidable task, and modern social scientists have so far made little advance over the speculations and conjectures of Plato, Machiavelli, and Mill. Although modern theorists have sometimes proposed that a "democratic personality" is either necessary to, or is produced by, democratic institutions, attempts to define the distinctive qualities of a democratic personality and to verify its relation to democratic regimes or practices have not met with much success. For example, the conjecture that political participation tends to create a stronger sense of self-worth, greater tolerance, and more public spiritedness is only weakly supported by systematic investigation, if at all (Sniderman 1975). The methodological obstacles to verifying the hypothesis are so great as to make this conjecture at best a weak and vulnerable justification for democracy—not one certainly that would carry much weight standing alone.

However, if we consider the previous justifications for democracy, we can look at the question in a different way. Suppose we believe adult persons should possess these qualities, among others: They should possess the capacity for looking after themselves, in the sense of being able to take care of their interests. They should so far as possible be morally autonomous, particularly on decisions of great importance to themselves and others. They should act responsibly, in the sense of weighing alternative courses of action as best they can, considering their consequences, and taking into account the rights and obligations of oneself and others. And they should be capable of engaging in free and open discussion with others in order to arrive at moral judgments. Both casual and systematic observation provide good grounds for believing that many, perhaps most, human beings at birth possess the potentiality for developing these qualities and that the extent to which they actually develop them depends primarily on the circumstances into which they are born and in which their development—or lack of it—takes place.

Among these circumstances is the nature of the political regime in which a person lives. And only democratic regimes can provide the conditions under which the qualities I have mentioned are likely to develop fully. For all other regimes reduce, often drastically, the scope within which adults can act to protect their own interests (much less the interests of others), exercise self-determination, take responsibility for important decisions, and engage freely with others in a search for the best decision. Because the existence of a democratic process in governing the state can hardly be a sufficient condition for these qualities to develop, and because in any case actual regimes are never by any means fully democratic, the methodological obstacles to empirical verification remain. But if the qualities I have described are desirable, then it seems reasonable to hold that, in order for them to develop among a large proportion of a people, it is necessary if not sufficient that the people govern themselves democratically.

## DEMOCRACY AS INSTRUMENTAL TO THE PROTECTION OF PERSONAL INTERESTS

Perhaps the most common justification given for democracy is that it is essential to the protection of the general interests of the persons who are subject to the regulations or actions of the officials of a state. While these include freedom and personal development, they also extend to a broad array of desires, wants, practices, and rights that people in a specific society and historical situation may believe to be important.

In his *Considerations on Representative Government*, Mill presented the following argument:

1. A principle "of as universal truth and applicability as any general propositions which can be laid down respecting human affairs . . . is that the rights and interests of every or any person are only secure from being disregarded when the person is himself able, and habitually disposed, to stand up for them. . . . Human beings are only secure from evil at the hands of others in proportion as they have the power of being, and are, self-*protecting*."
2. People can protect their rights and interests from abuse by government, and by those who influence or control government, only if they can participate fully in determining the conduct of the government.[13]
3. Therefore, "nothing less can be ultimately desirable than the admission of all to a share in the sovereign power of the state," that is, a democratic government.
4. "But since all cannot, in a community exceeding a single small town, participate in any but some very minor portions of the public business, it follows that the ideal type of perfect government must be representative" (Mill [1861] 1958, 43, 55).

Though Mill's utilitarian assumptions are conspicuously absent from his defense of representative government, and though he had come to reject the simple identification of happiness with pleasure espoused by his father and Bentham, he continued to believe that happiness was the supreme good. Consequently, he would have been obliged to say, I presume, that the protection of one's rights and interests is desirable because these rights and interests are instrumental to one's happiness. Mill's argument, however, does not strictly require this assumption, and one need not be a utilitarian in order to accept it. For example, one might simply contend that even if the protection of one's rights and interests is not necessarily conducive to one's happiness, it is morally proper that a person's fundamental rights and interests should be protected. It is important to keep in mind, then, that the validity of Mill's argument and its implicit premise do not necessarily depend on the validity of any form of utilitarianism.

It is nonetheless true that classical utilitarians like Bentham and James Mill, as well as innumerable successors, have justified democracy on the ground that satisfying one's wants is conducive to one's happiness; and that democracy is desirable because, and insofar as, it is a political process by means of which people may best satisfy their wants. The general form of their argument is exactly like Mill's, except that this species of utilitarianism speaks of wants where Mill speaks of rights and interests.

Widespread though it may be, the attempt to justify democracy as instrumental to satisfying wants has been attacked by some democratic theorists. John Plamenatz argued, for example, that there is "no good reason for believing that, the more successful I am in maximizing the satisfaction of my wants within the limits in which success is possible, the more happy I am likely to be." Moreover, we cannot compare governments and, as a reasonable empirical judgment, conclude that "the policies of one have in general done more than those of the other to enable their subjects to maximize the satisfaction of their wants," particularly if the governments are not of the same type and the values and beliefs of the people concerned differ greatly. Finally, people do not and should not prefer democracy to its alternatives because they believe it is better at maximizing the satisfaction of their wants. "Neither its champions nor its critics are concerned with maximizing the satisfaction of wants or the achievement of goals. They favor it because it gives men certain rights and opportunities; or they reject it because it does not. But these rights and opportunities are not valued because they make it easier for people to maximize the satisfaction of their wants" (Plamenatz 1973, 163, 164, 168).[14]

Now it is one thing to say that democracy cannot be justified on the ground that it maximizes want-satisfaction and it is quite another to insist that democracy has nothing to do with what people want. To begin with, one need not accept the simple psychology of classical utilitarianism in order to believe that one's happiness is to some extent dependent on satisfying one's wants, or some of them. I cannot conceive how people could be happy if none of their wants were ever satisfied. In the same way, it is hard to see why people would value a government that never did what they wanted it to do. If, as Plamenatz contended, people value democracy because of the rights and opportunities it provides, then they must want their government to provide, protect, and enforce these rights and opportunities. If, in their view, democracy did not satisfy these wants better than any feasible alternative to it, then insofar as they were rational they would prefer the alternative.

To speak of people wanting their government to do certain things and to avoid doing others is no doubt a long way from "maximizing the satisfaction of wants." A's wanting to satisfy his desire for a hamburger is certainly not equivalent to A's wanting the government to maximize his opportunities to eat hamburgers. Probably no sane person would expect a government to satisfy, or try to satisfy, all his wants. What people want a government to do or to refrain from doing is a special subset, and for many people a small subset, of their wants. This subset can nonetheless be highly important. For example, it can include what Mill referred to as one's rights and interests and Plamenatz as one's rights and opportunities. To avoid confusing this special but often important subset with the multiplicity of "wants" people may wish to satisfy, let me call these "urgent political concerns."

A more reasonable justification for democracy, then, is that, to a substantially greater degree than any alternative to it, a democratic government provides an orderly and peaceful process by means of which a majority of citizens can induce the government to do what they most want it to do and to avoid doing what they most want it not to do.[15] Instead of a claim that democratic governments respond by maximizing the satisfaction of wants, we might claim instead that they tend to satisfy a minimal set of urgent political concerns. Now it may well be that as a practical matter we cannot determine whether this justification is valid by rigorously comparing the performances of democratic and nondemocratic governments with evidence showing what citizens want their governments to do or not do. We might nevertheless be able to arrive at a reasonable judgment by comparing the opportunities that the democratic process (both in ideal form and in actuality) provides a majority of citizens for influencing the government to attempt to satisfy their urgent political concerns with the opportunities that a nondemocratic government, both in ideal form and in actuality, would provide. And on the basis of such a comparison, we would decide whether the claim is justified.

This is a substantial undertaking. Among other things, we would need to specify the institutions that, in practice, the democratic process requires. These tasks await later chapters. Meanwhile Plamenatz's criticisms do not seem to me to warrant our rejecting either Mill's argument or the belief that democratic governments provide citizens with better opportunities for satisfying their urgent political concerns than any feasible alternatives to them.

✦

I suggested earlier that the Idea of Intrinsic Equality is subject to two weaknesses: First, because it does not specify what are to be counted as human interests or goods, the limits it sets on inequalities are extremely loose and vague. Thus it is not by itself sufficient to uphold a claim to political equality of the kind required for democracy. The principle becomes more specific, and more closely related to the democratic process, when we interpret human interests to include claims to maximum feasible freedom, personal development, and opportunities to satisfy urgent political concerns more generally.

Even these goods, however, do not make the principle self-interpreting. Who then should determine more specifically what goods or interests ought to be given priority? In short, who should rule? Might not one reasonably argue, as Plato did in *The Republic*, that only a highly qualified minority of experts on such matters is truly qualified to make these decisions and thus to rule? Indeed, the question may be asked even within a "democratic" system. Would we want to call a system a "democracy" if the size of the demos is greatly exceeded by the number of adults who are excluded from the demos? Athens, as we saw in chapter 1, was just such a system, and the Athenians, who after all invented the term, called Athens a democracy. And for all their language of universalism, Locke, Rousseau, and Jefferson, like Aristotle earlier and Mill later, shrank from accepting universal inclusion in practice. For in their judgments the number of persons qualified to participate in political life were in many specific instances fewer than those who might properly be compelled to obey the laws.

That they could believe in popular government and yet believe that "the people" ought not to include all the people does not demonstrate that they were necessarily inconsistent or hypocritical. It reveals instead an incompleteness in the Idea of Intrinsic Equality as a justification for democracy.

# Chapter 7

◆◆◆◆◆◆◆◆

# Personal Autonomy

Democracy—rule by the people—can be justified only on the assumption that ordinary people are, in general, *qualified* to govern themselves. For it seems self-evident that people ought not to govern themselves if they are not qualified to do so. After all, because we believe that children are not qualified to govern themselves we insist that they be governed by others who, we presume, are more qualified to do so. Yet the assumption that people in general—ordinary people— are adequately qualified to govern themselves is, on the face of it, such an extravagant claim that critics of democracy have rejected it ever since the philosophical idea and practice of democracy appeared among the Greeks over two thousand years ago.

## A STRONG PRINCIPLE OF EQUALITY

The assumption that a substantial portion of adults are adequately qualified to govern themselves might be called a Strong Principle of Equality (to distinguish it, for example, from the weaker principle expressed in the Idea of Intrinsic Equality). We might also refer to it as an assumption of *roughly equal qualification*, and I shall use either expression as seems appropriate.

An assumption of roughly equal qualification immediately suggests three questions: What does it mean? How can it be justified as reasonable? To what persons should it apply?

## THE STRONG PRINCIPLE: A PRELIMINARY INTERPRETATION

Let me offer a preliminary interpretation, subject to modification later on. To begin with, it is important to note that the principle might be meant to apply only to a particular group, such as all citizens of Athens. But since the seventeenth century assertions along these lines have often been cast in a universal form, as in the famous declaration that all men are created equal. And today we would want to interpret "all men" as including all women, even though the authors of the renowned phrase did not.

Let us imagine, as we did earlier, that some human association, concrete or hypothetical, has a need for collective decisions binding on all members of the association. Which members of the association are qualified to participate in making these collective decisions, and under what conditions? Suppose we could provisionally agree on the following assumption:

*All members are sufficiently well qualified, taken all around, to participate in making the collective decisions binding on the association that significantly affect their good or interests. In any case, none are so definitely better qualified than the others that they should be entrusted with making the collective and binding decisions.*

Notice that the assumption consists of two sentences that are not strictly equivalent propositions. The first asserts that all the members meet an acceptable standard of competence. The second denies that any members possess such extraordinary qualifications that they alone should rule. The first implies a hypothetical *lower* limit, a *minimum* level of competence, that *all* members reach, the second a hypothetical *upper* limit, a *maximum* level of competence, that *no* members reach.[1]

The set of persons to whom such a principle may be applied could be called the demos, the *populus*, or the citizen-body. Its members are *full citizens*. (For brevity, I shall ordinarily refer to them simply as citizens.) We have provisionally assumed that the demos includes all the members of the association, that is, every member is also a full citizen. But it is possible that some members who are obliged to obey the rules of the association are nevertheless excluded from the demos and therefore are not full citizens. Children are an obvious example.

If we were to deny that the Strong Principle of Equality could properly be applied to all the members of an association, it would be extremely difficult, and perhaps impossible, to make a reasonable argument that all the members of the association ought to be full citizens, that is, entitled to participate fully in governing the association. For if, as with children, some persons are definitely not adequately qualified to govern, while others are, then should not these more qualified members, even if a minority, govern the rest? Conversely, however, if the Strong Principle does properly apply to all members, then on what grounds could one reasonably deny that all the members should participate, as equals, in governing themselves?

A rational belief in democracy thus presupposes that Strong Equality exists among (full) citizens. But who should be citizens, that is, among whom does Strong Equality exist? We seem to find ourselves trapped in a circle: Strong Equality exists among citizens because those members of an association among whom Strong Equality exists are (or should be) citizens. How are we to break out of this circle? How should we decide on the *range* of Strong Equality? Depending on the answer, democracy could be universally inclusive or as narrowly exclusive as the Republic of Venice, in which less than two thousand male members of the Venetian aristocracy were entitled to govern over the several hundred thousand residents of Venice. And what of the interests of the excluded? Are they to be cared for equally with the interests of the citizens? If so, why and how? Evidently the moral value of democracy, and thus much of its justification, will vary according to its inclusiveness.

Although strong in implications within its range, then, the Strong Principle is weak in implications outside its range. The import of the Strong Principle, it seems, cannot be separated from its range: unless the range is specified we are hard put to judge its significance. At the same time, our willingness to accept the principle will depend on its range. Extend the range far enough—to include infants, for example—and probably no one will accept it. Yet one who rejects a range as too inclusive would probably accept some version of a narrower range. For example, a member of the Venetian nobility would doubtless have excluded most adult residents of the Republic from the range of the Strong Principle; presumably, however, he would have assumed that the Strong Principle was perfectly applicable to the male members of the aristocracy. Thus the validity of the principle and the value we attribute to it both seem to depend on its range. What we need then is some reasonable way of determining simultaneously whether the principle is justified and what its range is.

I believe that two propositions, taken together, will help to solve this problem. Both are assumptions of the theory of the democratic process that will be described in chapter 8. One of these is the Principle of Equal Consideration discussed in the last chapter. As we saw, however, that principle, like the general idea of intrinsic equality, is weak in its implications: by itself, it could as readily justify guardianship as democracy.

Although the Idea of Intrinsic Equality, standing alone, is too weak to support the Strong Principle of Equality, a stout foundation can be constructed by joining it with a second assumption that has been a cornerstone of democratic beliefs (as it has also been of liberal thought). This is the assumption that no person is, in general, more likely than yourself to be a better judge of your own good or interest or to act to bring it about. Consequently, you should have the right to judge whether a policy is, or is not, in your best interest. The assumption is, further, that what holds for you holds, generally speaking, for other adults. By a "policy" I mean a decision to adopt certain *means* to bring about certain *results*.[2] On this assumption, then, no one else is more qualified than you to judge whether the results are in your interest—both the results expected from a decision before it is taken and the actual results following the decision. You may choose to delegate the choice of *means* to those you judge to be more qualified than yourself to select the most appropriate means.[3] But you could not, without acting contrary to the assumption, yield your right to judge whether the results (intended and actual) were in your interests. I am going to call this the Presumption of Personal Autonomy.

## THE PRESUMPTION OF PERSONAL AUTONOMY

It is much easier to interpret the Presumption of Personal Autonomy for individual decisions than for collective decisions. If we assume that under some conditions a collective decision may properly be made binding on those who disagree with the expected outcome because they believe that it will be harmful to their interests, then an individual's final choice cannot be decisive, as it can be with individual decisions. Such is often the case, for example, when binding collective decisions are made by majority rule: though the members of the losing minority may feel that the outcome is harmful to their interests, they may nonetheless be required to comply and indeed may even believe stongly that, having lost the vote, it is *right* that they be required to comply.

The implications of personal autonomy for collective decisions become clearer if we assume the validity of intrinsic equality and what it implies for the equal consideration of interests. If in making collective decisions the interests of each person ought to be weighed equally with the interests of every other, who is to say what the interests of each are? By adopting the Presumption of Personal Autonomy, we agree that each adult person whose interests are involved in the outcome ought to have the right to specify what those interests are. As I indicated in the last chapter, if A holds that her interest is best served by policy x rather than policy y, then insofar as the rules and procedures are intended to take A's interest equally into account, along with B's, C's, and others', then what is *counted* as A's interest is what A—not B, C, or any other—says are A's interests.

To accept the idea of personal autonomy among adults, then, is to establish a *presumption* that in making individual or collective decisions each adult ought to be treated—for purposes of making decisions—as the proper judge of his or her own interests. In the absence of a very compelling showing of incompetence, then, the presumption is assumed to be binding. In short:

THE PRESUMPTION OF PERSONAL AUTONOMY: *In the absence of a compelling showing to the contrary everyone should be assumed to be the best judge of his or her own good or interests.*

The practical effect of the presumption is to deny that paternalistic authority can ever be legitimate among adults, in either individual or collective decisions, except for presumably rare exceptions. And conversely, all legitimate authority relations involving adults must be consistent with—in that sense, must respect—the presumption of personal autonomy.

Unlike the Idea of Intrinsic Equality and the Principle of Equal Consideration of Interests, which are moral judgments about as unalloyed as we ever encounter, are universal in their range, and so admit of no exceptions, the Presumption of Personal Autonomy could best be described as a rule of prudence. It is not an epistemological principle: one could reasonably deny that A is acting in her own interests and still insist that the rule be upheld in A's case. Because a prudential rule is a mix of moral and empirical judgments it displays the inherent messiness of a contingent statement that is not derived rigorously from axioms or empirical laws. Instead a prudential rule draws upon a flawed and imprecise understanding of human experience. It displays all the imperfections of contingency. It does not lay down an absolutely inviolable right or duty, or purport to say what definitely will happen, or estimate precisely what is most likely to happen. It admits of exceptions. But it does tell us where the burden of proof must lie when a claim is made for an exception, that is, for replacing personal autonomy by a paternalistic authority.

Even among adults personal autonomy has sometimes been widely replaced by paternalistic authority. In the relation of master to slave, paternalistic authority was the general rule. And until quite recently half of all adults were legally subject to paternalism on grounds widely thought, and not merely by the other half, to be almost self-evident: that women were not competent to make decisions for themselves. Today, however, children are the only large group of people subject to comprehensive paternalistic authority; thus they constitute the only major exception to the Presumption of Personal Autonomy. For children, parents are the normal authorities, though in special cases paternalistic authority over a child may be awarded to other adults. For adults, on the other hand, paternalistic authority with respect to individual decisions is thought to be justified in only a small percentage of exceptional cases—persons so severely handicapped because of birth defects, brain damage, acute psychosis, senility, and so on that they are judged incapable of making the elementary decisions required for their own survival or minimal well-being. Even in these cases, the burden of proof is always legally placed on those who propose to replace personal autonomy by paternalism.

But why should we accept the presumption? Would it be just as reasonable to reject it? To reject it as a presumption for individual and collective decisions, however, we would have to believe *not only* that (1) some substantial proportion of adults are quite unable to understand, or are not sufficiently motivated to seek, their most fundamental interests, *but also* that (2) a class of paternalistic authorities could be counted on to do so in their behalf. An argument along these lines is subject to two grave defects. First, in apprehending the good or interests of the self, every other tends to be at a disadvantage. Second, human experience provides strong reasons for rejecting the second proposition.

## THE DISADVANTAGED POSITION OF THE OTHER

In examining the case for guardianship we saw that in order to justify a claim that some other person (or group of persons) possesses better knowledge than the self—yourself, for example—of the self's own good or interests would require a convincing account of what this knowledge consists of and why the other's knowledge is superior to the knowledge possessed by the self. We also saw that a satisfactory defense of such a claim would require an answer to one of the most difficult and contentious intellectual problems of our times: whether moral judgments can be intellectually justified, and, if so, how.

Fortunately, however, the justification for democracy does not depend, in my view, on a *specific* answer to the intractable epistemological and ontological questions about the nature of moral judgments. While it is illusory to think that a satisfactory demonstration of the general superiority of democracy to its alterna-tives can ever consist of a straightforward axiomatical argument from unimpeach-able premises to an "absolute" and "objectively valid" conclusion, it is equally mistaken, and even more absurd, to insist that all arguments with a moral flavor are equally arbitrary and therefore equally reasonable or unreasonable. My aim is to show why it is much more reasonable to believe in democracy than in any alterna-tive to it.

To be sure, specific cases may sometimes require difficult, complex, and highly debatable judgments; but that is always so in matters involving important moral issues, particularly if these are mixed with empirical uncertainties. Even then, the quality of one's judgments depends on one's understanding of the more general issues at stake.

Let me return to the disadvantaged position of the other. In judging whether some course of action or policy is in A's interests, either we must know something about A's preferences, wants, or needs, or we must possess knowledge of what is good for A independently of A's own preferences, wants, or needs—"ideal val-ues" for A, if you will. When we arrange preferences, wants, needs, and ideal values along a hypothetical axis, a significant shift occurs in the kind of knowledge required. Along most of the axis the self is uniquely privileged because only the self has direct access to its own awareness. The more that knowledge of A's interests requires direct access to A's awareness, the more advantageous is the position of A herself. If we were to assume that A's own interests are most accurately reflected by her immediate *preferences*, her claim to adequate, even superior knowledge of her interests is enormously strengthened. Likewise, though A's expressed preferences might reflect a mistaken view of her deeper or more enduring *wants*, with respect to her wants, too, her unique access to her own awareness again provides a definite advantage. Even if we were to hold that human interests consist ultimately not of preferences or wants but *needs*, as a general matter the self is probably in a better position than any other to know the relative order of urgency among its various needs.

Some psychologists have maintained that the needs of human beings form a hierarchy, a more or less universal "objective" hierarchy. But even if this were true (a by no means uncontroversial presumption), it would allow us to say only that some of a person's needs, say, for food, have to be met above a certain threshold before others take on equal urgency. But who is best qualified to judge when that threshold has been reached? The theory itself makes sense only on the presumption that the relative priorities work their way into the *self's* awareness, when they can be reported to others or inferred from the person's actions. In specific cases, the observer might perhaps make a better guess about the threshold, but if that were generally so then the whole empirical basis of the theory would be undermined. Thus whether interests are thought to be indicated by a person's preferences, wants, or needs, the knowledge of the self is likely to be superior to that of any other person and certainly, in general, no worse.

Up to now I have deliberately used the terms "interest" and "good" as if they were interchangeable. Suppose, however, that it could be shown that the *good* of a person consists of an end or ideal value that is not fully indicated by preferences, wants, or needs. Then the unique access of the self to its own awareness would be less of an advantage. Yet to demonstrate that any such assertion is true appears to be impossible. We are therefore entitled, indeed obliged, to look with the greatest suspicion on any claim that another possesses objective knowledge of the good of the self that is definitely superior to the knowledge possessed by the self.

An additional reason for doubting the validity of another's claim arises if one is confronted, as one at times almost certainly will be, by conflicts between several values, such as seeking one's own happiness or self-development, doing justice to one's family, or doing justice to others. Even if these value conflicts arise within a single, coherent system of values, like utilitarianism, they require judgments about trade-offs that depend in turn on detailed knowledge of the particularities of the concrete case. Once again, the self is privileged in its access to the particularities, even the uniqueness, of the self. But value conflicts may also arise because different *systems* of value can and often do specify different courses of action; and no higher order system for adjudicating these conflicts seems to exist (Nagel 1979, 129–34). Thus the claim of another to superior knowledge of what is good for me reflects nothing more than a particular value system, and not at all what would be best in the perspective of my own system of values.

## INTERESTS AND HUMAN EXPERIENCE

Not only are others ordinarily at a disadvantage in *understanding* the good or interests of the self. The *incentives* of others to seek the interests of the self are much weaker than those of the self. As we saw in the discussion of guardianship, paternalistic authorities need both knowledge and virtue.

And as to virtue, the record of human experience argues decisively, so it seems to me, against the view that, as a general matter, the protection and advancement of the good or interests of any significant proportion of adults can safely be entrusted to others. Earlier I mentioned the two historic cases that provide the bulk of human experience with comprehensive paternalism: slavery and the legal subjection of women. Do we have the slightest reason for believing that slaves and women would not have protected their own interests at least as well as their masters and in all likelihood far better?

Another example is provided by the exclusion of the working classes from the suffrage. Perhaps no one put the case more convincingly than Mill, for, perhaps overgenerously, he did not

> believe that the classes who do participate in [the government] have in general any intention of sacrificing the working classes to themselves. . . . Yet does Parliament, or almost any of the members composing it, ever for an instant look at any question with the eyes of a workingman? When a subject arises in which the laborers as such have an interest, is it regarded from any point of view but that of employers of labor? (Mill [1861] 1958, 44)

Considerations like these led Mill to formulate a principle that is essentially equivalent to the Presumption of Personal Autonomy. As Mill rightly saw, the argument from human experience, particularly in the three crucial cases of slavery, women, and working people, lends powerful support to the conclusion that both individual and collective decisions should respect the Presumption of Personal Autonomy.[4]

To these three cases we may now add two others. Although, as a result of the Civil War, slavery was abolished in the United States, the rights of the freed blacks to participate in political life were swiftly annihilated throughout the South during the Reconstruction period. As a result the liberated slaves and their descendants continued to live another full century in a condition of political subjection and oppression enforced ultimately by violence and terror. Not until the passage and vigorous enforcement of the civil rights acts of the 1960s were southern blacks at last permitted to transform their nominal citizenship into full political participation. Throughout this long period of political subjection, many southern whites sought to justify their rule—"white supremacy"—by the double claim that blacks were not competent to participate in political life *and* that they, the de facto white rulers, would in any case fully attend to the essential interests of the blacks. Few people, even southern whites, would regard these claims today as more than preposterous rationalizations for a system of rule that utterly failed to protect even the most elementary interests of most southern blacks.

The other case has been provided by South Africa. I cannot imagine a reasonable defense of the proposition that the white rulers of the Republic of South Africa ever adequately cared for the fundamental interests of the millions of blacks who were subject to their rule and yet lacked all means of participating in the making of the laws that subjected them to the misery, humiliation, and torment that was their lot.

If we accept the Idea of Intrinsic Equality, then no process of lawmaking can be morally justified if it does not take equally into account the interests of every person subject to the laws. While it cannot be shown, I think, that democracy is sufficient to ensure the protection of the basic interests of all people subject to its laws, the record of human experience provides convincing evidence that people who, because of their exclusion from citizenship, are deprived of the opportunity to defend their own interests will almost certainly not have their interests adequately taken into account by the demos from which they are excluded. While citizenship in a democratic polity does not ensure that one's interests are weighed equally in lawmaking, the historical record does at any rate demonstrate that citizenship is a necessary condition.

## PERSONAL AUTONOMY AND PERSONAL DEVELOPMENT

So too with personal development. The personal development that some writers attribute to citizenship in a democratic order is in large part *moral* development: gaining a more mature sense of responsibility for one's actions, a broader awareness of the others affected by one's actions, a greater willingness to reflect on and take into account the consequences of one's actions for others, and so on. Probably few people would contest the normative premise that it is desirable to promote the growth of these qualities. The extent to which these qualities are actually produced in citizens by democracy is, as I said in the last chapter, not a normative question but an empirical one; and how well the empirical claim holds up is at present unclear. The relevant point here, however, is that the argument presupposes that people ought to enjoy a high degree of personal autonomy in individual and collective decisions. Anyone whose personal autonomy is permanently replaced by paternalistic authority would be maintained in a perpetual state of childhood and dependence. Consequently, if collective decisions were always made by paternalistic authorities—by a body of guardians, let us say—then in the domain of public affairs people could never outgrow their childhood.

## PERSONAL AUTONOMY AND SELF-DETERMINATION

That personal autonomy and thus inclusion as a full citizen in a democratic order are necessary to self-determination is even more obvious. Lacking personal autonomy, one simply could not live under rules of one's own choosing; as a result, one would be neither self-determining nor morally autonomous and to that extent could not be a moral person. The minimum desirable range for personal autonomy must therefore be at least as broad as the minimum desirable range of self-determination and moral autonomy. And the minimum desirable range for self-determination and moral autonomy is all adults, with the usual rare exceptions for those lacking rational faculties.[5]

## THE STRONG PRINCIPLE RESTATED

If the good or interests of everyone should be weighed equally, and if each adult person is in general the best judge of his or her good or interests, then *every adult member* of an association is sufficiently well qualified, taken all around, to participate in making binding collective decisions that affect his or her good or interests, that is, to be a *full citizen* of the demos. More specifically, when binding decisions are made, the claims of each citizen as to the laws, rules, policies, etc. to be adopted must be counted as valid and equally valid. Moreover, no adult members are so definitely better qualified than the others that they should be entrusted with making binding collective decisions. More specifically, when binding decisions are made, no citizen's claims as to the laws, rules, and policies to be adopted are to be counted as superior to the claims of any other citzen.

Taken as premises, then, the Principle of Equal Consideration of Interests and the Presumption of Personal Autonomy justify our adopting the Strong Principle of Equality. The Strong Principle, in turn, is at once the most powerful and the most controversial assumption in the theory of the democratic process. By accepting the Strong Principle, in effect we accept the democratic process as a requirement for making binding decisions.

# Chapter 8

◆◆◆◆◆◆◆◆

# A Theory of the
# Democratic Process

"In democratic states," Aristotle wrote in *The Politics*, "the people [or *demos*] is sovereign; in oligarchies, on the other hand, the few [or *oligoi*] have the position" (1952, 110). Democracy means, literally, rule by the people.[1] But what does it mean to say that the people rule, the people is sovereign, a people governs itself? In order to rule, the people must have some way of ruling, a *process* for ruling. What are the distinctive characteristics of a democratic process of government? For example, how does it differ from rule by the few, or oligarchy?

To answer these questions it is useful to proceed in three stages. First, since democracy is a *political order* it is useful to set out the assumptions that justify the existence of a political order. Second, we need to specify the assumptions that justify a *democratic* political order. Although I shall describe these two sets of assumptions rather abstractly, they are not meant to be ahistorical, and they definitely do not presume the fiction, common in democratic theory since Locke, of a prior "state of nature" out of which a political society emerges by a social contract. Third, we need to describe the essential *criteria* of a democratic political order and indicate how these follow from the assumptions.

## ASSUMPTIONS OF A POLITICAL ORDER

To begin with, let us suppose that (say, in a concrete historical situation) some persons have in mind the idea of forming an association to achieve certain ends; or what is more likely, they want to adapt an already existing association to undertake these tasks. I use the term association loosely; as we shall see in moment, it need not be a state.

To achieve these ends, the association needs to adopt policies, with which members will be obliged to act consistently.[2] Ordinarily, their obligation to act consistently with the policies of the association is expressed in a rule or a law that includes penalties for noncompliance. Because members are obliged to obey the rules or laws, the decisions may be said to be *binding*. Taken collectively,

*106*

the decisionmakers who make binding decisions constitute the *government* of the association. These binding decisions might therefore also be called *governmental* or binding *collective* decisions.

That decisions are binding does not imply that the association is necessarily coercive, employs the threat of violent sanctions to bring about compliance, or possesses other similar characteristics that are often used to distinguish a state from other sorts of associations. Although the government of the association might create an expectation that violators will be punished by officials, in some circumstances decisions might be binding without punishments by officials or even by other members. To evoke an expectation of divine or magical sanctions might be sufficient. Or the mere process of enacting or announcing a rule might cause enough members to adopt it as a principle of conduct to produce a quite satisfactory level of compliance. In short, although the association could be a state in the usual sense of a coercive order, it might not be; likewise the government of the association need not be the government of a state. Thus we can describe a general theory of the democratic process applicable to associations whether or not they constitute a state.

The process for making binding decisions includes at least two analytically distinguishable stages: setting the agenda and deciding the outcome. *Setting the agenda* is the part of the process during which matters are selected on which decisions are to be made (including a decision not to decide the matter). *Deciding the outcome*, or the *decisive stage*, is the period during which the process culminates in an outcome, signifying that a policy has definitely been adopted or rejected. If setting the agenda is the first say, the decisive stage is the last say, the moment of sovereignty with respect to the matter at hand. Until the decisive stage is completed, the process of decisionmaking is tentative. It may lead to discussion, agreements, even outcomes of votes; but these are all preliminary, may be overruled at the decisive stage, and are not binding on the members. Decisions become binding only at the conclusion of the decisive stage. Although this analytic distinction would apply to any political order, it is essential in clarifying the nature of the democratic process, as will become clearer later on.

What constitutes the decisive stage in making collective decisions is far from self-evident. Adopting a constitution or a constitutional amendment is surely a decisive stage (or, if it is not, the constitution is a fictive or paper constitution). For most policies enacted in a constitutional order, however, the decisive stage occurs within the existing constitutional limits. In principle, a stage is decisive if all prior decisions can still be recalled or reversed. Thus, prior to the decisive stage decisions may be thought of as having been *delegated* but not *alienated* by those who participate in the decisive stage, a distinction we return to below.

## ASSUMPTIONS JUSTIFYING A DEMOCRATIC POLITICAL ORDER

Binding decisions are to be made only by persons who are subject to the decisions, that is, by members of the association, not by persons outside the association. No lawmaker is, in the familiar expression, above the law. The assumption rests on the elementary principle of fairness that laws cannot rightfully be imposed on others by persons who are not themselves obliged to obey those laws. Moreover, while this assumption is not sufficient to guarantee that freedom of self-determination will be respected, clearly it is necessary to self-determination; for laws and rules imposed by an outsider would violate the self-determination of all those subject to the laws.

The good of each member is entitled to equal consideration. This is a straightforward application to all the members of the Idea of Intrinsic Equality described in the last chapter.

No adult member of the association should ever be required to demonstrate adequate competence for protecting that member's own interests. Instead, the burden of proof would always lie with a claim to an exception, and no exception would be admissible, either morally or legally, in the absence of a very compelling showing. Thus this assumption presupposes that each member of the association is, taken all around, a better judge of his or her interests than others would be. The grounds for adopting this presumption were set out in chapter 5. Meanwhile, let us call the adult members who satisfy this presumption *citizens*; collectively the citizens constitute the *demos, populus,* or *citizen body.*

When binding decisions are made, the claims of each citizen as to the desirability of the policies to be adopted must be counted as valid and equally valid.[3] Thus by way of the two previous assumptions we are led to the conclusion that Strong Equality exists among the citizens.

Although the preceding assumptions might appear to be sufficient to justify the democratic process, formally they need to be complemented by an elementary principle of fairness that it will do no harm to make explicit. This principle, which few would contest, is simply that, in general, scarce and valued things should be fairly allocated. Fairness need not require equality in allocations; it might, for example, require allocation according to desert. Even when fairness does require equality, as we saw in chapter 6 fair equality might not require equal lots or shares. But in certain circumstances fairness does require that each person should receive an equal share or, if that is impossible, an equal chance to gain the scarce item.

## CRITERIA FOR A DEMOCRATIC PROCESS

Suppose, then, that some persons wish to constitute a political order. Suppose further that the assumptions justifying a *democratic* political order are valid with respect to this group. Because these assumptions are valid, we conclude that they ought to adopt a democratic order and therefore that the process by which the demos is to arrive at its decisions ought to meet certain criteria. When I say that the process ought to meet certain criteria, I mean that if one believes in the assumptions, then one must reasonably affirm the desirability of the criteria; conversely, to reject the criteria is in effect to reject one or more of the assumptions.[4]

The five criteria are standards—ideal standards, if you like—against which procedures proposed ought to be evaluated in any association to which the assumptions apply. Any process that met them perfectly would be a perfect democratic process, and the government of the association would be a perfect democratic government. I take for granted that a perfect democratic process and a perfect democratic government might never exist in actuality. They represent ideas of human possibilities against which actualities may be compared. Even if the criteria can never be perfectly satisfied, they are useful in appraising real world possibilities, as I shall show. Naturally they do not eliminate all elements of judgment in evaluation. For example, the criteria do not specify any particular procedures, such as majority rule, for specific procedures cannot be directly extracted from the criteria. And judgments will have to take into account the specific historical conditions under which a democratic association is to be developed. However, no one should be surprised that democratic theory, like all other normative theories, cannot furnish completely unambiguous answers for every concrete situation in which a choice has to be made between alternative proposals.

What criteria, then, will be uniquely consistent with our assumptions and thereby provide us with the distinguishing features of a democratic process?

## Effective Participation

*Throughout the process of making binding decisions, citizens ought to have an adequate opportunity, and an equal opportunity, for expressing their preferences as to the final outcome. They must have adequate and equal opportunities for placing questions on the agenda and for expressing reasons for endorsing one outcome rather than another.*

To deny any citizen adequate opportunities for effective participation means that because their preferences are unknown or incorrectly perceived, they cannot be taken into account. But not to take their preferences as to the final outcome equally into account is to reject the principle of equal consideration of interests.

## Voting Equality at the Decisive Stage

*At the decisive stage of collective decisions, each citizen must be ensured an equal opportunity to express a choice that will be counted as equal in weight to the choice expressed by any other citizen. In determining outcomes at the decisive stage, these choices, and only these choices, must be taken into account.*

Because the choices are, of course, what we ordinarily mean by voting, this criterion may be said to require voting equality at the decisive stage.

Obviously something like this requirement has been a mainstay of democratic theory and practice from classical Greece onward. But on what rational ground? Its justification rests, I think, on the practical judgment that voting equality at the decisive stage is necessary in order to provide adequate protection for the intrinsic equality of citizens and the Presumption of Personal Autonomy. Without it, citizens would face the prospect of an infinite regress of potential inequalities in their influence over decisions, with no final court of appeal in which, as political equals, they could decide whether their interests, as they interpreted them, were given equal consideration. Just as inequalities in other resources could give advantages to some persons in securing special consideration for their interests, and handicap others, so too, without a requirement of equal voting at the decisive stage, inequalities in votes could work cumulatively to violate the Principle of Equal Consideration of Interests.

Notice, however, what the criterion of voting equality at the decisive stage does not specify. To begin with, it does not require voting equality at preceding stages. A demos might reasonably decide that the interests of some persons could best be given equal consideration by weighing their votes more heavily at earlier stages. On the same grounds the demos might delegate some decisions to citizen bodies in which votes were unequally weighted. Arrangements like these might be exceptional, as they have been historically in democratic countries, but they would not necessarily violate the criterion. The criterion would be violated, however, if the demos were no longer free to alter such arrangements whenever they failed to achieve their purposes or threatened to cause the demos to lose its final control over collective decisions.

Moreover, the criterion does not specify a particular method of voting or elections. To require that citizens have equal opportunities to express their choices could be satisfied if the votes or voters were selected randomly, that is, by lot. Nor does equal voting mean that each citizen should necessarily be entitled to an equal vote in districts of equal numbers of voters or residents; a system of proportional representation might serve as well or better. How citizens may best express their choices, and what specific rules and procedures should be adopted, are questions that require additional practical judgments. But procedures that meet the criterion better ought to be chosen over those that meet it worse. That the better procedure should be preferred to the worse holds even if all the procedures proposed are in some respects defective, as might often be the case.

Finally, the criterion does not explicitly require an association to adopt the principle of majority rule for its decisions. It requires only that majority rule and alternatives to it be evaluated according to this and other criteria, including the principles and assumptions that justify this criterion, such as the principle of equal consideration of interests, and that the solution that best meets the criteria should be adopted. Whether majority rule is the best solution is thus left open. As we shall see in chapter 10, the problem posed by majority rule and the alternatives to it is one of extreme difficulty for which no completely satisfactory solutions have yet been found. Judging what decision rule best meets the criterion of voting equality, whether generally or in a specific context, is a question on which persons who are committed to voting equality continue to disagree.

I think it is consistent with historic usage to say that any association whose government satisfies the criteria of effective participation and voting equality governs itself, to that limited extent, by means of a democratic process. In order to leave room for some important distinctions to come, I want to say that such an association is governed by a *democratic process in a narrow sense*. Though the process is narrower in scope than a fully democratic process, the two criteria enable us to evaluate a large number of possible procedures. To be sure, they cannot be decisive in cases where a procedure is better according to one criterion and worse by the other. Moreover, any evaluation would ordinarily require additional judgments about the facts of the particular situation or about general tendencies and regularities of human behavior and action. Nonetheless, the criteria are far from vacuous. Although I will not introduce a rigorous argument here, it would be hard to deny that procedures providing for decisions by a randomly selected sample of citizens would satisfy the criteria better than a procedure by which one citizen makes binding decisions for all the rest; or that a voting scheme allocating one vote to each citizen at the decisive stage would be better than a scheme in which some citizens had ten votes and others none. I do not mean to imply, however, that judgments about alternatives like these would follow as unassailable conclusions from a perfectly rigorous argument.

## Enlightened Understanding

As I have already suggested, judgments about the existence, composition, and boundaries of a demos are highly contestable. Thus one might simply challenge such judgments outright by asserting that some citizens are more qualified than the rest to make the decisions required. This objection of course raises the challenge to democracy posed by guardianship, which we have already considered at length. What I wish to consider now, however, is a second objection that might run like this:

I agree—the objector might say—that the citizens are equally well qualified, taken all around. I agree also that none among them, or among the other members, or among nonmembers are so definitely better qualified as to warrant their making the decisions instead of the demos. Yet for all that, I think the citizens are not as well qualified as they might be. They make mistakes about the means to the ends they want; they also choose ends they would reject if they were more enlightened. I agree then that they ought to govern themselves by procedures that are satisfactory according to the criteria of a democratic process, narrowly defined. Yet a number of different procedures will satisfy the criteria equally well; among these, however, some are more likely to lead to a more enlightened demos—and thus to better decisions—than others. Surely these are better procedures and ought to be chosen over the others.

One might object, I suppose, that enlightenment has nothing to do with democracy. But I think this would be a foolish and historically false assertion. It is foolish because democracy has usually been conceived as a system in which "rule by the people" makes it more likely that the "people" will get what it wants, or what it believes is best, than alternative systems like guardianship in which an elite determines what is best. But to know what it wants, or what is best, the people must be enlightened, at least to some degree. And because advocates of democracy have invariably recognized this and placed great stress on the means to an informed and enlightened demos, such as education and public discussion, the objection is also historically false.

I propose therefore to amplify the meaning of the democratic process by adding a third criterion. Unfortunately, I do not know how to formulate the criterion except in words that are rich in meaning and correspondingly ambiguous. Let me, however, offer this formulation for the criterion of enlightened understanding:

*Each citizen ought to have adequate and equal opportunities for discovering and validating (within the time permitted by the need for a decision) the choice on the matter to be decided that would best serve the citizen's interests.*

This criterion implies, then, that alternative procedures for making decisions ought to be evaluated according to the opportunities they furnish citizens for acquiring an understanding of means and ends, of one's interests and the expected consequences of policies for interests, not only for oneself but for all other relevant persons as well. Insofar as a citizen's good or interests requires attention to a public good or general interest, then citizens ought to have the opportunity to acquire an understanding of these matters. Ambiguous as the criterion may be, it provides guidance for determining the shape that institutions should take. Thus the criterion makes it hard to justify procedures that would cut off or suppress information which, were it available, might well cause citizens to arrive at a different decision; or that would give some citizens much easier access than others to information of crucial importance; or that would present citizens with an agenda of decisions that had to be decided without discussion, though time was available; and so on. To be sure, these may look like easy cases, but a great many political systems—perhaps most—operate according to the worse not the better procedures.

### Control of the Agenda

If an association were to satisfy all three criteria, it could properly be regarded as a full procedural democracy with respect to its agenda and in relation to its demos. The criteria are to be understood as aspects of the best possible political system, from a democratic point of view; while no actual system could be expected to satisfy the criteria perfectly, systems could be judged more democratic or less, and to that extent better or worse, according to how nearly they meet the criteria.

Yet to say that a system is governed by a fully democratic process "with respect to an agenda" and "in relation to a demos" suggests the possibility that the three criteria are incomplete. The two qualifying clauses imply the possibility of restrictions—of democratic decisionmaking processes limited to a narrow agenda, or responsive to a highly exclusive demos, or both. To judge whether a demos is appropriately inclusive and exercises control over an appropriate agenda requires additional standards.

In order to see more clearly why a fourth criterion is needed, let us suppose that Philip of Macedon, having defeated the Athenians at Chaeronea, deprives the Athenian assembly of the authority to make any decisions on matters of foreign and military policy. The citizens continue to assemble some forty times a year and decide on many matters, but on some of the most important questions they must remain silent. With respect to 'local' matters, the Athenian polis is no less democratic than before, but with respect to foreign and military affairs the Athenians are now governed hierarchically by Philip or his minions. Would we want to say that Athens was now fully democratic or was as democratic as it had been before?

Although outside control makes the point more dramatically, control over the agenda may also be taken from citizens by some of its own members. Let us imagine an independent country where the three criteria we have discussed are relatively well met, and in addition there are no limitations on the matters that citizens may decide. Their agenda of collective decisions is completely open. Suppose that an antidemocratic movement somehow seizes power. In a move to placate the democratic sentiments of their fellow countrymen the new rulers leave the old constitution symbolically in place. However, they modify it in one respect. Hereafter, the people may use their old democratic political institutions for only a few matters—purely local questions, let us say, such as traffic control, street maintenance, and residential zoning. The rulers keep all the rest strictly under their own control. Even if the new system were to meet the first three criteria perfectly and thus was "fully democratic with respect to its agenda," it would be a travesty of democracy. For citizens could not democratically decide matters they felt to be important other than those the rulers had allowed to remain on the pitifully shrunken agenda of the neutered democracy. The control of nondemocratic rulers over the agenda could be much less blatant and more subtle. In some countries, for example, military leaders are under the nominal control of elected civilians who know, however, that they will be removed from office, and worse, unless they tailor their decisions to meet the wishes of the military.

These considerations suggest a fourth criterion, final control of the agenda by the demos.

*The demos must have the exclusive opportunity to decide how matters are to be placed on the agenda of matters that are to be decided by means of the democratic process.*

The criterion of final control is perhaps what is also meant when we say that in a democracy the people must have the final say, or must be sovereign. A system that satisfies this criterion as well as the other three could be regarded as having a fully democratic process in relation to its demos.

According to this criterion, a political system would employ a fully democratic process even if the demos decided that it would not make every decision on every matter but instead chose to have some decisions on some matters made, say, in a hierarchical fashion by judges or administrators. As long as the demos could effectively retrieve any matter for decision by itself, the criterion would be met. In this respect, then, the criteria for a democratic process presented here allows more latitude for delegation of decisionmaking than would be permissible by Rousseau's eccentric definition of democracy in the *Social Contract*. Because he defined democracy so as to make delegation impermissible, Rousseau concluded that "if there were a people of Gods, it would govern itself democratically. Such a perfect government is not suited to men" (Rousseau 1978, bk. 3, chap. 4, p. 85).

Thus the criterion of final control does not presuppose a judgment that the demos is qualified to decide every question requiring a binding decision. It does presuppose a judgment that the demos is qualified to decide (1) which matters do or do not require binding decisions, (2) of those that do, which matters the demos is qualified to decide for itself, and (3) the terms on which the demos delegates authority. To accept the criterion as appropriate is therefore to imply that the demos is the best judge of its own competence and limits. Consequently, to say that certain matters ought to be placed beyond the final reach of the demos—in the sense that the demos ought to be prohibited from dealing with them at all—is to say that on these matters the demos is not qualified to judge its own competence and limits.

By delegation I mean a revocable grant of authority, subject to recovery by the demos. Empirically, of course, the boundaries between delegation and alienation are not always sharp, and what begins as delegation might end as alienation. Moreover, the empirical problem of judging whether the final agenda is covertly controlled by certain leaders outside the democratic process—like the military, in the example given earlier—is necessarily complicated by the covert nature of the control. But, however difficult it may be to draw the line in practice, the theoretical distinction between delegation and alienation is nonetheless crucial. In a system employing a fully democratic process, decisions about delegation would be made according to democratic procedures. But alienation of control over the final agenda (or its appropriation by leaders outside the democratic process) would clearly violate the criterion of final control and would be inconsistent with the judgment that the full condition of equal qualification exists among citizens.[5]

The criterion of final control completes the requirements for *a fully democratic process in relation to a demos*. If all the members are judged equally qualified, in the full sense, and if the other conditions set out earlier are held to exist among them, then the procedures according to which these persons, the citizens, make binding decisions ought to be evaluated according to the four criteria.

## WHY EQUAL OPPORTUNITY?

The criteria specify that citizens or the demos ought to have adequate and equal *opportunities* to act in certain ways. I can readily imagine two objections to this formulation. First, it might be said that "equal opportunities" can be reduced to nothing more than formal or legal requirements that ignore important differences—in resources, for example. Suppose Citizen P is poor and Citizen R is rich. Then (the argument might go) both P and R may have "equal opportunities" to participate in collective decisions, in the sense that both are legally entitled to do so. Yet because R has far greater access to money, information, publicity, organizations, time, and other political resources than P, not only will R probably participate more than P, but R's influence on decisions will vastly outweigh P's.

The objection draws its force from the familiar fact that influence is a function of resources, and typically resources are unequally distributed. Nonetheless, it misses the point. For "equal opportunities" means "equal opportunities," and what the example shows is that R's and P's opportunities to participate are decidedly unequal. Though the idea of equal opportunity is often so weakly interpreted that it is rightly dismissed as too undemanding, when it is taken in its fullest sense it is extraordinarily demanding—so demanding, indeed, that the criteria for the democratic process would require a people committed to it to institute measures well beyond those that even the most democratic states have hitherto brought about. In the final chapters I shall suggest some possibilities that seem to me to fall within the range of feasibility.

A second objection might go like this: An opportunity to act to do something necessarily implies that one might choose *not* to act. If the democratic process is desirable, then should the criteria not specify *duties* as well as opportunities—duties of the citizen to participate, to vote, to become informed, and the duty of the demos to determine how the agenda is to be decided? While I believe the democratic process does imply duties like these, they are moral duties. They take their place among an array of obligations, rights, and opportunities that would confront citizens in a democratic order. I cannot say that it would always be wrong for a citizen to choose not to fulfill the political obligations implied by the criteria of the democratic process. It seems to me more consistent with the Presumption of Personal Autonomy and with freedom of self-determination and moral autonomy to ensure that citizens have the freedom to choose how they will fulfill their political obligations.

## PROBLEMS IN THE THEORY

The theory of the democratic process that I have just described might seem adequate as it stands. Yet it is radically incomplete. Several of the most crucial assumptions of the theory are much too debatable to be acceptable without further examination. The implications of the theory are also far from clear, and in any case important implications are themselves likely to be contested.

In the rest of this book therefore I take up the most important problems in the theory of the democratic process. Although there is no definitive solution for most of these problems, I shall try to arrive as close to a reasonable solution as may be possible at present.

1. The argument for the Strong Principle of Equality would appear to support the conclusion that everyone subject to the laws should be included in the demos. Everyone? Not quite: not children, for example: the Presumption of Personal Autonomy applies to adults. As we saw earlier, Athenian democrats did not find it anomalous that their demos included only a minority of adults. Well into the last century most advocates of democracy assumed that women were rightly excluded from the suffrage, that is, from the demos. In most countries women gained the suffrage only in this century, and in a few only after the Second World War. In

fact, not until our own century did democratic theory and practice begin to reflect a belief that all (or virtually all) adults should be included in the demos as a matter of right. Is a judgment as to who should be included in the demos, then, purely arbitrary or so strongly conditioned by history and culture that no general judgment is possible? Although democratic theory and practice both provide substantial support for such a conclusion, I believe it is mistaken. I take up this problem in the next chapter.

2. The criteria for a democratic process, as I have described them here, do not specify a *decision rule*. Historically, of course, it has usually been contended that the only decision rule appropriate to the democratic process is majority rule. Yet even the term "majority" rule does not refer to a single, well-defined decision rule: It refers to a family of possible rules. These range from the rule that the alternative to be accepted as binding is the one that gains the greatest number of votes, even if this number is less than 50 percent, to others that require at least 50 percent plus one or a matching of every alternative against every other alternative. But all such numerical rules are subject to potential defects, such as cycles in which no majority preference can definitely be established. And even if these problems can be solved, the question remains: Why should we accept any majority principle? These issues will be considered in chapter 10.

3. Advocates of guardianship contend that any process by which ordinary citizens rule is unlikely to achieve the public good, since ordinary citizens lack both the necessary knowledge and the necessary virtue. However, even advocates of democracy sometimes argue that no *process* is sufficient to ensure that the public good (the public interest, the good of all, etc.) will be achieved. What is sometimes referred to as the idea of *substantive democracy* gives priority to the justice or rightness of the substantive outcomes of decisions rather than to the process by which the decisions are reached. In one phrasing, substantive justice should take priority over procedural justice and substantive rights priority over procedural rights. Sorting out the issues involved in this dispute over priorities is, as we shall see in chapters 11 and 12, quite tricky. But on the face of it the argument for the importance of substance as against process clearly has merit.

4. If the democratic process is a means by which some collection of persons may rightfully govern itself, what constitutes an appropriate collection of persons for employing the democratic process? Is *any* collection of persons entitled to the democratic process? In short, if democracy means government by the people, what constitutes "a people"? There may be no problem in the whole domain of democratic theory and practice more intractable than the one posed by this innocent-seeming question. To grasp it, imagine an aggregate of persons. Adapting Jonathan Swift to our purposes, let us call them the Eggfolk. While many Eggfolk contend that the Eggfolk constitute a single "people," some insist that they are really divided into two distinct peoples, the Big Eggfolk and the Little Eggfolk, with such different ways and beliefs that they should govern themselves separately, each entitled to its own fully democratic system. How are we to decide? As

we shall discover in chapter 13, democratic theory supplies little by way of an answer. In fact, while historical answers exist, there may be no satisfactory theoretical solution to this problem.

5. As the problem of a decision rule illustrates, the democratic process must somehow be actualized in the real world—in actually existing procedures, institutions, associations, states, and so on. As we saw, in the long history of democracy in the Western world democratic ideas have been applied to two radically different types of political system, the city-state and the nation-state. These were radically different in scale, and they developed radically different political institutions. Is it possible, then, to specify a unique set of institutions necessary to the democratic process? Or do the institutional requirements vary according to the scale of a society as well as other factors? We return to these questions in chapters 14 and 15.

6. Inevitably, whenever democratic ideas are applied to the real world, actual democracy falls significantly short of ideal standards. For example, the criteria for the democratic process set out earlier have never been fully met and probably cannot be. What level of approximation are we to regard as in some sense satisfactory—sufficiently satisfactory, let us say, so that we may reasonably call some actual system a "democracy." This problem of the proper threshold of democracy is more than a mere matter of terminology. For example, if we feel an obligation to uphold democratic governments but not authoritarian governments, then the threshold becomes essential to a judgment about our obligations.

I shall argue in chapter 16 that an important threshold of democracy has been attained by a significant number of modern countries, as evidenced by a specific set of political institutions which, taken together, distinguishes the political system of these countries from all "democracies" and republics prior to the eighteenth century and from all "nondemocracies" in the contemporary world. Although these countries are ordinarily said to be "democracies," I will refer to their systems—distinguishable as I have said by virtue of their political institutions—as *polyarchies*. What conditions favor the emergence and persistence of polyarchy in a country—and conversely, the absence of what conditions reduces the likelihood that a country will arrive at this modern threshold of democracy? I explore these questions in chapter 17.

7. Since the threshold attained by polyarchy is well short of democratic ideals, would it be possible, and if possible would it be desirable, to close some of the gap between polyarchy and democracy—to establish and surpass yet another threshold on the way to democracy? A strong current of utopianism in democratic thought encourages one to answer yes. But a countercurrent in modern thought, which will be discussed in chapter 18, contends that other powerful tendencies, such as a universal tendency to oligarchy, set insuperable limits to the possibilities of further democratization.

8. The transformation in the scale of democracy that came about as a result of the attempt to apply the democratic process to the nation-state seems to have turned political life in democratic countries into a competitive struggle among individuals

and groups with conflicting ideas, ideals, and goals. What then is the fate of that ancient ideal of political virtue and the pursuit of a common good? This question is the subject of chapters 19 and 20.

9. Finally, then, what can we reasonably conclude as to the limits and possibilities of democratization, particularly in a world that does not stand still, where the limits and possibilities may be changing as profoundly as they did when the nation-state superseded the city-state as the locus of democracy? And what about the nondemocratic governments that now prevail and may continue to prevail in a majority of countries of the world? How ought we appraise political systems in countries that are *not* democratic—that have not even reached the threshold of polyarchy? In the final chapters I want to explore some of the limits and possibilities of democracy.

# Chapter 9

◆◆◆◆◆◆◆◆

# The Problem of Inclusion

A political order that met the four criteria described in the last chapter would be fully democratic in relation to its demos. But the demos might include all the members or range downward to an infinitesimally small proportion of them. In the extreme case, would we want to say that the political order was a democracy? If not, what requirements can we lay down, and how would we justify them? The problem is difficult, and democratic theory and ideas have by no means provided a satisfactory solution. The problem is, in fact, twofold:

1. The problem of inclusion: What persons have a rightful claim to be included in the demos?
2. The scope of its authority: What rightful limits are there on the control of a demos? Is alienation ever morally permissible?

The problems are interrelated. The extent to which a particular demos (a local community, for example) ought to have final control over the agenda evidently depends on a prior judgment as to the scope of matters that the demos is qualified to decide. A judgment as to the competence of the demos bears on the scope of its agenda; and the nature of an agenda bears on a judgment as to the composition of the demos. The demos being given, the scope of its agenda can be determined. The scope of an agenda being given, the composition of an appropriate demos to make decisions on those matters can be determined. But in principle, it seems, the one cannot be finally determined independently of the other.

In this chapter, however, I shall concentrate on the first. The second will be considered in the next two chapters. What then properly constitutes a demos? Who must be included in a properly constituted demos, and who may or may not be excluded from it?

The question of inclusion in (or exclusion from) a demos might present a less serious challenge if a demos could enact rules that were binding only on itself. Some associations do escape the problem in this way. Either all the members are also citizens, in which case the association is fully inclusive. Or every member is free to leave the association at any time with no significant difficulty, in ·which case a member who objects to a rule can simply escape its application by withdrawing from the association. To be sure, an outsider might argue that a self-regulating demos was acting unwisely or unjustly toward itself. But since that claim would hardly justify including the outsider the problem of inclusion would still be avoided.

However, it is not true of every association that its demos can enact rules binding only on itself. A trade union might enforce a rule preventing nonmembers from working at a particular trade or workplace. An even more obvious and certainly more important exception is of course the state. Even if a state met all four of the previous criteria for a democratic process, it could enact laws that were enforceable against persons who were not citizens, did not have the right to participate in making the laws, and had not given their consent either explicitly or implicitly to the laws they were forced to obey. Indeed every state has done so in the past, and there are convincing reasons for thinking that all states, even the most democratic states, will continue to do so in the future.

If some persons are excluded from the demos of a state and yet are compelled to obey its laws, do they have a justifiable claim either to be included in the demos or else to be excluded from the domain of enforcement? Are there criteria for judging when, if ever, exclusion is rightful or inclusion is obligatory? How inclusive should the demos be? The argument for the Strong Principle of Equality provides the grounds we need for a criterion of inclusion that a democratic process would have to satisfy: *the demos should include all adults subject to the binding collective decisions of the association.* This proposition constitutes the fifth and final criterion for a fully democratic process.

But before we accept it we should consider several alternative solutions that reach far back into the history of democratic theory and practice.

## CITIZENSHIP AS WHOLLY CONTINGENT

One solution is to say that the grounds for deciding who ought to be included in a demos are inherently particularistic and historical, often indeed primordial, and cannot be set forth as general principles. Thus citizenship is wholly contingent on circumstances that cannot be specified in advance.

As a description of historical practice, this view can hardly be faulted. And because political philosophers cannot entirely escape the tug of their own circumstances, their views on the question of inclusion often reflect some of the prejudices of their times. Thus Aristotle managed to furnish a philosophic rationalization for slavery by arguing that some persons "are by nature slaves, and it is better for them . . . to be ruled by a master." And, though he recognized that practices varied in different states, he did not think that laborers and mechanics should be citizens (1952, 11–17, 107–10). As we shall see in a moment, later political philosophers like Locke and Rousseau, who in their writings used universal terms (such as "all men") that implied a wide extension of citizenship, did not oppose the narrow boundaries on citizenship that actually existed in their own time.

But to describe an historical fact is not to answer a normative question. As Rousseau remarked about Hugo Grotius, "His most persistent mode of reasoning is always to establish right by fact. One could use a more rational method, but not one more favorable to tyrants" (1978, 47). Nonetheless, to rely on the contingencies of history to solve the problem of inclusion has its defenders. Perhaps the most explicit is Joseph Schumpeter.

Although democratic ideas often yield rather ambiguous answers to the question of inclusion, Schumpeter was an exception. It is an "inescapable conclusion," he asserted, that we must "leave it to every populus to define himself [sic]." He rested his argument on an incontestable historical fact: What had been thought and legally held to constitute a "people" has varied enormously, even among "democratic" countries. What is more, there are no grounds for rejecting any exclusion whatsoever as improper: "It is not relevant whether we the observers admit the validity of those reasons or of the practical rules by which they are made to exclude portions of the population; all that matters is that the society in question admits it." He pressed his argument relentlessly. The exclusion of blacks in the American South does not allow us to say that the South was undemocratic. The rule of the "Bolshevik party" in the Soviet Union "would not per se entitle us to call the Soviet Republic undemocratic. We are entitled to call it so only if the Bolshevik party itself is managed in an undemocratic manner—as obviously it is" (Schumpeter [1942] 1947, 243–45).[1]

The last two examples beautifully illustrate the absurdities to which we may be led by the absence of any criterion for defining the demos. It is undeniable that in the United States, southern blacks were excluded from the demos. But surely *to that extent* the South was undemocratic: *undemocratic in relation to its black population.* Suppose that in the South, as in Rhodesia or South Africa, blacks had been a preponderant majority of the population. Would Schumpeter still have said that the southern states were "democratic"? Is there not some number or proportion of a population below which a "people" is not a demos but rather an aristocracy, oligarchy, or despotism? If the rulers numbered 100 in a population of 100 million, would we call the rulers a demos and the system a democracy? On Schumpeter's argument, arguably Britain was already a "democracy" by the end of the eighteenth century, even though only one adult in twenty could vote.

Consider the monumental implications of the second example, in which Schumpeter asserts that "the Soviet Republic" would be a democracy if only the ruling party itself were internally democratic. Schumpeter imposes no minimum limits on the relative size of the party. Suppose it were 1 percent of the population? Or suppose that the Politburo were internally democratic and ruled the party, which ruled over the state, which ruled over the people. Then the members of the Politburo would constitute the Soviet populus, and the Soviet state would be, on Schumpeter's interpretation, a democracy.

His definition thus leaves us with no particular reason for wanting to know whether a system is "democratic" or not. Indeed, if a demos can be a tiny group that exercises a brutal despotism over a vast subject population, then "democracy" is conceptually, morally, and empirically indistinguishable from autocracy. Thus Schumpeter's solution is truly no solution at all, for its upshot is that there are simply no principles for judging whether anyone is unjustly excluded from citizenship. But the argument leads, as we have seen, to absurdities.

These consequences follow because Schumpeter failed to distinguish, indeed insisted on conflating, two different kinds of propositions:

System X is democratic in relation to its own demos.
System Y is democratic in relation to everyone subject to its rules.

Perhaps because he was convinced by historical experience that no state like Y had ever existed or was likely to, he felt that any "realistic" theory of democracy, such as he proposed, could scarcely require that a "democracy" be a system like Y. For if this requirement were imposed, then no democratic state would, or probably ever could, exist. But by carrying historicism and moral relativism to their limits, he obliterated the possibility of any useful distinction between democracy, aristocracy, oligarchy, and one-party dictatorship.

## CITIZENSHIP AS A CATEGORICAL RIGHT

Schumpeter's solution, or rather nonsolution, was to allow a demos to draw any line it chooses between itself and other members. Suppose instead that one were to insist that no one subject to the rules of the demos should be excluded from the demos. Then the demos would be exactly equivalent to the membership of the association.

It is possible to interpret Locke, Rousseau, and a long succession of writers they influenced as advancing a solution along these lines.[2] The argument is grounded on the moral axiom that no person ought to be governed without his consent, or, with Rousseau, required to obey laws that are not of his own making in some genuine sense. In developing the argument, writers have found it useful to distinguish between the initial act of forming the polity (society, association, community, city, or state) and the subsequent process of making and enforcing the rules of the polity. Thus both Locke and Rousseau held that the initial formation requires the agreement of everyone who is to be subject to it; thereafter, however, laws could be enacted and enforced if they are endorsed by a majority. Both sought to explain why, even though unanimity is required in the first instance, thereafter a majority is sufficient. I wish to ignore this question, for my concern here is a different one: In speaking of agreement by "all" or a "majority," what is the collection of persons to which they refer? Does "the consent of every individual" and "the determination of the majority" of such individuals[3] literally refer to every member, in the sense that a majority must be a majority of every person subject to the laws?

Clearly, neither Locke nor Rousseau meant to imply this conclusion. To begin with, children are of course to be excluded from the demos. The exclusion of children from the demos is so often taken as unproblematical that one hardly notices how much the claim to citizenship based on a categorical right of all persons is contradicted by this simple exclusion, for it is made on the grounds that children are not competent to govern themselves or the community. Yet if we permit the exclusion of children from the demos (and who seriously does not?) then we allow a contingent element, based on qualification for governing, to limit the universality of the claim based on categorical right. Never mind; let us momentarily ignore this difficulty, though I intend to return to it.

Suppose, then, that the claim based on a categorical right is revised to read: All *adults* subject to the laws of a state would be members of the demos of that state. Citizenship is no longer fully coextensive with membership, but all adult members are citizens by categorical right. Did Rousseau and Locke mean to justify such a claim?

Certainly Rousseau did not, though it is easy to see why the *Social Contract* is sometimes understood as saying so. There Rousseau occasionally appears to be asserting an unqualified right to membership in the demos.[4] Rousseau makes it clear that he means no such thing. Thus he lauds Geneva, even though its demos consisted of only a small minority of the population. Children were, of course, excluded. But so too were women. What is more, a majority of adult males were also excluded from the Genevan demos. Rousseau was well aware of these exclusions. Yet he neither condemned them as inconsistent with his principles nor provided grounds on which they might be justified. Rather, he seems simply to have taken them for granted.

Rousseau may, in fact, have anticipated Schumpeter's solution. In arguing that it is wrong to take the government of Venice as an instance of true aristocracy, he remarks that, although the ordinary people in Venice have no part in the government, there the nobility takes the place of the people. This is Schumpeter's populus defining itself. Rousseau then goes on to show that Venice and Geneva are truly alike. Thus the government of Venice is actually no more aristocratic than that of Geneva (1978, 4, chap. 3)!

What Rousseau does not feel it important to say is that in both cities the great bulk of the people subject to the laws were not only excluded from the execution and administration of the laws (the government, in Rousseau's terminology) but also from any participation in making the laws. In neither republic were the people—that is, most people—entitled to assemble in order to vote on the laws or even to vote for representatives who would make the laws. In both cities, most people were thus subject to laws they had no part in making.[5] One might conclude that neither republic could be legitimate in Rousseau's eyes. But this was not his conclusion, nor did he even hint at such an inference.

What Rousseau seems to have assumed, as other advocates of democracy had done since the Greek city-states of antiquity, is that a large number of persons in any republic—children, women, foreigners, and many male adult residents—will be subjects but are not qualified to be citizens. In this way, Rousseau himself undermined the categorical principle of inclusion that he appeared to set forth in the *Social Contract*.

Locke's language in the *Second Treatise* is as categorical and universalistic as Rousseau's, if not more so.[6] Yet his apparent assertion of an unqualified and categorical claim was limited both explicitly and implicitly by a requirement as to competence. Naturally, children were excluded; I shall return later to Locke's argument on "paternal power." It is highly doubtful that he meant women to be included as a matter of right.[7] As to adult males, he explicitly excluded "lunatics and idiots [who] are never set free from the government of their parents" (1970, chap. 6, para. 60). In addition, "slaves . . . being captives taken in a just war, are by the right of nature subjected to the absolute dominion and arbitrary power of their masters." He probably intended to exclude servants as well (chap. 7, para. 85). Thus a claim to citizenship was not categorical but, as it turns out, contingent on a judgment as to the relative qualifications of a person for participating in the government of the commonwealth. Like Rousseau, Locke torpedoed his own view (if indeed it was his view) that every person subject to the laws made by the demos possesses a categorical and unqualified right to membership in the demos.

## CITIZENSHIP AS CONTINGENT ON COMPETENCE

Locke and Rousseau appear to have advanced two different principles on which a claim to citizenship might be grounded. One is explicit, categorical, and universal; the other is implicit, contingent, and limiting:

CATEGORICAL PRINCIPLE: *Every person subject to a government and its laws has an unqualified right to be a member of the demos (i.e., a citizen).*

CONTINGENT PRINCIPLE: *Only persons who are qualified to govern, but all such persons, should be members of the demos (i.e., citizens).*

If some persons subject to the laws are not qualified to govern, then obviously the two principles lead to contradictory conclusions. Which principle should take precedence? As we have seen, Locke and Rousseau held, at least implicitly, that the second principle should take precedence over the first.

What was only or mainly implicit in the arguments of Locke and Rousseau was made explicit by John Stuart Mill, who openly confronted the conflict he believed to exist between the two principles. Like his predecessors he also insisted that in case of conflict the first must give way to the second.

To be sure, on a careless reading Mill could be interpreted as favoring the categorical principle.[8] Yet, although on casual inspection his language has a universalistic tone, in fact Mill does not endorse a categorical principle of general inclusion. It is hardly surprising that he argues not from principles of abstract right but rather from considerations of social utility. His judgments are meant to reflect a balancing of social utilities and disutilities. And while his argument is powerful, it does not lead him to a categorical principle but to a contingent and contestable judgment about social utility. But, because the question is one of social utility, relative competence is also a factor to be weighed.

As every reader of *Representative Government* soon discovers, it was Mill himself who undermined his own argument for universal inclusion by posing a counterargument based on considerations of competence. In the course of his discussion, he explicitly asserted that the criterion of competence must take priority over any principle, whether categorical or utilitarian, that makes inclusion in the demos a matter of general right among all adults subject to the laws. At a minimum, he argued, to demonstrate that persons are qualified to engage in governing requires a showing that they have "acquired the commonest and most essential requisites for taking care of themselves, for pursuing intelligently their own interests and those of the persons most nearly allied to them." It was Mill's judgment that, in the England of his day, many categories of adults could not meet this standard and ought therefore to be denied the suffrage until they acquired the competence they at that time lacked (Mill 1958, 131–38).

By giving priority to the criterion of competence, recognizing the contingent and socially specific nature of judgments about competence, and accepting a restricted demos as the consequence of his own judgment as to the qualifications of fellow Englishmen, Mill brought into the open a problem that had been glossed over by some of his most illustrious predecessors. Yet in justifying an exclusionary demos Mill did no more than make implicit what had generally been implicit in all previous democratic theory and practice.

The formal opportunities for participation available to citizens in the democratic city-states of Greece, the universalistic language in which democratic beliefs are often presented, and the emphasis on participation by Rousseau and Mill have induced some writers to interpret "classical" democratic ideas as much less "elitist" than they actually were.[9]

One might choose to dismiss these limits as transitory deficiencies in a revolutionary new political idea that transcended the historical limits of actual practice. But, as we have seen, Locke and Rousseau accepted, and Mill defended, the principle that a demos might properly exclude large numbers of adults who are subject to laws made by the demos. And in principle the qualified might be a tiny majority. Thus it is not only Schumpeter's solution that would permit the demos to shrink into a ruling elite. Rousseau himself, as we saw, regarded Geneva and Venice both as true republics, governed "by the people," even though in both cities the demos constituted a minority of the adults.

Modern admirers of "classical" democratic ideas seem to have reversed the relation between citizenship and competence as it was generally understood from the Greeks to Mill. In the "classical" perspective not every adult, much less every person, was necessarily qualified to govern and thus to enter into the demos. Rather, the demos consisted only of those who were, in their own view, qualified to govern. In this perspective, it was precisely because citizens were a qualified minority of the whole people that they were entitled to govern and could on the whole be counted on to govern well.

As a consequence, "classical" ideas leave the intellectual defense of democracy lethally vulnerable, as can be readily seen if we contrast it with the view that inclusion is a categorical right. If everyone subject to law has a categorical right to participate in the process of making laws, if the requirement of consent is universal and uncontestable, then the case for democracy is very powerful and the case against exclusionary alternatives—aristocracy, meritocracy, rule by a qualified elite, monarchy, dictatorship, and so on—is correspondingly weakened. If the claim to citizenship is a categorical and universal right of all human beings, then among any human group a demos always exists and that demos must always be inclusive. To put it another way, among any body of persons who wish to establish or maintain an association having a government capable of making binding decisions, the Strong Principle of Equality—the most crucial of the conditions for the democratic process set forth earlier—must necessarily exist.

But if the criterion of competence overrides a claim based on rights, then the argument for democracy rests on mushy grounds. Citizenship depends on contingent judgments, not categorical rights. And the contingent judgments need not lead to universal inclusion. Indeed, the boundaries between democracy on the one side and guardianship on the other become fuzzy and indeterminate. The arguments for the one or the other become indistinguishable except for a crucial judgment as to the relative magnitude of the competent members. And, as we have seen, even among political philosophers these contingent and practical judgments are easily swayed by the narrow prejudices of one's time.

## A CRITERION OF INCLUSIVENESS

Three questions arise: First, is it possible to get around the principle of competence in deciding on the inclusiveness of the demos? Second, if not, is it possible to avoid the contingent and contestable nature of a judgment as to competence? Third, if again not, can we develop strong criteria that such a judgment ought to satisfy?

That we cannot get around the principle of competence in deciding on the inclusiveness of the demos is decisively demonstrated by the exclusion of children. It is virtually never argued, no doubt because it would be so obviously untenable, that children either must be members of the state's demos or ought not to be subject to laws made by the demos. So far as I am aware, no one seriously contends that children should be full members of the demos that governs the state. An eight-year-old child can hardly be enlightened enough to participate equally with adults in deciding on laws to be enforced by the government of the state. Yet these laws are enforced on children without their explicit or implied consent. It is often held—and legal systems tend to reflect the force of the argument—that because of their limited competence children should not be subject to exactly the same laws as adults; they cannot, for example, enter into legally enforceable contracts. Yet they are not wholly exempt from the enforcement of all laws.

Children therefore furnish us with a clear instance of violation of the principle that a government must rest on the consent of the governed or that no one should be subject to a law not of one's own choosing or subject to a law made by an association not of one's own choosing. Yet this violation is nearly always either taken for granted or interpreted as not actually a violation. One way of interpreting it is to say that the principle of consent applies only to adults. But this is to admit that some persons who are subject to the rules of a state can nevertheless be properly excluded from the demos of the state.

On what grounds? The only defensible ground on which to exclude children from the demos is that they are not yet fully qualified. The need to exclude children on this ground was of course perfectly obvious to early democratic theorists. Locke devotes a whole chapter to "Paternal Power." After reminding us of "that equal right that every man hath to his natural freedom, without being subject to the will or authority of any other man," he immediately turns to the exceptions, of which children are the most numerous, obvious, and important (*Second Treatise*, paras. 55, 63, pp. 28, 31). Rousseau also recognizes, though merely in passing, the authority of the father over the children "before they reach the age of reason" (bk. 1, chap. 4, p. 49).

The example of children is sufficient to show that the criterion of competence cannot reasonably be evaded, that any reasonable bounding of a demos must, by excluding children, necessarily exclude a large body of persons subject to the laws, and that any assertion of a universal right of all persons to membership in a demos cannot be sustained. It might be argued, however, that children constitute a comparatively well-defined and unique exception.[10] Thus, once a distinction is allowed between children and adults, all *adults* subject to the laws must be included.

## A MODIFIED CATEGORICAL PRINCIPLE?

The categorical principle might then be restated as follows:

MODIFIED CATEGORICAL PRINCIPLE: *Every adult subject to a government and its laws must be presumed to be qualified as, and has an unqualified right to be, a member of the demos.*

There are, however, at least two sources of difficulty with the modified categorical principle. First, the boundary between childhood and adulthood presents some difficulty. There is the well-known arbitrariness of imposing a dichotomy—child/adult—on a process of development that is not only continuous but varies between different persons. Thus we may reasonably disagree about whether, on average, people become qualified at twenty-one, or eighteen, or whatever; and whatever age we choose, we may disagree over specific cases of persons who mature more rapidly or less rapidly than the average. There are also the troublesome cases for which experience, even when joined with compassion, points to no clear solution. As Locke put it:

if, through defects that may happen out of ordinary course of Nature, any one comes not to such a degree of Reason wherein he might be supposed capable of knowing the Law, and so living within the rules of it, he is *never capable of being a Free Man . . .* but is continued under the Tuition and Government of others, all the time his own Understanding is incapable of that Charge. And so *Lunatics* and *Idiots* are never set free from the government of their Parents. (*Second Treatise*, chap. 6, para. 60, pp. 325–26)

Thus the modified categorical principle runs the risk of circularity by defining "adults" as persons who are presumed to be qualified to govern.

A second source of difficulty with the modified principle is caused by the presence in a country of foreigners who might be adult by any reasonable standards, who are subject to the laws of the country in which they temporarily reside, but who are not thereby qualified to participate in governing. Suppose that France is holding an election on Sunday and I, an American, arrive in Paris on Saturday as a tourist. Would anyone argue that I should be entitled to participate in the election, much less acquire all the other political rights of French citizenship? I think not. On what grounds could I properly be excluded? On the ground that I am unqualified.[11]

To sum up:

1. Schumpeter's solution to the problem of the composition of the demos is unacceptable, because it effectively erases the distinction between democracy and a nondemocratic order dominated by a collegial elite.

2. A categorical principle of inclusion that overrides the need for a judgment as to competence is also unacceptable, for it is rendered untenable by such cases as children, feeble-minded persons, and foreigners of temporary residence. Insofar as Locke and Rousseau advanced a categorical principle, their defense of it is unconvincing. However, evidence suggests that they recognized these objections and never intended their argument to be taken as a rejection of the priority of a criterion of competence.

3. Because a judgment on competence is contingent on weighing evidence and making inferences as to the intellectual and moral qualifications of specific categories of persons, a decision based on competence is inherently open to question. To be sure, a reasonable argument may be presented in behalf of a particular judgment as to the proper boundaries of inclusion and exclusion. But the exact location of any boundary is necessarily a highly debatable judgment, and from Aristotle onward the practical judgments of political philosophers have tended to reflect the prejudices of their times. Even J. S. Mill, whose support for broadening the boundaries of political participation was exceptional for a person of his class, nonetheless presented persuasive reasons to justify the particular exclusions he advocated; yet probably few contemporary democrats would accept his exclusions as reasonable.

In short, if Schumpeter's solution leads to absurdities, the solutions found in earlier democratic ideas, whether in classical antiquity or in the works of early modern theorists like Locke, Rousseau, and Mill, provide all too fragile a foundation for a satisfactory normative theory of the democratic process. Though evidently we must accept the need for a judgment on competence, and its contingent and contestable nature, we require a criterion that will help to reduce the arbitrariness of such a judgment.

## A JUSTIFICATION FOR INCLUSIVENESS

Although the weaknesses of categorical principles of inclusion mean that we cannot avoid contingent judgments, the grounds for adopting the Strong Principle of Equality set out in the last chapter obviously justify a broad criterion of inclusiveness. As I have already said, in adopting the Strong Principle as an assumption of a democratic process, in effect we affirm that all adults should be included, subject only to such exceptions as may fail to satisfy the presumption of personal autonomy.

Experience has shown that any group of adults excluded from the demos—for example, women, artisans and laborers, the unpropertied, racial minorities—will be lethally weakened in defending its own interests. And an exclusive demos is unlikely to protect the interests of those who are excluded. "Universal teaching must precede universal enfranchisement," Mill wrote (1958, 132). But it was not until *after* the extension of the suffrage in 1868 that Parliament passed the first act establishing public elementary schools. The historical record since then demonstrates even more fully that when a large class of adults is excluded from citizenship their interests will almost certainly not be given equal consideration. Perhaps the most convincing evidence is provided by the exclusion of southern blacks from political life in the United States until the late 1960s.

In adopting the Strong Principle of Equality, we have already taken considerations like these into account. That principle, and the assumptions from which it is derived, provide reasonable grounds for adopting a criterion that approaches universality among adults. It is not only very much less arbitrary than Schumpeter's solution but far more inclusive than the restricted demos that was accepted, implicitly or explicitly, in the classical polis and by Aristotle, Locke, Rousseau, or Mill. The fifth and final criterion for the democratic process is, then, as follows:

*The demos must include all adult members of the association except transients and persons proved to be mentally defective.*

Admittedly the definition of adults and transients is a potential source of ambiguity. Probably no definition of the term "adult" can be completely watertight. A practical test might be to treat every member as an adult who does not suffer from a severe mental disability or who is considered an adult in criminal law. If a legal system assigns burdens, obligations, and punishments to persons when they reach an age at which they are legally presumed to have achieved the minimum threshold of reason and responsibility for their actions, then that age might also serve as the threshold at which the right to inclusion in the demos ought to begin.

The meaning of the criterion seems to me to be clear enough: A demos that permitted the concept of adulthood to be manipulated in order to deprive certain persons of their rights—dissenters, for example—to that degree would simply fail to meet the criterion of inclusiveness.

Taken with the other four criteria presented in chapter 8, inclusiveness completes the requirements for a democratic process. These five criteria fully specify the democratic process. For I find it impossible to say in what respects a process meeting these criteria would not be *democratic* or how any process that failed to satisfy one or more of the criteria could be regarded as *fully* democratic.

## THEORY OF THE DEMOCRATIC PROCESS

Let me now summarize the argument of this chapter and anticipate a few objections and problems.

The criteria help us to distinguish several thresholds that have often given rise to confusion. As we saw, Schumpeter failed to distinguish between a political system that is democratic in relation to its own demos and one that is democratic in relation to everyone subject to its rules. A political process that meets only the first two criteria, I have suggested, might be regarded as *procedurally democratic in a narrow sense*. In contrast, one that also meets the criterion of enlightened understanding can be regarded as *fully democratic with respect to an agenda and in relation to a demos*. At a still higher threshold, a process that in addition provides for final control of the agenda by its demos is *fully democratic in relation to its demos*. But only if the demos were inclusive enough to meet the fifth criterion could we describe the process of decisionmaking as *fully democratic*.

Just as the criteria fully specify the democratic process, so I believe they fully specify what we ought to mean by *political equality*. To the extent that the criteria are not met, then persons could hardly be said to be politically equal; and, insofar as any process of decisionmaking can ever ensure political equality, persons among whom the criteria are met would surely be politic equals.

The assumptions and the criteria for a democratic process do not specify any particular kind of association. The implication is that in *any* association for which the assumptions are valid, the democratic process, and only the democratic process, would be justified. Historically, however, advocates of democracy have focused their attention on the state. They were right to do so. Whether or not the state is the most important of all human associations, it is without question highly crucial. It is crucial because of its extraordinary influence, power, and authority, and thus because of the capacity of those who govern the state to control the resources, structures, agendas, and decisions of all other associations within the boundaries of the state. A people that alienates its final control over the agenda and decisions of the government of the state runs a very high risk of alienating its final control over other important associations as well.

Because a familiar objection discussed in the last chapter is likely to be renewed at this point, perhaps I need to dispose of it once again. Do the criteria merely specify a "formal" but not a "real" political equality and democratic process? Suppose citizens are highly unequal in their political resources—income, wealth, status, for example. Would they not be unequal politically? Of course they might and very likely would be. Yet it is a serious mistake to object to the criteria on this ground. For when differences in political resources cause citizens to be politically unequal, then that inequality necessarily reveals itself by a violation of the criteria. Indeed, to the extent that one believes that the criteria specify a desirable political order, then one must be concerned about the social, economic, and cultural prerequisites for such an order, a problem we examine later on.

One might also wonder whether any system can hope to meet the criteria fully. And, if not, of what relevance are the criteria? Now I take it for granted that, in the real world, no system will fully meet the criteria for a democratic process. At best any actual polity is likely to achieve something of an approximation to a fully democratic process. My guess is that any approximation will fall pretty far short of meeting the criteria. However, the criteria serve as standards against which one may compare alternative processes and institutions in order to judge their relative merits. The criteria do not completely define what we mean by a good polity or a good society. But to the extent that the democratic process is worthwhile, then the criteria will help us to arrive at judgments that bear directly on the relative worth or goodness of political arrangements.

# PART FOUR

◆◆◆◆◆◆◆◆◆

# PROBLEMS IN THE DEMOCRATIC PROCESS

# Chapter 10

◆◆◆◆◆◆◆◆◆

# Majority Rule and
# the Democratic Process

The theory of the democratic process described in the previous chapters does not specify the rule that should be followed if collective decisions are to be made according to the democratic process. Can we say what that rule should be?

This question suggests others:

1. Does the democratic process require the exclusive use of the majority principle? Many advocates of popular, republican, or democratic government have defended majority rule.[1] Locke and Rousseau, as I said earlier, prescribed unanimity at the time of the original contract by which the state was founded but majority rule thereafter. Contemporary writers—both advocates and critics of democracy—often hold that democracy "means" or requires majority rule (for example, Spitz 1984).

Of course virtually everyone assumes that democracy requires majority rule in the weak sense that support by a majority ought to be *necessary* to passing a law. But ordinarily supporters of majority rule mean it in a much stronger sense. In this stronger sense, majority rule means that majority support ought to be not only necessary but also *sufficient* for enacting laws.[2] Requiring majority rule in this strong sense, however, runs into a several perplexing problems for which no entirely satisfactory solutions have yet been found.

2. If majority rule in the strong sense is unsatisfactory, is there a clearly superior alternative? One possibility is to require for all collective decisions what Locke and Rousseau assumed to be necessary for the original founding: unanimity. Between strict majority rule and unanimity lie an indefinite range of possibilities—two-thirds, three-fourths . . . Unfortunately, however, all the alternatives to strict majority rule are also open to serious objection.

3. If no entirely satisfactory rule can be found, does this mean that the democratic process is, strictly speaking, impossible? And, if so, is there an acceptable substitute for the democratic process that escapes the objections to majority rule and its alternatives?

4. Finally, what rules do people who support democracy actually adopt in practice? For example, is majority rule pretty much the standard solution despite its difficulties?

I propose to undertake our search for answers by presenting the strongest arguments for majority rule I know and then considering the main objections and alternatives.

## PRELIMINARIES

MAJORITARIAN: Before showing you why I believe that strong majority rule is required by the democratic process, I want to make explicit some assumptions that, I'm sure, you'll have no trouble with. Let's assume that a collection of people exists with well-defined boundaries. They are committed to political equality and the democratic process. They have a need for collective decisions. Any problems so far?

CRITIC: None. In effect you've made assumptions I would make in justifying the democratic process.

MAJORITARIAN: I was well aware of that, of course. I'm sure you will also agree with me that the democratic process requires some decision rule or even several different rules. After all, when the final stage of decisionmaking is reached, and all the votes of equal weight have been counted, a rule is needed to specify which alternative is to be adopted.

CRITIC: Of course. What you say seems obvious to me.

MAJORITARIAN: And you agree, I'm sure, that among a people committed to the democratic process, an appropriate decision rule must of course be consistent with the criteria and assumptions of that process.

CRITIC: Naturally.

MAJORITARIAN: Would it not be reasonable also to insist that whatever decision rule is adopted, it should be *decisive*? By decisive I mean that it will ensure that *some* outcome is definitely selected.

CRITIC: A requirement of decisiveness seems entirely reasonable to me. May I also suggest that a good decision rule should also be practical or *feasible*? And that it ought to be *acceptable* to the participants?

MAJORITARIAN: Bravo! As I was sure you would, old friend, you've entered into the spirit of my quest for the best rule for making democratic decisions. I hope to show you why majority rule in the strong sense is the best decision rule, in fact the only decision rule fully consistent with the democratic process.

CRITIC: I eagerly await your demonstration.

MAJORITARIAN: Let me begin with an observation that isn't a "demonstration," as you call it, but does add some support to the principle. Any demos committed to the democratic process is likely to find majority rule intuitively appealing. Let me explain why. If the participants regard one another as political equals—if they firmly believe that no one among them ought to be treated as politically more privileged than another—then the weak version of majority rule will almost certainly seem desirable to them. For surely a minority among them, they will reason, should not be allowed to prevail over a majority. But if they accept that premise, then they are also bound to find the strong version appealing.

CRITIC: Why? The weak version doesn't logically imply the strong version.

MAJORITARIAN: Why not? If it's wrong to allow a minority to prevail over a majority, then isn't it also wrong to allow a minority to block a majority? Yet that's exactly what could happen without the strong version. Think about it for a moment: if a minority could always exercise a veto over majority decisions, then the practical effect would be minority rule, wouldn't it? The upshot is that once the members of some group see themselves as political equals who ought to govern themselves by the democratic process, the strong version of majority rule is likely to seem more appropriate and acceptable than any alternative to it.

CRITIC: Perhaps. Yet while your conjecture is quite plausible, I don't find it very rigorous. I think I can see several moves that would knock your argument off the board.

MAJORITARIAN: I'm quite aware that what I just said isn't a rigorous demonstration. However, to emphasize the intuitive appeal that majority rule is likely to enjoy among people who see themselves as political equals seems to me highly relevant. Among other things it speaks to the question of acceptability, which you yourself proposed as a criterion for a good decision rule.

I understand, though, that what you're asking is whether this intutitive sense of appropriateness can be rationally justified.

CRITIC: Exactly.

MAJORITARIAN: The answer is clearly yes, provided we agree on several entirely reasonable assumptions. In fact, a rational justification for majority rule can be arrived at in at least four different ways.

CRITIC: One would be enough.

MAJORITARIAN: I appreciate that. But since each of the four justifications I have in mind depends on somewhat different assumptions, I'd like to explain all four.

CRITIC: Of course. I learned long ago that there is more than one path to enlightenment. Perhaps you will show me one that I won't be able to resist.

MAJORITARIAN: I hope to. First, though, I'd like to ask you to accept a preliminary assumption. In exploring my four arguments for majority rule, it would be convenient to begin by assuming that the demos votes directly on the matters that are on the agenda for collective decisions. I'd also like to assume that the alternatives before the demos are in each case only two. If you'll allow me those assumptions initially, we can ignore some complications that would otherwise get in the way of an orderly exposition of the arguments.

CRITIC: Both assumptions drastically simplify the real world of democratic politics! Although I understand the usefulness of making assumptions that help to reduce the inordinate complexity of the real world, I'm going to insist that at some point we return to the world of actual experience. As you well know, in the real world for two centuries advocates of democracy have tried to apply the democratic process to representative governments. What's more, in the real world voters and legislatures often confront issues with more than two alternatives.

MAJORITARIAN: I don't deny that. But we can deal with those complications more intelligibly if we start off in a simpler though less realistic world.

## FOUR JUSTIFICATIONS FOR MAJORITY RULE

### Maximizing Self-Determination

MAJORITARIAN: To start with, majority rule maximizes the number of persons who can exercise self-determination in collective decisions. Given the boundaries of a particular political system, the composition of the demos, and the need for a collective decision on some matter, the strong principle of majority rule ensures that the greatest possible number of citizens will live under laws they have chosen for themselves. If a law is adopted by less than a majority, then the number who have chosen that law will necessarily be smaller than the number of citizens who would have chosen the alternative. Likewise, if more than a majority were required in order for a law to be adopted—let's say 60 percent—then a minority of 40 percent (plus one vote) could prevent a majority of 60 percent (less one vote) from adopting its preferred alternative. As a result, the alternative preferred by a minority would be imposed on the majority.[3]

CRITIC: I don't disagree with your argument, but let me make two observations. First, the justification you've just presented depends on the assumption that the freedom expressed through self-determination ought to be maximized in collective decisions. Isn't an argument of that kind too abstract to appeal to anyone except a philosopher? Are you saying that the acceptability of majority rule requires people to read and understand Rousseau or Immanuel Kant?

MAJORITARIAN: Of course not. While my justification may seem abstract I suspect that it implicitly underlies how lots of people think about majority rule. I can easily imagine an ordinary citizen saying something like this to his fellow citizens:

Look, we have to reach a decision on this matter. Some of us don't like the one option before us, and some don't like the other. We've tried as long and as hard as we can to find a solution we could all agree on, or, failing that, a solution more of us could agree on than seems to be the case with the alternatives before us. But we haven't turned up any better alternatives. So now we have to choose between the two best alternatives we've managed to put before us. Whichever way the decision turns out, some of us aren't going to like the law, though we'll all have to obey it anyway. So let the majority have its way. At least then more of us will live under the law we want than if we let the minority get what it wants. Isn't that the only right thing to do?

CRITIC: I can see how such an argument would appeal to many people. So let's pass on to my second observation. At the beginning of our conversation I agreed to assume that some collective decisions were necessary and that the boundaries of the collectivity were fixed. I now see that by doing so I may have given the store away. Those assumptions each conceal what might be called a boundary problem. The assumption that collective decisions are required presupposes a boundary between matters that require collective decisions and matters that don't. The assumption that the boundaries of the collectivity are fixed rejects the possibility that a collective unit with different boundaries—smaller, more local, more homogeneous, let's say, or larger and more heterogeneous—might be better.

MAJORITARIAN: If we try to consider all the problems of democratic theory and practice at the same time, we'll never get anywhere. Can't we treat your boundary problems later?

CRITIC: I yield.

MAJORITARIAN: Meanwhile, you do concede, do you not, that *if the members of an association need collective decisions to achieve their ends, and the boundaries of a democratic unit are taken as given*, then majority rule is required for maximum self-determination?

CRITIC: Yes. I'm quite willing to pass over my reservations for the moment, but I'll want us to come back to them later on.

MAJORITARIAN: As you wish. But the problems you pose must surely be distinguished from the problem of majority rule, must they not?

CRITIC: Perhaps I see the problems as more interdependent than you do.

## Majority Rule as a Necessary Consequence of Reasonable Requirements

MAJORITARIAN: My second justification is somewhat analogous to the first. But the argument is a bit more detailed and rigorous. Roughly stated, the argument is that, if you accept four reasonable criteria that ought to be met by a decision rule in a democratic association, then logically you must agree that the principle of majority rule, and only that principle, can satisfy those criteria. This proposition was nicely demonstrated in a simple, straightforward, and rigorous proof by a mathematician, Kenneth May, in 1952 (May 1952). If you will indulge me, I'd like to summarize his argument.

CRITIC: Please do.

MAJORITARIAN: First, we've already agreed that a democratic decision rule should be *decisive.* If the demos is confronted by two alternatives, x and y (as we've assumed to be the case), then the decision rule must definitely lead to one of three outcomes: either x is chosen, or y is chosen, or neither is chosen. Second, a democratic decision rule should not favor one voter over another. May calls this the requirement of *anonymity:* The outcome shouldn't depend on which specific persons favor or oppose an alternative.

CRITIC: Since what he calls anonymity is also implied by one of the criteria of the democratic process—voting equality—I find it an entirely reasonable assumption. The third requirement?

MAJORITARIAN: A voting procedure should also be *neutral* with respect to the alternatives. That is, it shouldn't favor or disfavor one alternative more than another. If there are two alternatives on the agenda, A and B, the decision rule should not have any built-in bias in favor of either. For example, suppose A is a proposal to adopt a new policy, while B means simply leaving the existing policy in place. The alternatives are to change the status quo in some respect or to preserve it. Neutrality requires that the decision rule shouldn't give any special advantage either to the proposed change or to the status quo.

CRITIC: A Burkean conservative might contend that the status quo should be given a built-in advantage.[4]

MAJORITARIAN: The status quo always has so many built-in advantages that surely it doesn't need the additional advantage of a biased decision rule! Since the point is immensely important, let me pursue it for a moment. Let's suppose, as once was the case in every country that is now democratic, that children are permitted to work in mines and factories. Being permitted to work, poverty drives them to do so. Let's suppose further that a referendum is scheduled in which voters may vote for or against a proposal to prohibit child labor in mines and factories. (Employing a referendum, you'll notice, allows us to set aside the question of representation, as we've been doing so far.) Call the proposal to ban child labor A. To vote against A in effect means voting for B, which is the status quo. If you want to abolish child labor, you support A; if you don't want it abolished, you support B, which means that child labor will continue to be allowed. I ask you, why should a decision rule favor the status quo over change, that is, favor child labor over its abolition? Suppose the constitution of a country requires that no law to regulate labor in mines and factories can be adopted in a referendum except by a two thirds vote. So let's now suppose that 66 percent of the voters support the abolition of child labor, while 34 percent oppose it. Child labor can't be abolished! Is there any earthly reason why the status quo should be so privileged? *cheap labor*

CRITIC: In choosing the example of child labor, you've managed to make a highly persuasive argument. Still, I can't help thinking that in some circumstances a minority might justifiably insist that certain matters, not necessarily so offensive to our contemporary sense of justice as child labor, should be made immune to ready change. Are you saying that the criterion of neutrality would necessarily prevent the adoption of a special decision rule for dealing with these matters? If so, I'm not fully convinced that neutrality is invariably a good criterion. However, I'm happy to set aside my reservations so that you can lay out the full argument.

MAJORITARIAN: Thank you. May's last assumption may strike you at first as rather finicky, but it does make sense. He proposed that a decision rule should be *positively responsive*, by which he meant the following. Suppose the members of a demos are initially indifferent between A and B. They have no preference for one over the other. Then (perhaps as a result of discussion or further reflection) one citizen comes to prefer A to B, while no citizen comes to prefer B to A. Surely, May reasoned, the decision rule must now lead to the selection of A.

CRITIC: I don't quite grasp the need for that assumption.

MAJORITARIAN: Let me see if I can give it some intuitive force. Imagine a

*voter apathy*

decision rule that meets the three criteria I mentioned earlier. It's decisive, neutral with respect to citizens (May's anonymity criterion), and neutral with respect to issues. But it specifies that the policy to be adopted is the alternative preferred not by the majority but by the minority. Perversely making the minority the winner would certainly violate May's notion of positive responsiveness. Or consider a less obvious case. Suppose no one cares whether A is adopted or B is adopted. I suppose the citizens could then choose by tossing a coin if they felt a decision had to be made. But if just one citizen, Robinson, now decides that A really is better than B, it seems fair that Robinson's choice should tip the scales. No one else cares; Robinson does. Having A adopted rather than B matters to her; it doesn't harm anyone else. So shouldn't A be adopted? To go back to the previous argument, self-determination would be maximized. To jump ahead to a utilitarian perspective, one person would be more satisfied with the outcome, and no one would be any worse off. So reasonableness dictates that A should be selected.

CRITIC: Put that way, I'm inclined to agree.

MAJORITARIAN: Well, if you accept that and the other three as reasonable criteria, then, May demonstrated, only one decision rule could satisfy all four criteria. As I said earlier, that unique decision rule is nothing other than the strong version of majority rule. Since each of the axioms seems highly reasonable—all the more so to anyone committed to the democratic process—May's demonstration provides a rational justification, and one of very considerable intellectual power, for the adoption of majority rule in its strong form.

CRITIC: I've indicated my reservations about the assumption of neutrality with respect to all issues, but otherwise I find the argument impressive. You have several others, I believe.

## More Likely to Produce Correct Decisions

MAJORITARIAN: Yes. My third justification for majority rule is that under certain conditions it is more likely than any other to lead to *correct* decisions. As you'll recall, it was Aristotle's view that the pooled judgments of many different persons are likely to be wiser on the whole, and certainly less subject to gross error, than the judgments of one person or a few. I think some such view is really rather common. In fact, one rather like it can be found in parts of Mill's celebrated defense of freedom of ideas. The justification for a trial by a jury of one's peers rests on the same notion.

CRITIC: Are you saying that truth is whatever a majority decides is true?

MAJORITARIAN: Not at all. What I'm saying is that under certain conditions the best test we have of whether an assertion is true, or correct, is whether a majority of those who are familiar with the evidence judge it to be true or correct.

CRITIC: If we looked carefully at your qualifier—"under certain conditions"—it might prove to be a can of worms.

MAJORITARIAN: To explain my argument I'm going to make use of a demonstration advanced in the eighteenth century by the French philosopher and mathematician the Marquis de Condorcet.[5] Let's assume that in some situations a citizen's choice may be right or wrong, as when a member of a jury decides whether or not the defendant is guilty of a criminal charge. Let's also suppose that, over a number of such decisions, while every citizen is sometimes right and sometimes wrong, more often than not each citizen makes a correct choice. Then the probability that a majority will make the correct choice is greater than the probability that a minority will do so. Consequently, the judgment of the majority, not the minority, ought to prevail, shouldn't it?

CRITIC: I suppose so, provided the only alternatives are majority rule or minority rule.

MAJORITARIAN: Fine. But Condorcet showed something even more interesting. The probability that the majority is right increases dramatically the larger it is. Suppose the probability of each member's being right is only a trifle better than chance, say 0.51. Then in a group of 100 the probability of a majority of 51 being right is a modest 0.52. But if the majority increases to 55 the probability of its being right rises to almost 0.60. For a majority of 60, the chances of its being right are nearly 70 percent! Likewise, as the probability that an individual citizen is correct goes up, even by small amounts, the probability that the majority is correct rises very swiftly. Take the same starting point as in the example I just gave: In a group of a hundred, where the chance of each member's being right is only 0.51, the probability that the majority will make the right judgment is only 0.52. But if the chance of a member's being right is 0.55, then the probability of the majority's being right is 0.60.[6]

CRITIC: Bravo! But on Condorcet's showing, shouldn't we insist on supermajorities—a two-thirds rule, say, or even a rule of unanimity?

MAJORITARIAN: No, for this reason. If the probability that a majority is right is greater, the larger it is, then the smaller the minority the lower the probability that *it* is right. A rule requiring a supermajority necessarily means that a minority could block a majority. But, the larger the supermajority the rule requires, the smaller the minority that would be sufficient to veto and so to impose *its* judgment. But, the smaller the minority, the greater the probability that it is wrong.

CRITIC: Let's not forget that your whole argument depends on the dubious assumption that the average voter is more likely right than wrong. If I reject that assumption, then your proof would point in the opposite direction—toward replacing strict majority rule with a supermajority rule. And if I recall correctly, Condorcet himself went on to show that majority voting can get into deep difficulties if there are more than two alternatives. We really ought to get on to those problems.

## Maximizing Utility

MAJORITARIAN: Before we do, I want to present my fourth justification, a utilitarian argument based on assumptions about costs and benefits.[7]

Maintaining the simplifying assumptions we initially agreed on, let's suppose that the demos votes directly on the laws. Now let's also suppose that, on any proposals supported by a majority, if the proposal is adopted then each citizen in the majority will gain at least as much benefit (or utility, or satisfaction, or whatnot) as each citizen in the minority will lose. On this assumption, majority rule would necessarily maximize the average benefit of the laws among all citizens.

CRITIC: Given your assumption, your conclusion obviously follows. What isn't at all obvious is the validity of your assumption.

MAJORITARIAN: I accept that. Nonetheless, I'd like to drive my point home with an extreme case. I'm going to assume that the net benefit to each member of the majority and the net loss to each member of the minority is exactly the same—just one unit of satisfaction. Even if only 51 citizens in a demos of 100 favor a law and 49 oppose it, the net gain under the majority principle would be, let's say, two units of satisfaction. *No alternative decision rule could do as well*. Let me push the point even further. If we assume that the boundaries of the system can't be changed, then in the extreme case where the same citizens are in the majority or in the minority on *all* issues decisions by majority rule would be superior to every alternative. Brutal and unjust as such a political system would surely seem to the permanent minority, given the boundaries of that particular system any alternative to majority rule would necessarily be worse.

CRITIC: Here we are, back to the boundary problem again. I think we really must confront that problem squarely.

MAJORITARIAN: I agree. But notice once again that, if a permanent minority were to secede and establish its own independent democratic system, and if my assumption about relative gains and losses were still valid, then the best decision rule for the new system would still be the majority principle.

CRITIC: Yes, but your assumption seems to me arbitrary. Anyway, how could one ever know? You realize as well as I that we can't really measure relative satisfaction. Your units of satisfaction—the famous "utiles" of the classical utilitarians—are a fiction.

MAJORITARIAN: That may be. Yet we do nonetheless constantly make such judgments about relative costs and gains. I'd guess that, most of the time when we reach a judgment as to whether or not something would be in the public good, our judgment is essentially utilitarian. Despite all the well-known difficulties, we try to arrive at a rough estimate of overall costs and benefits. Precisely because of the well-known difficulties, we can't determine them at all precisely. As a rule of thumb, therefore, we conclude that a policy ought to be adopted if more people gain than lose; it shouldn't be adopted if more people lose than gain. Judgments like these may be too soft and fuzzy to convince a philosopher or a social choice theorist. But since these folks have never been able to tell us how we can really measure utility or satisfaction in a hard-nosed way, most of the time we really have no alternative to soft and fuzzy judgments. Going back to my previous justification for majority rule, in making these difficult judgments I think a majority is more likely to be right than a minority.

CRITIC: Perhaps so. But your utilitarian justification seems to me to be much weaker than the others. Unless you've more to say I'd like to explain why.

MAJORITARIAN: Before you do, I have one more point to make. A utilitarian justification for majority rule is considerably strengthened by a second assumption. Suppose citizens who lose on one issue have a reasonable expectation that they will win on the next. In other words, there are no permanent majorities or permanent minorities. More precisely, let's assume that on each question the chance that a particular citizen is in the majority is equal to the proportion of citizens in the majority favoring the law. For example, if 60 percent of the citizens favor a law, the chances are six out of ten that any given citizen is in the majority. Over time, therefore, every citizen stands a better than even chance of winning on a particular issue. The greater the consensus (that is, the larger the average majority), the greater the probability that the typical citizen will be on the winning side. So, if the average majority were around 75 percent, the typical citizen would vote with the majority about three times out of four.

On the first assumption about gains and losses, from a utilitarian perspective no alternative to majority rule could ensure as good an outcome on a particular issue. If the second assumption is also valid, no alternative could assure the average citizen as good an outcome over all issues.

## DIFFICULTIES

CRITIC: Your justifications for majority rule all depend on certain assumptions. I confess that if I could fully accept those assumptions your arguments would compel me to conclude that majority rule is rationally justified and that no alternative to it is as good. In short, I would have to say that the democratic process necessarily entails the principle of majority rule.

But, as I've indicated in the course of our discussion, I believe many of your key assumptions are open to serious objections.

MAJORITARIAN: Which ones do you have in mind?

CRITIC: Though I agreed with you that some simplifying assumptions might be useful, you'll agree with me, I'm sure, that the complications created by the real world of democratic life do have to be taken into account.

MAJORITARIAN: Of course. If I thought that the majority principle could not be justified in actual political life, I'd reject it.

### More Than Two Alternatives

CRITIC: Well, your assumption that the demos confronts only two alternatives is obviously highly unrealistic. Yet whenever citizens must vote on three or more alternatives the principle of majority rule runs into serious difficulties. For one thing, the principle is no longer always decisive.[8]

With only two alternatives, what majority rule requires is perfectly clear: The alternative supported by the larger number of voters should be adopted. But let's suppose that voters face three alternatives, A. B, and C. Let's suppose further that each voter ranks the alternatives in the order of their desirability. We can now interpret the majority principle in several different ways, depending on how the various voters rank the alternatives.

The easiest case exists if one alternative is ranked first by an *absolute majority* of voters. Then under the majority principle that alternative ought of course to be adopted. Here's a clear-cut instance:

| | | Group | |
|---|---|---|---|
| | I | II | III |
| Ranking of | A | C | B |
| alternatives | B | B | C |
| | C | A | A |
| Votes: | 55 | 25 | 20 |

A is ranked first by 55 voters, an absolute majority. Alternative A is therefore adopted—a pretty unambiguous interpretation of majority rule.

But what are we to say if none of the alternatives is ranked first by an absolute majority? For example, suppose that Group I consists of 40 voters, Group II of 35, and Group III of 25:

| | | Group | |
|---|---|---|---|
| | I | II | III |
| Ranking of | A | C | B |
| alternatives | B | B | C |
| | C | A | A |
| Votes: | 40 | 35 | 25 |

MAJORITARIAN: One possible solution in that case would be to employ Condorcet's criterion in order to define a "majority." The winning outcome would be the alternative that defeats each of the others in a vote on every pair of alternatives. In your example that would mean pitting A against B, B against C, and C against A. Applying this decision-rule to your example, B would beat C by 65–35 (Groups I and III against Group II); and B would also beat A by 60–40 (Groups II and III against Group I). In the third pairwise vote, C would beat A by 60–40. So B would beat A and C, and C would beat A. By the Condorcet criterion B is the clear winner.

## Cyclic Majorities

CRITIC: Condorcet pulled you out of that hole, but I don't think he can get you out of a far deeper one. In some circumstances the rankings of the voters might not allow a demos to employ the Condorcet criterion, much less to insist on an absolute majority. Let me show you an example:

| | | Group | |
|---|---|---|---|
| | I | II | III |
| Ranking of | A | C | B |
| alternatives | B | A | C |
| | C | B | A |
| Votes: | 40 | 30 | 30 |

In this case, A will defeat B, 70–30 (Groups I and II against Group III); B will defeat C, 70–30 (Groups I and III against Group II); and C will defeat A, 60–40 (Groups II and III against Group I). We now confront an instance of *cyclic majorities,* which your mentor Condorcet also discussed. As you know, this intractable problem in democratic theory and practice has received an extraordinary amount of attention since Kenneth Arrow directed attention to it in 1951. Arrow's famous Impossibility Theorem demonstrates that unless you allow one person to dictate to all the rest, no solution to a cyclic majority exists that doesn't violate at least one of several other reasonable assumptions.[9] To my knowledge, no one has ever succeeded in showing that any of Arrow's assumptions are unreasonable or discovered a solution to cyclic majorities consistent with those assumptions. So, unless you're prepared to replace majority rule with dictatorship, you can't provide any way out of a majority cycle that isn't arbitrary.

MAJORITARIAN: Well, one possible solution would be to interpret the majority principle as requiring the adoption of the alternative preferred by the largest number of voters—what Americans call a "plurality" and the British a "relative majority." If a plurality or relative majority were acceptable, then in your last example A would be adopted, since it's ranked first by the largest number of voters.

CRITIC: But as my example shows, and as we all know from common experience, a plurality of voters can be a minority of voters. To insist in this case that the majority principle requires a minority to have its way seems to me self-contradictory. How can majority rule be rationally justified if no majority exists?

### Controlling the Agenda

CRITIC: Cyclic voting creates still another problem for the democratic process: Control over the agenda can be used to manipulate the outcome. As you can see from my last example, the sequence in which people vote on the alternatives could arbitrarily ensure a winner. Suppose that a clever advocate of one of the alternatives controls the agenda, perhaps as moderator or chairman of the meeting. Let's say the chairman wants A to win. She first asks the citizens to vote between B and C. B wins 70–30. Then she asks them to vote between B and the remaining alternative, A. This time A beats B 70–30. She then pronounces A the winner. A chairman who could manipulate the agenda this way could just as well have brought about a victory for either of the other two alternatives. Doesn't that nullify the criterion of final control?

MAJORITARIAN: No, because the criterion requires that the citizens have an opportunity to determine *how* the agenda is to be determined. They might decide, for example, that when voting cycles occur a plurality of votes will suffice or the matter is to be decided by a lottery of some sort or by any other method that seems to them fair and reasonable.

### Boundary Problems

CRITIC: Let me now turn to the two boundary problems I mentioned earlier. One, you may recall, has to do with the boundary between matters decided collectively and matters not so decided: the boundary for *collective decisions*. The other has to do with the boundaries of the collective *unit* itself. Considering the boundary for collective decisions in the light of your first justification, might it not sometimes be possible to maximize self-determination by allowing individuals or groups to decide certain matters autonomously rather than submitting them to a collective decision?

MAJORITARIAN: Of course! But deciding how a particular matter is to be decided, whether collectively or autonomously, will itself require a collective decision, will it not, at least if and when the question becomes a public issue? Unless you want to contend that no matters whatsover will require collective decisions, the assumption we agreed to is perfectly valid. And if nothing requires collective decisions we surely don't need a democratic process, do we?

CRITIC: I accept your point. But I don't want us to forget that for a democratic association to maximize self-determination among its members requires far more than their adoption of a satisfactory principle for collective decisions.

MAJORITARIAN: I fully agree. I'm now wondering whether the question of the unit's boundaries won't also prove to be a problem not in the majority principle but rather in democratic theory and practice more generally.

CRITIC: To find out, let's examine the problem. Like the democratic process itself, the majority principle assumes the existence of a political unit, within which a body of citizens must arrive at collective decisions. But nothing in the idea of majority rule provides a rational justification for the boundaries around any specific unit. To say that a decision should be made by majority rule simply does not—and cannot—answer the question: a majority of what democratic unit?

MAJORITARIAN: True. But I don't see how the point bears on the justification for majority rule.

CRITIC: Let's suppose a country exists that governs itself by the democratic process, adopts the majority principle for its collective decisions, and yet contains a permanent majority and a permanent minority. So the same people always win and the same people always lose. Let's say the permanent majority are 60 percent, leaving a permanent minority of 40 percent. So 60 percent of the citizens live under laws they've chosen, while 40 percent always live under laws they don't like, laws imposed on them by the majority. I would hardly call that a way of maximizing self-determination. What you have instead is self-determination for the majority and external determination for the minority: majority domination, I'd say. Wouldn't self-determination be maximized instead if the two groups were to separate into two independent political associations? Since the people in each would now agree among themselves on the laws they wanted, *everybody* would live under laws they'd chosen for themselves, while none would be obliged to obey laws imposed on them by others.

MAJORITARIAN: Your solution is obviously the correct one, at least formally. So let's assume that instead of one association we now have two. But please notice an interesting consequence of the change: The citizens in each association now confront exactly the same question as they did before! What decision rule do you believe they should now adopt for governing themselves in their new and more homogeneous units? Naturally if you want to postulate a fairy tale conclusion, in which perfect harmony exists in each unit forever after, then you won't need an answer. But politics, the state, and the need for a democratic process would also vanish in a wisp of smoke. You've implied that the assumptions I've been suggesting might not apply to the real world. Well, the "harmony forevermore" scenario is to the real world as the tooth fairy is to a toothache. All I'm arguing is that in any democratic unit that lacks perfect unanimity, in other words, in any real democratic unit, self-determination would be maximized by majority rule in collective decisions.

CRITIC: And what I'm arguing is simply this: No matter how democratic their convictions, a minority might reject majority rule *in a particular political unit.* Instead, they might insist on *altering the unit itself,* maybe by decentralizing decisions on certain matters to more homogeneous units, possibly even by gaining complete independence. In fact I would generalize the argument: Assuming that the democratic process is desirable among any given collection of people, the values of the democratic process might sometimes be better achieved by changing the boundaries of the unit.

MAJORITARIAN: I've already conceded your point. If one way of bounding a political unit would serve democratic values better than another, then other things being equal the better unit obviously ought to be selected. In the real world, though, other things aren't equal and boundary questions aren't easily solved. But can't we distinguish the question of majority rule from the question of the unit's boundaries? What constitutes the best unit within which to achieve democratic values is itself so difficult and complex a question that to do it justice would require an extended discussion ranging far beyond the majority principle.[10] However, I must insist on this point: My argument is that, once a particular unit is taken as given, even if only tentatively, then among the members of that unit the majority principle provides on balance a better democratic decision rule than any alternative to it.

### The Attenuation of Majority Rule in the Real World

CRITIC: Let me turn to another assumption. I don't believe that a reasonable justification can be made for majority rule without explicitly taking representation into account. I'm quite willing to admit that, in order to simplify the discussion at the outset, it was helpful to ignore the complexities that representation entails. But majority rule would have only limited relevance to the modern world if it couldn't be justified for representative systems.

MAJORITARIAN: I can hardly deny what you say. In order to present a more straightforward argument, it is useful to consider democratic associations in which citizens would assemble and vote directly on the laws. But I readily concede that in today's world direct democracy is the exception. Consequently if the majority principle is to be relevant to modern democracy we have to be able to apply it to representative democracy. But I don't see why that should create insuperable difficulties.

CRITIC: Yet wasn't Rousseau dead right about representation? Doesn't representation seriously attenuate majority rule?

MAJORITARIAN: What do you mean, "attenuate"?

CRITIC: I mean that conditions in the real world generally weaken the translation of majority preferences into law and administration. When you speak of majority rule in the real world, what majority do you have in mind—a majority of citizens, a majority of voters, or a majority of legislators? Even in systems of direct democracy, majority rule is attenuated if many citizens abstain from participating. For example, in the New England town meetings that I'm familiar with, only a small minority of citizens attend the meetings, and they aren't particularly "representative" of the others. As to Athenian democracy, no one can say with confidence what percentage of citizens came to the assemblies or how representative they were. Some advocates of direct democracy argue that in large systems referenda can substitute for assemblies; but referenda are notorious as instruments of minorities. When we turn to modern representative systems, we notice that in some, such as the United States, the turnout in midterm congressional elections is under 50 percent. Even where electoral turnout is relatively high, a majority of the voters may slim down into a minority of legislators. What's more, a minority of voters may sometimes win a majority of seats.

MAJORITARIAN: I'm aware of that. But electoral systems can be designed to ensure that electoral majorities end up as legislative majorities. Fortunately, a democratic country doesn't have to adopt the highly defective type of electoral system employed in Britain, the United States, Canada, Australia, and New Zealand. In those countries, the electoral systems make it possible, and not uncommon, for representatives of a minority of voters to win a majority of seats. But it's just because of these defects in the electoral systems of the English-speaking countries that almost all other democratic countries have instead adopted systems of proportional representation, which generally produce a pretty close fit between electoral and legislative majorities.

CRITIC: But even under PR, in a country with three or more significant parties in parliament, as is almost invariably the case, the process of forming a cabinet supported by a majority of members is by no means completely determined by the preceding election. In fact, governing coalitions may fall apart between elections and new ones, different from the old, may take their place without a new election. I'd say that's rather a sizable attenuation of majority rule.

MAJORITARIAN: I agree. But isn't the majority principle an important criterion against which we can judge the legitimacy of the government that is eventually formed?

CRITIC: No doubt it's one criterion. But when we apply it we see how frequently actual practice in real world democratic countries falls short of the abstract principle. And the majority principle is attenuated in practice not only by representation; it's further attenuated by all the other factors that impede political equality and consensus in the real world.

MAJORITARIAN: It seems to me you're only saying what we already know perfectly well: To achieve anything close to the democratic process in the real world is difficult and in some times, places, and conditions virtually impossible. But to the extent that we *can* achieve it, then the majority principle, even if attenuated in practice, is the best decision rule.

CRITIC: Only up to a point. I'm suggesting that, even if we believe that the majority principle is the best decision rule for an ideal democracy, the more that majority rule is attenuated in practice the weaker its justification also becomes *in practice*. Under some conditions, majority rule might be so attenuated that we could reasonably prefer an alternative.

MAJORITARIAN: What do you have in mind?

CRITIC: Nothing specific. But I would suggest that from a realistic perspective perhaps more often than not governmental decisions in democratic countries are not instances of majority rule at all but of minorities rule.

MAJORITARIAN: Are you now asserting that actual democracies are really systems of minority domination, as writers like Gaetano Mosca, Vilfredo Pareto, Robert Michels, V. I. Lenin, and many other critics of "bourgeois" democracy have contended? If so, you surprise me. I know we disagree somewhat about the majority principle, but until now I hadn't supposed that in your view a reasonable approximation to democracy is impossible to achieve in the real world!

CRITIC: Hold on! No, in my view theories of minority domination, like those of the people you just mentioned, profoundly misrepresent the nature of government in modern democratic countries.[11] I mean something rather different. I mean that if you carefully examine specific decisions of governments, often they can't be correctly described as *majority* decisions. They're more accurately described as decisions by a minority or a minority coalition of minorities. In theories of minority domination the dominant minority is roughly the same in all key decisions. In systems of "minorities rule" the minority or minority coalition varies significantly in composition and interests from one decision or type of decision to another.

MAJORITARIAN: Maybe "minorities rule" is a correct empirical description of decisionmaking in some democratic countries. But once again, wouldn't we judge a system of "minorities rule" to be inferior to a system of majority rule? What you call minorities rule is definitely a second-best system, isn't it?

CRITIC: Not necessarily. It might allow more people to achieve more of the policies they most strongly prefer than they would under a more majoritarian system. To that extent, it might maximize self-determination, average utility, and fairness more than would be possible under strict majority rule.

MAJORITARIAN: Or it might not. That would depend on empirical circumstances, right?

CRITIC: Exactly. But if "minorities rule" is better than majority rule in some circumstances, then we can't say that the principle of majority rule is always the best, can we?

## Does Majority Rule Maximize Average Utility?

CRITIC: Let me turn to your justification of majority rule as a way of maximizing average net benefits from collective decisions—or average satisfaction, utility, or whatever word you prefer.

MAJORITARIAN: Net benefits will do.

CRITIC: To make your case, you had to stipulate that, if alternative A were adopted, the average net benefit to persons in the majority would be at least equal to the average net benefit to the members of the minority if A were rejected (and B adopted). But that assumption seems to me dreadfully arbitrary. When it doesn't hold, majority rule won't guarantee that the majority will necessarily judge policies according to the net gains for everyone concerned. A majority, after all, isn't exactly the same as a neutral, benevolent, and omniscient judge who opts for the policies that will maximize average utility (or pleasure, happiness, or whatever). A majority might instead choose policies that provide only modest benefits to its members and yet are so harmful to a minority that on a strictly utilitarian calculation—maximizing average welfare, let us say—they should be rejected. The less the average benefit to members of the majority, the greater the average loss to members of the minority, and the less the difference in numbers between majority and minority (at the limit 50 percent plus one versus 50 percent minus one), the worse the outcome by strictly utilitarian standards. In these cases, if a neutral arbiter were to make the decision, she would reject the majority's policies and instead choose the minority's.

MAJORITARIAN: But your neutral arbiter also does away with the democratic process and replaces it with some form of guardianship. Is that what you're proposing as an alternative to majority rule?

CRITIC: I'm not proposing an alternative. I simply used the artifice of the neutral arbiter to show why your utilitarian justification for majority rule is seriously defective. I should also add that whenever a majority fails to give equal consideration to the interests of a minority, it thereby violates a principle on which the legitimacy of the democratic process and majority rule both depend.

MAJORITARIAN: I'm pretty sure I could specify certain conditions under which a majority wouldn't act as you've described it.

CRITIC: I don't doubt it, but that's no answer. If you have to require "certain conditions" in order for the majority principle to be justified, you thereby concede that if these conditions are absent the process of majority rule is no longer justified. Yet nothing in the majority principle ensures that these conditions will exist and the majority will choose the outcomes that satisfy utilitarian criteria. Whenever a system lacks your hypothetical conditions, you can't justify majority rule as necessary or sufficient for morally right outcomes, at least judged by utilitarian criteria. You're not going to say that the conditions you would specify are invariably present, are you?

MAJORITARIAN: Of course not.

### Neutrality with Respect to Issues

CRITIC: Finally, I want to question an assumption that is crucial to May's argument for majority rule: the assumption of neutrality with respect to issues. The question of neutrality is of exceptional practical import, since in most democratic countries the decisionmaking process is not neutral with respect to all issues: constitutional amendments, for example. Another instance: In federal systems, the states, provinces, or cantons that constitute the system can't be abolished by simple majority rule. Yet another: In some democratic countries, questions bearing on important religious, linguistic, or regional subcultures can't be decided by majority rule. In fact, whether constitutionally or by agreement, each subculture may be entitled to exercise a veto on matters crucial to the values or interests of the subculture. In short, a comparative analysis of democratic countries would show that majority rule over all issues is comparatively rare.[12]

MAJORITARIAN: Which shows how few countries are fully committed to the democratic process.

CRITIC: Your answer is too facile. Like many advocates of majority rule, you assume that people can't be committed to the democratic process unless they're also committed to majority rule. But I believe you would concede that, in some democratic countries where the scope of majority rule is restricted, the people are as fully committed to political equality and the democratic idea as in majoritarian democracies. And, unless you make majority rule your definitional touchstone, you'd have to concede that the political institutions of the nonmajoritarian countries achieve the democratic process as fully as the political institutions of the more majoritarian countries.

✦

The flaws in majority rule pointed out by Critic do great damage to the contention of majoritarians that the democratic process necessarily requires majority rule in all collective decisions. However, from the unassailable proposition that majority rule is imperfect—perhaps indeed highly imperfect—we cannot move directly to the conclusion that it should be replaced by an alternative rule for making collecting decisions. Before arriving at that conclusion, we would want to know whether a generally superior alternative can be found. As we shall see, the alternatives to majority rule are also deeply flawed.

# Chapter 11

♦♦♦♦♦♦♦♦♦

# Is There a
# Better Alternative?

Given the difficulties in majority rule indicated in the dialogue between a majoritarian and a critic, is it possible to find an alternative that is clearly superior and still consistent with the moral assumptions and values of democracy?

## SUPERMAJORITIES

One proposed solution is a decision rule that would require a supermajority for the adoption of collective policies—a practice, as Critic pointed out, that is common in democratic countries. In the extreme case, unanimity could be required. But it is one thing to say that if everyone approves of a policy it surely ought to be adopted (the Pareto principle). And it is quite another to say that a policy should be adopted *only if* everyone approves. By giving a veto to any person opposed to a policy, a unanimity rule would in effect make a state impossible. Since we have already considered and rejected the case for anarchism, it is unnecessary to repeat that discussion here.[1]

What about a rule requiring less than unanimity but more than a bare majority? Might not a rule be found, as Rousseau suggested, that would balance the need for speed with the seriousness of the matter to be decided? These intermedidate supermajority solutions are, however, subject to several objections. First, by allowing a minority to veto a majority decision they reduce the number of citizens who can exercise self-determination, which as Majoritarian pointed out is maximized by majority rule. Second, nothing short of unanimity will get around the intractable problem of voting cycles. Third, as Majoritarian also pointed out, supermajority requirements privilege the status quo and thus preserve existing injustices against reform by a majority decision.

If the members were willing to accept the last consequence, then under certain conditions a rule requiring a majority of 64 percent or more would solve the problem of voting cycles and ensure that a "winner always exists."[2] Yet while a requirement of this kind might appeal to conservatives strongly committed to the status quo, and quite possibly to others if the rule were restricted to certain kinds of decisions, the highly privileged position it assigns to the status quo lacks a convincing moral justification. And empirically speaking the rule is likely to offend the moral sensibilities and policy goals of enough people in many democratic associations and countries to prevent its general adoption.

A solution might be to combine the advantages of majority rule with the possibilities of supermajorities by using majority rule as a first and last resort. The members could decide in advance, by majority rule, that in certain cases a supermajority would be required. These cases might include special issues of great consequence and explosiveness, touching for example on enduring linguistic or religious differences; and they might also include voting cycles, if and when these were detected. But the decision as to which issues were to require a supermajority would itself be made by majority rule.

## LIMITED DEMOCRACY

The democratic process obviously could not exist unless it were self-limiting, that is, unless it limited itself to decisions that did not destroy the conditions necessary to its own existence. (I return to this point in the next chapter.) However, the extraordinary difficulty of finding a satisfactory decision rule has prompted some critics of the democratic process to propose limits that would go far beyond the self-limits necessary to the process itself.

In this spirit William Riker, a leading student of the theory of social choice, contends that no rule for collective decisions can be discovered that does not produce arbitrary or meaningless outcomes (Riker 1982). Consequently, we must reject as unfeasible, and indeed impossible, all attempts to attain a political system that would satisfy the requirements of the democratic process or, in his terminology, "populist democracy." What is possible, and in his view desirable, is a considerably more limited objective—a system sufficiently democratic to enable citizens voting in periodic elections to remove elected officials when they become discontented with the officials' performance (181–200). To Riker, a democratic system limited in this way (what he calls "liberal democracy") serves the fundamental values expressed in the democratic idea even if the government does not achieve the impossible goal of uniquely representing the popular will.

As a rough description of the realities of the democratic process when it is applied to large-scale systems, and of the values of large-scale democracy, Riker's argument has much to be said for it (cf. chap. 16 below). However, his argument is subject to some grave difficulties. First, as critics have pointed out, his "liberal democracy" does not escape the difficulties of "populist democracy." If his criticisms of the ambiguity of social choice are correct, then simply because citizens vote to remove officials from office in an election does not provide adequate grounds for determining what the outcome means.[3] Second, the extent to which voting cycles are a genuine problem in democratic associations is unclear; some social theorists have concluded that the importance Riker and others have attributed to voting cycles is exaggerated.[4]

## QUASI GUARDIANSHIP

Because of difficulties in voting rules, some critics of the democratic process have argued that the capacity of legislatures to make laws is inferior to that of a body of nonelected quasi guardians, such as the United States Supreme Court. Thus Riker and Barry Weingast (1986) reject the standard argument in the United States that the Supreme Court should defer to Congress on questions of economic choices and economic rights, particularly property rights. Their critique, they argue, "provides a more complete underpinning of judicial review of legislative decisions over rights of all kinds" (26).

Yet the authority they offer the quasi guardians on the Court with one hand, they promptly take back with the other.

> Judicial scrutiny that allows judges to substitute their own logic for that of the legislature merely transfers the problem of unpredictability and insecurity of economic rights from the legislative to the judicial stage; it does not solve the problem of protecting rights (26).[5]

Thus they recognize, if only implicitly, that as an alternative to the majority principle quasi guardianship suffers from two fatal flaws. First, though the scope of the guardians' authority is more limited, within that scope their authority is subject to most of the objections that, as we saw in chapter 5, provide strong grounds for rejecting guardianship. Second, like full guardianship, quasi guardianship cannot escape the difficulties of majority rule unless one is prepared to adopt one of two heroically implausible assumptions: either the number of guardians is reduced to one or they always agree perfectly. To assume that only one person is qualified to rule by virtue of superior wisdom and virtue is even more implausible than the assumption that only a minority are qualified. It is equally implausible to suppose, particularly given the historical record, that the judges sitting on a high court will always agree. Yet if a court consists of several judges, and if they disagree, as surely they will, then the court will need a decision rule. If disagreements are to be settled by voting, and if the justices' votes are counted equally, then all problems of majority rule and its alternatives will exist in microcosm (Shapiro 1989).

## MAJORITY TYRANNY VERSUS MINORITY TYRANNY[6]

While defenders of nonmajoritarian systems sometimes gesture fearfully toward a specter of majority tyranny they contend is hovering overhead, awaiting the slightest invitation to attack minority rights, these advocates usually fail to notice the less visible indications of a second specter—minority tyranny. Yet, just as a majoritarian democratic system offers no constitutional guarantee of minority rights and privileges beyond the primary political rights of all citizens, so nonmajoritarian democratic arrangements by themselves cannot prevent a minority from using its protected position to inflict harm on a majority. In a majoritarian country, the protection of minority rights can be no stronger than the commitment of the majority of citizens to preserving the primary democratic rights of all citizens, to maintaining respect for their fellow citizens, and to avoiding the adverse consequences of harming a minority. So too in a democratic country with a nonmajoritarian system, the protection of majorities against abusive minorities can be no stronger than the commitment of protected minorities not to abuse their opportunities to veto majority decisions they dislike. The argument that a minority veto can be employed negatively only in order to block majority threats to minority rights and welfare but cannot be used to inflict positive harm on a majority or on another minority is, as Majoritarian demonstrated in the dialogue with Critic, false.

Thus by themselves neither majoritarian nor nonmajoritarian arrangements can ensure justice in collective decisions. Despite their advocates, neither majority rule nor various nonmajoritarian arrangements can be prescribed as invariably the best system for arriving at collective decisions in a democratic country.

## MAJORITY RULE IN DEMOCRATIC COUNTRIES

Since theoretical reasoning evidently cannot be made to yield a firm conclusion that majority rule is necessarily superior or inferior to some alternatives to it, it would be surprising if associations whose members are committed to the democratic idea had arrived at a single solution to the problem of decision rules. Casual observation of "democratic" organizations appears to confirm this judgment, since they seem to follow a tremendous variety of different practices.

One relevant body of evidence bearing on this conclusion is Arend Lijphart's analysis of patterns of majoritarian and consensus government in twenty-one countries, which comprise all that have been "continuously democratic since about World War II" (Lijphart 1984).[7] Lijphart's democracies are essentially what I define as "polyarchies" in chapter 15. Anticipating chapter 15, I am going to call these countries "stable polyarchies."[8]

Lijphart contrasts two models of democracy—the "Westminster model," derived from an idealized version of Great Britain's parliamentary system,[9] and the "consensus" model, represented, for example, by Switzerland and Belgium. By "consensus" Lijphart does not necessarily mean unanimity. Consequently the systems of decisionmaking in the countries that fit his consensus model are for the most part not open to the objections to unanimity that were discussed in the last chapter, though like all supermajority rules their arrangements do privilege the status quo with respect to at least some issues. Thus while "the essence of the Westminster model is majority rule" (4), the guiding principle of the consensus model is to achieve the explicit consent of the major social groups in the country.[10]

The details are illuminating. For example, if majoritarianism were the norm in stable polyarchies, on theoretical grounds one would expect that in countries with cabinet systems (that is, all but the United States) cabinets would typically include only members of the majority party or party coalition. To include members of minority parties whose votes were not strictly necessary to passing laws would be an overture to consensualism. Yet in only eight countries are cabinets limited to the minimal winning size more than 85 percent of the time (table 11.1). Likewise, in a strictly majoritarian system a second chamber makes little sense; indeed, precisely because each chamber virtually duplicated the other, the Scandinavian countries abolished the redundant second house. But bicameralism remains far and away more common in democratic countries (table 11.1).

Advocates of the Westminster model as the very epitome of modern democratic institutions have long lauded two-party systems as essential to majority rule. The party that gains a majority of votes and seats is entitled to govern, while the minority party constitutes the loyal opposition. Yet two-party systems are a rarity; today only New Zealand and the United States can be so characterized (and the fragmented parties of the United States are a far cry from the centralized parties of the original Westminster model). Even the original home of the two-party system, Britain, is no longer so (table 11.1).

Supporters of a majoritarian system also tend to assume that party conflict will tend to occur over a single type of issue (typically socioeconomic questions) that allows voters to array themselves pretty consistently at about the same place on the political spectrum from left to right. Thus the outcome of an election will reflect a consistent majority and minority in the electorate, and it will produce a majority government and a minority opposition in parliament. Moreover, since the policy alternatives are typically framed to require one to vote either for or against a proposal, the defects of majority rule in the face of more than two alternatives are avoided. By contrast, when political activists disagree along two or more issue dimensions, such as socioeconomic matters *and* religious issues, a majority on one issue is likely to differ in composition from a majority on another issue. Forming a parliamentary majority capable of maintaining itself over a series of different questions therefore requires leaders to extend themselves to build coalitions and consensus; at the limit, the outcome may be a grand coalition of all the major parties. In such a political environment, then, the majoritarian Westminster model is likely to give way to a consensus system. By Lijphart's measure, in only five countries with polyarchal governments is partisan conflict predominantly along a single-issue dimension (table 11.1).

Although the Westminster model prescribes a plurality or majority electoral system—parliamentary seats go to candidates who win the most votes in single-member districts—this feature seems to me an historical peculiarity of the English-speaking countries rather than a strict requirement for majoritarianism.[11] It is often argued, however, that the Westminster electoral arrangements favor two parties, while PR tends to generate multiparty systems. Two parties will ensure that voters, confronted by only two alternatives, will coalesce into a majority, represented by the majority party, and a minority, represented by the loyal opposition. By reward-

*Table 11.1. Majoritarian and Nonmajoritarian Systems in Twenty-Two Stable Polyarchies*

| | | Number of Countries | | |
| --- | --- | --- | --- | --- |
| | | Majoritarian | Mixed | Consensus |
| Size of Cabinets[a] | Minimal winning size More than 85 percent of the time | 8 | | |
| | 85 percent of the time or less | | 6 | |
| | Oversized cabinets | | | 7 |
| Unicameral and Bicameral Parliaments[b] | Unicameral | 6 | | |
| | Hybrid | | 2 | |
| | Bicameral | | | 14 |
| Party Systems[c] | Two parties | 2 | | |
| | More than two, fewer than three[d] | | 6 | |
| | Three or more | | | 14 |
| Number of Issue Dimensions Involved in Partisan Conflicts[e] | Predominantly one issue dimension[f] | 5 | | |
| | Two or more issue dimensions | | | 17 |
| Electoral Systems[g] | Plurality and majority systems | 6 | | |
| | Semiproportional[h] | | 1 | |
| | Proportional representation | | | 15 |
| Unitary and Federal Systems[i] | Unitary | 16 | | |
| | Federal | | | 6 |
| Judicial Review and Minority Veto[j] | Neither | 4 | | |
| | Judicial review, no minority veto | | 6 | |
| | Minority veto, no judicial review | | 5 | |
| | Minority veto and judicial review | | | 7 |

[a]Excludes United States. *Source:* Lijphart 1984, 152.

[b]*Source:* Lijphart 1984, 92.

[c]*Source:* Lijphart 1984, 121, 122.

[d]Systems in which the third party is weaker than the other two.

[e]*Source:* Lijphart 1984, 130.

[f]Includes all countries scoring less than 2 on Lijphart's measure of issue dimensions: Canada, Ireland, New Zealand, United Kingdom, and the United States.

[g]*Source:* Lijphart 1984, 152.

[h]Japan.

[i]*Source:* Lijphart 1984, 178.

[j]*Source:* Lijphart 1984, 193.

*Table 11.2. National Referendums (1945–80)*

| Number of Referendums | Number of Countries |
|---|---|
| 169 | 1 (Switzerland) |
| 20–169 | 0 |
| 10–19 | 3 |
| 2–9 | 5 |
| 1 | 4 |
| 0 | 9 |

ing the winning party with more seats than its percentage of popular votes would warrant, the Westminster arrangement also enhances the majority party's prospects for a stable cabinet that is capable of carrying out the policies that a majority of voters had presumably supported, in broad outline at least. Although these arguments are of doubtful validity,[12] the fact is that outside the English-speaking countries proportional representation is the norm (table 11.1). PR and multiparty

*Table 11.3.*

Majoritarian
  New Zealand
  United Kingdom
  Ireland
  Luxembourg
  Sweden
  Norway
Majoritarian-Federal
  United States
  Canada
  Germany
  Austria
  Australia
  Japan
Consensual-Unitary
  Israel
  Denmark
  Finland
  France (Fourth Republic)
  Iceland
Consensual
  Switzerland
  Belgium
  Netherlands
  Italy
  France (Fifth Republic)

*Source:* Lijphart 1984, 216.

systems do tend to go together.[13] Typically in PR countries electorates are fragmented. A single party rarely wins a majority of seats, much less a majority of
electoral votes. Coalition cabinets are the rule. And stable coalitions typically
require consensus building.

The political institutions of some countries impede majority rule in still other
ways. In federal countries national majorities cannot always prevail over minorities concentrated in certain states or provinces. Though only six countries have
federal systems, these include several of the oldest "stable polyarchies" (table
11.1). Other forms of minority veto over majority decisions are even more widespread. In most democratic countries the political system allows minorities to
exercise a veto over policies by means of judicial review, which allows a high
court to set aside legislation that in its view contravenes the constitution, or by
pacts and understandings that create consociational arrangements of some sort, or
sometimes by both (table 11.1).

The various limits on the scope of majoritarian government might be transcended if referenda were commonly employed. But national referenda are confined almost exclusively to Switzerland. Elsewhere they are either rare or nonexistent (table 11.2).

Most stable polyarchies, then, have not adopted strictly majoritarian systems.
Of the twenty-one countries analyzed by Lijphart, he judges only six to be more or
less fully majoritarian. An additional six are "majoritarian-federal," that is, national majorities are limited by federalism. All the rest are "consensual" rather than
majoritarian (table 11.3).

## WHY MAJORITY RULE IS LESS POPULAR IN DEMOCRATIC PRACTICE THAN IN DEMOCRATIC THEORY

How are we to account for the predominance of limited majority rule and
consensual systems over strictly majoritarian systems in modern "democratic"
countries?

To argue convincingly that the people in nonmajoritarian countries are less
committed to democratic ideas than people in majoritarian countries would require
a rigorous comparative analysis that to my knowledge no one has made. A casual
inspection of table 11.9 seems to me sufficient to discredit the argument. Likewise, unless strict majoritarianism is by definition a requirement of the democratic
process, which the previous chapter argues it is not, to demonstrate that the
political systems of the stable nonmajoritarian polyarchies are less democratic than
those of the more strictly majoritarian countries would also require a comparative
analysis that has never been performed. Once again, casual comparisons do not, I
think, support that view.

A more satisfactory explanation is suggested by the dialogue between Critic and
Majoritarian. As Critic shows, under some conditions, justifications for the majority principle fail. In these circumstances, the democratic process does not neces-

sarily exclude alternatives to strict majority rule. Whether people committed to the democratic process find it reasonable to adopt majority rule for all collective decisions, impose limits on majority rule, or move toward consensual arrangements therefore depends in part on the conditions under which they expect collective decisions will be made. If and as these conditions change, arrangements judged suitable in previous circumstances may be modified in one direction or another—toward stricter majoritarianism or toward greater nonmajoritarianism. When political conflicts endanger national unity, for example, political leaders may replace majoritarian practices with consociational arrangements that ensure a veto to all significant subcultures. If and when the conflict subsides, these consociational arrangements may in turn give way to a less consensual, more majoritarian system, which is roughly the history of the Netherlands from the First World War to the 1980s.

The main conditions that favor majoritarian practices in a country are these. First, the more homogeneous the people of a country are, particularly in characteristics that are strongly associated with political attitudes, the less likely it is that a majority will support policies harmful to a minority and therefore the more likely it is that a broad consensus on the desirability of majority rule will exist. At the limit, a country's people would be so homogeneous that no majority could ever harm a minority without simultaneously harming its own members, an assumption of Rousseau's, I believe, that allowed him to entrust collective decisions about the general good so confidently to the majority.

Second, the stronger the expectations among the members of a political minority that they will enter into tomorrow's majority, the more acceptable majority rule will be to them, the less they will feel a need for such special guarantees as a minority veto, and the more likely they are to see these as impediments to their own future prospects as participants in a majority government.

Finally, whether as a consequence of the first two or for other reasons, majority rule is likely to gain greater support among members of a minority if they are confident that collective decisions will never fundamentally endanger the basic elements of their way of life, whether in matters of religion, language, economic security, or others.

Conversely, to the extent that one or more of these conditions is absent, some groups are likely to resist strict majority rule and to deny legitimacy to majority decisions. As we shall see in chapter 18, most countries of the world do lack these conditions (as well, often, as others favorable to democracy); this is therefore one reason, among others, why so many countries are not democratic. But even in countries with (otherwise) democratic, or polyarchic, institutions, the conditions favorable to majoritarianism just mentioned are frequently weak or absent. As a consequence, in these democratic countries strict majoritarianism has usually been rejected in favor of various nonmajoritarian and consensual arrangements for collective decisionmaking.[14]

Confronted by conditions that would seriously undermine the general acceptability and legitimacy of majority rule, then, democrats commonly prefer to adopt limitations on majoritarianism. To insist that by doing so they must *necessarily* violate the requirements of the democratic process seems to me unwarranted.

◆

The upshot of our exploration of majority rule, then, is this: The quest for a single rule to specify how collective decisions must be made in a system governed by the democratic process is destined to fail. No such rule, it seems, can be found.

On the other hand, the defects in majority rule are far too serious to be brushed aside. They oblige us to look with the utmost skepticism on the claim that democracy necessarily requires majority rule. Yet we are entitled to be just as skeptical about claims that an alternative would be clearly superior to majority rule or more consistent with the democratic process and its values. For all the alternatives to majority rule are also seriously flawed.

We may reasonably conclude, then, that judgments as to the best rule for collective decisions ought to be made only after a careful appraisal of the circumstances in which these decisions are likely to be taken. This conclusion is consistent with actual experience in different democratic countries, where people have adopted a variety of different rules and practices.

In adopting or rejecting majority rule, the people in democratic countries have not necessarily violated the democratic process or the values that justify it. For under different conditions, the democratic process may properly be carried out under different rules for making collective decisions.

# Chapter 12
++++++++++
# Process and Substance

A possible defect in almost any process for making decisions is that it may fail to achieve desirable results. Even a just process might sometimes produce an unjust outcome. A process might in principle meet all the requirements set out in the last chapters as fully as may be humanly possible. Yet might it not in some circumstances lead to morally undesirable results?

The possibility suggests two fundamental objections to the democratic process. (1) It may do harm. (2) It may fail to achieve the common good. Critics of the first persuasion often argue that in order to prevent harm from being done by means of collective decisions, the democratic process should be limited, restricted, or replaced in some important respects. Critics of the second persuasion often contend that the conflicts of interest and the poverty of civic virtue endemic in modern societies make the democratic process serve mainly particularistic interests and unable to achieve the common good.

We shall examine the first objection in this chapter and the next. I postpone our examination of the second objection to chapters 20 and 21, after we have had an opportunity to consider the consequences for democratic institutions and practices resulting from the shift of the democratic idea to the large scale of the nation-state.

Carried to an extreme, the insistence that substantive results take precedence over processes becomes a flatly antidemocratic justification for guardianship and "substantive democracy" becomes a deceptive label for what is in fact a dictatorship. But these antidemocratic arguments can be dealt with for what they are, as I have tried to do in discussing guardianship. Much more relevant for democratic theory and practice are disputes well within the democratic tradition among those who firmly believe that the best state is one governed by the democratic process but disagree about the proper balance between procedural and substantive values, and particularly over the extent to which substantive limits ought to be imposed on the democratic process. In the dialogue that follows the dispute is not between a democrat and an antidemocrat; they are both democrats. But one defends the democratic process on the ground that it is strongly substantive as well as procedural, while the other, his critic, contends that standing alone it provides insufficient protection against injury to substantive interests.

## SOME MISTAKEN NOTIONS

ADVOCATE: Though I agree that the problem of process and substance is a serious one for democratic theory and practice, I also think that the nature of the problem is often obscured by certain mistaken assumptions.

First, it is a mistake to think that procedures are somehow devoid of moral significance. I hear people say, for example, that "procedures should not be permitted to stand in the way of justice." Yet justice is procedural as well as substantive. Often, as in criminal trials, no process can guarantee that the outcome will be substantively just: A fair trial may still lead to a mistaken verdict. Nonetheless, it is possible to conclude that one process is more likely than another to arrive at the right result. Thus we may decide that in criminal cases a jury of one's peers is superior to any feasible alternative. At most, however, even the best-designed judicial system can guarantee only procedural justice; it cannot guarantee substantive justice. A constitution can ensure a right to a fair trial; it can't absolutely guarantee that a fair trial will always lead to the right verdict. But it is precisely because no such guarantee is possible that we place such a high value on a fair trial.

Second, and following from the first point, it is a profound mistake to speak as if the requirements of justice conflict with the "merely formal" procedures of democracy. The justification for the democratic process allows us to say that, given certain assumptions, the democratic process is itself a form of justice: It is a just procedure for arriving at collective decisions. Moreover, insofar as the democratic process allocates the distribution of authority, it also provides a form of distributive justice: A proper distribution of authority is a just product of a good constitution. Distributive justice requires a fair distribution of crucial resources—power, wealth, income, education, access to knowledge, opportunities for personal development and self worth, and others. Among the most crucial resources in any society is power. And the distribution of power is partly determined by the distribution of authority over the government of the state and over other associations. This authority is important, among other reasons, because these governments help to influence the way many other resources are distributed. Consequently a choice between the democratic process and substantive outcomes is not a simple choice between procedures and justice nor even between procedural justice and substantive justice. It is a choice between the justice of the democratic process, both procedural and distributive, and other claims to substantive justice. What I'm saying is, in short, that the democratic process is packed to the hilt with substantive values.

CRITIC: But you do admit that the democratic process hardly exhausts all claims to substantive justice. As you just said, there are other claims, too. If so, isn't it perfectly reasonable to ask that these claims be protected in some way from being violated by decisions made through the democratic process?

ADVOCATE: Whether it's reasonable to ask for limitations on the democratic process depends on whether you can supply an alternative. That points to a third mistake. *Unless you can specify a feasible alternative process that is more likely to produce just outcomes* it is wrong to contend that a process for making collective decisions is defective solely because it may lead to unjust outcomes. Even if we could establish independent criteria of justice against which to compare the performance of a process, it looks to be the case that no process for making collective decisions can, in John Rawls's terms, do more than provide imperfect procedural justice.

I'd like to use some of Rawls's categories to clarify the possible relation between procedural and substantive justice. We'll say that, if a procedure were able to guarantee an outcome that we independently define as just, then we have *perfect* procedural justice. An example would be a trial procedure that would always find the guilty to be guilty and always acquit the innocent. As Rawls says, "Pretty clearly, perfect procedural justice is rare, if not impossible, in cases of much practical interest" (1971, 85). So ordinarily we have to make do with the most feasible procedure we can design, even though it will sometimes fail, as in a criminal trial. That's *imperfect* procedural justice. Sometimes where we just don't have an independent criterion for the right result we can design "a correct or fair procedure such that the outcome is likewise correct or fair" (86). Rawls calls that *pure* procedural justice. An example might be if we were to divide a cake between us and you first sliced the cake, and afterward I chose which slice I wanted.

Often, though, neither "perfect," "imperfect," nor "pure" procedural justice is feasibly attainable. Independent criteria may exist but they aren't enough to enable us to say which is the right outcome, except within a range of possibilities. Within that range, various outcomes may be equally just. Rawls somewhat confusingly calls "quasi-pure" a procedure that ensures a choice within that range. More often than not, quasi-pure procedures may be the best we can arrive at. For example, even if a country were to adopt Rawls's famous two principles of justice as the proper criteria for legislation, "on many questions of social and economic policy," he concludes, "we must fall back upon a notion of quasi-pure procedural justice" (201). It may be helpful to put Rawls's categories into a table (table 12.1).

*Table 12.1. Procedural and Substantive Justice*

| Form of Procedural Justice | Independent Criterion? | A Perfect Procedure? |
|---|---|---|
| Perfect | yes | yes |
| Imperfect | yes | no |
| Pure | no | yes |
| Quasi-pure | yes | quasi[a] |

*Source:* Adapted from Rawls 1971, 85–86, 201.

[a]Indeterminate within a range of choices acceptable according to the criterion.

Let me read one of Rawls's conclusions, because I think he's dead right on this point:

Clearly any feasible political procedure may yield an unjust outcome. In fact, there is no scheme of procedural political rules which guarantees that unjust legislation will not be enacted. In the case of a constitutional regime, or indeed of any political form, the ideal of perfect procedural justice cannot be realized. The best attainable scheme is one of imperfect procedural justice. (198)

But even imperfect procedural justice may elude us. As Rawls admits, if his two principles of justice were adopted as constitutional principles, their generality would leave a large area of indeterminacy in their application to specific decisions. Consequently, as he says, the most we can often reasonably expect is his "quasi-pure procedural justice" (201). And if we can't discover independent principles for judging the outcomes, then we might have to fall back on pure procedure.

CRITIC: I hope you're not going to try to argue that a majority decision is such a procedure. You begin to sound like Rousseau when he says: "The general will is always right and always tends toward the public utility" (1978, bk. 2, chap. 3, p. 61). Surely you will admit that majorities have often done a lot of harm to minorities.

ADVOCATE: I'm not so foolish as to deny that. Nonetheless, I want to call your attention to a misleading implication in your comment. I wonder if you meant to imply that a procedure for making collective decisions is defective if it harms the interests of some persons; for by harming the interests of some persons it necessarily fails to give equal consideration to their interests. If so, I think your conclusion is mistaken. A collective decision that harms the interests of some people doesn't necessarily violate the principle of equal consideration of interests. In making collective decisions it's virtually impossible *not* to harm some of the interests of some persons. No solution, procedural or substantive, can guarantee that no one's interests will ever suffer in any way. Neither the democratic process nor any other feasible process for arriving at collective decisions can always, or even often, satisfy the requirement that no one should be made worse off. The important point is, however, that if the process by which these decisions are made gives equal consideration to the interests of everyone, then even though the interests of some persons were harmed the principle wouldn't be violated.

CRITIC: But now look what you're assuming: a perfect democratic process in which everyone gets equal consideration. But you know as well as I that political processes in all democratic countries are a long way from measuring up fully to the criteria of the democratic process. You seem to be talking about democracy in an ideal world, not democracy as we know it in the world we know.

ADVOCATE: I can't deny that politics in democratic countries isn't by any means perfectly democratic. In fact, that's a crucial point to keep in mind. I think advocates of substantive limitations on the democratic process often confound situations in which substantive injustice is the outcome of a well-functioning democratic process with situations in which injustice results from a failure of the decision process to meet democratic criteria. I agree that in the first case no solution consistent with the democratic process is attainable. In the second case, though, the best solution might be to achieve the democratic process more fully.

CRITIC: But it's the first case that I'm interested in. So far you have danced around it. Isn't it time you really faced up to it?

## THE DEMOCRATIC PROCESS VERSUS EQUAL CONSIDERATION

ADVOCATE: We're almost there. But when we do explore the significance of possible conflicts between substantive claims and the democratic process, I would like us to make a distinction between three different kinds of claims to a substantive interest or good:

1. The substantive interest is a right, entitlement, or other claim to something integral to the democratic process. By "integral" I mean that it is an essential part of the very conception of the democratic process itself, such as the right to free speech or freedom of assembly.
2. The substantive right or good is *external* to the democratic process but necessary to it. By "external" I mean that it is not a part of the conception of the process itself, yet it is essential to the proper functioning of the process. For example, from Aristotle onward political theorists have recognized that the functioning of democratic processes will be impaired if citizens are vastly unequal in economic means or in other crucial resources.
3. The substantive right or good is external to the democratic process and not necessary to it; but it is necessary if the Idea of Intrinsic Equality is to be respected. Thus a fair trial in criminal cases is not an element of the democratic process, and arguably is not necessary to it, but it is clearly necessary for equal consideration.

CRITIC: The last seems to me particularly important, because it opens up the possibility that the democratic process might sometimes violate one of its own assumptions, an assumption essential to its very justification as a process for collective decision. It might do so in two ways: (1) It might directly fail to provide equal consideration for the interests of all, by, for example, giving insufficient attention to the interests of the poor because they were less articulate, organized, and effective. (2) From the Idea of Intrinsic Equality we might be able to specify certain interests so fundamental that they just shouldn't be overridden, even by the democratic process.

## CLAIMS TO GOODS INTEGRAL TO THE DEMOCRATIC PROCESS

ADVOCATE: Naturally you've gone directly to the hardest case. But the others are important too. Suppose you could show that the substantively good outcome you seek is really an integral part of the democratic process itself: for example, a right to free speech. Then the conflict between the democratic process and the proper substantive outcomes would vanish. In this case, the solution is not to displace the democratic process but to bring it about or further perfect it.

The conflict between substantive outcomes and the democratic process would vanish if (1) majority rule in some form necessarily leads to the best substantive outcomes; (2) the substantive outcome in question is a right, privilege, opportunity, or obligation that is an integral part of the democratic process; or (3) insofar as the criterion of enlightened understanding is satisfied, the democratic process necessarily leads to the best substantive outcomes.

## Majority Rule

CRITIC: The first solution is surely wrong. At the outset I think we must both reject the view that we have no external criteria against which to judge majority decisions and therefore whatever the majority decides is necessarily right. If this were so, then majority rule would provide what Rawls termed "pure procedural justice." But this contention is ultimately self-defeating. For, if we have no external criteria by which to judge the actions of a majority, it follows that we also have no criteria by which to judge whether majority rule is superior to any alternative or indeed whether the democratic process is superior to any alternative, such as guardianship.

ADVOCATE: We do agree on that. I find it mindless to suppose that we could justify the democratic process on moral grounds if we believed that no moral grounds exist external to the process itself.

CRITIC: Then majority rule isn't a form of Rawls's "pure procedural justice"?

ADVOCATE: No, nor would I contend that it is "perfect procedural justice" either. It may be "imperfect" or "quasi-pure," in Rawls's terms. But look: the problem of majority rule is a bog through which we could trudge until we were both exhausted. I hope that we can manage to bypass most of that swampy terrain. It would help if we could agree that hereafter when we talk about majority decisions we mean decisions in which the votes of the greater number of citizens are entitled to prevail, though we leave open the tricky question whether this requires strict majority rule. I think we can agree that, under any reasonable interpretation of the democratic process, majorities would ordinarily be entitled to prevail over minorities in collective decisions. What we're both saying is that even in this loose sense majority rule doesn't always and necessarily lead to the best substantive outcomes.

CRITIC: And majorities may sometimes do harm to minorities?

ADVOCATE: As I said earlier, and since you didn't object I assumed you agreed, no process for making collective decisions—even if it attained perfect procedural justice—can always avoid harming the interests of some persons. Even Tocqueville, who saw majorities as a standing danger to fundamental liberties, nonetheless believed that "the moral power of the majority is founded upon . . . [the principle] . . . that the interests of the many are to be preferred to those of the few" (Tocqueville [1835] 1961, 1:300). The question is not whether majorities, acting by means of the democratic process, might sometimes harm the interests of a minority. They surely will. But the question is whether and how they may best be prevented from *wrongfully* harming the *fundamental* rights and interests of a minority.

CRITIC: Aren't you now saying that in some circumstances the right course of action doesn't depend on weighing its consequences for utility, pleasure, happiness or whatnot? Killing innocent persons, for example, can't be justified because killing them is necessary to some collective end. Likewise, it would be wrong to weigh fundamental rights or principles of justice on strictly utilitarian scales, where they might often be overbalanced by the utility gains of the majority (Dworkin 1978, 271; Rawls 1971, 22–27, 356–62). But in contending that certain basic rights and principles should be regarded as inviolable, and certainly should be inviolable by any political process, aren't you agreeing with me that they ought not to be violated by the democratic process?

## Rights

ADVOCATE: Yes, but when we come to the question of fundamental rights, the case for the democratic process is much stronger, and much stronger than people like you seem to appreciate. You critics who contend that substantive outcomes are superior to the democratic process often argue, especially in the United States, that citizens in a democracy possess "certain fundamental rights against their government." In the case of Americans, for example, these are said to include "certain moral rights made into legal rights by the Constitution" (Dworkin 1978, 191). The prototypical example is the right of free speech (192). Thus the right of free speech is often seen as a substantive claim superior to the democratic process and entitled to protection, if need be, against the democratic process. So too with a number of other fundamental political rights—exercising a vote in a free and fair election, freedom of the press, freedom of assembly, and so on. I would call this a *theory of prior rights*.

CRITIC: I'm inclined to that theory myself. I believe that many fundamental rights (including political rights) possess a moral standing, an ontological basis if you will, altogether independent of democracy and democratic processes. They serve as limits on what can be done, properly at least, by means of democratic processes. A citizen is entitled to exercise these rights, if need be, *against* the democratic process. Because the liberty they make possible is potentially threatened *by* the democratic process, to preserve fundamental political rights and liberties we ought to protect them from infringement even by means of the democratic process itself.

ADVOCATE: Your view is often called a theory of limited democracy, in supposed contrast to unlimited democracy. But I think that contrast is misleading.

CRITIC: But if you don't believe in limiting the democratic process, then obviously you believe that democracy doesn't have any proper limits.

ADVOCATE: I think that's a false contrast. The right to self-government through the democratic process is itself one of the most fundamental rights a person can possess. If any rights can be said to be inalienable, surely you'd agree that this must be among them. Consequently, any infringement of the right to self-government must necessarily violate a fundamental, inalienable right. But if people are entitled to govern themselves, then citizens are also entitled to all the rights that are necessary in order for them to govern themselves, that is, all the rights that are essential to the democratic process. On this reasoning, a set of basic political rights can be derived from one of the most fundamental of all the rights to which human beings are entitled: the right to self-government through the democratic process.

CRITIC: That has a very lofty sound to it, but a "right to self-government through the democratic process" is so general as to be meaningless. How can a right as general as that ever be enforced? I mean by a court of law, not by a revolution.

ADVOCATE: Of course the "right to self-government" is general. It's a general moral right, not a specific right enforceable by a court of law. But that general moral right translates into an array of moral *and* legal rights, many of which are specific and legally enforceable. To understand why this is so, consider the criteria for the democratic process. These necessarily require that persons affected by collective decisions possess certain rights; if the rights are absent, the criteria are not met and the democratic process does not exist. Each criterion specifies a broad moral right: a right to be included as a full citizen of the association engaged in making collective decisions to which one is subject; as a full citizen, rights to voting equality and equal opportunities for participating effectively in the process of decisionmaking, acquiring an enlightened understanding of one's personal interests, and exercising with other citizens final control over binding collective decisions.

In practice, each of these broad moral rights in turn requires a set of more specific rights, both moral and legal, such as a right to free expression. In some cases these more specific rights are essential not only to one but to several of the broad moral rights. Freedom of speech, for example, is necessary both for effective participation and for enlightened understanding; so too are freedom of the press and freedom of assembly. In large democratic systems the right to form political parties and other political associations is necessary to voting equality, effective participation, enlightenment, and final control over the agenda.

CRITIC: That's all very well but aren't you being rather formalistic? After all, what if a majority acting by perfectly democratic procedures deprives a minority of its freedom of speech?

ADVOCATE: But don't you see that in such a case the majority would not—could not—be acting by "perfectly democratic procedures"? These specific rights—let me call them *primary political rights*—are integral to the democratic process. They aren't ontologically separate from—or prior to, or superior to—the democratic process. To the extent that the democratic process exists in a political system, all the primary political rights must also exist. To the extent that primary political rights are absent from a system, the democratic process does not exist.

The upshot is that we don't confront a straightforward conflict between substantive rights and liberties on the one side and the democratic process on the other. For if democracy itself is a fundamental right, then a person's fundamental liberty consists, in part, of the opportunity to exercise that right. We've already agreed that in exercising its rights and liberties a majority may rightfully protect its interests against damage by a minority, though that means restricting the harmful activities of a minority.

But the democratic process isn't completely open-ended. If a majority were to deprive a minority, or even itself, of any of its primary political rights, then in the very act of doing so it would violate the democratic process. If the decision of the majority wasn't simply a mistake on their part, then it would necessarily be true that they weren't fully committed to the democratic process itself. Or, putting it the other way around, if citizens were committed to the democratic process, they would not, except perhaps by mistake, infringe on the primary political rights of any citizens.

CRITIC: Are you trying to say that majority tyranny is simply an illusion? If so, that is going to be small comfort to a minority whose fundamental rights are trampled on by an abusive majority. I think you need to consider seriously two possibilities: first, that a majority will infringe on the rights of a minority, and second, that a majority may oppose democracy itself.

ADVOCATE: Let's take up the first. The issue is sometimes presented as a paradox: If a majority is not entitled to do so, then it is thereby deprived of its rights; but if a majority is entitled to do so, then it can deprive the minority of *its* rights. The paradox is supposed to show that no solution can be both democratic and just. But the dilemma seems to me spurious.

Of course a majority might have the power or strength to deprive a minority of its political rights. In practice, though, I would guess that a powerful minority strips a majority of its political rights much more often than the other way round. But that's an empirical question, and it's not the issue we're discussing. The question is whether a majority may *rightly* use its primary political rights to deprive a minority of its primary political rights.

The answer is clearly no. To put it another way, logically it can't be true that the members of an association ought to govern themselves by the democratic process, and at the same time a majority of the association may properly strip a minority of its primary political rights. For, by doing so, the majority would deny the minority the rights necessary to the democratic process. In effect therefore the majority would affirm that the association ought not to govern itself by the democratic process. They can't have it both ways.

CRITIC: Your argument may be perfectly logical. But majorities aren't always perfectly logical. They may believe in democracy to some extent and yet violate its principles. Even worse, they may *not* believe in democracy and yet they may cynically use the democratic process to destroy democracy. In your theory of rights, what's to prevent people from deciding that they simply don't want to be governed by democratic processes? Mightn't they deliberately use the democratic process to replace democracy with a nondemocratic regime? Don't you now confront a paradox for which you have no solution? Either a people does not have the right to use the democratic process to destroy democracy, in which case it is unable to govern itself democratically, or it does have the right, in which case it may democratically choose to be governed by a dictator. In either case, the democratic process is bound to lose. Without some limits, both moral and constitutional, the democratic process becomes self-contradictory, doesn't it?

ADVOCATE: That's exactly what I've been trying to show. Of course democracy has limits. But my point is that these are built into the very nature of the process itself. If you exceed those limits, then you necessarily violate the democratic process. Let me explain what I mean by using your example of a majority that is hostile to democracy itself. Empirically, it's obviously true that people might choose to employ the democratic process to destroy that process. After all, if the democratic process exists it can hardly be an insuperable barrier to a majority doing so. The immediate question, however, is whether a demos may *rightfully* do what it clearly *can* do or, to use a different terminology, whether it has the authority to do what it has the power to do. Posed this way, the argument that a demos may rightfully employ the democratic process in order to destroy democracy is as badly conceived as the previous argument that a majority may rightfully deprive a minority of its rights. Since the two arguments are in essence the same, the dilemma is as spurious in the one case as in the other. If it's desirable that a people should govern itself democratically, then it cannot be desirable that it should be governed undemocratically. If people believe that democracy is desirable and justified, logically they can't simultaneously believe that it is undesirable and thereby justify the destruction of the democratic process.

Nothing in human experience tells us that democracy can't break down. But people committed to the democratic process would be bound, logically, to uphold the rights necessary to the democratic process. If they knowingly infringe on these rights they thereby declare that they want to reject the democratic process.

CRITIC: You continue to elude the point I've been trying to make. Your artful exercises in logic provide no more than feeble barriers to majority tyranny. Here we are again: We need institutional guarantees for substantive rights and results, not merely your formal procedures!

ADVOCATE: I couldn't agree more. In practice, though, the democratic process isn't likely to be preserved for very long unless the people of a country preponderantly believe that it's desirable and unless their belief comes to be embedded in their habits, practices, and culture. The relation between the democratic process and primary political rights isn't really terribly abstract. It's well within the reach of practical reason and common sense. Thinking about the requirements of their political system, a democratic people, its leaders, its intellectuals, and its jurists would see the practical need for primary political rights and would develop protections for them. As a result, among a people generally democratic in their commitments, a belief in the desirability of primary political rights might well become interwoven with their belief in democracy itself. In a stable democracy a commitment to the protection of all the primary political rights would become an essential element of the political culture, particularly as that culture was borne, interpreted, and transmitted by persons bearing a special responsibility for the interpretation and enforcement of rights—as jurists do, for example.

Unless the democratic process and the primary political rights necessary to it were supported in this way by the political culture of a people, it's unlikely that the democratic process would persist.

CRITIC: But maybe what's needed to ensure that it really does persist is a judiciary with the constitutional authority to uphold the fundamental rights no matter what the majority want.

ADVOCATE: When the democratic process can no longer be sustained in the face of a weak or hostile political culture, it strains credulity to believe that primary political rights will be preserved for long by courts or any other institution. Surely you aren't going to ask me to believe that a supreme court with authority to enforce substantive rights would have prevented the overthrow of democracy by the forces of dictatorship in Italy in 1923, Germany in 1933, Chile and Uruguay in 1973, and so on!

CRITIC: Even if no conflict exists between the democratic process and a broad array of fundamental rights necessary to it—the primary political rights— it's possible that in a moderately well-functioning democratic system supported by a democratic political culture, lapses may occur from time to time in protecting the primary political rights—free speech, for example. Isn't it also possible that an alternative process could correct these errors without greatly displacing the democratic process? Many Americans believe that just such a process exists in an independent judiciary with authority to declare unconstitutional legislation that infringes on constitutionally prescribed rights.

Your treatment of primary political rights also leaves open the possibility that the democratic process could harm *other* rights and interests beyond those counted among primary political rights. Earlier I suggested that the democratic process might violate the Principle of Intrinsic Equality either by failing to give equal consideration to the interests of all or by harming an interest so fundamental that it ought to be constitutionally inviolable. In this case, even while perfectly preserving every citizen's primary political rights and in other ways ensuring equal consideration, the democratic process would infringe upon an inviolable good, interest, or right.

## INTERESTS, ENLIGHTENMENT, AND FREE DISCUSSION

ADVOCATE: You people who insist that substantive outcomes ought to have priority over the democratic process must believe that you know what those outcomes ought to be. But what exactly entitles you to claim such superior knowledge? Don't you run aground on the same reef as the claim that guardianship is superior to democracy?

Ultimately your claim to knowing what substantive interests ought to be protected against the democratic process is self-contradictory. You could not possibly acquire knowledge of the interests of others, not to say your own, except through extensive acquaintance and discussion with others. The discussion would have to be free, unfettered, and uncoerced. But if such a discussion were to take place, then surely the others, unless severely impaired in cognitive capacities, would acquire an understanding of their interests fully as enlightened as yours. How then could you justify a claim to a more enlightened understanding of their interests than they would acquire themselves in the course of discussion?

CRITIC: You might be right if we all engaged in the free, unfettered, and uncoerced discussion you speak of. Unfortunately, we don't live in that kind of world.

ADVOCATE: I agree. The point I want to make, however, is that the democratic process is far superior in that respect to any alternative. While the criteria of the democratic process are of course never perfectly satisfied, they can be satisfactorily met only to the extent that citizens do possess opportunities for free, unfettered, and uncoerced discussion. No alternative to the democratic process proposes such a severe standard against which its performance is to be judged.

CRITIC: You keep circling around my main point. You continue to portray the democratic process in ideal terms. Yet you know as well as I that in actual practice political life in democratic countries never fully meets ideal standards for the democratic process. Often, maybe most of the time, actual practice falls very far short of the ideal. When that happens, even on your showing serious injustices may occur. The interests of some citizens simply are *not* given equal consideration. Even if there were no other violations of that principle, those cases surely require an alternative process to guarantee the right substantive outcomes.

ADVOCATE: If I have seemed to avoid your point, it's because I wanted you to see that much of the conflict that you suppose to exist between process and substance is not truly a conflict between substantive justice or right and the democratic process. On the contrary, it reflects a failure of the democratic process. That conclusion is not merely of theoretical significance. It's of practical importance, for it informs us that the solution may not be to impose limits on the democratic process or to guarantee the right outcomes by means of an alternative and presumably less democratic process. The solution may be instead to improve the operation of the democratic process: to make it more truly democratic.

CRITIC: It's obvious to me that we haven't yet confronted the main differences between us. Early in our discussion you suggested that we distinguish between three different kinds of rights or goods. So far we've talked only about substantive rights and goods *integral* to the democratic process itself, assuming that the process comes reasonably close to meeting its criteria. Your last point reminds me, however, that we still need to consider the question of feasibility. What you say about improving the democratic process is all very well as an ideal goal, but in practice that solution may be less feasible than, say, a set of constitutional guarantees and a supreme court with the final authority to interpret them.

Second, you haven't confronted the problem raised by substantive rights or goods *external* to the democratic process but necessary to it. I think I can see the makings of a nice paradox there.

Third, you haven't confronted the problem of rights or goods external to the democratic process, and not necessary to it, but necessary if the Idea of Intrinsic Equality and the Principle of Equal Consideration of Interests are to be upheld.

You mentioned as an example a fair trial in criminal cases, and I could probably furnish others.

◆

Although the discussion between Advocate and Critic breaks off at this point leaving some crucial problems unsolved, before turning to these in the next chapter I want to emphasize the importance of Advocate's argument.

The supposed failure of the democratic process to guarantee desirable substantive outcomes is in important respects spurious. We need to reject, as Advocate does, the familiar contrast between substance and process. For integral to the democratic process are substantive rights, goods, and interests that are often mistakenly thought to be threatened by it.

Among these is the right to self-government by means of the democratic process. This is no trivial right but one so fundamental that the authors of the American Declaration of Independence called it inalienable. Nor is the right to self-government a right to a "merely formal process," for the democratic process is neither "merely process" nor "merely formal." The democratic process is not "merely process," because it is also an important kind of distributive justice. For it helps to determine the distribution of the crucial resources of power and authority and thereby influences the distribution of all other crucial resources as well. The right to the democratic process is not "merely formal," because in order to exercise this right all the resources and institutions necessary to it must exist; To the extent that these are absent the democratic process itself does not exist. Nor is the right to the democratic process "merely an abstract claim." It is instead a claim to all the general and specific rights—moral, legal, constitutional—that are necessary to it, from freedom of speech, press, and assembly to the right to form opposition political parties. That authoritarian rulers bend every effort to destroy all the institutions necessary to the democratic process demonstrates how fully aware they are that the democratic process is not "merely formal" but would lead a structural transformation of their regimes.

Viewed in this way the democratic process endows citizens with an extensive array of rights, liberties, and resources sufficient to permit them to participate fully, as equal citizens, in the making of all the collective decisions by which they are bound. If adult persons must participate in collective decisions in order to protect their personal interests, including their interests as members of a community, to develop their human capacities, and to act as self-determining, morally responsible beings, then the democratic process is necessary to these ends as well. Seen in this light, the democratic process is not only essential to one of the most important of all political goods—the right of people to govern themselves—but is itself a rich bundle of substantive goods.

# Chapter 13

◆◆◆◆◆◆◆◆◆

# Process versus Process

The conclusion of the last chapter does not eliminate the possibility that the democratic process may impair important important substantive rights or other requirements of justice. As Critic pointed out, it might do so in three ways. First, some groups, possibly a majority, might employ an imperfect democratic process to violate rights essential to the democratic process—free speech, for example. Since in practice the exacting criteria of the democratic process are never fully met, even the best democracies are sure to be imperfect. Second, rights and goods external to the process, but necessary to it, may be inadequately protected. For example, illiteracy, poverty, and low status may deny some citizens equal and adequate opportunities to participate in decisions. Third, decisions made by a democratic process, perfect or imperfect, might nonetheless injure rights, interests, or goods not necessary to the democratic process but required by the principle of equal intrinsic worth. For example, alleged criminals might not be ensured a fair trial. These three possibilities I want to call, in shorthand, "violations" or "failures."

However, if we assume, as realism demands, that collective decisions need to be made, then any alternative to a perfect or imperfect democratic process for making collective decisions will require some *other* process for making collective decisions. We saw in the last chapter that what appeared to be a simple and straightfoward conflict between process and substance actually involves a much more complex conflict between one set of substantive goods and other possible goods. What we now see is that reasonable solutions to these conflicts will require weighing the values of the democratic process against the values of an alternative process. What began as substance versus process turns out to be process versus process. What process for making collective decisions can be counted on to achieve the best substantive results? Do feasible alternatives exist that would provide better solutions than the democratic process?

As Advocate insisted, it would be wrong to displace the democratic process only

*176*

because it sometimes fails to achieve morally right results. It would be wrong to displace the democratic process if its failures could be corrected by a feasible improvement in the process. Even if they could not, it would be wrong unless a feasible alternative with a significantly greater likelihood of success could be put in its place.

To put these points more schematically, the failures of the democratic process to achieve desirable substantive results can be corrected in only four ways. (1) The democratic regime could be replaced by a different kind of regime. But since we have rejected this option, I am going to assume that the point is not to replace democracy with an alternative political system. Instead, a feasible alternative would have to be designed to rectify only certain specific decisions, laws, or policies within a largely democratic system. Thus (2) an imperfect democratic process might be improved. Or (3) specific failures resulting from the democratic process (perfect or imperfect) might be rectified by a nondemocratic process. Or finally, (4) if neither (2) nor (3) were feasible, some level of violation might be accepted as a tolerable price for the advantages of the democratic process. If the price were thought to be too high, however, then the only option would be to reconsider (1).

## THE INEVITABLE IMPERFECTIONS IN DEMOCRATIC PERFORMANCE

In the actual world, as Advocate and Critic agree, "democracies" are never fully democratic: they invariably fall short of democratic criteria in some respects. Yet our judgment about feasible alternatives depends in part on how well the democratic process functions in practice. A solution that would be appropriate for a country in which democracy functions barely and badly we might reasonably reject for a country where the democratic process functions well.

Evidently we need to have some concrete systems in view. What are they to be? I propose that the systems in view should be the set of countries that we ordinarily count as "democracies." Because this solution may strike some readers as vague and arbitrary, let me anticipate later chapters once again by saying that what I mean by a "democratic" country is one in which the government of the state is a poly-archy. As we shall see later, a polyarchy is a regime with a unique set of political institutions that, taken together, distinguish it from other regimes. Polyarchies may be thought of as governments in which the institutions necessary to the democratic process exist above a certain threshold. Although polyarchies are the most complete historical achievement of the democratic process on the large scale of the nation-state, what polyarchies have achieved is far from complete judged by the criteria of the democratic process in chapter 8. As a system of real world large-scale democracy, polyarchy is the best so far, but by ideal standards it is second-best.

Our question is, then, how substantive failures might best be corrected in a country where the government of the state is a polyarchy, that is, an imperfect democracy. Our four possible solutions now become: (1) to replace polyarchy with nonpolyarchy; (2) to improve the performance of polyarchy; (3) in specific cases of failure to replace the imperfect democratic processes of polyarchy with a feasible nondemocratic alternative, such as a supreme court; (4) if none of these is feasible, to continue to make the relevant collective decisions through the imperfect democracy of polyarchy.

Many readers may wonder at this point whether any general treatment of our problem, taking polyarchies as a class, can be very illuminating or whether instead the most crucial elements of a solution will be found, as I am inclined to think they will, in the particularities of a specific country. But if we keep that caveat in mind, it is useful, I think, to consider some of the general aspects of the problem. Further dialogue between Advocate and Critic may help to illuminate these.

## VIOLATIONS OF RIGHTS AND GOODS EXTERNAL TO THE DEMOCRATIC PROCESS BUT NECESSARY TO IT

CRITIC: Although you have dealt at length with the question of rights or goods integral to the democratic process itself, so far you've failed to confront the possibility that failures or violations might occur with respect to rights and goods external to the democratic process but necessary to it.

ADVOCATE: I'm not sure what you have in mind.

CRITIC: Do you agree that in order for the democratic process to be fully achieved, certain conditions must exist?

ADVOCATE: That's perfectly obvious.

CRITIC: Then what are these conditions?

ADVOCATE: Well, ideally citizens would engage in political life as political equals. As I said earlier, for citizens to be political equals would require that they have all the rights, obligations, and opportunities implied by the criteria of the democratic process. But—and this I think is what you're asking for—those rights, duties, opportunities, and so on could not exist unless, for example, many crucial political resources were distributed pretty equally among them. I have in mind the degree of equality that Tocqueville thought he had found among Americans in the 1830s or anyway among adult white male citizens. I mean property, wealth, income, education, social status, information, and the like.

CRITIC: Are there other conditions?

ADVOCATE: As I mentioned a while ago, democracy couldn't exist if people didn't believe in it. In fact, Tocqueville put beliefs, mores, habits as even more important than the Constitution and the laws, because without the support of beliefs legal systems would become meaningless, as he thought they were in some countries of South America in his time.

CRITIC: So to the extent that beliefs, socioeconomic equalities, and other essential conditions are lacking, then a process for making collective decisions is bound to be less than perfectly democratic?

ADVOCATE: That is undeniably so.

CRITIC: And is it not also undeniable that what we call polyarchy is an imperfect or second-best democracy because the conditions necessary to a perfect democratic process do not exist?

ADVOCATE: Absolutely!

CRITIC: But why don't the necessary conditions exist? Would you agree that they don't exist for one of two reasons: either because the conditions are impossible and simply can't be brought about or because, though they are possible, they have not been brought about?

ADVOCATE: I don't see how I could quarrel with such a self-evident proposition.

CRITIC: And why haven't they been brought about? Either a majority of citizens would like to bring them about but can't do so because of imperfections in the democratic process or a majority of citizens don't wish to bring them about. Isn't that so?

ADVOCATE: Your logical argument would find favor with a medieval philosopher. Yes, I think you must be correct so far.

CRITIC: Yet if imperfections in the democratic process prevent a majority of citizens from bringing about the necessary conditions for political equality, then wouldn't the only way to bring them about be through some nondemocratic process? Likewise, if a majority of citizens don't want to create the conditions necessary for the democratic process, then isn't it also true that the necessary conditions can't be created except by a nondemocratic process?

ADVOCATE: I suppose they can't, at least in the short run. In the long run, beliefs do change. But I think you have neatly constructed a trap that will catch your own argument. Take the first alternative you just proposed. In that case, the minority that is capable of preventing the majority from governing must also be opposed to further democratization. So these putative guardians surely can't be counted on to bring about greater democracy. In the second case, the minority favorable to greater democratization would have to impose its rule on the reluctant majority. Paraphrasing Rousseau, the minority would have to force the majority to be free. But in a generally democratic system, I don't see how that would be politically feasible. The upshot is that, while you have nicely stated a problem, you have blocked the possibility of a feasible solution.

CRITIC: Who is now the scholastic? You have just proved by abstract reasoning that the U.S. Supreme Court does not exist. Congratulations!

ADVOCATE: We may differ on whether the Supreme Court really disproves my argument.

CRITIC: I'm sure we do disagree on that point. But if you are right, then aren't you also left without a solution?

ADVOCATE: No, I still have two. First, I'm prepared to accept some failures and violations as a tolerable price to pay for the democratic process, even in its imperfect realization. You might call that a nonsolution, but your nonsolution could be my solution. Second, a moment ago when I agreed with you about the short run, I brought up the possibility of long-run changes in public opinion. I think that public opinion in democratic countries tends to move toward an ever more inclusive commitment to ideas like intrinsic equality and equal consideration.

Democratic cultures have considerable capacity for correcting their own failures. And in the long run general opinion does generally prevail in democratic countries.

CRITIC: I can see that the differences between us may turn on practical judgments about the feasibility of alternative solutions, not on more theoretical questions. But we still have the third type of failure to consider: injury to a fundamental interest, good, or right that is neither integral to the democratic process nor essential to its proper functioning.

## INTERESTS NOT ESSENTIAL TO THE DEMOCRATIC PROCESS

In the last chapter, Advocate argues that people like Critic, who insist that substantive outcomes should have priority over the democratic process, need to explain how they know what these outcomes ought to be. Advocate's remarks suggest three questions. The first is epistemological. How can we *know* what a person's interests are, particularly a person's "fundamental" interests? The second is substantive. It is all very well to speak airily of interests so fundamental that they should be inviolable by the democratic process (or any other), but concretely, *what* are these interests and on what grounds do we justify their inviolability? The third is procedural or institutional. What *processes* or *institutions* can best be counted on to protect these interests?

### How Can We Know?

One argument in defense of the democratic process asserts that the first question has no rationally justifiable answer. At the same time, however, it attempts to disarm the antidemocratic potentialities of this position by assuming it as a starting point: (1) If no moral claim is more valid than any other, then all such claims are on an equal footing. (2) But if all claims are on an equal footing, all persons who advance different claims are also on an equal footing: No one can be reasonably regarded as superior or inferior to another in the validity of his or her claims. (3) Hence everyone should participate as an equal in the process of arriving at a consensus. (4) And decisions that depend on moral claims should therefore be arrived at by a participatory process eventuating, ideally at least, in consensus.[1]

A lethal defect in an argument of this kind, as some critics of complete moral skepticism have insisted, is that it is self-defeating. If no moral proposition is better than any other, then (3) and (4), which surely are (or directly depend on) moral assumptions, are no better than any other. In short, why *should* people participate as equals? Would it not be just as reasonable to say that, since no moral statement is superior to another, to assert (3) and (4) is no more justified than to assert that the stronger should prevail?

Still, the question persists. How can we know what a person's interests are? Like both Critic and Advocate I reject the view that all claims to moral understanding are inherently invalid. I propose to say instead:

*A person's interest or good is whatever that person would choose with fullest attainable understanding of the experience resulting from that choice and its most relevant alternatives.*

To say that it is in A's interest to have a fair trial in criminal cases is equivalent to saying that if A understood the consequences of having or not having a fair trial he would insist on a fair trial.

The criterion of enlightened understanding can now be given more substance by interpreting it to mean that persons who understand their interests in the sense just given possess an enlightened understanding of their interests.[2] By saying the "fullest attainable understanding" I have deliberately drawn back from the abyss of impossibility into which we would be drawn by saying "full understanding," since full understanding presumably would require one to undergo the actual experience itself, as well as its relevant alternatives, which is, in a strict sense, impossible in advance.[3]

But is the definition vacuous? If not, how are we to apply it to another person? We can do so only by a process of enlightened sympathy through which we try to grasp the desires, wants, needs, and values of other human beings, and, by a thought experiment, try to imagine what they would choose to do if they understood the consequences of their choices. To the extent that we succeed in this effort, we possess an enlightened understanding of the interests of others. However, since we ourselves are limited by our own understanding, our thought experiments are inherently imperfect—based on our own inadequate knowledge and biased by our own views, convictions, and passions. Even our enlightened understanding is fallible.

Should we reject the idea of enlightened sympathy because of its inescapable fallibility? Does enlightened sympathy compel us to make judgments that are in any case impossible for us to make? The fact is that we do make judgments about the interests of others. What is more, we distinguish between reasonable and unreasonable judgments about the interests of others. How could we justify parental authority if we believed it impossible for parents to make better judgments about the interests of their children than the children themselves? In making such judgments we assume that we can employ enlightened sympathy. We also assume we can do so when, for example, we attempt to judge whether certain adults are so incapable of attending to their own basic interests that they should be placed under the care of a paternalistic authority. We also use enlightened sympathy post hoc in order to judge whether those charged with paternalistic authority have properly used their authority or abused it. Presumably, too, we use enlightened sympathy when we try to dissuade other adults—a family member or a friend, perhaps— from engaging in a course of action that we believe they will come to regret. Except by monstrously deforming our ordinary, everyday, garden variety human qualities we cannot avoid making judgments about the interests of others or reject enlightened sympathy as a means for doing so.

What I have just said is meant to be a solution to the epistemological problem of interests: how we can know what they are. One might wonder how this solution bears on the Presumption of Personal Autonomy, which, as I pointed out earlier, is not an epistemological assumption but a prudential rule to be employed in making collective decisions. But suppose we were confident that all citizens actually do base their judgments in collective decisions on an enlightened understanding of their interests, including their concerns for others and for their community. How then could we possibly justify saying that what A is choosing is not in A's interests? To do so would presuppose that we possess privileged knowledge, not accessible to A, of an absolute standard independent of A's own enlightened understanding of her desires, wants, needs, and ideal values. But, as I have already said, in the past century all attempts to prove such a claim have crumbled under the attacks of their critics. Given the assumption of enlightened understanding, an appeal beyond A's own judgments to a higher court of independent judges armed with superior knowledge of A's good could never be justified.

Conversely, however, if we cannot assume that all citizens are guided by an enlightened understanding of their interests, then the claim to personal autonomy in determining what is best for oneself can hardly be treated as an epistemological principle. And it is precisely because we cannot assume that citizens are invariably guided by an enlightened understanding of their interests that the presumption of personal autonomy in collective decisions is not an epistemological assumption but only a prudential rule.

## What Interests Are Superior to the Democratic Process?

What interests, then, can be justifiably claimed to be inviolable by the democratic process or, for that matter, any other process for making collective decisions? It seems to me highly reasonable to argue that *no* interests should be inviolable beyond those integral or essential to the democratic process. A democratic people would not invade this extensive domain except by mistake; and such a people might also choose to create institutional safeguards designed to keep mistakes from occurring. But outside this broad domain a democratic people could freely choose the policies its members feel best; they could decide how best to balance freedom and control, how best to settle conflicts between the interests of some and the interests of others, how best to organize and control their economy, and so on. In short, outside the inviolable interests of a democratic people in the preservation of the democratic process would lie the proper sphere for political decisions. By means of the democratic process and all the requirements of that process, citizens would maximize their collective freedom to decide on the laws and principles under which they wished to live.

It is quite natural for A to feel that all *his* most deeply cherished interests and goals should be inviolable. And for B to make a similar claim. And C . . . Members of a highly privileged group are likely to claim that their interests surely ought to be inviolable, particularly since, in their view, their interests coincide with the interests of the society as a whole. Not surprisingly, therefore, property rights are often asserted to be prior or superior to the democratic process. Members of a disadvantaged group may also lay claim to a superior interest that ought to be advanced by other means if the democratic process fails to do so.

As Advocate insists, in protecting or advancing the interests of some persons, collective decisions generally harm the interests of others. Decisions on public issues are in large part decisions about allocating costs and gains, benefit and harm. In these contests it is highly advantageous to any group to succeed in putting its interests beyond the reach of collective decisions or, failing that, within the reach of a body of decisionmakers who are beyond the reach of the democratic process. But, given the extensive range of rights, interests, goods, and protections built into the democratic process, how can we reasonably justify going beyond the reach of that process?

Although I find this view attractive, it leaves open a disturbing question. Can we truly say that human beings have no inviolable interests beyond their right to the democratic process and whatever is essential to it? For example, does not everyone have a right to a fair trial in criminal cases? If so, should not this right be inviolable even by the democratic process? These questions bring us back almost full circle to the third question I posed a moment ago. If certain rights or interests ought to be treated as inviolable and therefore superior to the democratic process itself, what process or institutions can best be counted on to protect them?

This question moves the argument to entirely different ground. Because we now confront a conflict between fundamental rights, we need to find a process for resolving that conflict. If people possess a fundamental right to self-government, then would it not be wrong to impair that right by placing restrictions on the scope of the democratic process, beyond the requirements of the process itself? When the right to the democratic process conflicts with another fundamental right, by what process should the conflict be decided? To offer a purely philosophical answer, such as that one must be balanced against another, is not enough. The conflict must be dealt with (I do not say settled) by a decisionmaking process of some kind—a "political" process in the broad sense of the term. And presumably that process would be embedded in political institutions.

Thus what begins by posing substance as an alternative to process must sooner or later turn to practical judgments about feasible alternative processes.

## SOME PROCESSES

Drawing on the distinctions employed by Advocate and Critic, we can imagine that the democratic process might injure three types of interests: interests integral to the democratic process, interests not integral to it but necessary to its functioning, and interests neither integral to it nor necessary to its functioning. What kinds of institutional arrangements might be adopted in order to prevent violations of these kinds? I propose to examine four general solutions.

If four solutions can be called on to deal with three types of possible violations, then formally speaking we have at least twelve possible arrangements. Despite this plethora of possibilities in our theoretical universe, the fact that each solution is of a general character and not tailored to a concrete situation provides grounds for thinking that specific solutions will depend less on theoretical considerations than on practical judgments about what is appropriate to a particular country, given its political culture, historical development, and constitutional structure. General principles can take us only so far, and we are rapidly approaching the limits of their usefulness. My purpose now, therefore, is to point out the four general solutions and to mention some of the problems associated with each.

Critics who insist on the primacy of substantive outcomes over the democratic process are prone to assume that, since the democratic process cannot guarantee the results they want, it must therefore be superseded by an alternative to it, which must necessarily, then, be a nondemocratic alternative. But as Advocate pointed out in the last chapter, this conclusion is unwarranted, since the best solution may sometimes be to improve the democratic process. I want therefore to mention three democratic solutions and one alternative nondemocratic solution.

## Expanding or Reducing the Demos

In some circumstances violations of fundamental rights or interests might be minimized by changing the composition of the citizen body, either by inclusion or by exclusion, by enlarging it or by reducing it. Because I have assumed that the democratic process is in place, the problem could not be solved by enlarging the citizen body; for a minority whose rights were invaded by laws adopted by a majority would be, by assumption, already included in the demos. It is nonetheless worth pausing to take note that probably the worst invasions of fundamental rights, including of course the primary political rights themselves, result when those who are subject to the laws of the demos are excluded from it. In these cases extending the democratic process is often exactly the right solution: Let the demos be expanded to include those who are excluded yet harmed by laws to which they are subject. Exercising their political rights, the newly included members may now succeed in modifying laws injurious to their fundamental rights.

But suppose the injured citizens are a minority and the majority does not respond? Sometimes the solution lies in allowing such a minority to form its own democratic unit. This solution may be appropriate when the minority is well defined, conflict between majority and minority is persistent, and the majority principle allows the majority to infringe upon some right the minority believes to be of transcendent importance. In a separate democratic unit, the members of the onetime minority can now govern themselves without infringing upon the majority principle, which, if they choose, they now can apply among themselves. As for the members of the earlier majority, they continue to govern themselves, but they no longer govern over the now autonomous minority. At one extreme, this solution may require complete independence: One state becomes two. At the other extreme, only authority over certain specific questions is decentralized: For example, the majority and the minority each form separate local governments with narrowly restricted authority.

This solution is not only perfectly consistent with the democratic process, but by making it possible for more citizens to achieve their goals and to choose their own laws it can also increase freedom and self-determination. Yet emotional ties—feelings of nationalism, for example—may prevent a majority from accepting this solution. What is more, it would not necessarily be a desirable solution if the freedom gained by the new demos, the previous minority, enabled it to act in ways harmful to the good of the majority now excluded from the smaller demos.

## Voting, Election, and Legislative Procedures

Sometimes the best solution may be to design voting, election, or legislative procedures that will protect the interests of a minority or of minorities generally.

As we saw in chapter 10, the claim that strict majority rule is the only principle of decisionmaking consistent with the democratic process and its assumptions is highly suspect. Moreover, a variety of voting arrangements, each with quite different consequences, can reasonably claim to achieve political equality.[4] Of course we have yet to confront the crucial question we take up in the next chapter, a question that is implicit in the solution of changing the unit: majority of what unit? Because the criteria of the democratic process do not prescribe a unique arrangement of voting and election procedures, these create a rich field of opportunities for minimizing violations of fundamental interests without impairing the democratic process.

So too with legislative procedures. It is a common practice for democratic bodies to impose procedures on themselves that help to ensure that they act carefully, not hastily; wisely, not foolishly. These procedures often delegate to some minority the authority to halt, delay, or modify what might otherwise be enacted by simple, untrammeled majority rule. Accepting a moral obligation to respect certain fundamental rights, sensitive to its own frailties, concerned that it might act unwisely, a demos might therefore adopt procedures of this kind as a means of protecting fundamental rights.

Experience suggests a vast array of possibilities. Although in most polyarchies today second chambers serve mainly to rectify errors in measures passed by the other house, a second chamber that represents or reflects different interests from the first has sometimes been recommended, as it was at the American Constitutional Convention, as a bastion of minority rights and a barrier to majority tyranny. So too has the qualified veto given to a chief executive by many constitutions. Voting rules in a legislative body may also have the same end: By requiring a special majority such as two-thirds, the procedures grant a minority the power to prevent legislation it holds objectionable.

Whenever it is not feasible or desirable to solve the problem by expanding the demos or changing the democratic unit, arrangements like these may be the best solution. For, if the demos effectively retains its final authority over its own procedures, then these procedures do not violate democratic criteria. Indeed, they may help to satisfy the criterion of enlightened understanding by making it more likely that a majority will understand the consequences of its actions better before it finally decides to enact and enforce a law, policy, or principle.

In practice, however, arrangements like these carry two serious risks. First, it is all but impossible to ensure that these special arrangements are employed by a minority solely to protect their fundamental rights. Generally, the arrangements grant some minority the power to modify the decisions of the majority on questions of *policy* in ways that a majority of citizens would not, on reflection, choose; or the arrangements are used to protect rights of minorities at the expense of equally valid or superior rights of majorities. Many of the framers of the American Constitution, for example, seem to have believed that in order to preserve fundamental rights the president needed a veto over legislation enacted by the Congress, a veto that could be overridden only by a two-thirds majority in each house. But from the beginning American presidents have regularly used their power to veto *policies* of which they disapprove; no one contends that the president uses, indeed probably no one today contends that the president should use, the veto exclusively on legislation demonstrably invading fundamental rights. Likewise it was argued both at the convention and later that in order to protect the rights of minorities each state ought to be equally represented in the Senate, even though this requirement necessarily means unequal representation for individual citizens. Yet the extra weight given small states in relation to their population has rarely if ever served to protect primary political or social rights.

The second grave drawback to these procedures is that in practice it is often extraordinarily difficult for a majority to alter them when a minority abuses the power it enjoys thanks to the special procedures. For example, the rules of the United States Senate make it difficult, and for a number of years made it virtually impossible, to cut off unlimited debate. A few determined and suitably long-winded senators could not only block legislation supported by the president, a large majority of senators, the House, and the country but could also prevent remedial changes in the procedures themselves. Contrary to the argument that the right to unlimited debate is essential to the protection of fundamental rights, in the Senate unlimited debate was used for generations to prevent the passage of legislation intended to protect the fundamental rights of blacks. Yet the very rules that enabled a minority of senators to defeat civil rights legislation supported by a majority—sometimes a preponderant majority—of senators were also used to defeat majority proposals to alter the rules.

Thus one problem with special procedures is that they rarely can be counted on to work as they should in order to be acceptable according to democratic criteria, that is, to ensure delegation but prevent alienation of final control by the demos. Insofar as special procedures do satisfy democratic criteria and final control over the agenda is retained by the demos, or a majority thereof, then in a strict sense they do not solve the problem with which we began: how to protect fundamental rights and interests from violation by the democratic process if those rights or interests are invaded by means of the democratic process.

## The Evolution of Public Opinion

If neither changing the demos nor designing special voting, election, or legislative procedures is sufficient, then another possible solution may be to rely on the evolution of public opinion. Our Critic would no doubt reject this idea at once, saying that since public opinion is precisely the problem it can hardly be the solution. But this would be too hasty a view.

In later chapters (17 and 18), we shall see how and why the attempt to apply the democratic process to the large scale of the nation-state sometimes succeeded and sometimes failed. In some countries the institutions of polyarchy evolved more or less steadily, took root, and endured. We encountered these twenty or so countries in a previous chapter, where they were called stable polyarchies. By contrast, in most countries, polyarchy has not developed. In some, where the institutions have developed recently, they remain precarious or uncertain. In others, they came into being and then broke down, in a few cases to be restored once again.

In the historical development of the first group, the stable polyarchies, we can detect a rough pattern in the evolution of public opinion—an evolution, it should be stressed, without which stable polyarchy could not have developed. (What I offer now is intended as a loose empirical account, not a normative argument.) The experience of these countries reveals that with the passage of time the protection of fundamental rights and interests is deepened and expanded, and violations earlier supported by public opinion prove in due time to become unacceptable. In this sense, the Idea of Intrinsic Equality, which requires equal consideration of the interests of all who are subject to the laws, has steadily gained strength as an element in the constitutional consensus and political culture. In saying this I do not mean to overlook the shortfalls and violations of the principle, the frustrating slowness with which grave injustices are corrected, and the occasional regressive moves. But in taking a longer view, the general historical movement in these countries has been toward an expansion of the institutional protections for many fundamental rights and interests. Were this not so, they would never have become polyarchies, much less stable polyarchies. But the evolution has not stopped with the rights and opportunities necessary to the institutions of polyarchy but has also gone on to include social and economic rights and guarantees and many other rights and interests (see Marshall 1950 for Britain).

I do not mean to suggest that this evolution comes about as a result of nothing more than well-mannered philosophical debate. On the contrary, it comes about after struggle and contestation, often protracted and sometimes laced with violence and dangers to the stability of the polyarchy (or emerging polyarchy) itself. In this process of struggle and contestation, the belief in intrinsic equality and the right to equal consideration grows ever deeper roots; discriminations of all kinds are ever more under attack; what is accepted as a proper distinction by a majority of citizens at one time is perceived as arbitrary and unfair by a later majority, quite possibly a majority of a demos that previous battles over the suffrage have succeeded in expanding to include those whose rights had hitherto suffered invasion.

The historical record thus lends considerable support to the argument that, given time, in a country with a generally democratic culture public opinion may rectify blatant disregard for the equal consideration of interests. Yet our Critic is unlikely to be persuaded that the slow evolution of public opinion in a democratic country is a sufficient guarantee. And if it is not, and other democratic solutions are insufficient, then we must turn to nondemocratic solutions.

## Quasi Guardianship

If fundamental rights and interests cannot be adequately protected by means consistent with the democratic process, then the remaining alternative is to ensure their protection by officials not subject to the democratic process. Because these officials would make their decisions within the context of a generally democratic system, yet would not be democratically controlled, they might be called quasi guardians. The most common form of quasi guardianship in democratic countries is a judiciary with final authority over certain substantive and procedural protections. The finality of the judicial decision is ordinarily derived from its authority to declare unconstitutional legislation enacted by the parliament—what Americans call "judicial review." Of twenty-one stable polyarchies, thirteen have some form of judicial review (cf. table 11.7, supra).

Probably the best-known exemplar of the solution of judicial quasi guardianship is the American federal judiciary, and in particular the U.S. Supreme Court, which since 1803 has successfully asserted its claim to authority to declare legislation unconstitutional, therefore not law, and thus not binding. In no other democratic country are the courts as powerful an instrument for imposing collective decisions as are the federal courts in the United States. Elsewhere, even though the courts may be constitutionally entitled to exercise judicial review, typically they are more cautious about striking down laws enacted by parliament. To protect fundamental rights and interests, in most stable polyarchies citizens rely mainly on the democratic process as reflected in parliament, elections, and sometimes national referenda.

Accustomed as they are to the key role of the courts, most Americans, including most lawyers,[5] tend to take for granted that a vigilant judiciary empowered and willing to strike down national policies adopted by the national legislature and executive is essential to the preservation of fundamental rights. Even if confronted by the fact that stable polyarchies exist without judicial review, many informed Americans would be inclined to argue, I suspect, that the American solution ought to be seen not as unique but rather as a general solution to the problem of protecting inviolable rights and interests. How satisfactory, then, is the solution of quasi guardianship by the judiciary?

American and comparative experience, together with more general considerations, seem to me to justify the following judgments about quasi guardianship as a general solution.

1. There is necessarily an inverse ratio between the authority of the quasi guardians and the authority of the demos and its representatives. If the authority of the quasi guardians were comprehensive, then the demos would alienate its control over the agenda of public affairs and the democratic process would be gutted. Even if the authority of the guardians were restricted solely to certain questions of fundamental rights and interests, on these matters the demos would necessarily alienate its control. On questions within a narrower range, the inverse ratio still holds: The broader the scope of rights and interests subject to final decision by the quasi guardians, the narrower must be the scope of the democratic process. Moreover, even within a restricted range the power of the quasi guardians may be more than merely negative, more than a veto of unconstitutional laws. As the experience of the U.S. Supreme Court shows (in school desegregation, for example), in

seeking to enforce superior rights and interests a court may find it necessary to go beyond mere negative restraints and attempt to lay down positive policies, sometimes in great detail. From preventing the execution of policies it decides are harmful to fundamental rights, a court may be impelled to move on to imposing policies it judges are necessary to fundamental rights and the common good. The broader the scope of the rights and interests the quasi guardians are authorized to protect, the more they must take on the functions of making law and policy.

2. In federal systems, a standard solution is a high court with authority to strike down laws of the lower federal units that violate the national constitution. However, only a minority of stable polyarchies are federal; a substantial majority are unitary. In about half the unitary systems the judiciary is denied authority to declare parliamentary acts unconstitutional.[6] Even in a federal system the courts might be denied the power to declare unconstitutional laws passed by the national parliament; their authority to do so could be restricted only to laws passed by the lower units. Such, in fact, is the solution adopted by the Swiss (Codding 1961, 33, 105–06, 112).

3. To demonstrate that a judiciary with the power to negate laws passed by the *national* legislature is essential to the protection of fundamental rights in democratic orders would require showing one of two things. Either the democratic countries in which courts lack such powers are not really democratic or at any rate are not as democratic as the United States or in these countries fundamental rights are less well protected than in the United States. No one has shown that countries like the Netherlands and New Zealand, which lack judicial review, or Norway and Sweden, where it is exercised rarely and in highly restrained fashion, or Switzerland, where it can be applied only to cantonal legislation, are less democratic than the United States, nor, I think, could one reasonably do so.

4. It has not been shown either that fundamental rights and interests are better protected in polyarchies with judicial quasi guardianship than in polyarchies without it. Presumably in a country without quasi guardians the demos and its representatives would have to exercise more self-restraint. In such a country, a fundamental right or interest would have to be recognized as a norm, and the norm would have to be enforced by social and political processes rather than by legal restraints imposed on the parliament by judicial guardians. Quasi guardianship may therefore require less self-restraint on the part of the demos and its representatives and more externally imposed restraint by judicial guardians. Over time, the political culture may come to incorporate the expectation that the judicial guardians can be counted on to fend off violations of fundamental rights, just as greater self-restraint on the part of the demos and its representatives may become a stronger norm in the political culture of polyarchies without judicial guardianship.

5. Judging from the whole history of judicial review in the United States, judicial guardians do not in fact offer much protection for fundamental rights in the face of persistent invasions by the national demos and its representatives. The reputation of the U.S. Supreme Court for doing so rests mainly on a period of judicial activism beginning in 1954 when the Court was presided over by Chief

Justice Earl Warren. Yet most of the famous cases of the Warren Court involved state or local laws, not acts of Congress.

Over against these decisions are a substantial number of cases in which the Court used the protections of the Bill of Rights, or the constitutional amendments enacted after the Civil War to protect the rights of the newly freed blacks, not to uphold the rights of those who were too weak politically to protect themselves through electoral politics but quite the reverse. Tbe victors were chiefly slaveholders at the expense of slaves, whites at the expense of nonwhites, and property holders at the expense of wage earners and other groups. Unlike some of the relatively unimportant cases mentioned earlier, these cases all involved rights and interests of genuinely fundamental importance, where an opposite policy would have meant basic shifts in the distribution of rights, liberties, and opportunities in the United States.

6. That, despite its reputation, the U.S. Supreme Court has not regularly stood as a bulwark against violations of fundamental rights and interests by congressional legislation (as distinct from state and local laws or ordinances) is accounted for by a fact of great relevance to the broader issues of quasi guardianship: The Supreme Court inevitably becomes a part of any national political coalition that steadily wins majorities in national elections. Jurists known to be sharply at odds with the basic outlook of the president or a majority of senators are not nominated by the president and confirmed by the Senate. Thus the views of a majority of the justices of the Supreme Court are never out of line for very long with the views prevailing among the lawmaking majorities of the country. To suppose that it might be otherwise is highly unrealistic. The quasi guardians of the Supreme Court rarely hold out more than a few years at most against major policies sought by a lawmaking majority. What the American experience indicates, then, is that in a democratic country, employing quasi guardians to protect fundamental rights from invasion by the national legislature (as distinct from state, provincial, cantonal, or municipal legislatures) does not provide a promising alternative to democratic processes, except perhaps in the short run.

It is easy to see why. Either the quasi guardians are so insulated from prevailing public opinion and can mobilize such great resources for coercion that they can impose their views despite opposition from national electoral majorities and their representatives or they cannot and at most can only fight a rearguard delaying action until they are overwhelmed by the dominant coalition of nationally elected officials. Is the first politically possible in any democratic country? American experience argues that it is not.[7] And if it were possible, would not the legitimacy of the quasi guardians ultimately be undermined? If, on the other hand, the function of quasi guardians is only to delay changes in national policies, it would surely be possible to design a more feasible and less arbitrary means for doing so.[8]

7. If nonetheless the solution of judicial quasi guardianship is adopted, it can be made consistent with the democratic process if the authority of the judicial guardians is sufficiently restricted. To see how judicial review and the democratic process might be reconciled, we need to consider once again the distinction be-

tween interests or rights integral to the democratic process, those external but nonetheless necessary to it, and those external and not necessary to it, yet necessary if the Idea of Intrinsic Equality and the Principle of Equal Consideration of Interests are to be respected. The criteria for the democratic process do not specify how the process itself is to be maintained. For a court to strike down laws that violate the criteria themselves would surely not be inconsistent with those criteria. Consequently a court whose authority to declare laws unconstitutional was restricted to rights and interests integral to the democratic process would be fully compatible with the democratic process.[9]

As we move away from the first category, the role of the quasi guardians grows more doubtful. Even so, for an independent body to strike down laws that seriously damage rights and interests that while external to the democratic process are demonstrably necessary to it would not seem to constitute a violation of the democratic process. With the third category, however, the conflict is irreconcilable. Once the rights and other interests necessary to the democratic process have been effectively secured, then the more the quasi guardians extend their authority to substantive questions, the more they reduce the scope of the democratic process.

◆

What are we to conclude from this examination of alternative arrangements for protecting fundamental rights and interests in a democratic order?

We have seen that it is wrong to pose the problem of protecting fundamental rights and interests as if the issue were one of substance versus process, of fundamental rights and interests against mere procedures. The democratic process not only presupposes a broad array of fundamental rights: It is itself a form of distributive justice, since it directly influences the distribution of power and authority over the government of the state and, because of the importance of the decisions made by the government of the state, over other substantive goods as well.

It is therefore a mistake, as we have seen, to interpret a conflict between substantive claims and the democratic process as a conflict between fundamental rights on the one hand and mere procedures on the other. If such conflicts occur, they are conflicts between one right or interest and another right that is one of the most fundamental rights human beings possess, a right so basic that it has been called inalienable: the right of people to govern themselves.

It follows also that to assert that a particular right or interest should be inviolable by the democratic process is not, as is sometimes said, to assert a right against "the state," as if "the state" were any state. It is rather to assert a right against the democratic process in the government of a democratic state, presumably therefore a good state, and possibly the best feasible type of state.

Moreover, it would be wrong to limit the democratic process solely on the ground that it might be or is in fact employed to harm fundamental rights and interests. For any such limitation would require an alternative process for making collective decisions, and presumably therefore a nondemocratic process. If it would be wrong for the democratic process to violate a fundamental right or interest, then it would also be wrong for any other process to do so. Therefore the democratic process ought not to be displaced by a nondemocratic process unless (at the very least) a convincing showing is made that over the long run the nondemocratic process will be superior to the democratic process.

It is misleading to suggest that there is one universally best solution to the problem of how best to protect fundamental rights and interests in a polyarchy. Although American lawyers typically assume that the solution must include a supreme court with the authority to strike down national legislation that violates fundamental rights and interests, such a system of quasi guardianship is neither necessary nor, on American experience, sufficient. In the absence of a universally best solution, specific solutions need to be adapted to the historical conditions and experiences, political culture, and concrete political institutions of a particular country. Quasi guardianship in the form of a supreme court with the power of judicial review is a solution that Americans have accepted as desirable. It cannot be shown to be generally desirable in polyarchies. Obviously, then, to make a reasonable decision about the trade-offs requires not only an empirical assessment of the probable consequences of alternative processes in the concrete setting of a particular country, but also a judgment about the relative weight to assign to the democratic process in comparison with other values.

A heavy burden of proof should therefore be required before the democratic process is displaced by quasi guardianship. It should be necessary to demonstrate that the democratic process fails to give equal consideration to the interests of some who are subject to its laws; that the quasi guardians will do so; and that the injury inflicted on the right to equal consideration outweighs the injury done to the right of a people to govern itself.

This judgment should depend partly on one's view of the potentialities for collective moral responsibility and growth in a good political order. If a good political order requires that the demos must in no circumstances have the opportunity to do wrong, at least with respect to fundamental rights and interests, then one may be tempted to suppose that the demos and its representatives ought to be restrained by quasi guardians who, like true guardians, possess superior knowledge and virtue. If however the best political order is one in which the members individually and collectively gain maturity and responsibility by confronting moral choices, then they must have the opportunity to act autonomously. Just as individual autonomy necessarily includes the opportunity to err as well as to act rightly, so too with a people. To the extent that a people is deprived of the opportunity to act autonomously and is governed by guardians, it is less likely to develop a sense of responsibility for its collective actions. To the extent that it is autonomous, then it may sometimes err and act unjustly.

The democratic process is a gamble on the possibilities that a people, in acting autonomously, will learn how to act rightly.

# Chapter 14

◆◆◆◆◆◆◆◆◆

# When Is a People
# Entitled to the
# Democratic Process?

To say that all people—all adults, anyway—are entitled to the democratic process begs a prior question. When does a collection of persons constitute an entity—"a people"—entitled to govern itself democratically?

To the extent that the persons composing a political system are combined together in an unjustifiable way, the value of democracy for that system is reduced. If Costa Rica were forcibly annexed by the United States and compelled to become the fifty-first state, why should the people of Costa Rica—or we as external judges—value their new federal democracy as highly as their previously independent democratic system? And the principle of majority rule, as I remarked earlier, presupposes that the unit itself is appropriate for majority rule. To the extent that the unit within which majority rule operates is unjustifiable, then majority rule is unjustifiable in that unit. Would a majority of citizens of the United States be entitled to decide policies for the Costa Ricans if they were coerced into becoming citizens of a fifty-first state?

In the main, democratic theorists have either ignored these puzzling and difficult questions or provided facile answers. Can it be that there are no satisfactory answers?

## THE PROBLEM OF THE UNIT

What is it about a particular collection of people that entitles it to a democratic government? The question poses the problem of the appropriateness of democracy for various aggregations of persons—units, so to speak—with different boundaries.[1] However, what looks at first blush to be one question breaks down on examination into several different questions:

1. What type (or types) of associations should be governed democratically by the members of the association? Democrats have usually assumed that at the very least the government of a territorial state should be subject to democratic control.[2]

*193*

However, many modern democrats argue that other types of associations should also be internally democratic: trade unions, political parties, economic enterprises, and so on. Some advocates of "participatory democracy" appear to believe that virtually all associations should be democratic. I am going to assume, however, that the type of association we have in mind is a territorial state.

2. Even if we limit ourselves to states, given the long history of democratic ideas and practices one might reasonably wonder whether the type of state might have a bearing on the suitability of the democratic process. To the Greeks, as we have seen, it was self-evident that, if democracy were desirable, it would have to exist in a city-state, since a good state could exist only in a city. As late as the eighteenth century Rousseau and Montesquieu agreed that the best state for a self-governing people could not be larger than a city. Since their day, democratic orthodoxy has claimed the national state or country as the proper unit even if the country in question is no more than a fragile aggregate of regions or tribes. But, like its predecessors, the national state is a moment in history. In the year 2100 will it still seem to be the natural site and limit of the democratic process?

In chapter 22 I am going to discuss the consequences for democracy of the shift in scale from city to national state—and beyond. Here I shall begin by assuming that what we have in mind is a world of national states, though I want to relax that restriction as the argument unfolds.

Even national states may vary in form. Federal systems generate some questions for democratic theory and practice that unitary systems do not. Since the difference between federal and unitary systems is directly related to the central problem of this chapter, I shall return to it in a moment.

3. Having put these questions to one side for the time being, we can now more easily home in on the problem of the democratic unit and its boundaries. When advocates of democracy describe or recommend a democratic system, they take for granted that democracy would exist in certain concrete political units: city-states, national states, or whatever. They can point to historical or existing examples of these units, certain specific aggregations of person living within more or less clearly bounded territories: Athens, Geneva, France, Sweden . . . But they rarely ask why we ought to accept these particular aggregations as appropriate for democracy rather than different aggregations with different boundaries. Why should ancient Athenians have been entitled to democracy but not ancient Greece as a whole? Or why modern Greeks rather than Athenians, or Norwegians rather than Scandinavians? Alaska and Hawaii have gained statehood in the United States. Why not Puerto Rico—or Costa Rica? Is it simply a matter of consent rather than coercion?

Consider, for a moment, claims like these:

CLAIM 1: *The people living in Quebec are entitled to their own democratic government, independent of Canada.* (For Quebec and Canada you may substitute the southern states and the United States of America; Norway and Sweden; Ireland and the United Kingdom; North Ireland and the Irish Republic; Brittany and France; Turkish Cypriots and Greek Cypriots . . .)

CLAIM 2: *The people living in Quebec ought to be citizens of the democratic government of Canada.* (This is merely the mirror image of the first claim, which it rejects, and the same substitutions may be made.)

CLAIM 3: *With respect to matters involving birth control the people of Connecticut are entitled to employ the democratic process among themselves, independent of the federal government of the United States.* (For the United States you may substitute any democratic country; for Connecticut any locality within that country; for birth control an indefinite list of matters that might be subject to determination by units smaller than the national state. For a democratic country you might also substitute a transnational political system, such as the European Community, and for the locality, the constituent countries; the range of matters subject to country control might be very broad.)

CLAIMS 4, 5. . . n: *Claims to local autonomy like those just mentioned could be met by counterclaims asserting that control over the particular matters in dispute should be exercised by the larger and more inclusive unit. These counterclaims are of course merely mirror images of claims to local autonomy.*

When we inspect claims and counterclaims like these we see that they are twofold: They are simultaneously claims to control, or to autonomy, with respect to certain matters—police, health, housing, foreign affairs, and so on—and claims to control over these matters by a certain aggregate of persons, who ordinarily occupy a common territory but conceivably might not.[3] We might call the first a claim as to the proper *scope* of control, the second a claim as to the proper *domain* of persons entitled to exercise control with respect to matters falling within the proper scope. The scope might range all the way from a single narrow question—parking, for example—to complete autonomy, total sovereignty, full independence. Likewise the domain might be as tiny as the people of a village or a neighborhood or as vast as the inhabitants of a giant country or an association of countries like the European Union. Scope and domain are usually highly interdependent: The claim to the one is explicitly linked to the claim to the other.

Although claims about the domain and scope of authority clearly rest on value judgments of some kind, what immediately strikes the eye when we examine specific claims is how much a reasonable solution will necessarily depend on concrete circumstances. Like the claims themselves, feasible solutions are strongly conditioned by the particular beliefs, traditions, myths, historical experiences, in short by the complex tapestry of empirical reality existing among a concrete aggregate of human beings. Often, too—perhaps more often than not—disputes about scope and domain are settled not by the force of reasoned appeals to justice, freedom, democracy, self-determination, efficiency, and other abstract ideas but by the force of violence and coercion. The abstract values then serve only as convenient rationalizations for the legitimacy of the winning outcome.

Once again one might well wonder whether the problem admits of a general solution or indeed whether general principles can have any bearing at all on feasible solutions. When one begins to search for general solutions, one's doubts about their utility are likely to grow stronger.

## TWO NONSOLUTIONS

Let me mention two illusory solutions, both of which we encountered in a different context when we considered the problem of inclusion.

### Every People Defines Itself

One nonsolution is analogous to Schumpeter's answer to the problem of who ought to be included in the demos, except that in this case every *people* defines itself. Thus Athenians defined themselves as a distinct group of Greeks living together in an autonomous and democratic polis. Two millenia later modern Greeks have defined themselves as a people and Athenians are now citizens of greater Greece. At the time of the American Revolution, Virginians defined themselves more as Virginians than as Americans; in 1861 they saw themselves as citizens of the Confederacy rather than of the Union; today they regard themselves as unquestionably citizens of the United States. So ancient Athenians, modern Greeks, eighteenth-century Virginians, the people of the Confederate States in the Civil War period, Americans today—all have defined themselves and their fellow citizens in historically unique ways. After describing these historical changes, what more can be said?

Just as with membership in the demos, however, here too the aphorism that every people defines itself may succinctly summarize historical experience, but it provides no grounds for judging whether one claim is better than another or whether the historical outcome should be preserved or overthrown. To remain content with the aphorism we should have to allow every claim and its counterclaim to stand on an equal footing. But then the only means for reaching solutions would be propaganda and coercion. In that sense, the aphorism fails as a solution; it merely declares that there is none.

### Political Autonomy as an Absolute Right

What about the venerable notion of consent? Is not one of the crucial differences between bringing Alaska and Costa Rica into the United States simply that Alaskans gave their consent, whereas (I assume) Costa Ricans would not give theirs?

From the seventeenth century onward, the notion of consent was used to provide a moral foundation for the idea of a democratic state. How can we ensure consent? To do so, why not regard political autonomy as an absolute right? By absolute I mean that autonomy would always be granted to any group wishing it, provided only that the group made a convincing showing that its new unit, whether partly or fully independent, would be governed by the democratic process.

Imagine that a democratic country were actually to declare political autonomy to be an absolute right. Granting such a right would make a state, or any coercive organization, impossible (or at any rate illegitimate), since any group facing coercion on any matter could demand and through secession gain autonomy. In effect anarchism would be legitimized. While this conclusion will delight philosophical anarchists, if the argument of chapter 3 is correct and a democratic state is better than no state at all, then it would be a mistake to concede political autonomy as an absolute right. For an autonomous organization, even an autonomous and inclusive democracy, could do great harm to the interests of nonmembers. Since an absolute right to political autonomy would mean that no organization could properly exercise power to prevent damage to nonmembers, whether or not damage would occur would depend wholly on the action of the members of the autonomous group. As to that, human experience provides little ground for optimism.

## FEDERALISM

Federalism is sometimes a solution but, as the example of Costa Rica suggests, not necessarily always. By federalism I mean a system in which some matters are exclusively *within* the competence of certain local units—cantons, states, provinces—and are constitutionally *beyond* the scope of the authority of the national government, and where certain other matters are constitutionally outside the scope of the authority of the smaller units.

Federal systems have a somewhat ambiguous standing in democratic ideas, partly for purely historical reasons but also because they reflect in their constitutions certain aspects of the problem of this chapter.

### Federalism and Democratic Ideas

The older doctrine, which insisted that the most appropriate unit for republican or democratic government was the small city-state, often also stressed the harm to the public good that must result when relatively autonomous associations exist within the city-state. Thus Rousseau, the last great exponent of views like these, contended that a republic would be best served by a small state without associations. This prescription helped Rousseau, as it had his predecessors, to bypass the sticky problem of the nature of the public good in a state where each citizen belongs simultaneously to several different political associations, as would be the case, for example, with someone who is a citizen of a municipality, a state, and a country. If the public good of one municipality (or of some other association) is X and the public good of another municipality or association is Y, what is the public good of all citizens in a state that includes these and many other local units as well as other kinds of associations?[4]

Yet even in Rousseau's day the historical focus of democratic ideas was shifting from the city-state to national state and countries. It happened, however, that the countries in which democratic ideas most deeply influenced institutions and practices were, constitutionally speaking, of two kinds: unitary and federal. In unitary systems, local units are merely creations of the national parliament, fully subject, in constitutional principle at least, to its control. The national government delegates authority to local governments; it does not alienate its authority. Thus the constitutional arrangements would permit the national demos to exercise full control over the agenda of political life. A national majority may, if it chooses, overrule the decisions of local units, for example, by removing the matters in question from the agenda of local governments.

Yet democratic ideas and practices also flourished in federal systems—earlier, in fact, than in unitary systems. Indeed in both Switzerland and the United States, where federalism antedates many of the institutions necessary to the democratic process, the federal system was widely thought to be specially favorable to democracy. So Tocqueville argued in his famous analysis of democracy in the United States. In the twentieth century, however, with the growth of the welfare state and the expansion of national controls over economic life it was sometimes said that federalism had become obsolete (Laski 1939). Yet this view proved to be premature, among other reasons because of the emergence of federal institutions on a transnational scale in the European Community.

Transnational federalism is the mirror image of federalism within a country. When a nation with a unitary constitution, such as France or Britain, enters into a transnational federal system, such as the European Community, then its national demos no longer has final control over the political agenda. Yet the agenda of the transnational unit is also strictly limited. Consequently, even if the larger community were to operate according to the majority principle, on many questions a majority of citizens in that community could not overrule a minority if the minority of the community happened to be a majority in a local unit, that is, a country. If we assume that over the next century transnational federalism will grow stronger, then the questions that federalism generates for democratic theory and practice are far from transitory or obsolete.

To explore these questions it may be helpful to imagine a conversation between two contemporary democrats, one an exponent of democratic federalism and the other a critic of federalism. Let me call the federalist James and his monistic critic Jean-Jacques.

### The Agenda Problem

JEAN-JACQUES: I know you to be something of an admirer of federal systems, James, isn't that so?

JAMES: Yes, I think they have some special virtues, if that's what you mean.

JEAN-JACQUES: But, as I know well, you are also a strong believer in democracy, are you not?

JAMES: Yes, that is so.

JEAN-JACQUES: Well, I don't quite see how the two fit together.

JAMES: You'll have to explain.

JEAN-JACQUES: I'll try. I know that many Americans seem to believe that the United States is the embodiment of democracy, and so whatever the U.S. Constitution specifies must necessarily be essential to democracy. I suppose some Americans might believe that, because the United States is federal, therefore federalism is necessary to democracy. You wouldn't go so far as to argue that, would you?

JAMES: That would be absurd. Even the most convinced federalist can hardly contend that the political system of Norway, being unitary, is inherently less democratic than the political system of Switzerland. If federalism is necessary to democracy, then unitary constitutional systems are necessarily undemocratic. To show that unitary constitutional systems are necessarily undemocratic, I would have to show that a small, autonomous city-state with no need for decentralization to even smaller units would *necessarily* be undemocratic. That would be downright silly.

JEAN-JACQUES: Might not the converse be true: that federal systems are *necessarily* undemocratic?

JAMES: I find that just as absurd as the other.

JEAN-JACQUES: But you do agree, James, that one requirement of a fully democratic process is that the demos exercise final control over the agenda?

JAMES: I can hardly deny that.

JEAN-JACQUES: Yet in a federal system no *single* body of citizens can exercise final control over the agenda. Don't you agree, then, that in federal systems the processes by which people govern themselves can't even in principle ever be fully democratic?

JAMES: I don't quite grasp your reasoning, Jean-Jacques.

JEAN-JACQUES: Ah, the Anglo-American political mind: Naturally you mistrust my appeal to reason rather than experience. So let me try to make the problem more concrete with a hypothetical example. Let's invent a so-called democracy with a very limited agenda, say, the schooling of children. Let's call it Sylvania, for no particular reason. Now if our Sylvanians want to act on other things than schools, but have no opportunity to put those matters on the Sylvanian agenda or on the agenda of any other government they control, then even if they are active and vigorous participants in decisions about education, wouldn't you regard them as oppressed?

JAMES: Yes, of course. But why *can't* the Sylvanians put other matters on the agenda?

JEAN-JACQUES: Well, suppose that Sylvania is controlled by a foreign nation. Let's just call it the Union. The Union excludes the hapless Sylvanians from citizenship but lets them do what they want with their schools. No matter if the Union is the very perfection of the democratic process: Sylvanians are colonials and their thin little "democracy" is a pretty piece of window-dressing staged by their rulers. The Sylvanians may admire the democracy of their rulers, but they can never emulate it.

JAMES: That's not only a rather far-fetched example, but it has nothing to do with federalism. Let's suppose that the Sylvanians *aren't* excluded from citizenship in the Union, which is more likely than your assumption. They are now citizens of both Sylvania and the more inclusive unit, which I'll now call the Federal Union. If, as Sylvanians, they govern themselves democratically on school matters, and, as citizens of the Federal Union, they govern themselves democratically on all other questions, and if the Federal agenda is completely open, so that Sylvanians may place matters of interest to them on the Federal agenda, then I don't see any objections from a democratic point of view. I don't say there may not be other problems, but the opportunities the Sylvanians have to govern themselves satisfy all the requirements of the democratic process. Taking their two governments together, the Sylvanians control a completely open agenda. If we assume, as we have, that all the other criteria are met, then must we not also conclude that the Sylvanians enjoy a fully democratic process?

JEAN-JACQUES: But haven't you just turned your Federal Union into a unitary rather than a federal system? If so, you've shown how the Sylvanians might be citizens of a democratic system, but you haven't shown how federalism can be reconciled with democracy. In particular, you haven't shown that a federal system can satisfy the requirement of final control over the agenda by the demos. Hasn't the demos of the Federal Union merely *delegated* control over school questions to Sylvania and other local governments? But if that is the case, then your reconciliation of federalism with democracy is spurious. You've demonstrated what we knew all along: that the problem of final control need not arise in unitary systems. But you still haven't shown how the demos can exercise final control over the agenda in federal systems. In fact, I think your solution may imply something extremely interesting: that the problem can't be solved *except* by turning federal systems into unitary ones!

JAMES: I compliment you on your dazzling logic, but I'm afraid you've missed the target. Let's suppose that, under the constitutional arrangements reached when Sylvania joined the Federal Union, Sylvania's control over schools is permanent and inalienable. Wouldn't you concede that under these conditions the system is definitely federal? And definitely not unitary?

JEAN-JACQUES: Yes, I'd have to agree that the system is not unitary but federal. A definition is a definition is a definition . . . But I'm not sure what conclusions you are trying to draw. I still don't see that your Federal Union is fully democratic.

JAMES: Well, looked at from one perspective, you could say that the demos of the Federal Union has alienated control over schools to Sylvania and other local governments. Just as the agenda of Sylvania is completely closed on everything except schools, so the agenda of the Federal Union is permanently closed on matters involving schools. Nonetheless, even though the government is for these reasons clearly federal, the solution looks very much like that provided by a unitary system with local governments! Yes, the agenda of the Federal Union *is* closed with respect to the schools. But on everything else it's completely open. Let's call the federal agenda quasi open.

JEAN-JACQUES: I suppose I must tolerate a slight pollution of the language so that you may get on with your argument.

JAMES: Thank you. Now, exactly as in a unitary system, if we take the two governments together then Sylvanians control a completely open agenda. Whatever they can't put on the Sylvanian agenda they can put on the Federal agenda. If every citizen of the Federal Union has a local equivalent of Sylvania, then there is nothing in the federal system that prevents its citizens from exercising final control over the agenda of public affairs. In deference to your preference for abstract argument, I'll now sum up my argument in a general proposition. Provided that in one of their units all citizens have access to a quasi-open agenda, federalism is not inherently less capable of meeting the criteria of the democratic process than a unitary system.

JEAN-JACQUES: Not inherently, perhaps. In some circumstances, though your solution won't be satisfactory. And it is more likely to be unsatisfactory the more robust the federal system.

JAMES: What do you mean, "robust"?

JEAN-JACQUES: I mean that the local units exercise exclusive control over some really important questions. I don't mean the anemic federalism of the United States today, for example, where constitutionally the federal government can directly or indirectly regulate or control most of the activities of the states and municipalities. De facto, the United States is pretty close to being a unitary system. So let's imagine that in the Federal Union, Sylvania and the other thirty provinces possess final authority over policies that the citizens of the Union think are very important. Pollution, let's say, or conservation of natural resources. Now suppose that while a majority of Sylvanians and other Union citizens want strong controls over pollution, strip mining, and the like, in one province, Carbonia, the citizens are opposed to all such controls. In these circumstances, there is no agenda on which the people in Sylvania and the other provinces can place the question of pollution by Carbonia.[5] In these circumstances, a unitary system—or an anemic federal one—satisfies the criteria of the democratic process better than a robust federal system.

JAMES: Yes, that is so. But your argument seems to imply that a larger and more inclusive group always has a right to impose its will on a smaller group, simply because it is larger. Do you really believe that? Doesn't the larger group have to be in some sense *legitimate* as a democratic entity?

JEAN-JACQUES: I believe so. But we seem to have come full circle back to the problem with which we began. So far neither of us has provided a satisfactory answer. And we still haven't talked about the problem of majority rule.

## Federalism and the Majority Principle

JAMES: It's not obvious to me what the problem is.

JEAN-JACQUES: All right, suppose a political system were to give a specially privileged minority the power to overrule the majority on questions of policy. You would hardly regard that system as democratic, would you?

JAMES: Putting aside the debatable matter of a supreme court with authority over constitutional issues, no. If a specially privileged minority could enforce its preferences as to policies over against those the majority wanted to adopt, I'd say the system was not only a flat violation of majority rule but plain undemocratic.

JEAN-JACQUES: I was sure you would. Let's assume, then, that we're now talking about policies, not basic constitutional issues: A majority wants policy X, a minority wants policy Y. The essence of the majority principle, we agree, is that, if a majority prefers policy X to policy Y, then policy X should be adopted. Yet isn't it true that in federal systems a national majority can't always prevail over a minority even on straightforward policy questions?

JAMES: I think I see where you're heading. This is simply another way of looking at the question of control over the agenda, isn't it?

JEAN-JACQUES: Yes, but from the perspective of majority rule. Suppose that matters like X and Y are a constitutional prerogative of the local units—states, provinces, cantons, regions, or whatever. Suppose the people in the minority who want Y happen to be concentrated in a constitutionally protected local unit where they make up a majority. If we assume for purposes of discussion that a majority in the national parliament more or less accurately reflects the policies of a national majority of citizens, then in a unitary system the national parliament could, by perfectly legal processes, override a local government. If a majority of all citizens prefer policy X to policy Y, the national parliament can adopt policy X and enforce it in a local unit even if a majority in that particular local unit happens to prefer Y. In a federal system, in some cases the minority would prevail, and the national majority could do nothing about it, constitutionally speaking.

JAMES: In some cases, yes. But I wonder whether nowadays in federal systems the national government couldn't find a way to prevail if the matter were really important.

JEAN-JACQUES: Thank you. You make my case. What you're saying is that in some countries like the United States federalism has become pretty anemic. In anemic federal systems, the authority of the national government over local policies has increased so greatly that they hardly differ in that respect from unitary systems. So it seems that, in order to cope with the problems of modern society, federal systems have had to turn themselves de facto into unitary systems. Can I rest my case?

JAMES: Not quite yet. In the United States, for example, public education is still pretty much within the exclusive jurisdiction of the states, which in turn delegate authority to municipal governments. In fact, the biggest item of expenditure in state budgets is education.

JEAN-JACQUES: Because education *is* important, your example helps me to complete my argument. Consider our hypothetical polities, Sylvania and the Federal Union. You'll remember that the agenda of Sylvania is closed to everything except schools, while the agenda of the Federal Union is closed only to school matters but to nothing else. Now let's suppose that a majority of citizens of the Federal Union come to the conclusion that their schools are in such a deplorable state that more uniform educational standards must be imposed on the country. If the Union were unitary, I doubt whether either of us would think it tyrannical or even undemocratic if national policies were imposed in order to bring local school systems up to scratch. Many democratic countries do exactly that. But, because the Federal Union is not unitary but federal, the majority of the country is barred from acting to improve the schools. Yet the Sylvanians might well be a small minority of all citizens; and even in Sylvania those who oppose federal control might be no more than a bare majority.

I can imagine lots of instances in which justice would support the claims of Sylvania for autonomy on some particular matter. But, in this particular instance, wouldn't it be both unjust and undemocratic if the minority—possibly a very tiny minority—were permitted to have its way about standards for the schools? If, in fact, the federal government were helpless to act? If the majority principle is ever justified, isn't it justified in this instance? And, if it can't be justified in this instance, how can it ever be justified?

JAMES: Answers to your questions may be more elusive than you think. To show you why, I want to put Sylvania and the Federal Union to one side and discuss a highly abstract political system. This abstract system may also force us to reconsider the agenda question.

JEAN-JACQUES: A highly abstract political system? Are you now shifting your allegiance to the goddess of Reason, after all?

JAMES: I've always admired her. Anyway, here's my abstract system: Imagine two squares, one within the other. S is a smaller system in B, the bigger and more inclusive system. S for smaller, B for bigger. Get it? Nothing could be simpler.

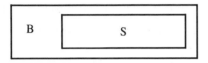

I ought to warn you not to think that I've reproduced Sylvania and the Federal Union all over again. Now let's assume that both B and S are governed democratically within the limits of their agendas and that the primary political rights of all citizens are fully respected. Should the majority of B always be entitled to prevail against the local majority in S—on, say, schools? Or, to put it the other way round, should the local majority in S be constitutionally entitled to prevail on some matters—say, schools—against the larger majority in B?

JEAN-JACQUES: I suppose that depends on what you mean by "entitled."

JAMES: By "entitled" I mean to exclude mere convenience, efficiency, or utility. It might be convenient or efficient for people in B to allow the people in S to govern themselves on certain matters, such as schools. This is simply to say that B is a unitary system and the majority in B finds it useful to delegate authority to S. Obviously that's not the problem we're concerned with here. To say that the majority in S is sometimes *entitled* to prevail over the majority in B is to say, in effect, that the people in S have a *right* to govern themselves on certain matters and that B ought not to infringe on that right. At the same time, however, by assumption all citizens in B, including those in S, are fully protected in exercising their primary political rights.

JEAN-JACQUES: But if the entitlement isn't merely convenience or efficiency, and if it's not a primary political right—a right necessary to the democratic process—then what sort of a "right" is it? Do people have a fundamental moral "right" to a "local" government, like the "right" to free speech—a moral right so basic that it should be constitutionally guaranteed? I'm not sure I can see how such a "right" could be justified.

JAMES: Nor do I. Yet I believe both of us believe in such a right nonetheless. Let me explain why. I imagine that, in spite of my warning a moment ago, you've really been thinking of S as a local unit and B as a national unit. As a result, from your earlier argument I'd suppose that you feel rather sympathetic with the claim of the people of B to exercise some control over the schools in S.

JEAN-JACQUES: Yes, I do, rather. I confess I was thinking of B as, say, France, or even the United States, and S as a municipality or maybe a state or *departement*.

JAMES: But suppose instead that S is a country like France or Britain, and B is a transnational system like the European Community. Where do your sympathies lie now? Do you want the French educational system to be controlled by the European Community? Now, I suspect, you are more sympathetic to the claims of the people in S to exercise control over the education of their children than you are with the claims of B to govern over the people of S on these matters?

JEAN-JACQUES: As I just said, that is so.

JAMES: So: are we to say that B merely *delegates* authority over education to S? But in what sense does B possess this authority to begin with? Certainly not legally or constitutionally. Morally? Ought any larger unit *always* to have authority over any smaller unit? Even as severe a critic of federalism as I take you to be will dig in and resist somewhere.

JEAN-JACQUES: I now realize that it was not the goddess of Reason you paid homage to but the goddess of Muddle. I can't see that we've gotten anywhere on this question of federalism and majority rule.

JAMES: No, I think we have. Whether through reason or muddle we've arrived at a very important conclusion. The majority principle itself depends on prior assumptions about the unit: that the unit within which it is to operate is itself legitimate and that the matters on which it is employed properly fall within the jurisdiction of that unit. In other words, whether the scope and domain of majority rule are appropriate in a particular unit depends on assumptions that the majority principle itself can do nothing to justify. The justification for the unit lies beyond the reach of the majority principle and, for that matter, mostly beyond the reach of democratic theory itself.

## THE BIGGER THE BETTER?

JEAN-JACQUES: I think our muddle may be the result of failing to distinguish between two different questions: Is one unit of a given domain and scope in some reasonable sense more democratic than another? And is one unit in some reasonable sense more desirable? As to the first, I see two possibilities. One is sheer numbers. As Rousseau suggested long ago, it is necessarily the case that the greater the number of citizens, the smaller the weight of each citizen in determining the outcome. If we accept the view that the greater the weight of each citizen, the more democratic a system is, then other things being equal a larger system is bound to be less democratic than a smaller system. So, given a choice, a democrat should always prefer the smaller unit.

JAMES: My dear Jean-Jacques, I fear your goddess has abandoned you. If it were true that a smaller system must always be more democratic than a larger, then the most democratic system would consist of one person, which is absurd.

JEAN-JACQUES: You might have noticed that my conclusion was strictly contingent: "If we accept the view," I said. And we don't. So that leaves us only with the second of the two possibilities I mentioned a moment ago. Let us say that a system is more democratic to the extent that it permits citizens to govern themselves on matters that are important to them. Then in many circumstances a larger system would be more democratic than a smaller one, since its capacity to cope with certain matters—pollution, fiscal and monetary policy, unemployment, social security, defense, and so on—would be greater. On this view, a unit large enough to deal with matters of importance to the people concerned will always be more democratic than any smaller unit.

JAMES: I think you're still making a case with tongue in cheek. Isn't it obvious that just as numbers alone lead to absurdity, taken by itself the criterion of system capacity compels us to say that an absurdly large system is the most democratic—quite possibly one consisting of the entire human population of the globe?

JEAN-JACQUES: To avoid the absurdities of each criterion taken alone, suppose we take the two criteria together and search for an optimum balance between system size and capacity?

JAMES: A splendid idea! I think you may have discovered the direction in which to look for a solution, if there is one. But notice two things. First, I don't see any way in which theoretical reasoning will take us very far in our search for an optimum. We'll need a lot more help than your goddess alone can provide. We'll have to make complex and debatable empirical and utilitarian judgments. What's more, since empirical conditions will vary, there is every reason to suppose that even if an optimum can be found it will not be the same in different circumstances and historical periods. Finally, we can't assume that a single aggregate of persons would be best served by only one system. Garbage removal, water supply, schools, pollution, defense—each of these might produce a different optimum. The result might well be a complex system with several or many layers of democratic government, each operating with a somewhat different agenda.

JEAN-JACQUES: Certainly a system more complex than the rather inflexible boundaries of a federal system would provide, don't you agree?

JAMES: I'm afraid I must. However, I now want to bring up the second point your proposal suggests to me. Notice how the two questions you urged us to distinguish—what unit is more *democratic*? and what unit is more *desirable*?—become confounded in our search for an optimum. Suppose that on balance one solution might be more desirable than another but less democratic. How are we to decide which is better?

JEAN-JACQUES: So far we haven't even discussed what we might mean by saying that a more *desirable* system might sometimes be less democratic. Evidently we have assumed that we can judge the desirability of a political system by other standards than the democratic process. Presumably we can also judge it by its results. We have also assumed that in some circumstances it would be justifiable to trade off a bit of democracy to obtain more of certain other desirable ends: a little less democracy in the process, a little more achievement of good results.

JAMES: Yes, we surely do seem to be making those assumptions. But trade-offs aren't always required. Surely you'll agree that it would be desirable if we could enhance democracy, self-determination, and freedom all at once?

JEAN-JACQUES: How could I disagree?

JAMES: And if federal arrangements could make that possible, you would have to agree that they would be desirable, would you not?

JEAN-JACQUES: If only federal arrangements could make it possible, I'd have to agree. But please tell me what you have in mind.

JAMES: I've already implied it. Let's suppose the Sylvanians are members of a unitary state. Call it Union. But suppose they happen to believe far more passionately than other Union citizens in the importance of education and unlike other Unionists they're prepared to pay high taxes to achieve the best possible schooling for their children. They also believe strongly in certain educational methods and subjects that other Unionists don't share. Unfortunately for the Sylvanians, they're a minority in the Union and they can't ever get their policies adopted. Finally, however, because of these and other disagreements the Unionists decide they want their unitary Union to become a Federal Union, which, among other things, will allow the Sylvanians control over their educational system and the taxes needed to support it. Federalism makes everyone better off: The Sylvanians get what they want, but so do the other citizens of the Federal Union. Now Jean-Jacques, you agree, do you not, that the federal solution is a clear gain for democracy, self-determination, and freedom?

JEAN-JACQUES: I am of course compelled to agree. But I don't agree that these same results could be achieved only by federalism, as you seem to imply. Couldn't the Unionists have achieved exactly the same thing by granting the Sylvanians authority over schools and adequate powers of taxation? But they wouldn't need to alienate that control. If beliefs changed, or the Sylvanians bankrupted themselves and thereby damaged the national economy, then the Union could try something else.

JAMES: I suppose it's a question of how secure the Sylvanians would feel about their future, if a national majority could take back their authority whenever they chose to. What you call "robust" federalism would prevent that, and even anemic federalism would inhibit it.

JEAN-JACQUES: I think we're now retracing our steps.

JAMES: You will also notice that we've pushed solutions still further from the domain of purely theoretical reasoning. Applying standards of performance in judging the relative value of alternative arrangements will require empirical knowledge—or plain guesswork—that we can't possibly discover in any abstract description of the alternatives. So it seems impossible to arrive at a defensible conclusion about the proper unit of democracy by strictly theoretical reasoning. I realize this conclusion may distress you, Jean-Jacques, but theoretical reason can't provide our answers: We shall have to rely on practical judgment. Yet even practical judgment, it seems, can't yield a general answer that will hold for all times and places. A satisfactory answer depends too much on particularities.

JEAN-JACQUES: Before we desert general principles altogether, I want to insist that, while an answer can't be derived theoretically, this doesn't mean that judgments need be arbitrary. If that were so, then almost all political judgments would be arbitrary. Certain assumptions on which the validity of the democratic process itself depends can be brought into play. In particular, a reasonable judgment would require us to appraise alternative solutions in the light of two prior principles: that the interests of each person are entitled to equal consideration and that in the absence of a compelling showing to the contrary an adult is assumed to understand his or her own interests better than any other person. These principles are too general to lead to conclusive answers, particularly in the face of great empirical complexity. But I think they may help us to find reasonable answers.

## CRITERIA FOR A DEMOCRATIC UNIT

As Jean-Jacques and James have concluded, we cannot solve the problem of the proper scope and domain of democratic units from within democratic theory. Like the majority principle, the democratic process presupposes a proper unit. *The criteria of the democratic process presuppose the rightfulness of the unit itself.* If the unit itself is not proper or rightful—if its scope or domain is not justifiable— then it cannot be made rightful simply by democratic procedures. And as James and Jean-Jacques also conclude, to make a reasonable judgment about the scope and domain of democratic units requires us to move well beyond the realm of theoretical reason and deep into the realm of practical judgment.

Yet as Jean-Jacques has hinted, it would be a mistake to conclude that nothing more can be said.[6] It seems to me reasonable to say that a claim as to the proper domain and scope of a democratic unit is justified to the extent that it satisfies seven criteria. Conversely, the less well it satisfies the criteria, the less justifiable is the claim.

However, none of these criteria standing by itself is adequate. The hidden clause of each is the famous "all other things being equal," and in particular "the other six criteria being equally well satisfied."

1. The domain and scope can be clearly identified. It is particularly important that the domain—the persons who comprise the unit—be clearly bounded. This is doubtless one reason why territorial boundaries, although not strictly essential, are so often used to specify the domain of a unit, particularly if they reflect obvious historical or geophysical factors. Conversely, the more indeterminate the domain and scope, the more likely that the unit would, if established, become embroiled in jurisdictional squabbles or even civil wars.

2. The people in the proposed domain strongly desire political autonomy with

respect to the matters falling within the proposed scope, whether the scope is to be as limited as local control over a school board or as broad as complete sovereignty. To impose political autonomy on a group whose members do not want it (because, for example, they want to retain or acquire membership in a more inclusive or less inclusive unit) can be as coercive as refusing autonomy to a group that does. Moreover, to the extent that the members of the proposed unit disagree—some persons want political autonomy, while others do not—then any solution will be coercive.

3. The people in the proposed domain strongly desire to govern themselves according to the democratic process. Conversely, the claim of a group to political autonomy is less justifiable the more likely it is that their new government will not respect the democratic process. The right to self-government entails no right to form an oppressive government.

4. The proposed scope is within justifiable limits, in the sense that it does not violate primary political rights (a restatement of the third criterion) or other fundamental rights and values. Conversely, a group's claim to autonomy is less justifiable the stronger the reasons for believing that if it gains autonomy the group will inflict serious harm, whether to its own members or to persons outside its boundaries.

5. Within the proposed scope, the interests of the persons in the proposed unit are strongly affected by decisions over which they have no significant control. As we have seen, claims to the right to participate in important decisions might best be satisfied in some cases by including those who are now excluded from an existing unit. In other cases a better solution might be to allow persons who are already included in an existing unit to form a relatively (or even fully) autonomous unit with respect to matters within a given scope. Conversely, a claim—whether to inclusion or independence—cannot be justified if it is advanced by persons whose interests are not significantly affected by the decisions of that unit.

6. Consensus among the persons whose interests are significantly affected will be higher than it would be with any other feasible boundaries. By this criterion, all other things being equal (the other criteria being equally well met), one set of boundaries is better than another to the extent that it permits more persons to do what they want to do: In this sense, the criterion reasserts the value of personal freedom. And, as James pointed out, the best solution may sometimes simultaneously enhance freeom, self-determination, and democracy. Conversely, of course, a proposed unit is less desirable the more that it will increase conflict over goals and thereby increase the number of persons who cannot achieve theirs.

7. Measured by all relevant criteria, the gains must outweigh the costs. This is of course no more than a general criterion of rational choice, and as such it is all but empty: It is a catchall that has already been largely fleshed out by the previous criteria. But it does serve to remind us that any solution to the problem of the scope and domain of a democratic unit will almost certainly produce costs as well as gains. To estimate costs and gains, as we have just seen, requires us to use a number of different criteria. In addition to net benefits as measured by the previous

six criteria, still others are relevant: costs and gains for communication, negotiation, administration, economic efficiency, and so on. For the most part the criteria will require qualitative judgments. Quantitative estimates will be illusory, since they will usually omit, fudge, or obfuscate most of the crucial judgments. Thus it will rarely if ever be possible to demonstrate conclusively that one solution is definitely the best. Because a clearly best solution cannot be determined, the advocates of a particular solution will exaggerate the gains and ignore the costs; meanwhile their opponents will exaggerate the costs and minimize the gains.

In the real world, then, answers to the question, what constitutes "a people" for democratic purposes? are far more likely to come from political action and conflict, which will often be accompanied by violence and coercion, than from reasoned inferences from democratic principles and practices. For as we have seen, in solving this particular problem democratic theory cannot take us very far. Democratic ideas, as I have said, do not yield a definitive answer. They presuppose that one has somehow been supplied, or will be supplied, by history and politics.

To say that adult persons have a right to participate in a democratic process for arriving at the collective decisions they may be compelled to obey is not to say that every person has a right to citizenship in a political unit that is best designed to protect and advance his or her interests. Because a world of perfectly consensual democratic systems is impossible to attain, the political units that citizens of a democratic polity can construct for themselves will never perfectly correspond to the interests of every citizen. Every specific, concrete, and feasible alternative solution to the problem of the best unit will, almost certainly, on balance benefit the interests of some citizens more than others. Here again, despite the perfectionist promises of democratic ideas, the best attainable unit will be for some citizens the second best.

Yet within the historical limits of time and place, judged according to reasonable criteria, some alternative units *are* better than others. The difficulty is not that reasonable judgments as to better and worse are impossible. It is only that they are very likely to be inconclusive and highly disputable.

# PART FIVE

◆◆◆◆◆◆◆◆

# THE LIMITS AND
# POSSIBILITIES OF
# DEMOCRACY

# Chapter 15

◆◆◆◆◆◆◆◆◆

# The Second Democratic Transformation: From the City-State to the Nation-State

Modern democratic ideas and practices are a product of two major transformations in political life. The first, as we saw, swept into ancient Greece and Rome in the fifth century B.C., and receded from the Mediterranean world before the beginning of the Christian Era. A thousand years later some of the city-states of medieval Italy were also transformed into popular governments, which however receded during the Renaissance. In both cases, the locus of democratic and republican ideas and practices was the city-state. In both cases, popular governments were ultimately submerged in imperial or oligarchic rule.

The second major transformation, to which we are the heirs, began with the gradual shift of the idea of democracy away from its historic locus in the city-state to the vaster domain of the nation, country, or national state.[1] As a political movement and sometimes as an achievement—not merely an idea—in the nineteenth century this second transformation acquired great momentum in Europe and the English-speaking world. During the twentieth century the idea of democracy ceased to be, as it had been heretofore, a parochial doctrine embraced only in the West by a small proportion of the world's people and actualized for a few centuries at most over a tiny portion of the earth. Though it is far from a worldwide achievement, in the last half-century democracy in the modern sense has gained almost universal force as a political idea, an aspiration, and an ideology.

## THE TRANSFORMATION

This seond great movement of democratic ideas and practices has, however, profoundly transformed the way in which the notion of a democratic process has been, or can be, achieved. The most powerful, though not the only, cause of this transformation is the shift in its locus from the the city-state to the national state. Beyond the national state now lies the possibility of even larger and more inclusive supranational political associations. Though the future is conjectural, the increase in the scale of the political order has already produced a modern democratic state profoundly different from the democracy of the city-state.

For over two thousand years—from classical Greece to the eighteenth century—it had been a dominant assumption of Western political thought that in democratic and republican states the size of the citizen body and of the territory of the state must both be small, indeed by modern standards minuscule. Democratic or republican government, it was usually assumed, was suitable only for small states.[2] Thus the idea and the ideals of the polis, the small unitary city-state of kinfolk and friends, lived on well after city-states themselves had all but disappeared as a historical phenomenon.

Despite the impressive defeats of the Persians by the Greeks, in the long run the small city-state was no match for a larger neighbor bent on empire, as Macedon and Rome adequately demonstrated. Much later, the rise of the national state, often accompanied by an expanded conception of nationhood, superseded city-states and other tiny principalities. Only a few exceptions like San Marino and Liechtenstein survive today as quaint legacies of a vanished past.

As a result of the rise of national states, from about the seventeenth century onward the idea of democracy would have had no feasible future if its locus had not been transferred from the city-state to the national state. In the *Social Contract* (1762), Rousseau still clung to the older vision of a people wielding final control over the government of a state that was small enough in population and territory to enable all the citizens to gather together in order to exercise their sovereignty in a single popular assembly. Yet less than a century later the belief that the nation or the country was the "natural" unit of sovereign government was so completely taken for granted that in his *Considerations on Representative Government* John Stuart Mill, stating in a single sentence what to him and his readers could be taken as a self-evident truth, dismissed the conventional wisdom of over two thousand years by rejecting the assumption that self-government necessarily required a unit small enough for the whole body of citizens to assemble (Mill [1861] 1958, 55).

Even Mill, however, failed to see fully how radically the great increase in scale would necessarily transform the institutions and practices of democracy. At least eight important consequences have followed from that epochal change in the locus of democracy. Taken together they set the modern democratic state in sharp contrast to the older ideals and practices of democratic and republican governments. As a result, this modern descendant of the democratic idea lives uneasily with ancestral memories that unceasingly evoke the mournful plaint that present practices have fallen far away from ancient ideals. (Never mind that ancient practices themselves hardly conformed to ancient ideals.)

## EIGHT CONSEQUENCES

Let me summarize briefly the major consequences of the enormous increase in scale. In the chapters that follow, I shall discuss several of them at greater length.

## Representation

The most obvious change, of course, is that representatives have largely displaced the citizen's assembly of ancient democracy. (Mill's one-sentence dismissal of direct democracy occurs in a work on *representative* government.) I have already described how representation, in origins a nondemocratic institution, came to be adopted as an essential element of modern democracy (chapter 2). A few more words may help to put representation in perspective.

As a means for helping to democratize the governments of national states, representation can be understood both as a historical phenomenon and as an application of the logic of equality to a large-scale political system.

The first successful efforts to democratize the national state typically occurred in countries with existing legislative bodies that were intended to represent certain fairly distinctive social interests: aristocrats, commoners, the landed interest, the commercial interest, and the like. As movements toward greater democratization gained force, therefore, the design for a "representative" legislature did not have to be spun from gossamer fibers of abstract democratic ideas; concrete legislatures and representatives, undemocratic though they were, already existed. As a consequence, the advocates of reform, who in the early stages rarely had the slightest intention of creating an inclusive democracy, sought to make existing legislatures more "representative" by broadening the franchise, adopting an electoral system that would make members more representative of the electorate, and ensuring that elections were free and fairly conducted. In addition, they sought to ensure that the highest executive officer (whether president, prime minister, cabinet, or governor) would be chosen by a majority of the legislature (or the popular house) or by the electorate at large.

Although this brief description of a general path to democratization cannot do justice to the many important variations in each country, something roughly along these lines took place in the first national states to be democratized. It took place, for example, in the American colonies prior to the revolution—a hundred-and-fifty-year period of predemocratic development the importance of which is often underestimated—and, after independence, in the thirteen American states. To be sure, in designing the Articles of Confederation after independence, American leaders had to create a national congress virtually from scratch; and shortly thereafter the U.S. Congress was cast in its more lasting form at the Constitutional Convention of 1787. Yet in designing the Constitution the delegates to the convention always assumed as a starting point the specific features of the British constitutional system—notably king, bicameral parliament, prime minister, and cabinet—even as they altered the British model to fit the novel conditions of a country formed from thirteen sovereign states and lacking both a monarch to serve as head of state and the hereditary peers needed for a house of lords. Although their solution to the problem of choosing a chief executive—an electoral college—proved to be inconsistent with the democratizing impulses of the times, in practice the president quickly came to be chosen in what was, as a practical matter, a popular election.

In Britain, where the prime minister had already come to be dependent on the confidence of parliamentary majorities by the end of the eighteenth century, a major goal of democratizing movements from 1832 onward was to broaden the right to vote for members of Parliament and to ensure that parliamentary elections were fair and free.[3] In the Scandinavian countries, where as in England legislative bodies had existed since the Middle Ages, the task was both to make the prime minister dependent on parliament (rather than the king), and to expand the suffrage for parliamentary elections. So too in Holland and Belgium. Although from the revolution in 1789 to the Third Republic in 1871 France followed a somewhat different path (expansion of the suffrage usually accompanied executive despotism), what democratic movements demanded was not dissimilar to what was taking place elsewhere. The political institutions of Canada, Australia, and New Zealand were shaped by their own colonial experiences, which included significant elements of parliamentary government, and by the British and American constitutional systems.

The point of this thumbnail history is to emphasize that movements to democratize the governments of national states in Europe and America did not begin with a tabula rasa. In the countries that were the main centers of successful democratization from the end of the eighteenth century until about 1920, legislatures, systems of representation, and even elections were already familiar institutions. As a consequence some of the most distinctive institutions of modern democracy, including representative government itself, were not merely a product of abstract reasoning about the requirements of a democratic process. They resulted instead from specific and successive modifications of already existing political institutions. Had they been produced only by advocates of democracy working exclusively from abstract blueprints of the democratic process, the results would probably have been rather different.

It would be a mistake, however, to interpret the democratization of existing legislative bodies as nothing more than ad hoc adaptations of existing institutions. Once the locus of democracy shifted to the national state, the logic of political equality, now applied to countries enormously greater than the city-state, clearly implied that most legislation would have to be enacted not by the assembled citizens but by their elected representatives.[4] For it was as obvious then as now that, as the number of citizens increases beyond a rather small if imprecise limit, the proportion of citizens who can assemble together (or, even if they can, have an opportunity to participate by anything more than voting) must necessarily grow smaller and smaller. I want to say more about the problem of participation in a moment. My point here is that representative government was not grafted onto the democratic idea simply because of the inertia and familiarity of existing institutions. Those who undertook to modify these institutions were well aware that, in order to apply the logic of political equality on the large scale of the national state, the "direct" democracy of citizen assemblies had to be replaced (or at least supplemented by) representative governments. That observation was made repeatedly until, as with Mill, it could be utterly taken for granted. Even the Swiss, with their long tradition of assembly government in the ancient cantons, recognized that national referenda could not adequately perform the functions of a national parliament.

Yet, as Rousseau rightly foresaw in the *Social Contract*, representation was bound to alter the nature of citizenship and the democratic process. As we shall see, large-scale democracy lacks some of the potentialities of small-scale democracy. What is often lost sight of is that the converse is also true.

### Unlimited Extension

Once representation was accepted as a solution, the barriers to the size of a democratic unit set by the limits of an assembly in a city-state were eliminated. In principle, no country could be too extensive, no population too vast for a representative government. In 1787, the United States had a population of about four million, already gigantic by the standards of the ideal Greek polis. Some delegates to the Constitutional Convention daringly forecast a future United States with a hundred million or more inhabitants, a figure finally surpassed by 1915. In 1950, when India established its republican parliamentary system, its inhabitants numbered around 350 million and were still multiplying. So far it has been impossible to specify a theoretical upper limit.

### Limits on Participatory Democracy

As a direct consequence of greater size, however, some forms of political participation are *inherently* more limited in polyarchies than they were in city-states. I do not mean to say that participation in democratic or republican city-states actually achieved anything like the limits of its potentialities for participation. But theoretical possibilities existed in many ancient and medieval city-states that do not exist in a democratic country, even a relatively small country, because of the sheer magnitude of its citizen body and (of less importance) its territory. The theoretical limit of effective political participation, even with modern electronic means of communication, rapidly diminishes with scale. The consequence is that on average a citizen of the United States, or even of Denmark, cannot participate in political life as fully as the average number of a very much smaller demos in a much smaller state. I want to return to this point in the next chapter.

### Diversity

Although the relation between scale and diversity is not linear, the larger and more inclusive a political unit, the more its inhabitants tend to exhibit greater diversity in ways relevant to political life: in local and regional loyalties, ethnic and racial identities, religion, political beliefs and ideologies, occupations, lifestyles, and so on. The relatively homogeneous population of citizens united by common attachments to city, language, race, history, myth, gods, and religion, which was so conspicuous a part of the ancient city-state vision of democracy, now became for all practical purposes impossible. Yet what is possible, as we can now see, is a political system beyond the conception of premodern advocates of popular government: representative governments with inclusive electorates and a broad array of personal rights and liberties, existing in large countries of extraordinary diversity.

### Conflict

As a consequence of diversity, however, political cleavages are multiplied, political conflict is an inevitable aspect of political life, and political thought and practices tend to accept conflict as a normal and not aberrant feature of politics.

A striking symbol of the change is James Madison, who at the American Constitutional Convention in 1787, and later in his defense of it in *The Federalist*, met head-on the historical view, which was still reflected in anti-Federalist objections to the absurdity and iniquity of the attempt to form a democratic republic on such a grotesque scale as a federal union of the thirteen states would create. In a brilliant polemic, Madison contended that, because conflicts of interest were in the nature of man and society, and the expression of these conflicts could not be suppressed without suppressing freedom, the best cure for the mischiefs of faction was to enlarge the scale. As he of course intended, it followed that, contrary to the traditional view, a positive advantage of republic government on the larger scale of the national state was that political conflicts would be much less likely to produce acute civil strife than in the tighter compass of the city-state.

In contradiction to the classical vision, then, in which a more homogeneous body of citizens could be expected to share rather similar beliefs about the common good, and to act on those beliefs, the notion of the common good is stretched much more thinly in order to encompass the heterogeneous attachments, loyalties, and beliefs formed among a body of diverse citizens with a multiplicity of cleavages and conflicts. It is stretched so thinly, in fact, that we are compelled to ask whether a concept of the common good can now be much more than a poignant reminder of an ancient vision that irreversible change has made irrelevant to the conditions of modern and postmodern political life. We return to this problem in chapters 20 and 21.

### POLYARCHY

The change of scale and its consequences—representative government, greater diversity, the increase in cleavages and conflicts—helped to bring about the development of a set of political institutions that, taken together, distinguish modern representative democracy from all other political systems, whether nondemocratic regimes or earlier democratic systems. This kind of political system has been called *polyarchy*, a term that I use frequently.[5]

Polyarchy can be understood in several ways: as a historical outcome of efforts to democratize and liberalize the political institutions of nation states; as a distinctive type of political order or regime different in important ways not only from nondemocratic systems of all kinds but also from earlier small-scale democracies; as a system (à la Schumpeter) of political control in which the highest officials in the government of the state are induced to modify their conduct so as to win elections in political competition with other candidates, parties, and groups; as a system of political rights (discussed earlier in chapter 11); or as a set of institutions necessary to the democratic process on a large scale. Though these ways of interpreting polyarchy are different in interesting and important ways, they are not inconsistent. On the contrary, they complement one another. They simply emphasize different aspects or consequences of the institutions that serve to distinguish polyarchal from nonpolyarchal political orders.

In a moment I shall examine polyarchy in the last sense, as a set of political institutions necessary to large-scale democracy. In later chapters we shall see how the development of polyarchy depends on certain essential conditions; how in the absence of one or more of these conditions polyarchy may break down; and how, following upon civil strife and authoritarian rule, polyarchy may sometimes be restored. We shall also consider the present extent of polyarchy in the world and its possibilities in the future.

### Social and Organizational Pluralism

A further concomitant of the greater size of the political order and the consequences so far described—diversity, conflict, and polyarchy—is the existence in polyarchies of a significant number of social groups and organizations that are relatively autonomous with respect to one another and to the government itself: what has come to be called *pluralism* or, more specifically, social and organizational pluralism.[6]

### The Expansion of Individual Rights

Although less directly related to the change in scale, one of the most striking differences between polyarchy and all earlier democratic and republican systems is the astounding expansion of individual rights that has occurred in countries with polyarchal governments.

In classical Greece, as we saw in chapter 1, freedom was an attribute of membership in a particular city, within which a citizen was free by virtue of the rule of law and the right to participate in the decisions of the assembly (supra, p. 22, and p. 345, notes 16 and 17). Arguably, in a small and relatively homogeneous group of citizens bound by ties of kinship, friendship, neighborhood, market, and civic identity, participating with one's fellow citizens in all the decisions affecting their common life, and thus exercising self-determination over the life of the community, is so fundamental and comprehensive a freedom that other rights and liberties lose much of their importance. Yet to offset this idealization it needs to be added that small communities are generally less renowned for their freedom than for their oppressiveness, particularly to nonconformists. Even Athens found itself unwilling to tolerate Socrates. Exceptional as Socrates' conviction was, he had no "constitutional right" to preach dissenting views.

By contrast, as I indicated in chapter 13, in countries with polyarchal governments the number and variety of individual rights that are legally specified and effectively enforced have increased with the passage of time. In addition, because citizenship in polyarchies has been expanded to include almost the entire adult population, virtually all adults are entitled to primary political rights; the slaves, metics, and women excluded from full citizenship in the Greek democracies have all gained the rights of citizenship in modern democratic countries. Finally, many individual rights, like the right to a fair trial, are not restricted only to citizens; they extend to others as well, in some cases to the entire population of a country.

It would be absurd to attribute this extraordinary expansion of individual rights in polyarchies simply to the effects of size. Yet even if the greater scale of society is only one among several causes, and probably not the most important, it has undoubtedly made some contribution to the expansion of individual rights. For one thing, democracy on a large scale requires the institutions of polyarchy, and as we have seen these institutions necessarily include primary political rights—rights that go well beyond those that citizens were entitled to in earlier democratic and republican orders. Moreover, the greater scale probably stimulates a concern for rights as alternatives to participation in collective decisions. For, as the social scale increases, each person necessarily knows and is known by an ever smaller proportion of all the people. Instead, each citizen is a stranger to an ever greater number of other citizens. Social ties and personal acquaintance among citizens give way to social distance and anonymity. In these circumstances, personal rights attached to citizenship—or simply to personhood—can ensure a sphere of personal freedom that participation in collective decisions cannot. Further, as diversity and political cleavages grow, and adversarial political conflict becomes a normal and accepted aspect of political life, individual rights may be seen as a substitute for political consensus. If a society could exist in which there were no conflicts of interest, no one would have much need for personal rights: What any citizen wanted, everyone would want. While no society has ever been so homogeneous or consensual, even where consensus is imperfect but nonetheless high most people could count on being in the majority so often that their basic interests would always be preserved in collective decisions. But, if conflicts of interests are normal and the outcomes of decisions are highly uncertain, personal rights provide a way of ensuring for everyone some free space that cannot be easily violated by ordinary political decisions.

## POLYARCHY

Polyarchy is a political order distinguished at the most general level by two broad characteristics: Citizenship is extended to a relatively high proportion of adults, and the rights of citizenship include the opportunity to oppose and vote out the highest officials in the government. The first characteristic distinguishes polyarchy from more exclusive systems of rule in which, though opposition is permitted, governments and their legal oppositions are restricted to a small group, as was the case in Britain, Belgium, Italy, and other countries before mass suffrage. The second characteristic distinguishes polyarchy from regimes in which, though most adults are citizens, citizenship does not include the right to oppose and vote out the government, as in modern authoritarian regimes.

## The Institutions of Polyarchy

More specifically, and giving greater content to these two general features, polyarchy is a political order distinguished by the presence of seven institutions, all of which must exist for a government to be classified as a polyarchy.

1. *Elected officials.* Control over government decisions about policy is constitutionally vested in elected officials.
2. *Free and fair elections.* Elected officials are chosen in frequent and fairly conducted elections in which coercion is comparatively uncommon.
3. *Inclusive suffrage.* Practically all adults have the right to vote in the election of officials.
4. *Right to run for office.* Practically all adults have the right to run for elective offices in the government, though age limits may be higher for holding office than for the suffrage.
5. *Freedom of expression.* Citizens have a right to express themselves without the danger of severe punishment on political matters broadly defined, including criticism of officials, the government, the regime, the socioeconomic order, and the prevailing ideology.
6. *Alternative information.* Citizens have a right to seek out alternative sources of information. Moreover, alternative sources of information exist and are protected by laws.
7. *Associational autonomy.* To achieve their various rights, including those listed above, citizens also have a right to form relatively independent associations or organizations, including independent political parties and interest groups.

It is important to understand that these statements characterize actual and not merely nominal rights, institutions, and processes. In fact, the countries of the world may be assigned approximate rankings according to the extent to which each of the institutions is present in a realistic sense. Consequently the institutions can serve as criteria for deciding which countries are governed by polyarchy today or were in earlier times. These ranking and classifications can then be used, as we shall see later, to investigate the conditions that favor or harm the chances for polyarchy.

### Polyarchy and Democracy

However, it is obvious that we are not concerned with polyarchy merely because it is a type of political order distinctive to the modern world. It interests us here primarily because of its bearing on democracy. How then *is* polyarchy related to democracy?

Briefly, the institutions of polyarchy are necessary to democracy on a large

*Table 15.1. Polyarchy and the Democratic Process*

| The following institutions . . . | are necessary to satisfy the following criteria |
|---|---|
| 1. Elected officials<br>2. Free and fair elections | I. Voting equality |
| 1. Elected officials<br>3. Inclusive suffrage<br>4. Right to run for office<br>5. Freedom of expression<br>6. Alternative information<br>7. Associational autonomy | II. Effective participation |
| 5. Freedom of expression<br>6. Alternative information<br>7. Associational autonomy | III. Enlightened understanding |
| 1. Elected officials<br>2. Free and fair elections<br>3. Inclusive suffrage<br>4. Right to run for office<br>5. Freedom of expression<br>6. Alternative information<br>7. Associational autonomy | IV. Control of the agenda |
| 3. Inclusive suffrage<br>4. Right to run for office<br>5. Freedom of expression<br>6. Alternative information<br>7. Associational autonomy | V. Inclusion |

scale, particularly the scale of the modern national state. To put the matter in a slightly different way, all the institutions of polyarchy are necessary to the highest feasible attainment of the democratic process in the government of a country. To say that all seven institutions are necessary is not to say that they are sufficient. In later chapters I want to explore some possibilities for the further democratization of countries governed by polyarchy.

The relation between polyarchy and the requirements of the democratic process are set out in table 15.1.

## APPRAISING POLYARCHY

Typical of democrats who live in countries governed by authoritarian regimes is a fervent hope that their country will one day reach the threshold of polyarchy. Typical of democrats who live in countries long governed by polyarchy is a belief that polyarchy is insufficiently democratic and should be made more so.

Yet, while democrats describe many different visions of what the next stage of democratization should be, so far no country has transcended polyarchy to a "higher" stage of democracy.

While intellectuals in democratic countries where polyarchy has existed without interruption for several generations or more often grow jaded with its institutions and contemptous of their shortcomings, it is not hard to understand why democrats deprived of these institutions find them highly desirable, warts and all. For polyarchy provides a broad array of human rights and liberties that no actually existing real world alternative to it can match. Integral to polyarchy itself is a generous zone of freedom and control that cannot be deeply or persistently invaded without destroying polyarchy itself. And because people in democratic countries, as we have seen, have a liking for other rights, liberties, and empowerments, that essential zone is enlarged even more. Although the institutions of polyarchy do not guarantee the ease and vigor of citizen participation that could exist, in principle, in a small city-state, nor ensure that governments are closely controlled by the citizens or that policies invariably correspond with the desires of a majority of citizens, they make it unlikely in the extreme that a government will long pursue policies that deeply offend a majority of citizens. What is more, those institutions even make it rather uncommon for a government to enforce policies to which a substantial number of citizens object and try to overturn by vigorously using the rights and opportunities available to them. If citizen control over collective decisions is more anemic than the robust control they would exercise if the dream of participatory democracy were ever realized, the capacity of citizens to exercise a veto over the reelection and policies of elected officials is a powerful and frequently exercised means for preventing officials from imposing policies objectionable to many citizens.

Compared then with its alternatives, historical and actual, polyarchy is one of the most extraordinary of all human artifacts. Yet it unquestionably falls well short of achieving the democratic process. From a democratic point of view, many questions can be raised about the institutions of large-scale democracy in the national state as they exist today. The most important of these are, in my view, the following, to which the rest of this book is devoted:

1. In the conditions of the modern and postmodern world how, if at all, can we realize the possibilities of political participation that were theoretically present, though often not fully achieved in practice, in small-scale democracies and republics?

2. Does polyarchy presuppose conditions that most countries lack and will continue to lack? Are most countries therefore unsuitable for polyarchy and prone instead to democratic breakdown or authoritarian rule?

3. Is large-scale *democracy* possible at all, in fact, or do tendencies toward bureaucratization and oligarchy necessarily rob it of its essential meaning and justification?

4. Does the pluralism inherent in large-scale democracy lethally enfeeble the

prospects for achieving the common good? In fact, does a *common* good really exist to any significant degree?

5. Finally, would it be possible to move beyond the historic threshold of polyarchy to a more completed attainment of the democratic process? In short, given the limits and possibilities of our world, is a third transformation a realistic possibility?

# Chapter 16

◆◆◆◆◆◆◆◆◆

# Democracy, Polyarchy, and Participation

One consequence of transferring the idea of democracy from the city-state to the national state is that opportunities for citizens to participate fully in collective decisions are more limited than they would be, theoretically at least, in a much smaller system. For most people nowadays, these limits seem to be pretty much taken for granted. Yet the nature of the democratic idea, and its origins, prevent the hope from ever dying out that the limits can be transcended by creating new (or recreating ancient) democratic forms and institutions. Consequently a strong countercurrent favoring the ideal of a fully participatory democracy persists among advocates of democracy, who often hark back to the older democratic vision that was reflected in Rousseau's *Social Contract* and in images of the Greek democracy (as it existed not so much in historical reality as in the idealized polis).

Some of the central issues appear as Jean-Jacques and James renew their dialogue:

JAMES: I have often noticed, Jean-Jacques, that while you accept all the benefits of modern democracy, including the right to say whatever you please—a right you obviously cherish, since you exercise it so often—you nonetheless always seem to denigrate its institutions and achievements. I sometimes think that in democratic countries the breakdown of democracy is less likely to be brought about by its opponents than by its utopian advocates. With friends like you . . .

JEAN-JACQUES: . . . democracy doesn't need enemies. Definitely below the belt, James. That was unlike you and unworthy of you, good friend. You speak of democracy. If I'm critical it's because what you and others insist on calling "modern democracy" is not and cannot be very democratic. Why not give things their honest names and call modern democracy "oligarchy"?

JAMES: I'm sorry if I offended you, Jean-Jacques. I thought my remark perfectly exact. But I can see that you're loaded for bear today, so I'll take cover while you aim and fire. Please proceed.

JEAN-JACQUES: Thank you. Isn't it perfectly obvious why what you call "poly-archy" is a pitiful substitute for real democracy?

JAMES: Excuse me, but I have learned that the phrase "real democracy" usually means either unreal democracy or real oppression, and usually both. However, I await your enlightenment. I'll even ask the question you're fishing for: Why is polyarchy a pitiful substitute for real democracy?

JEAN-JACQUES: Because no government on the scale of a country can really be democratic. Democracy as it was classically understood meant above all direct citizen participation; either democracy was *participatory*, or it was a sham. As Rousseau argued, following the ancient tradition, if citizens are to be truly sovereign they must be able to gather together to rule in a sovereign assembly. To do so, the citizen body- and in those days the territory of the state as well—had to be small. As he pointed out, the greater the number of citizens the smaller must necessarily be the average share each has in ruling. In a large state that share is infinitesimally small. "The English people," he remarked, "thinks it is free. It greatly deceives itself. It is free only during the election of the members of Parliament. As soon as they are elected, it is a slave, it is nothing" (Rousseau 1978, bk. 3, chap. 15, p. 102). I know this is hard for people accustomed only to polyarchy to grasp, but an Athenian would have understood it immediately.

JAMES: I don't want to divert us from your argument by starting an interminable discussion of "what Rousseau really meant," which I'll happily leave to those who relish that sort of thing. So I'll ignore his perverse definition of democracy in the *Social Contract* where he stipulates that in a "democracy" the people must not only make the laws but administer them also. So "democracy" was impossible. "If there were a people of gods, it would govern itself democratically. Such a perfect government is not suited to men." On his definition, he's perfectly right. But what he called a republic we would call direct democracy or, even more to the point, assembly democracy. I'll also ignore the fact that he regarded representation as totally unacceptable only in the *Social Contract*. In his previous work he had regarded it as a reasonable solution; he did so again in his later work. I suppose it was as obvious to him as it is to us that without representative governments Poland and Corsica, for example, could never be republics (see especially Fralin 1978).

JEAN-JACQUES: I agree that the argument can't be advanced by scholarly disquisitions on Rousseau. I didn't mention him in order to persuade you by citing a Great Name on my behalf, which we both agree proves nothing, though heaven knows it's a common form of argument in these matters. I mentioned him only because I happen to believe that he was perfectly correct about the consequences of size for political participation.

JAMES: It may surprise you, but so do I. I don't see how anyone can deny that the opportunity for every citizen to participate *directly* in collective decisions, except by voting, has to be inversely related to size. That's exactly why advocates of large-scale democracy so much admired representation. Representation is the obvious solution to an otherwise insoluble problem.

JEAN-JACQUES: But haven't you just conceded that representation doesn't solve the problem of participation? And haven't you also conceded by implication that the problem of participation simply can't be solved in a large system? Therefore it can be solved only on classical terms: by small-scale democracy.

JAMES: What you and most other advocates of assembly democracy don't seem to recognize is how swiftly your own argument turns against you. I've already agreed that, as the number of citizens grows larger, the opportunities for them to participate directly in decisions must necessarily decline. This is because, if nothing else has an upper limit, time does. Elementary arithmetic shows that if ten citizens were to meet for five hours—a long time for a meeting!—the maximum equal time each may be allowed for speaking, for parliamentary maneuvers, and for voting is thirty minutes. Small committees are the perfect example of participatory democracy, or at least they can be. Even so, as most of us know from experience, people who have other things to do would not look forward to attending many five-hour committee meetings a month. But you and Rousseau aren't talking about committees. You're talking about governing a *state*, for heaven's sake!

JEAN-JACQUES: Well, not only states. Other organizations and associations might also be democratically run.

JAMES: That is so, of course. But let's go back to the arithmetic of participation. Once you go beyond the size of a committee, the opportunities for all the members to participate necessarily decline rapidly and drastically. Look: If the length of the assembly meeting remains at five hours and the number of citizens goes up to no more than a hundred, then each member has three minutes. At three hundred members you approach the vanishing point of one minute. The number of citizens who were eligible to attend the assembly in classical Athens was twenty thousand, according to one common estimate; the best guesses of some scholars are two or three times that. With just twenty thousand, if time were allocated equally in a five-hour meeting each citizen would have less than one second in which to participate!

JEAN-JACQUES: Now, James, I can do arithmetic. I'm aware of calculations like these. But aren't they misleading? After all, not everyone wants to or has to participate by actually speaking. Among twenty thousand people there aren't twenty thousand different points of view on an issue, particularly if the citizens assemble after days, weeks, or months of discussions going on prior to the assembly. By the time of the meeting, probably only two or three alternatives will seem worth discussing seriously. So ten speakers, say, with about a half hour each to present their arguments, might well be plenty. Or let's say five speakers with a half hour each; that would leave time for brief questions and statements. Let's say five minutes for each intervention. That would allow thirty more people to participate.

JAMES: Bravo! Notice what you have just demonstrated. Thirty-five citizens actively participate in your assembly by speaking. What can the rest do? *They can listen, think, and vote.* So, in an assembly of twenty thousand, less than two-tenths of 1 percent actively participate and more than 99.8 percent participate only by listening, thinking, and voting! A great privilege, your participatory democracy.

JEAN-JACQUES: I find these arithmetical calculations tedious. Depending on the numbers you start with, they come out as you wish. As they say about computers, garbage in, garbage out.

JAMES: Tedious these school exercises may be, but advocates of participatory democracy just don't want to face up to what they demonstrate. All I ask is that the True Believers in participatory democracy plug in their own numbers and then think hard about the results. If they do, they can't rationally escape the conclusion that a democratic system in which most members have full and equal opportunities to participate is possible only in *very* small groups. It's silly to debate precise numbers, but can I assume that you don't intend to restrict democratic government to political systems with less than a few hundred people? Let me be generous and suppose your upper limit is a thousand, perhaps even ten thousand. On that scale most citizens will be unable to participate in any given assembly by more than listening, thinking, and voting. *And that is what they could also do in a representative system.* What's the difference? A large meeting—say, a thousand or more people—is inherently a kind of "representative" system because a few speakers have to represent the voices of all those who can't speak. But without rules of fair representation, the selection of speakers—representatives—could be arbitrary, accidental, and unfair. Establish rules for selecting speakers and you're already close to a representative system. An obvious solution is to create a system in which any citizen may be selected to speak, and let all the citizens vote to choose the ones to speak on their behalf. Or let representatives be chosen by lot, if you prefer. Either way, you'll end up with a fairer system than your attempt to avoid representative government.

JEAN-JACQUES: There would still be one important difference between my solution and yours. In a representative system, the representatives would vote on the policies to be adopted. In an assembly with elected or randomly chosen speakers, the citizens would vote on the policies. So citizens would still exercise more direct control over decisions than under a representative government.

JAMES: I don't deny that. But I wonder if you don't have to reflect on why Rousseau believed "democracy," as he perversely defined it, was impossible: you really can't expect citizens to spend all their time, or even most of their time, in assemblies. The world's work has to be done. Periodic elections of representatives allow the world's work to be done. Are you assuming a pastoral society in which all the work of government might be accomplished by citizen assemblies meeting once a month or so?

JEAN-JACQUES: No, I'm not. Participatory democracy works in the kibbutzim of Israel, and the kibbutzim are highly efficient productive units, not just in agriculture but also in manufacturing and marketing.

JAMES: Are you assuming, then, that your participatory democracy would require a society composed exclusively of communes like the kibbutzim? And that people could freely choose whether they wanted to live and work on the communes? So far as I know, no such society has ever existed. Even in Israel 95 percent of the people don't live on the kibbutzim. In no country have purely voluntary communes ever attracted more than a tiny percentage of the population. The Chinese communes, we now know, were created by heavy coercion and did not survive when the people in the countryside were no longer compelled to join them.

JEAN-JACQUES: Human consciousness isn't forever fixed, you know. Anyway, the commune isn't the only model. Participation could occur in producer cooperatives, town governments, and so on.

JAMES: Town governments? Don't we need to distinguish between two radically different prescriptions for participatory democracy? In one—the one usually advanced by True Believers—it is a comprehensive solution: *All* governments are fully participatory. From our arithmetical exercises, it follows that governments could exist only in small and completely autonomous units. No units could be so large as to make a highly participatory assembly government impossible. In my view that solution is absolutely utopian. In a more modest view of participatory democracy, on the other hand, only *some* units are governed as fully participatory democracies. Others, which are too large for assembly government, are governed by representative systems. If it is true that all the institutions of polyarchy are essential for the democratic process in the government of a large system, then the governments of these large systems would be polyarchies. Which of these two solutions do you have in mind?

JEAN-JACQUES: Though I don't expect it to arrive tomorrow morning, naturally I would prefer the first.

JAMES: I assumed you would. I really can't imagine how, starting with the world we now have, such a world would come about. I suppose a nuclear holocaust might do it, but I don't think you're proposing that particular means. Let's play God, though, and assume that a world with something like its present levels of population and technology will be inhabited only by people living in very small and politically autonomous units, each governed by a highly participatory assembly of all its citizens. Depending on the parameters we play with, there would be thousands or tens of thousands of these small participatory democracies.

JEAN-JACQUES: I distrust your playing God. I'd distrust you even more if you *were* God. But I suppose I have to let you have your fun. Go ahead and play God, if you insist.

JAMES: I appreciate your confidence. Now imagine that people in one of the independent units fall to quarreling with the people in another, or hankering after their goodies, or otherwise wanting to exercise greater control over them. In due time, one unit dominates another. Now that it has become larger than all its neighbors and has more resources, its people begin to experience the rewards of empire. So they vanquish a few more tiny neighbors. Their little empire expands. Still, except for our little empire, none but tiny states cover the globe. What a dazzling prospect lies before this new and growing imperial power! All the other tiny states wait to be consumed like delicious tidbits. Let the Lobsterman weep ever so much for the poor oysters, but he will eat them all the same.

JEAN-JACQUES: As God, I suppose you can create what you wish. But your creation strikes me as artificial, unimaginative, or simply culture-bound. Why do you assume the inevitability of aggression and empire?

JAMES: I don't assume they're inevitable, just highly probable. Do you really think my scenario is improbable, Jean-Jacques? Then reflect on Athens. Reflect on Rome. Reflect on the history of mankind. Or do you want me, playing God, to restore us to Eden and banish evil from the world—this time, forever?

JEAN-JACQUES: No, but please return to earth. In your Jovian stratosphere the shortage of oxygen is making you lose your usual sense of realism. Don't you think that people in the independent self-governing units would resist? Of course they would. In fact, they would surely construct alliances to protect themselves from conquest or absorption by the empire.

JAMES: Exactly! And so they would take the first steps toward creating a larger system, a system too large for participatory democracy. Being democrats, reasoning from the logic of political equality they would create not only representative government but all the institutions of polyarchy.

JEAN-JACQUES: I hope not. Starting from a belief in the importance of full participation, reasoning from the logic of equality, and unburdened by the inertia of the institutions of a large national state, I believe they could find ways of transcending the participatory limits of polyarchy.

JAMES: I want you to explain how they might do that. But first I want you to see how far we have come. Unless you assume that the whole world might exist indefinitely in the form of very small and completely autonomous states (or if not states, then entirely voluntary associations), then you must believe that some associations too large for full participatory democracy are bound to exist. But, if so, then won't these associations need governments?

JEAN-JACQUES: Of course they will have to be governed.

JAMES: Then must you not make one of two choices? Either you will insist that these governments, even if not fully participatory, should satisfy the criteria of the democratic process so far as that may be possible, given their large scale. Or you will not insist that they be democratic, in which case presumably you must be prepared to accept their being governed nondemocratically. But everything in your political philosophy repels you from the second, whereas everything in your political philosophy must surely draw you toward the first. From your point of view, these large-scale governments cannot be perfectly democratic; but, if they must exist, better that they be as democratic as may be feasible than that they be nondemocratic. You will conclude that a second-best democracy is better than the best nondemocracy. So, if polyarchy is essential to the democratic process in these large-scale systems, you will advocate polyarchy. That's the final upshot of my argument. Perhaps we finally agree on that conclusion?

JEAN-JACQUES: Perhaps. But that isn't the end of the problem of participation. Even if I were to concede that large-scale systems are desirable and that polyarchy is necessary if the governments of large-scale systems are to be democratized, I do not have to conclude that the institutions of polyarchy are sufficient for democracy, even in large-scale systems.

JAMES: You're right, of course. So we agree on that, too.

JEAN-JACQUES: Yet I think we still disagree about the possibilities of participation. Even in large systems, opportunities for political participation could be immeasurably greater than the institutions of polyarchy now provide for. I'm certain that democracy hasn't reached its maximum feasible limits with polyarchy. Changes are surely possible that would go beyond polyarchy and produce a new level of democratization. We need to search for a new form of democracy that will expand opportunities for participation and democratic control not only in smaller units where the democratic process could be greatly strengthened but in the larger units as well.

JAMES: I approve of your ends. It is the means that elude me.

JEAN-JACQUES: Then we must both give thought to the problem. For surely we both must reject the complacent view that the democratic idea has finally reached its highest feasible level of attainment with the institutions of polyarchy in the nation-state.

JAMES: On that much we are fully agreed. Sometime we must explore both the limits and the possibilities of democracy under conditions we can reasonably expect to exist in the kind of world that we and our descendants are likely to inhabit.

# Chapter 17

**♦♦♦♦♦♦♦♦♦**

# How Polyarchy Developed in Some Countries and Not Others

In its most general form, democracy is an ancient form of government. Indeed, if as some anthropologists have suggested our ancestral hunter-gatherers governed themselves by discussion and by leadership that depended on continuing consent, democracy in a broad sense may well be the oldest form of government practiced by human beings. For millennia democracy may have been well-nigh universal—the "natural" and standard form of tribal government. But, if so, it was followed by tribal despotism, which perhaps emerged along with the evolution of human society from the subsistence economies of the hunter-gatherers to settled agriculture and herding (Glassman 1986). In the more complex and partly urbanized societies that were present at the dawn of recorded history, democracy had long been superseded as the "natural" solution to the problem of government by monarchy and aristocracy, by despotism and oligarchy.

Although the appearance of popular government in the fifth century before the Christian era among the city-states of Greece and in the city-state of Rome was epochal in the evolution of political possibilities, the assembly-governed cities of Greece contained only a minuscule proportion of humankind. While the inhabitants of the Roman Republic at the peak of its expansion before it degenerated into imperial rule were far more numerous than the Greeks, they too comprised a small fraction of the world's people. Even so, Romans exceeded the total population of the later Italian republics of the late Middle Ages and early Renaissance, which once again were but drops in the great ocean of humanity. A large measure of popular control was not only historically rare in governing the state, it was still more uncommon in governing other associations—religious, economic, social—which often were hierarchies in form and despotisms in practice. Seen in a large historical perspective, then, living under a democratic government is not a "natural" condition for humankind; it is, or at least has been, aberrant. Nor until recently have prevailing ideologies, political philosophies, and recorded beliefs considered democracy to be a "natural" form of government. On the contrary, prevailing ideologies have generally regarded hierarchy as the natural order in human society.

However, as I remarked in the introduction, as an ostensible ideal, a component of prevailing ideologies, and a justificatory myth for rulers, "democracy" has become nearly universal today. In authoritarian countries, in an attempt to lend legitimacy to the regime, "democracy" is often simply redefined, as it has been in the Soviet Union, Eastern Europe, Indonesia, and elsewhere; or, as in Latin America, military regimes may justify their rule as necessary in order to purify political life so that democracy can ultimately be created or restored. Yet however much they distort and qualify the idea of democracy, in all except a handful of countries today government leaders not only claim that their government is for the good of the people, as leaders tend to claim everywhere and always; but beyond that, in most countries they also claim to be responsive to the will of the people; and in many countries they define government by the people to mean mass mobilization under the aegis of a single party. In ideological claims, at least, government of the people, by the people, and for the people has not perished from the earth; it is the standard that almost all regimes now claim to uphold.

Yet countries vary enormously in the extent to which their governments meet the criteria of the democratic process or, more narrowly, sustain the institutions necessary to polyarchy. It may be helpful at this point to recall what these institutions are:

1. Control over governmental decisions about policy is constitutionally vested in elected officials.
2. Elected officials are chosen and peacefully removed in relatively frequent, fair, and free elections in which coercion is quite limited.
3. Practically all adults have the right to vote in these elections.
4. Most adults also have the right to run for the public offices for which candidates run in these elections.
5. Citizens have an effectively enforced right to freedom of expression, particularly political expression, including criticism of the officials, the conduct of the government, the prevailing political, economic, and social system, and the dominant ideology.
6. They also have access to alternative sources of information that are not monopolized by the government or any other single group.
7. Finally they have an effectively enforced right to form and join autonomous associations, including political associations, such as political parties and interest groups, that attempt to influence the government by competing in elections and by other peaceful means.

Although the number of countries with these institutions has greatly increased in the twentieth century, nondemocratic regimes still greatly outnumber polyarchies. As for the governments of systems other than the state, the minimal requirements for the democratic process are exceptional even in polyarchies.

## THE GROWTH OF POLYARCHY

Full polyarchy is a twentieth-century system. Although some of the institutions of polyarchy appeared in a number of English-speaking and European countries in the nineteenth century, in no country did the demos become inclusive until the twentieth century.

Polyarchy has seen three periods of growth: 1776–1930, 1950–59, and the 1980s. The first period begins with the American and French revolutions and closes a few years after the end of the First World War. During this period the institutions that distinguish polyarchy evolved in North America and Europe. Yet in most countries that reached the threshold of polyarchy by 1920, the institutions were often defective, by present standards, until the last third of the nineteenth century or later.

In many of these countries it was not until the end of the century or even later that control over governmental decisions about policy was constitutionally vested in elected officials. This crucial development was often prevented until they had gained national independence; until then, of course, some control over their decisions was vested in foreign rulers. Of seventeen European countries that were full or male polyarchies by 1920, only seven had created elected governments independent of foreign control before 1850. Three more established independent elected governments before 1900 and the remaining seven only after the turn of the century.[1]

Elections in many of these countries also failed to meet our present conception of what is required in order to be free and fair. For example, the secret ballot came into general use some years after it was first introduced in elections in South Australia in 1858. In Great Britain, the secret ballot was not introduced in parliamentary and municipal elections until 1872. In the United States, where open voting was not uncommon, the Australian ballot was widely adopted only after the presidential election of 1884 led to widespread charges of voting frauds. In France, until 1913 ballots were openly provided by candidates to voters who then folded them and placed them in the ballot box.

Another obstacle to polyarchy in many European countries was the dependence of prime minister and cabinet on the approval of a monarch and in some cases a nonelective second chamber.[2] Of the seventeen European countries mentioned earlier, in only France, Italy, and Switzerland were cabinets or prime ministers fully responsible to an elective legislature before 1900. In Britain, to be sure, the dependence of the prime minister and cabinet on parliamentary majorities rather than the monarch had already been established as a constitutional principle by the end of the eighteenth century; but it was not until 1911 that the power of the House of Lords to modify, delay, and prevent legislation was virtually brought to an end. In the Netherlands, accountability was attained during the first decade of the century, while in the Scandinavian countries parliament gained control from the monarch only after acute and prolonged constitutional crises: Norway in 1884 (though it did not gain independence from Sweden and the Swedish monarchy until 1905), Denmark in 1901,[3] and Sweden not until 1918.

Yet because none had an inclusive demos, even countries that otherwise satisfied the requirements of polyarchy failed to achieve full polyarchy until the twentieth century. Not only were large percentages of the adult male population excluded from the suffrage in most countries, but until the second decade of the twentieth century only New Zealand (1893) and Australia (1902) had extended the suffrage to women in national elections. (South Australia did so in 1894). In France and Belgium, in fact, women did not gain the suffrage in national elections until after the Second World War. In Switzerland, where universal suffrage was legally established for males in 1848, well before any other country had done so, the suffrage in national elections was not guaranteed for women until 1971. Exclusion from the suffrage meant exclusion from many other forms of participation as well. Thus until the twentieth century all "democratic" countries were at best governed as male polyarchies.[4] The proportion of adults who actually voted (or, certainly, participated in other ways) was even smaller. In only a few countries did the voters exceed 10 percent of the total population, and even in those—with the single exception of New Zealand—they were less than about 20 percent at most (figure 17.1).

Each decade from 1860 to 1920 saw an increase in the number of countries possessing all the institutions of polyarchy except an inclusive suffrage. By 1930, eighteen full polyarchies and three male polyarchies existed, all either in Europe or in countries of predominantly European origins—the four English-speaking countries and ex-colonies (Australia, Canada, New Zealand, and the United States), together with Costa Rica and Uruguay in Latin America (table 17.1).

The end of this initial period of growth was punctuated, however, by the first instances of democratic breakdown and transition to dictatorship, as fascism was consolidated in Italy (1923–25), the Pilsudski dictatorship was established in Poland (1926), and the military seized power in Argentina (1930). The 1930s witnessed further authoritarian takeovers in Germany, Austria, and Spain, together with the Nazi occupation of Czechoslovakia. As a result, it became commonplace to see democracy in the grip of a deep and lasting crisis. After many decades of steady expansion, the breakdown of polyarchies in what were seen as advanced European countries appeared to presage a profound decline in the prospects for democracy in the world.

Yet as World War II receded, the number of countries governed by polyarchy—with women included in the demos, they were now full polyarchies—jumped to a second plateau of 36–40 countries, where it remained for about thirty years (table 17.2). During this same period, however, breakdowns and authoritarian takeovers also took place: in Czechoslovakia, Poland, and Hungary in the 1940s, in Brazil, Ecuador, and Peru in the 1960s, and in Chile, South Korea, Uruguay, and Turkey in the 1970s. Meanwhile with the collapse of outright colonialism the number of nominally independent countries in the world grew steadily; and new countries

*Figure 17.1. Restricted Suffrage and Full Suffrage Polyarchies, 1840–1930*

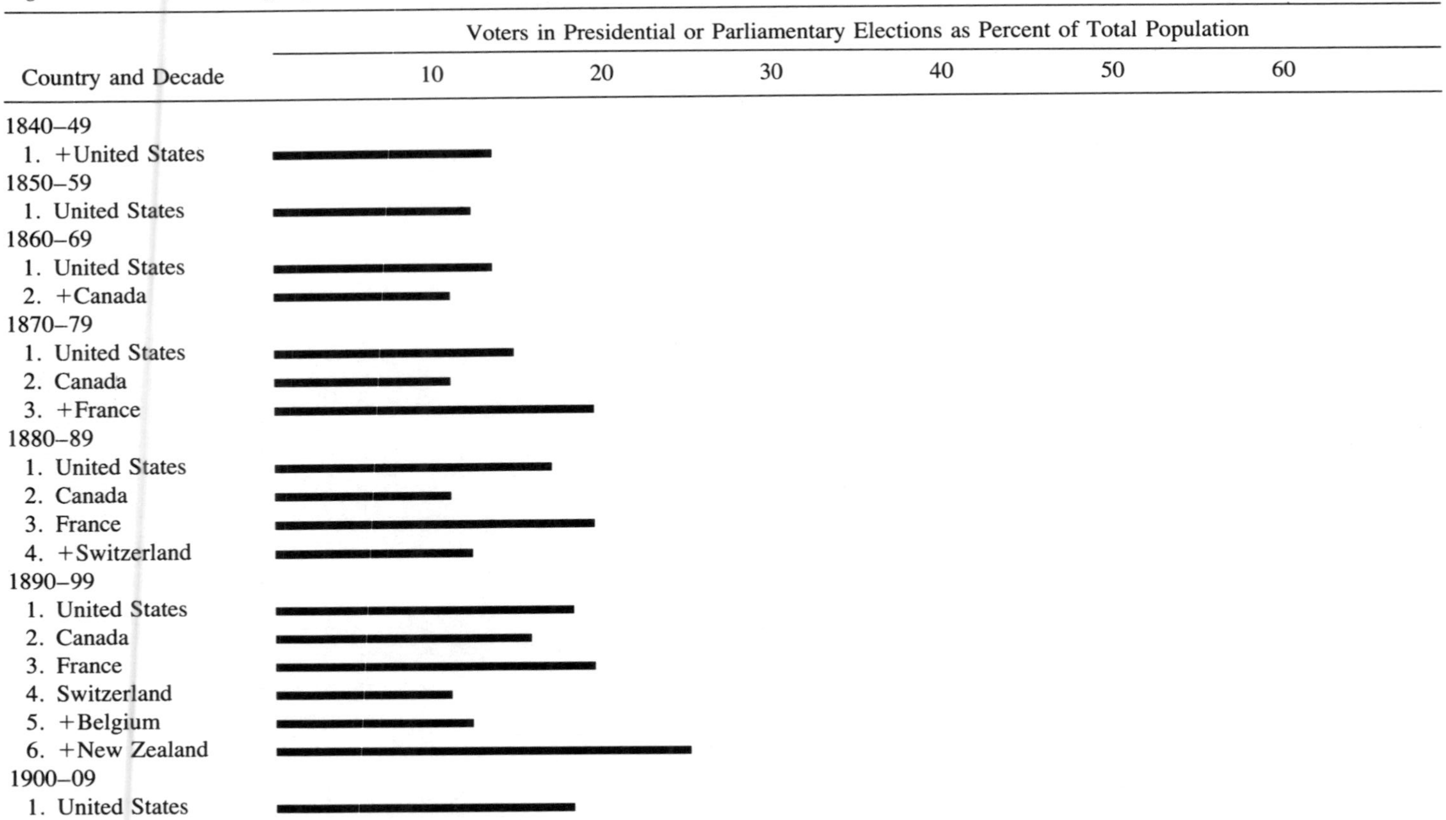

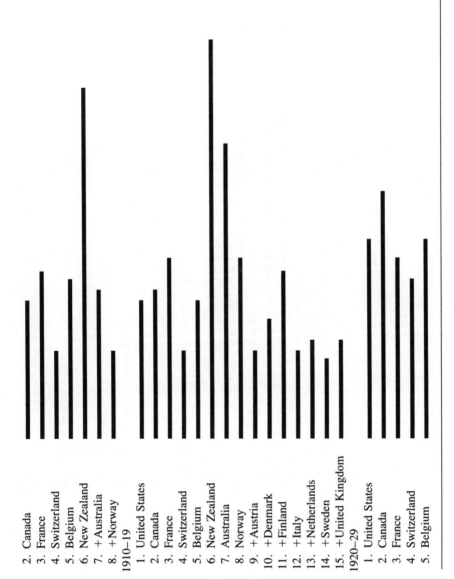

2. Canada
3. France
4. Switzerland
5. Belgium
6. New Zealand
7. +Australia
8. +Norway
1910–19
1. United States
2. Canada
3. France
4. Switzerland
5. Belgium
6. New Zealand
7. Australia
8. Norway
9. +Austria
10. +Denmark
11. +Finland
12. +Italy
13. +Netherlands
14. +Sweden
15. +United Kingdom
1920–29
1. United States
2. Canada
3. France
4. Switzerland
5. Belgium

(continued)

*Figure 17.1.* (*Continued*)

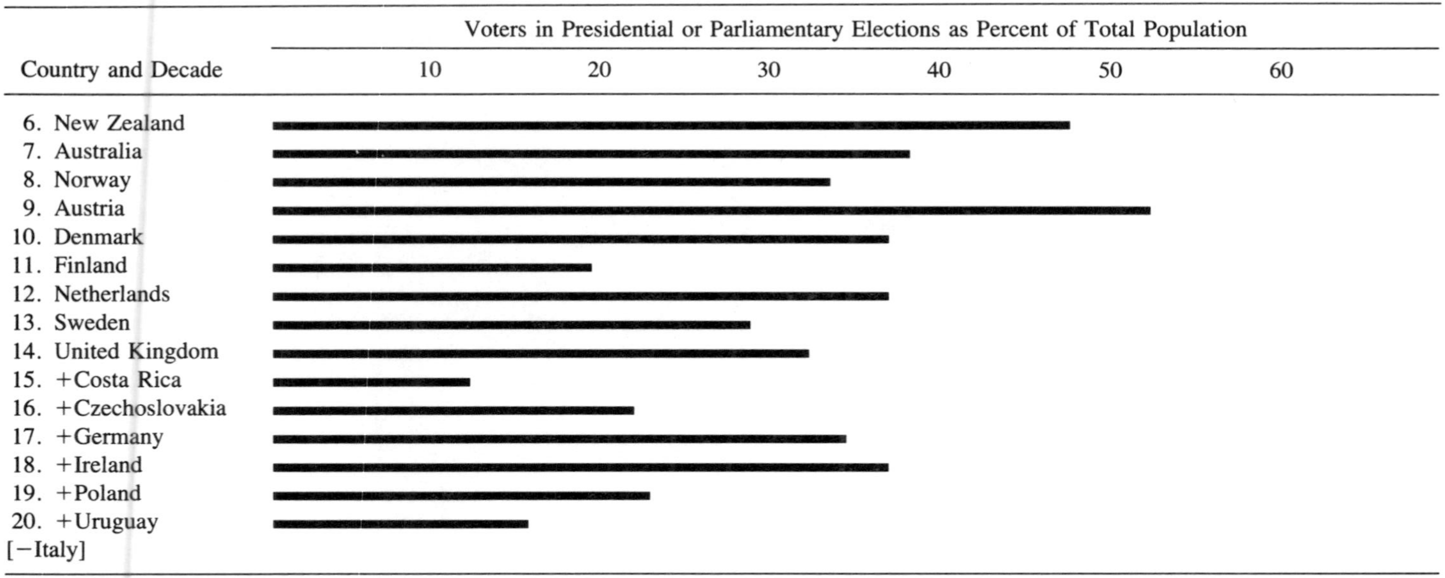

Voters in Presidential or Parliamentary Elections as Percent of Total Population

| Country and Decade | 10 | 20 | 30 | 40 | 50 | 60 |
|---|---|---|---|---|---|---|

6. New Zealand
7. Australia
8. Norway
9. Austria
10. Denmark
11. Finland
12. Netherlands
13. Sweden
14. United Kingdom
15. + Costa Rica
16. + Czechoslovakia
17. + Germany
18. + Ireland
19. + Poland
20. + Uruguay
[− Italy]

*Sources:* Except for United States 1840–49 all data are from Vanhanen 1984. Data for United States 1840–49 are from Congressional Quarterly 1979 and U.S. Bureau of the Census 1960.

*Note:* For further description of the data, see note to table 17.2.

*Table 17.1. Polyarchies, 1930*

| Full Polyarchies | Male Polyarchies | Failed Polyarchies |
|---|---|---|
| Europe | | |
| 1. Austria | 1. Belgium | 1. Italy |
| 2. Czechoslovakia | 2. France | 2. Poland |
| 3. Denmark | 3. Switzerland | |
| 4. Finland | | |
| 5. Germany | | |
| 6. Iceland | | |
| 7. Ireland | | |
| 8. Luxembourg | | |
| 9. Netherlands | | |
| 10. Norway | | |
| 11. Sweden | | |
| 12. United Kingdom | | |
| Other | | |
| 13. Australia | | 3. Argentina |
| 14. Canada | | |
| 15. Costa Rica | | |
| 16. New Zealand | | |
| 17. United States | | |
| 18. Uruguay | | |

*Source:* Unpublished data provided by M. Coppedge and W. Reinicke.

typically began independence with a full set of democratic political institutions. Not surprisingly, however, in many new countries polyarchy was soon replaced by authoritarianism. Thus the newly independent countries of Africa, which invariably were launched with ostensibly democratic constitutions, swiftly plunged into dictatorship; by the 1980s, on the entire continent only Botswana remained in the ranks of the polyarchies. As a partial offset to this decline, microstates among the islands of the Caribbean and the Pacific helped to swell the ranks of the polyarchies. Together with transitions and redemocratization in Latin America, by the mid-1980s the number of polyarchies had reached about fifty, or slightly less than a third of the one hundred and sixty-eight nominally independent countries then in existence (table 17.3), a proportion barely different from what it had been a half-century earlier (table 17.2).

## THEORETICAL CONSIDERATIONS

As these examples show, countries are not static and conditions may change. For example, conditions that initially favor polyarchy may weaken and thereby cause the breakdown of a polyarchy, as in Chile between 1970 and 1973. Or

Table 17.2. Number of Polyarchies (Male or Full) and Nonpolyarchies (by decades)

| Decade | Polyarchies (Male or Full) | NonPolyarchies | Total | Percent Polyarchies |
|--------|-----------------------------|----------------|-------|---------------------|
| 1850–59 | 1 | 36 | 37 | 3 |
| 1860–69 | 2 | 37 | 39 | 5 |
| 1870–79 | 3 | 38 | 41 | 7 |
| 1880–89 | 4 | 38 | 42 | 10 |
| 1890–99 | 6 | 37 | 43 | 14 |
| 1900–09 | 8 | 40 | 48 | 17 |
| 1910–19 | 15 | 36 | 51 | 29 |
| 1920–29 | 22 | 42 | 64 | 34 |
| 1930–39 | 19 | 46 | 65 | 29 |
| 1940–49 | 25 | 50 | 75 | 33 |
| 1950–59 | 36 | 51 | 87 | 41 |
| 1960–69 | 40 | 79 | 119 | 34 |
| 1970–79 | 37 | 84 | 121 | 31 |

Source: Adapted from data in Vanhanen 1984, table 22, p. 120. I have added Iceland and Luxembourg, which Vanhanen omits because of their size. For comments on the data, see note following.

Note: As indicated in the source notes to figure 17.1 and to this table, the data are from Vanhanen 1984. Although Vanhanen's study is an impressive and useful work, the indicators have some drawbacks that ought to be kept in mind in interpreting figure 17.1 and table 17.2.

The indicator of "democracy" is ID, or index of democratization, which is *Competition* multiplied by *Participation* and divided by 100. The threshold value for transition to "democracy" is 5.0.

*Competition* is the percentage of the smaller parties' total share of the votes cast in parliamentary or presidential elections, or both. Thus in a one-party system it would be 0, in a highly competitive two-party system it would approach 50 percent, and in a multiparty system it could go well over 50 percent (as in the Netherlands in 1970–79, when it was 71.1). Vanhanen adopts 30 percent as a threshold value.

*Participation* is the percentage of the total population that actually voted in the elections. Vanhanen adopts 10 percent as a threshold value.

Thus in order for a country to qualify as a democracy,

(i) 10 percent or more of the total population must participate in elections (P)

(ii) 30 percent or more of the vote must go to parties other than the largest party (C)

(iii) ID, or P × C, must not be less than 5.0. Thus if P is at the 10 percent threshold, then C must be at least 50 percent. If C is at the 30 percent threshold, then P must be at least 16.6 percent.

The measures and thresholds are therefore somewhat arbitrary. ID does not necessarily reflect the legal and constitutional situation of a country or a satisfactory level of institutional achievement of polyarchy. Nevertheless, as an inspection of the table shows, a classification based on legal suffrage and the institutions of polyarchy would probably not greatly alter the countries in the table or the decades of their emergence as "democracies."

*Table 17.3. A Classification of 168 Countries, circa 1981–85 (According to four criteria of polyarchy: free and fair elections, freedom of organizations, freedom of expression, and existence of alternative sources of information)*

| Classification | N | Anomalies | Percent of All Countries |
|---|---|---|---|
| 1. Full polyarchies | 41 | 1 | 25 |
| 2. Polyarchies with minor restrictions | 10 | | 6 |
|     Total polyarchies | 51 | | 31 |
| 3. Quasi-polyarchies (major restrictions) | 13 | | 8 |
| 4. Dominant party regimes | 12 | 4 | 10 |
| 5. Multiparty nondemocratic regimes | 7 | | 4 |
| 6. Nondemocratic with limited freedom of expression | | | |
|     Type A[a] | 8 | 1 | 5 |
|     Type B | 18 | 1 | 11 |
|     Type C | 17 | 2 | 11 |
|     Type D | 5 | 2 | 4 |
| 7. Nondemocratic with total control of organizations, expression, and media | 26 | | 15 |
|     Totals | 157 | 11 | 100 |

*Source:* Unpublished data provided by Coppedge and W. Reinicke

[a]Type A is a nondemocratic regime (NDR) with limited freedom of expression that practices near-total repression of organizations or the media, but not both.

Type B is an NDR with limited freedom of expression that exercises near-total control of organizations and the media.

Type C is an NDR with limited freedom of expression that practices near-total control of the media and total control of organizations.

Type D is an NDR with limited freedom of expression but total control of organizations and the media.

initially weak conditions may grow stronger and thus favor the stability of an existing polyarchy, as in West Germany and Japan in the decades after World War II. Increasingly favorable conditions may also bring about a transition to polyarchy in a country that hitherto has experienced only nondemocratic regimes, as in Britain in the nineteenth century, or may support the redemocratization of a country in which polyarchy had broken down, as in Uruguay in the 1980s. In addition to these changes in specific countries, more widespread and often slower-moving changes also occur: The late twentieth century, for example, provides an environment for democratization, as we shall see in the next chapter, that is in some respects less favorable, and in some more favorable, than the first period of growth in polyarchy.

What conditions favor the development, consolidation, and stability of polyarchy in a country or, on the other hand, limit the prospects for polyarchy? Although uncertainties still remain despite the rapidly accumulating results of research over the past several decades, nearly two centuries of experience help us to identify some of the most important of these conditions.

Until the 1960s attempts to account for the existence, absence, and failure of democracy either depended on the experience of only a few countries, of which the relevance of the democratic failures in Italy and Germany for breakdowns elsewhere was vastly overemphasized, or relied on such "hard" data as was readily available, was assumed to be valid and reliable, and consisted of such things as per capita income, literacy, telephones, hospital beds, and the like. Other conditions that were theoretically crucial, such as attitudes, beliefs, political culture, and similar "soft" variables, were omitted or remained highly conjectural. Thereafter, however, the nearly worldwide expansion of political science as an academic field, together with the adoption of newer techniques for systematically gathering and analyzing data, helped to provide better evidence on the experiences of a much wider range of countries.[5] As a consequence, and even though the demands of theory continue to exceed the supply and quality of data, it is now possible to anchor theory somewhat more firmly in experience.

Turning first to theory, it is hardly debatable that the likelihood of polyarchy in a country depends on the strength of certain conditions. The problem is to determine what those conditions are and how variations in them affect the likelihood of polyarchy. The most relevant patterns of development are these:[6]

1. In a country with a nonpolyarchal regime, favorable conditions develop and persist. Therefore it is highly likely that a transition to polyarchy occurs, that the institutions of polyarchy are consolidated, and that the polyarchal system persists, that is, is stable.[7] Thus,

    Given favorable conditions:
    then a nonpolyarchal regime (NPR) → stable polyarchy

2. In a country with a nonpolyarchal regime, favorable conditions do not develop or are weak. Therefore it is highly unlikely that a transition to polyarchy takes place and highly likely that a nonpolyarchal regime persists. Thus,

    Given unfavorable conditions:
    then NPR → NPR

3. In a country with a nonpolyarchal regime, the conditions are mixed or temporarily favorable. If under these conditions polyarchy develops, the likely possibilities are:

    3.a. Polyarchy breaks down within a short time (less than twenty years), a transition to a nonpolyarchal regime occurs, and a nonpolyarchal regime persists:

        Given mixed or temporarily favorable conditions:
        then NPR → polyarchy → NPR

    3.b. As in 3.a, except that the nonpolyarchal regime also breaks down, another transition to polyarchy occurs (*redemocratization*), polyarchy is consolidated, and it persists:

*Figure 17.2. Transitions from Nonpolyarchal Regimes*

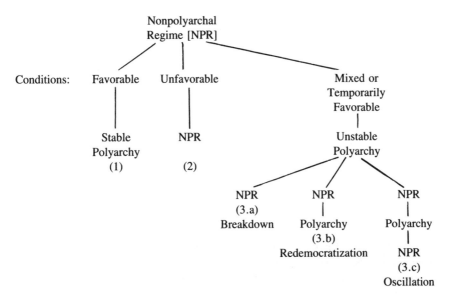

Given mixed or temporarily favorable conditions:
then NPR → polyarchy → NPR → polyarchy
3.c. As in 3.b, except that polyarchy is not consolidated, and the system oscillates between polyarchy and nonpolyarchy:
Given mixed or temporarily favorable conditions:
then NPR → polyarchy → NPR → polyarchy →
NPR → etc.

The five sequences are illustrated in figure 17.2.

What conditions favor the first sequence—the development, consolidation, and stability of polyarchy? In principle, we can answer this question by comparing the countries in which the first sequence has occurred with countries in which it has not. Though difficult in practice, the comparisons help us to arrive at some fairly well grounded judgments. This is the task we undertake in the following chapter.

# Chapter 18

◆◆◆◆◆◆◆◆◆

# Why Polyarchy Developed in Some Countries and Not Others

Why has stable polyarchy developed in some countries and not others? To put the question in another way, what conditions increase or decrease the chances for polyarchy? Because the experiences of different countries during the last century and a half have generated all the sequences described at the end of the last chapter, we can specify the most important conditions with considerable confidence. While no single condition can account for the existence or absence of polyarchy in a country, if all the conditions that I am about to describe are strongly present then polyarchy is almost a sure thing; while if all of them are absent or extremely weak, the likelihood is close to zero. In many countries, however, the outcome is more uncertain; while some of the conditions may be relatively strong and therefore relatively favorable, others are weak and therefore unfavorable. Then too conditions may change, either strengthening or reducing the chances for stable polyarchy in a country.

## CIVILIAN CONTROL OF VIOLENT COERCION

As we saw in an earlier chapter, all states, including democratic states, employ coercion. States employ coercion internally to enforce laws and policies and externally in their relations with other states. The means of coercion are of many kinds—economic, social, psychological, physical. The typical and distinctive capacities of a state are its instruments for physical coercion—military and police organizations whose task is to apply (or threaten to apply) systematic violence to maintain order and security.

But what is to prevent leaders from employing coercive violence to establish and maintain a nondemocratic regime? Throughout recorded history, military and police forces have often actively engaged in political life; and even when these forces have been controlled by civilians, civilian leaders have sometimes used them to install and uphold a nondemocratic regime. So too in the modern world, in many countries nondemocratic regimes are sustained, at least in part, by organized instruments for violent coercion. Yet in the past as in the present, in some political systems popularly chosen leaders have been able to exercise enough control over the military and police to permit the institutions of polyarchy to exist.

In order for a state to be governed democratically, evidently two conditions are required: (1) If military and police organizations exist, as they surely will, then they must be subject to civilian control. But civilian control, while necessary, is not sufficient, for many nondemocratic regimes also maintain civilian control. Therefore, (2) the civilians who control the military and police must themselves be subject to the democratic process.

That control over military and police forces by popularly chosen civilian leaders is sometimes possible can be accounted for largely by two factors: the existing state of military organization and techniques and the use of appropriate means for civilian control. The first is a broad historical condition that helps to determine the options open to political leaders during a historically specific and possibly very lengthy period. The second is a set of possible means that political leaders may choose, more or less deliberately and intentionally, to employ in order to ensure civilian control.

### The Political Consequences of Military Organization and Techniques

Historically speaking, the chances for popular government have depended partly on the existing state of military organization and technology. Military organization and technology have helped to determine whether the military forces were controlled by civilians and whether the civilians in control were themselves subject to the democratic process. The tendency to adopt the democratic process in governing the state has been stronger during periods when military organization and technology have required that large numbers of combatants be drawn from the general population. One writer has even proposed a Military Participation Ratio that links the breadth of participation in military affairs to the likelihood of self-government and individual rights (Andreski 1968). Although this "ratio" suggests a more exact correspondence than can be confirmed by historical experience, we do find a rough correspondence (at least in the Western world) of the following kind: The more that military superiority has depended on the capacity of a state for mobilizing large numbers of lightly armed foot soldiers, the greater have been the prospects for popular government.[1]

To understand why democracy developed in Greece in the early fifth century B.C., for example, but not in previous centuries or in thirteenth-century England or France, we would need to take account, among other things, of military organization and technology. From Homeric times to the seventh century B.C. the city-states of Greece were dominated by the nobility. An important part of the explanation is to be found in the prevailing military technology: the horse and chariot. For only the nobles could afford to own horses and war chariots. And the nobles' superior means of violent coercion in war facilitated their domination in political life as well, since they could easily intimidate poorly organized groups of commoners lightly armed with little more than clubs and farm tools. During the seventh century, however, the military and political supremacy of the aristocracy was undermined by the emergence of a new and superior fighting force, the infantry—the famous hoplites portrayed on innumerable Greek vases. More well-to-do commoners could afford the equipment of the hoplite—helmet, shield, corselet, greaves, and spear—and they also had enough leisure to engage in the training necessary for attack and defense in the disciplined close order of the hoplite phalanx. Although the details of the process are unclear, the commoners on whose loyalty and bravery the polis now depended gained increasing influence in political life.[2] The overthrow of aristocratic rule was often facilitated by popular tyrants, who may have drawn support from the hoplite class (Ste. Croix 1981, 282). Ultimately, too, it was the hoplite stratum that brought about the transition to democracy (Fine 1983, 59–61, 99–100; Sealey 1976, 30, 57).[3] In Athens democracy was deepened further by another military development: The growth of the Athenian navy meant that even those too poor to obtain the equipment of the hoplite could now serve as rowers in the galleys—as free men, not slaves. "Those who drive the ships," wrote a fifth-century pamphleteer, "are those who possess the power in the state" (Finley 1972, 50).

The Greek solution to the problem of civilian control over military forces was, then, the citizen militia. The militia could be rapidly mobilized for war and just as rapidly disbanded in peace. What is more, it was led by generals who were elected by the popular assembly. As a result, during the two centuries in which the system endured in Athens, no political leader could possibly govern for long without popular support. Even when democracy was briefly overthrown in 411 and 404, the oligarchies were swiftly displaced when they failed to gain the steady support of the military forces, that is, the citizens in the hoplite ground forces or the navy and their elected generals. When Athenian democracy was finally subjected to military domination, the coercive forces were not internal but external—first Macedon and then Rome.[4]

Although the military organization and technology of the Roman Republic differed in important ways from that of Greece, the solution was fundamentally the same: The legions of the early Roman Republic consisted of a citizen militia composed of ordinary Roman citizens.[5] But when in the terminal stages of the republic the citizen militia had become what amounted to a permanent and independent military establishment of professional and even mercenary soldiers, and the use of violence applied by the legions and by "gangs of hired professional thugs" came to be commonplace in Roman political life, the republic was doomed (Finley 1983, 117–18). Ambitious leaders, often military leaders themselves, now discovered that they could readily transform military resources into political resources. After republican government was replaced by the principate, under the emperors the praetorian cohorts, which during the republic had been the bodyguard of the generals, became an active political force; together with the frontier legions they engaged in political executions and terror and sometimes made and unmade emperors. What recent writers have called "praetorianism"—military intervention in government and domination over the executive—had made its appearance (Huntington 1957; Huntington 1968; Nordlinger 1977; Perlmutter 1977).

In the Middle Ages, changes in military organization and techniques once again vested superiority in the few who could afford the highly trained horse and equipment of the mounted knight. The citizen-soldier was eclipsed, and with him, for many centuries, the historical opportunities for democratic or republican government in most of Europe. In the Swiss cantons, however, the citizen militia supported by universal military service, armed with the pike and defending a terrain that strongly favored the foot soldier, could defeat the mounted knight. Not surprisingly, then, assembly democracy took root in mountain cantons that centuries later formed the core of the Swiss Confederation.

In the fourteenth and fifteenth centuries, by demonstrating the vulnerability of the mounted knight English foot soldiers armed with the longbow destroyed the military foundation of feudalism. The critical importance of foot soldiers was later enhanced by the development of the musket and in due course the rifle. In the eighteenth century military organization and technology came to depend on the employment of great masses of infantry soldiers whose ranks could be filled only by drawing extensively on the entire male population. For a half-century or so, given about equal training, what counted heavily in battle was sheer numbers of rather lightly armed men—a crude and violent achievement of majority rule. But the advantages of sheer numbers could be increased by commitment, and commitment could be enhanced by evoking loyalties to the country or the nation.[6] Yet to see oneself as a member of a nation, a privilege for which one was expected to make sacrifices, could also justify one in making a more expansive claim, including a right to a fair share in governing. The citizen-soldier was both soldier and citizen, or at any rate entitled to the franchise (Janowitz 1978, 178–79). Countries with mass armies now found that they had ushered in the Age of Democratic Revolutions. It was under these historical conditions in which military organization and technology were more favorable to democratization than they had been for many centuries that, as we saw in the last chapter, the institutions of polyarchy took root in one country after another.

In the United States particularly, the prospects for ruling by coercive violence were lower than they had ever been in any state, with the possible exception of Switzerland. As we shall see in a moment, the standing military establishment was tiny. But beyond that, existing military organization and technology favored the foot soldier armed with the musket and later the rifle. These weapons were so easily accessible and widely owned that Americans were virtually a nation in arms. In a quite concrete sense, the consent of the governed was absolutely essential if there were to be any government at all, for no government could have been imposed on the people of the United States over the opposition of a majority.

However, the state of military organization and technology that was on the whole so favorable to polyarchy in North America and Europe shifted once again—now to a more unfavorable balance. Military advantage gradually shifted away from numbers of lightly equipped troops to forces equipped with new and costly weapons of increasing lethality—heavy artillery, mortars, machine guns, tanks, and air and sea power, to which nuclear weapons were finally added. Unlike the pike, longbow, musket, or rifle, these could never become widely dispersed household items. Concentrated in a relatively few hands, they would provide enormous resources of violent coercion to a minority willing and able to use them for political ends. A growth in capacities for creating and employing bureaucratic organizations (Max Weber's "rational-legal bureaucracy"), together with new technologies for surveillance, further increased potentialities for centralized coercion. Centralized police systems could now be employed for destroying opposition more effectively than ever before in recorded history.

Thus the development of military and police organization and technology in the twentieth century has created a potential for centralized coercion much greater than existed during the eighteenth and nineteenth centuries, if not, in fact, greater than ever before. Yet as we saw in the last chapter, not only have the older polyarchies survived in this century but new ones have come into existence. If the state of military organization and technology does not account for this phenomenon, what does?

### Taming Violent Coercion

Democratic states have used several means, often in combination, to ensure that military and police forces are not employed to destroy democratic rule.

1. A democratic state may eliminate the coercive capabilities of military or police forces or reduce them to virtual insignificance. In rare cases, military forces have actually been abolished outright. Japan, where the military had become a powerful political actor in the 1930s, declared in its 1947 constitution (largely a creation of the United States military occupation) that it would never maintain land, sea, and air forces. Although the provision was weakened by the subsequent development of a national "police reserve" and then a "national defense force," its effect was to prevent the reemergence of the military as a significant political actor in the new polyarchy. Costa Rica, which had enjoyed popularly elected governments since 1889 except for two brief periods when governments took office with the aid of military forces, concluded the second of these by abolishing its armed forces in 1948–49 (Blachman and Hellman 1986, 156–60).

Although unlike Japan and Costa Rica the United States never formally abolished its armed forces, throughout most of its national history they have been minuscule. Until the Second World War, both Britain and the United States maintained tiny standing armies on the assumption that their power on the sea was sufficient to prevent invasion, and naval forces were poorly adapted to the task of coercing the population at home. In the United States the figures for 1830 are typical of the peacetime forces for the entire period from 1789 to the period following the Second World War. In 1830 the total armed forces of the United States—army, navy, and marines—amounted to one of every 1080 persons in the country; only one of every 2073 persons was in the army; army officers, numbering 627 in all, were one out of 20,575. In 1860, on the eve of the Civil War the figures were little different. At the outbreak of World War II in 1939, the total military force of the United States stood at 334,473 in a population of 131 million; army officers numbered under 15,000, or one person in 9045.[7]

2. A democratic state may disperse control over military or police forces among a multiplicity of local governments. Thus in the English-speaking polyarchies, police forces have been for the most part under local control.[8] Historically, in both Britain and the United States, even the military land forces have been partly dispersed as local or state militia. During the period when parliamentary supremacy evolved in predemocratic Britain, the militia was a counterweight to the standing forces led by officer-aristocrats; the militia was locally controlled and manned by local subjects who remained in service for brief terms solely for purposes of local defense. The militia was not integrated with the standing forces until the end of the nineteenth century (Perlmutter 1977, 40). During the nineteenth century in the United States, the state militias were for all practical purposes independent units under the control of state officials. In Switzerland, the constitutions of 1848 and 1874 (now in force) prohibited the confederation from maintaining a standing army and provided instead for a citizen militia under the peacetime control of the cantons.

3. Military forces may be formed of persons who share the civilian and democratic orientations of the general population. As we saw, this was the solution in Athens, where the hoplites on land and the rowers at sea were citizens called briefly into service in defense of the polis. It was the solution in predemocratic Europe of the seventeenth and eighteenth centuries.[9] It was also the solution of the Swiss Confederation, which in 1848 and 1874 made universal military service a constitutionally imposed obligation. With the exception of the top officers and a few other military personnel who are now full-time professionals, the Swiss military is still composed of citizens on temporary duty. In most other European countries, since World War II the land forces have been composed primarily of troops raised by conscription for brief terms of service—civilians in uniform.

4. Finally, indoctrination of professional soldiers, particularly officers, may help to ensure civilian control by elected democratic leaders. Military professionalism as such does not ensure civilian control, much less democratic control. Military professionalism does however tend to create and sustain beliefs about the regime to which the military owes loyalty and obedience and which it is obligated to defend. Obviously these beliefs may vary, depending on the regime; the professional revolutionary soldier may be loyal to the idea of a future regime that has yet to be created. In a democratic country not only may professional military personnel have received their early socialization as civilians, and as a result share civilian beliefs as to the legitimacy of the constitutional order and the idea and practices of democracy, but their sense of obligation to obey the constitutionally elected civilian leadership may be strengthened by the professional code of the military establishment.

Under certain circumstances, however, civilian control of a professional military establishment in a democratic country is likely to be jeopardized. Civilian control is endangered if professionalism creates a deep social and psychological gulf between military professionals and civilians, so that, as in Brazil in the 1950s and 1960s (Stepan 1973, 64), the military becomes a distinctly separate social order, a military caste cut off from civilian society. Or again, if the military professionals believe that the fundamental interests of the military establishment are endangered by the civilian leadership, they are likely to resist civilian control and may cast it off entirely, as in Brazil in 1964, Ghana in 1965, and Argentina repeatedly from 1955 to 1983 (Nordlinger 1977, 66–78; Stepan 1971, 153ff.; Stepan 1973, 50–65; Cavarozzi 1986, 31ff.). Civilian control also becomes more difficult as the size and complexity of the military establishment increase. Thus it has become notoriously difficult for a U.S. secretary of defense to control the enormous defense establishment and even more difficult for Congress to do so.

Finally, military leaders may reject civilian control if they believe that the stability, health, or existence of the system they are obligated to preserve—whether state, nation, society, or constitutional order—is endangered by democratically elected leadership. In many Latin American countries the constitution even assigns a certain responsibility to the military to ensure law and order or the proper functioning of the constitution. In Brazil, Alfred Stepan remarks, these constitutional obligations have "meant that in any clash between the president and the legislature, appeals have been made by civilians to the military to fulfill their constitutional obligation to defend the prerogatives of the Congress" (Stepan 1971, 75). Disorder, civil strife, guerrilla activity, acute polarization, continuing economic crisis, the prospect or actuality of government by leaders or movements ideologically unacceptable to the military—all may help to trigger off a military takeover, as in Brazil in 1964, Chile and Uruguay in 1973, and Argentina in 1976.[10]

The prevailing state of military technology and organization has in some times and places (classical Greece and nineteenth century Europe and America, for example) favored popular government and in other times and places (Greece before about 650 B.C. and medieval Europe, for example) has been highly unfavorable in its effects. In this century, military technology and organization are, on the whole, unfavorable. Yet in this century not only have older polyarchies managed to survive but new polyarchies have come into existence. It is obvious, then, that the prevailing state of military technology and organization does not adequately account for the presence or absence of polyarchy.

Clearly, civilian control over the military and police is a necessary condition for polyarchy, and the failure of civilian control is sufficient to account for the existence of nondemocratic regimes in many countries. But civilian control is not sufficient for polyarchy, since some nondemocratic regimes also maintain civilian control over their military and police forces; indeed, leaders in these nondemocratic regimes employ the superior coercive resources of the military and police to maintain their rule.

It is obvious, then, that we cannot explain the presence or absence of polyarchy in a country by civilian control alone.

Thus while the concentration and control of coercive violence is a part of the explanation we seek, it cannot be the whole explanation.

## A MODERN, ORGANIZATIONALLY PLURALIST SOCIETY

Historically, polyarchy has been strongly associated with a society marked by a host of interrelated characteristics: a relatively high level of income and wealth per capita, long-run growth in per capita income and wealth, a high level of urbanization, a rapidly declining or relatively small agricultural population, great occupational diversity, extensive literacy, a comparatively large number of persons who have attended institutions of higher education, an economic order in which production is mainly carried on by relatively autonomous firms whose decisions are strongly oriented toward national and international markets, and relatively high levels of conventional indicators of well-being, such as physicians and hospital beds per thousand persons, life expectancy, infant mortality, percentage of families with various consumer durables, and so on. Societal measures like these are so highly intercorrelated as to justify the conclusion—if further justification of a rather obvious historical judgment were necessary—that they are all indicators of a more or less distinguishable type of social system (for example, see table 1 in Vanhanen 1984 showing the intercorrelations of explanatory variables). In the extensive and growing body of research on the conditions of democracy, probably nothing is more firmly established than the correlations between any of these societal measures and indicators of democracy or polyarchy (see, for example, Vanhanen 1984).

What are we to call this type of society, one that is evidently so favorable to polyarchy? It bears many labels: liberal, capitalist, bourgeois, middle-class, business, modern (and postmodern), competitive, market-oriented, open . . . Most of these terms, however, lay too much stress on subordinate features or special aspects of the society. Some of the essential qualities are perhaps best conveyed by the idea of *modernity* (for example, historically high average levels of wealth, income, consumption, and education, great occupational diversity, large urban populations, a marked decrease in the agricultural population, and the relative economic importance of agriculture). Other aspects are captured by the *dynamic* nature of the society (economic growth, increasing standards of living), and some by its *pluralist* character (numerous relatively autonomous groups and organizations, particularly in the economy). I am therefore going to refer to this particular kind of society as a *modern dynamic pluralist society* and a country with these features as a *modern dynamic pluralist country* (for convenience, MDP.)

### Why an MDP Society Favors Polyarchy

So many characteristics of an MDP society are favorable to polyarchy that it would be a mistake to single out one or two as primary or causal. However, the multiplicity of favorable aspects may be boiled down to two general features: (1) An MDP society disperses power, influence, authority, and control away from any single center toward a variety of individuals, groups, associations, and organizations.[11] And (2) it fosters attitudes and beliefs favorable to democratic ideas. Though these two features are independently generated, they also reinforce one another.[12]

What is crucial about an MDP society is that on the one hand it inhibits the concentration of power in any single unified set of actors, and on the other it disperses power among a number of relatively independent actors. Because of their power and autonomy, the actors can resist unilateral domination, compete with one another for advantages, engage in conflict and bargaining, and pursue independent actions on their own. Characteristic of an MDP society is a dispersion of *political resources*, such as money, knowledge, status, and access to organizations; of *strategic locations*, particularly in economic, scientific, educational, and cultural affairs; and of *bargaining positions*, both overt and latent, in economic affairs, science, communications, education, and elsewhere.

Among the many ways in which an MDP society favors democratic beliefs let me emphasize several. The economic growth characteristic of an MDP society fosters the belief that joint gains may be shared from an increase in outputs; in political life, the game of politics need not be zero-sum; if politics is not zero-sum, political opponents are not necessarily implacable enemies; and negotiation and bargaining can lead to mutually beneficial compromises. Thus even when the government of the state is restricted to elites, as it generally was in countries that were later to become polyarchies, in an MDP society a competitive political system in which compromise is a normal feature is very likely to emerge. But confining this competitive process strictly to elites is difficult to maintain in an MDP society. For the dispersion of wealth, income, education, status, and power creates various groups of persons who perceive one another as essentially similar in the rights and opportunities to which they believe themselves entitled, while it simultaneously blurs or frequently changes the boundaries that distinguish the members of one such group from those of another.[13] An MDP society therefore presents an excluded group with the opportunity to appeal to the logic of equality in order to justify their admission into political life; and at the same time it weakens the capacity of a privileged group to justify its exclusive rights to participate in political life. The admission of an excluded group is further facilitated by political rivalry and competition among the elites. If members of an excluded group possess political resources that can be turned to advantage, as they usually do, some members of the governing class find it profitable to demand their entry into political life in return for their support.

Consequently, once the members of a privileged minority begin to govern the state by a rudimentary application of the democratic process restricted to themselves, as the British aristocracy did in the eighteenth century, the development of an MDP society makes it increasingly difficult for them to prevent the entry of excluded groups, particularly those closest to them in social and economic positions. But expanding the boundaries of citizenship is difficult to stop short of full inclusion. Hence in a system where political competition is narrowly restricted, the dynamic of an MDP society tends to drive it toward full inclusion. As MDP societies have developed in one country after another, then, they supported the development of polyarchy.

### Qualifications

The relation between an MDP society and polyarchy is not, however, one of simple cause and effect. Strictly speaking, an MDP society is neither necessary nor sufficient for polyarchy.

1. While an MDP society disperses power sufficiently to inhibit its monopolization by any single group, it does not eliminate significant inequalities in the distribution of power. As a result, citizens in polyarchies are far from equal in their influence on the government of the state. Several questions therefore arise: Is power so unequally distributed that polyarchies are in fact ruled by a dominant elite? Should polyarchies be more fully democratized, and if so how? These questions are deferred to later chapters.

2. Moreover, since polyarchies have developed in countries without MDP societies, evidently an MDP society is not strictly necessary to the existence of polyarchy. Thus a leading contemporary exception to the general relation between polyarchy and MDP society is India, where polyarchy was established when the population was overwhelmingly agricultural, illiterate, occupationally much less specialized than in an MDP country, and highly traditional and rule-bound in behavior and beliefs. Although polyarchy was superseded after a quarter century by the quasi-authoritarian rule of the elected prime minister, Indira Gandhi, after a few years it was restored.

Even more telling, however, are countries in which the institutions of polyarchy became strongly rooted well before they developed MDP societies, while they were still preponderantly agrarian. For example, when the institutions of white male polyarchy took form in the United States in the early nineteenth century, the population was overwhelmingly rural and agricultural. In 1800, 94 percent of the population lived in rural territory, and in 1830 (only a few years before Tocqueville's famous visit) 91 percent; in 1820, 72 percent of the working population (as defined by the U.S. census) worked on farms, and a decade later it was 70 percent. Indeed, it was not until 1880 that nonfarm workers outnumbered farm workers, not until 1890 that the census reported a slight majority of the population in urban territory (places with 2500 persons or more) (U.S. Bureau of the Census, Historical Statistics, Series A 195209, p. 14, and Series D 36–45, p. 72). Yet as Tocqueville observed (among many others), the agrarian society of the United States possessed the two crucial features that make an MDP society favorable to polyarchy: It produced a wide dispersion of power and it strongly fostered democratic beliefs. In fact, ideologues of agrarian republicanism like Thomas Jefferson and John Taylor were so firmly convinced that an agrarian society of independent family farmers was absolutely essential to the existence of a democratic republic that they were unable to foresee the possibility that a republic might continue to exist in the United States even after farmers became a minuscule minority.

As in the United States, polyarchy also developed in other countries in which independent farmers were numerically preponderant: among newly settled countries—Canada, Australia, and New Zealand—and among old European countries—Norway, Sweden, Denmark, and Switzerland.[14]

Although these examples demonstrate that an MDP society is not essential to polyarchy, we can scarcely doubt that the two critical features of an MDP society—that it disperses power and fosters attitudes favorable to democracy—are essential to the long run stability of a polyarchy.

3. In the last century, the two critical features of an MDP society were most marked in agrarian societies of independent farmers. But in this century, free farming societies have all but vanished, having been replaced by MDP societies, which like polyarchy itself are mainly a product of the twentieth century. Today, countries with predominantly agricultural populations possess neither the free farming societies of the nineteenth century nor the MDP societies of this century, and typically they lack the two features essential to democratic stability. Consequently, unlike the free farming societies of the nineteenth century, agrarian societies today do not provide a promising basis for polyarchy.

4. Finally, an MDP society is obviously not *sufficient* for polyarchy, since not all MDP countries have become polyarchies. Leading examples in the 1980s included Yugoslavia, South Korea, and Taiwan. In each of these countries the development of an MDP society fostered democratic ideas, movements, and oppositions, but the leadership of the regime managed to overcome them. To understand why an MDP society is not always sufficient to produce polyarchy, additional factors must obviously be taken into account. One of the most important of these I have already discussed: the concentration of control over the means of violence. We now turn to the others.

## THE CONSEQUENCES OF SUBCULTURAL PLURALISM

Imagine a dispute in which a large segment of a country believes that its way of life and highest values are severely menaced by another element of the population. Faced with a conflict of this kind, a polyarchy is likely to dissolve into civil war or to be displaced by a nondemocratic regime or both. While a nondemocratic regime might successfully suppress the public manifestation of the latent conflict by employing its resources for violent coercion, a polyarchy could not do so without ceasing to be a polyarchy.

It is reasonable to suppose, then, that the prospects for polyarchy are greatly reduced if the fundamental beliefs and identities among the people of a country produce political conflicts and are correspondingly increased if beliefs and identities are compatible and therefore not a source of conflict. Thus as the strength and distinctiveness of a country's subcultures increase, the chances for polyarchy should decline. Subcultures are typically formed around ethnic, religious, racial, linguistic, or regional differences and shared historical experience or ancestral myths. Though less common, in some countries strong and distinctive subcultures have also been formed primarily around the nexus of political party and ideology.[15] The stronger and more distinctive a subculture, the more its members identify and interact with one another, and the less they identify and interact with nonmembers. In extreme cases, most members of a subculture live out their lives in nearly total isolation from nonmembers. They comprise a separate nation within the country. Marriage, friendships, play, sports, commensalism, festivals, education, ceremonial occasions, religious activities, even economic tasks take place more or less exclusively among members of the subculture.

Thus when members of one subculture come to believe that their common life is seriously endangered by the actions or plans of others, their situation is not unlike that of people in a country whose existence is threatened by a foreign power. Like people in such a country, members of a subculture will strongly oppose any settlement on terms that fail to ensure the preservation of their subcultural heritage. If their opponents also constitute a separate subculture whose members feel equally threatened by *their* opponents in the other subculture, then the conflict is certain to be even more explosive. Because subcultural conflicts threaten personal and group identities and ways of life, because such threats evoke deep and powerful emotions, and because the sacrifice of identities and ways of life cannot readily be settled by negotiation, disputes involving different subcultures often turn into violent, nonnegotiable conflicts. In a country where conflicts are persistently violent and nonnegotiable, polyarchy is unlikely to exist.

These theoretical speculations are well supported by empirical evidence. Polyarchy is indeed significantly less frequent in countries with marked subcultural pluralism.[16]

### Qualifications

Yet the relation of polyarchy to subcultural pluralism is complex. Since subcultural pluralism is relatively more common among countries that gained their independence after 1945, have therefore been going through the trauma of nation building, and also are at lower levels of economic development, some of the association can reasonably be attributed to other factors (Dahl 1971, 112). Moreover, while cultural homogeneity facilitates polyarchy, it is clearly not sufficient to bring about and sustain polyarchy. That cultural homogeneity does not automatically produce polyarchy can be readily seen by the examples of North and South Korea, both of which have been governed by nondemocratic regimes though they are culturally among the most homogeneous countries in the world. To the list of comparatively homogeneous countries with nondemocratic regimes we can also add Southern Yemen, Yemen, East Germany, Poland, the United Arab Republic, and through most of its history Haiti.[17]

What is even more important, cultural homogeneity is also not strictly necessary to polyarchy. To put the point more strongly, under certain conditions polyarchy can survive, and even function fairly well, despite extensive subcultural pluralism.

One solution that has proved successful in several countries is "consociational democracy."[18]

### Consociational Democracy as a Solution

The most significant examples of polyarchies persisting under conditions of extreme subcultural pluralism are Switzerland, Belgium, Austria, and the Netherlands. The Swiss are highly fragmented in both religion and language. In addition, with a few exceptions the twenty-five cantons are highly homogeneous internally with respect both to religion and language; as a consequence, the country as a whole is highly fragmented along territorial lines. The Belgians are divided linguistically into the Dutch-speaking Flemish and the French-speaking Walloons. While most Belgians are nominally Catholic, the language divisions tend to coincide with Catholic or anticlerical orientations. Moreover, the Catholic Flemish speakers and the more anticlerical francophone Walloons are, except for the Brussels region, quite concentrated geographically. Austria was historically divided into three distinct and antagonistic *lager* or "camps," formed along the axis of ideology, reinforced by religious views and somewhat by region and urban-rural residence, and mainly concentrated in three parties. In the Netherlands, the crosscutting of religion and ideology produced four separate blocs or *zuilen* (Catholic, Calvinist, Liberal, and Socialist), each a sharply bounded subculture with its own beliefs, friendships, marriage partners, newspapers, schools, political party, trade union organization, radio and television organizations, and voluntary associations, whether for cultural activities, recreation, sports, youth, or charitable purposes. [19]

How can we account for the persistence of polyarchy in these countries despite their subcultural cleavages? The explanation is twofold. First, political leaders created "consociational" arrangements for resolving conflicts, by which all important political decisions required agreement among the leaders of the major subcultures; as a result these systems prevented subcultural cleavages from producing explosive conflicts. However, had it not been for the presence of certain conditions, consociational systems could not have been introduced or would have failed, as they did in several other countries. Thus the presence of these favorable conditions constitutes the second part of the explanation. A brief focus on these two explanatory factors will help us to understand why consociationalism has succeeded in a few countries, but only a few.

### Characteristics of Consociational Democracy

While the political systems of countries in which consociationalism has been practiced vary considerably, Lijphart has identified four characteristics of consociational democracy (1977, 25–44).

Although taking different forms in different countries, "the first and most important element is government by a grand coalition of the political leaders of all significant segments of the plural society." The second element is the mutual veto: Decisions affecting the vital interests of a subculture will not be taken without the agreement of its leaders. Thus the mutual veto constitutes a minority veto as well and a rejection of majority rule. Third, the major subcultures are represented in cabinets and other decisionmaking bodies roughly in proportion to their numbers; proportionality may extend also to civil service appointments. Fourth, each subculture enjoys a high degree of autonomy in dealing with matters that are its exclusive concern. This principle "is the logical corollary to the grand coalition principle. On all matters of common interest, decisions should be made by all of the segments with roughly proportional degrees of influence. On all other matters, however, the decisions and their execution can be left to the separate segments" (41).

Austria, Belgium, the Netherlands, and Switzerland all bear testimony to the success of consociational systems in reducing the potentially destabilizing effects of subcultural conflicts. A consociational system may be permanent, as it appears to be in Switzerland; or after having mitigated subcultural conflicts over a period sufficient to establish (or reestablish) an adequate national consensus, consociational arrangements may give way to the more usual practices of party contestation and competition among the political elites, as happened in Austria after 1966 and in the Netherlands in the 1970s.[20]

In Colombia and Venezuela, successful transitions to democracy after brutal periods of civil war and dictatorship were greatly facilitated by pacts among party leaders that embodied some elements of consociationalism. In Colombia leaders of the two historic parties, the Conservatives and the Liberals, entered formally into such a pact after a decade of virtual civil war between them that cost between 100,000 and 200,000 lives and is remembered as *La Violencia*.[21] In 1957 in the Pact of Sitges the leaders of the two parties agreed to form a "National Front" setting aside their destructive rivalry. The main terms of the pact were adopted by a national plebiscite in 1958 and embodied in the constitution, which guaranteed that for twelve years seats in both houses of Congress, departmental assemblies, and municipal councils were to be divided equally between the two parties. All cabinet offices, seats on the Supreme Court, government offices, and public positions were also to be equally divided. In all elective bodies substantive measures were to require a two-thirds vote. Subsequently the party leaders also agreed that the presidency would alternate between the parties every four years until 1972 (Dix 1967, 134–35). This consociational system lasted until the 1970s, when it was gradually dismantled and replaced by a competitive and adversarial system.

Venezuela had been ruled by a dictatorship during the half-century from 1908 to 1946, when the dictatorship was briefly replaced by polyarchy. However, three years of bitter conflicts so completely undermined the legitimacy of civilian government that the military again overthrew the fledgling polyarchy in 1948 and a decade of severe and bloody dictatorship ensued. Upon the fall of this dictatorship in 1958, the leaders of the three major parties, chastened by their failure to establish enduring democracy during the *trienio*, entered into an agreement—the Pact of Punto Fijo—in which they pledged to abide by the results of the forthcoming elections and to seek and support a minimum program of legislation on which they could all agree. The pact also gained the support of the employers association, the trade unions, the church, and the armed forces. The transition to polyarchy, initially with a coalition government under presidential leadership, was successfully completed according to the terms of the Pact of Punto Fijo, which formed the framework for Venezuelan political life for the next thirty years (Levine 1973, 43, 235–43, and passim; Karl 1986, 213ff.; Bautista Urbaneja 1986, 229). Although Venezuelan consociationalism was less comprehensive than in the other countries mentioned, it greatly facilitated the development of stable polyarchy in a country that had hitherto failed to achieve it.

Over against these successes are a number of failures. In Lebanon a complex system of consociationalism that had maintained social peace among the country's numerous subcultures for thirty years collapsed in 1975 and was succeeded by savage internecine warfare. In Malaysia fourteen years of consociationalism broke down in 1969 and the arrangements were not restored. A constitutional system of consociationalism that endured in Cyprus from 1960 to 1963 ended in civil war. Consociational arrangements have never been acceptable to the Protestant majority in North Ireland. Nigeria's experience with polyarchy, which included a weak version of consociationalism, ended in military rule after ten years.[22]

### Favorable Conditions

What conditions favor consociationalism as a means of mitigating the intense conflicts that would otherwise arise because of subcultural pluralism (Lijphart 1977, 53–103; Nordlinger 1972)?

To begin with, while consociational arrangements can sometimes overcome an otherwise dangerous threat arising from subcultural cleavages in a country where polyarchy would otherwise not be at great risk, they cannot singlehandedly create or preserve polyarchy in a country where conditions are generally unfavorable to it. Hence consociationalism can succeed only in countries where the other conditions that favor polyarchy are present.

In addition, political elites must believe that consociational arrangements are highly desirable and feasible, and they must possess the skills and incentives to make them work. Though this requirement may seem obvious, its absence in many countries makes consociationalism impossible. It evidently ceased to exist in Lebanon in 1975 and has never existed in North Ireland. Development of the beliefs, skills, and incentives among political elites is helped by the existence of overarching values, notably a commitment to democratic institutions and the country's independence; the conviction that the alternative to consociationalism is a fearful Hobbesian struggle with disastrous consequences; and traditions within the elite culture favoring conciliation, mutual accommodation, and compromise. These traditions existed among the political elites in the Netherlands, Switzerland, and Belgium and to some extent in Austria under the Hapsburg monarchy. The necessary beliefs, skills, and incentives did not exist in Colombia prior to and during *La Violencia* or in Venezuela during the *trienio*, and they were too weak to guide party leaders in Austria during the First Republic between 1918 and 1933. In these three countries the brutal experiences of destructive conflict were evidently instrumental in creating a strong belief among the political elites that consociationalism was essential if the far worse alternative of Hobbesian strife were to be avoided. Once entered into, the arrangements themselves helped to strengthen the attitudes, behavior, and skills required in order to make consociationalism work.

Consociational arrangements are also favored if the relative strength of the different subcultures, most notably the numbers in each, are politically somewhat in balance, or at any rate not so widely out of balance that one of them can nourish realistic hopes of governing without the collaboration of one or more of the others. The chances for consociationalism are therefore better if none of the subcultures comprises a majority of the population or, because of the electoral system, can gain a majority of seats and so form a government by itself. Two subcultures, then, are less favorable than three or four, none of which is a majority.

Where three or more subcultures exist, multiparty systems are more favorable than two-party systems.[23] In a multiparty system, when negotiations take place among the leaders of the subcultures, each subculture can be represented by party leaders who reflect the orientations of that subculture; who therefore seem trustworthy; and whose agreements are likely to be acceptable to the mass followings. If the parties are also centralized, party leaders are likely to possess the authority to enter into binding agreements and to insulate their negotiations from public discussion and participation. As a result, agreements may be reached, and later accepted by followers, that could not have been reached in public or by negotiations by rank-and-file members of the subcultures.

Is consociationalism more suited to small countries than large? Lijphart suggests two reasons why this may be so. First, "the elites are more likely to know each other personally and to meet often." Second, "small countries are more likely to be and feel threatened by other powers than large countries. Such feelings of vulnerability and insecurity provide strong incentives to maintain internal solidarity" (1977, 65–66).

### Alternative Solutions?

Although consociational arrangements have been most clearly successful in overcoming the potential divisiveness of subcultural pluralism, polyarchy has survived in several countries with distinctive subcultural differences. The most conspicuous examples are Canada, the United States, and India. In all three, subcultural conflict has at times been acute. In Canada the preponderantly French-speaking population of Quebec is sharply distinguished from other Canadians not only by language but by history, traditions, and culture, all of which are reinforced by its Catholicism in a largely Protestant country. Although some writers have discerned elements of consociationalism in Canadian politics (McRae 1974, Noel 1974, Ormsby 1974), the key element of its solution is the high degree of autonomy granted to Quebec within the federal system.

In the United States ethnic identities are politically important; but though the melting pot is more myth than reality, much stronger and more distinctive political subcultures might have developed among the country's numerous ethnic groups had it not been for the rapid assimilation (both voluntary and coerced) of immigrants and their children into the dominant political and general culture. Far more consequential, however, were the regional and ethnically quite homogeneous subculture of white southerners and the historically, socially, and racially distinguishable subculture of blacks. Coercively combined in slavery they formed a society within which peaceful accommodation proved impossible, despite far-reaching proposals for compromise. These included John C. Calhoun's anticipation of consociationalism in the form of a system of "concurrent majorities" and mutual vetoes (from which blacks were of course to be excluded). Despite its defeat in the Civil War and the prohibition of slavery, the South remained a distinctive subculture that could be accommodated only on its own terms, "white supremacy," which was preserved for a full century after the end of the Civil War by what amounted to a southern veto—a belated and ironic triumph for Calhoun's idea of concurrent majorities. With the admission of southern blacks to political life in the 1960s, after bitter and often violent conflicts, blacks formed the most homogeneous voting bloc in the country. But as a comparatively small minority they have not had the power to bring about consociational arrangements (except weakly within the Democratic party) and instead have operated largely within the loose two-party system of competitive and adversarial politics.

Although subcultural conflicts in India are frequent, often deadly, and sometimes a threat to the unity of the country, the extraordinary number of subcultures formed by language, caste, region, and religion make it impossible for any one of them, or even a coalition among a few, to win elections, much less to govern. Party leaders are therefore powerfully motivated to shape policies, programs, and propaganda that will appeal to voters across a broad spectrum of subcultures. As a result, subcultural conflicts have not destroyed polyarchy in India, though they constantly endanger its survival.

## Why Polyarchy Often Fails in Culturally Segmented Countries

If conditions are otherwise favorable, a country with strong and distinctive subcultures may succeed in moderating subcultural conflicts sufficiently to permit polyarchy to survive. Although consociational arrangements provide the most conspicuous instances of success, other solutions are also possible. But in many countries either the conflicts are so acute or the other conditions are so highly unfavorable to polyarchy, or often both of these, that no means of accommodation can be devised. In general, then, polyarchy is less likely, and is certainly less frequent, in countries with relatively strong and distinctive subcultures, particularly if the political triumph of one poses a fundamental threat to another. Because many less developed countries not only are riven by subcultural conflicts but also lack other strongly favorable conditions, their prospects for developing stable polyarchies are rather slim.

## THE BELIEFS OF POLITICAL ACTIVISTS

No satisfactory explanation of why polyarchy exists in some countries and not in others can ignore the pivotal role of beliefs. No one, I imagine, would deny that how people act is strongly influenced by what they believe about the way the world functions, its limits and possibilities, and the relative worth and probability of success of possible courses of action. But some accounts reduce beliefs to mere epiphenomena that are fully caused and fully explained by other factors. In social science jargon, beliefs are no more than intervening variables. I think this notion is mistaken. All theoretical attempts to reduce beliefs, ideas, ideologies, or cultures completely to other general factors seem to me to fail badly as satisfactory explanations for a range of particular cases. However, the matter is far too complex to deal with here. My point is only to indicate that in explaining the presence or absence of polyarchy, I consider beliefs to be relatively independent to about the same extent as the other factors described in this chapter are relatively independent. Of course this does not mean that these factors are uncaused prime movers. It means only that they cannot, now at least, be further explained by any general theory.

Having said this, I am now compelled to say also that evidence on variations in beliefs among and within countries is still limited to a few countries, most of which, as might be expected, are polyarchies. Strictly speaking, therefore, assertions about the impact of beliefs on the character of a country's regime are at best plausible hypotheses that cannot yet be tested satisfactorily against reliable and relevant data.

Good evidence from several countries combined with common observation does strongly support the judgment that the political beliefs of most people everywhere are likely to be rather rudimentary. Rich and complex systems of political belief are, it seems, held only by small minorities. Knowledge of a variety of aspects of political life, including the rules of the game, is likely to be markedly greater among leaders and activists than among the general population of a country and certainly far greater than among the politically apathetic inhabitants. Political activists and leaders are more likely than most other people to have moderately elaborate systems of political beliefs, to be guided in their actions by their political beliefs, and to have more influence on political events, including events that affect the stability or transformation of regimes. To take one example, consociational arrangements for overcoming deep subcultural conflicts have invariably been directly created and managed by leaders and activists, not by their followers or the general public, among whom passionate conflicting beliefs may remain strong even as their leaders pursue pragmatic and accommodative tactics. Just as the breakdown of polyarchy in Venezuela during the *trienio* might justifiably be laid to quarrels among the elites, so the successful transition to stable polyarchy in 1958 was a self-conscious creation of essentially the same leaders who had failed during the *trienio*.[24]

## The Legitimacy of Polyarchy

Such evidence as we have supports three propositions. First, countries vary a great deal in the extent to which activists (and others) believe in the legitimacy of polyarchy. Second, these variations are to some extent independent of the social and economic characteristics of a country: Two countries with a great many similarities in their social and economic orders may vary significantly in the extent to which activists (and others) believe in the legitimacy of polyarchy. Third, the greater the belief within a country in the legitimacy of the institutions of polyarchy, the greater the chances for polyarchy.

While the third proposition seems self-evident, the first, and the second in particular, are less so. As to the first, the most likely alternative favored by political leaders is, as it has always been, some form of guardianship. As I mentioned in the introduction, with few exceptions political leaders everywhere today justify their regimes as democratic in some special sense or as preliminary to a transition to democracy at some later stage. But their rejection of the concrete institutions of polyarchy is usually justified by an argument for guardianship, even when the guardianship is said to be only temporary or transitional. In the Soviet Union, Eastern Europe, Cuba, and China, the hegemony of the single party has been defended essentially by appeals to guardianship principles. Military regimes in Argentina, Brazil, Chile, Peru, Uruguay, Turkey, Nigeria, and elsewhere justify their rule as a guardianship by those most qualified to rule in the particular if transitory historical circumstances of the country. Indeed, in few if any non-democratic regimes today do rulers appear to believe that their rule needs no justification; and the most readily available justification for nondemocratic rule is, as it has always been, the need for guardians of superior knowledge and virtue.

The second proposition is nicely illustrated by Argentina, where a half-century of military regimes, punctuated by brief periods of unstable polyarchy, cannot be fully explained without taking into account the weak commitment to democratic principles among the political activists (cf. O'Donnell 1978; Smith 1978). Throughout this period, Argentina had the attributes of an MDP society to a greater extent than any other country in Latin America; yet while its MDP society was favorable to the emergence and stability of polyarchy, it could not overcome the weakness of democratic commitments. Likewise, the Soviet Union has developed all the attributes of an MDP society except for the relatively low level of organizational autonomy and hence of pluralism.[25] Though it is modern and dynamic, even the liberalization under Mikhail Gorbachev has not yet brought about a highly pluralistic society. One cannot fully explain the rejection of greater pluralism by the leadership, I believe, without taking into account the weakness of democratic ideas, beliefs, and traditions in Russia throughout its history and the commitment of the leadership since 1918 to a Leninist view of the world.

### Political Culture

Although the evidence grows weaker, it is plausible that the chances for polyarchy in a country are influenced by other beliefs as well: beliefs about authority, for example; the effectiveness of the government and the relative effectiveness of alternative regimes in dealing with crucial problems; the extent of trust or confidence in fellow citizens or political activists; attitudes toward conflict and cooperation; and no doubt others.

Taken together, beliefs, attitudes, and predispositions form a political culture, or perhaps several political subcultures, into which activists and citizens are socialized in varying degrees. A country with a political culture strongly favorable to polyarchy will make its way through crises that would bring about a breakdown of polyarchy in a country with less supportive political culture. In many countries, indeed in most, a political culture favorable to democratic ideas and practices does not exist. This is not to say that polyarchy cannot exist in such a country, but it is likely to be unstable. Nor is it to say that a more favorable political culture cannot evolve in a country now lacking it. As a country develops an MDP society, for example, it is likely to develop and sustain beliefs, attitudes, and authority relationships more favorable to polyarchy. But the evolution of political culture is necessarily slow and lags behind the more rapid changes in structures and processes of a developing MDP society. And in any case, for a great many countries an MDP society is still a long way off.

## FOREIGN INFLUENCE OR CONTROL

Even if all of the conditions mentioned so far were present in a country, it would not possess the institutions of polyarchy if a more powerful country intervened to prevent them. Though the proposition is obvious, it is often neglected because of an implicit assumption that polyarchy results from purely internal factors. Were it not for the actual or potential intervention of the Soviet Union, is it not possible that Poland, Czechoslovakia, Hungary, and East Germany would have been governed by polyarchy? Although we cannot answer with certainty, we can say with certainty that moves toward democratization in the first three were reversed by the threat or actuality of Soviet intervention. Likewise, might not Guatemala have solidified the institutions of polyarchy if the United States government had not intervened to overthrow the elected government of Jacopo Arbenz in 1954?

While one might suppose that external domination is invariably harmful to polyarchy, its effects on political change are actually quite complex.

It is true that in order to acquire full constitutional authority over their own national agendas, many countries that became polyarchies first had to gain their independence from a superior power. Examples are the United States, Canada, Australia, New Zealand, Norway, Finland, Iceland, the Philippines, and India. Yet foreign intervention and even outright domination are by no means always detrimental to the advance of polyarchy. If the dominant country is itself a polyarchy, or moving toward polyarchy, its rule may contribute to the development of local institutions favorable to polyarchy, as with Britain in Canada, Australia, New Zealand, and India and the United States in the Philippines. If economic and international factors warrant, the dominant country may even deliberately set out to implant the institutions necessary to polyarchy, as was true with the U.S. occupation force in Japan in 1945 and the Western Allies in Italy, Germany, and Austria after the defeat of the Axis powers, or may yield in a timely and constructive way to local demands for democracy, as Britain did in its Caribbean colonies.[26]

The fact that the dominant country is itself a polyarchy does not guarantee, however, that it will foster polyarchy in another country. The policies of the dominant country are likely to be influenced more strongly by strategic, economic, and geopolitical considerations than by any special preference for democracy. Thus the military and economic intervention of the United States in Central America from 1898 onward typically weakened independence and popular governments and strengthened military dictatorships.[27]

## PROSPECTS FOR DEMOCRACY IN THE WORLD

A country is very likely to develop and sustain the institutions of polyarchy

- if the means of violent coercion are dispersed or neutralized;
- if it possesses an MDP society;
- if it is culturally homogeneous,
  or, if it is heterogeneous, is not segmented into strong and distinctive subcultures,
  or, if it is so segmented, its leaders have succeeded in creating a consociational arrangement for managing subcultural conflicts;
- if it possesses a political culture and beliefs, particularly among political activists, that support the institutions of polyarchy;
- and if it is not subject to intervention by a foreign power hostile to polyarchy.

By the same token, if a country lacks these conditions, or if the obverse conditions are strongly present, a country will almost certainly be governed by a nondemocratic regime. In countries with mixed conditions, if polyarchy exists at all it is likely to be unstable; in some countries, the regime may oscillate between polyarchy and a nondemocratic regime.

That no more than a third of the countries in the world are governed by polyarchy should not be surprising. It would be surprising, on the other hand, if the proportion were to change greatly over the next twenty years. Yet the the democratic idea is likely to maintain a strong attraction for people in nondemocratic countries, and if and as modern, dynamic, and more pluralistic societies develop in these countries, their authoritarian governments will find it increasingly difficult to resist the pressures for greater democratization.

# Chapter 19

◆◆◆◆◆◆◆◆◆

# Is Minority
# Domination Inevitable?

After reading in the last two chapters my account of the development of polyarchy and the conditions that have facilitated it, a critic of a certain persuasion might respond something like this:

I fully accept your account. I can even go along with your explanation as to why the kind of modern regime you call polyarchy has developed in some countries and not others. What I don't accept is that polyarchy takes a country very far along the path to democracy. However different these modern regimes may be from previous ones in their institutions and structures, they certainly aren't very democratic. I'd say instead that "democracy" is mainly an ideological facade. When you look carefully behind the facade you find the same old familiar phenomenon of human experience: domination.

In support of such a view, our critic might cite a predecessor, Gaetano Mosca:

Among the constant facts and tendencies that are to be found in all political organisms, one is so obvious that it is apparent to the most casual eye. In all societies—from societies that are very meagerly developed and have barely attained the dawnings of civilization, down to the most advanced and powerful societies—two classes of people appear—a class that rules and a class that is ruled. The first class, always the less numerous, performs all political functions, monopolizes power and enjoys the advantages that power brings, whereas the second, the more numerous class, is directed and controlled by the first, in a manner that is now more or less legal, now more or less arbitrary and violent, and supplies the first, in appearance at least, with material means of subsistence and with the instrumentalities that are essential to the vitality of the political organism. In practical life we all recognize the existence of this ruling class (or political class . . .). (Mosca [1923] 1939, 52)

Gaetano Mosca advances an argument that poses a fundamental challenge to the possibility that the democratic idea can ever be realized.[1] The argument, to put it somewhat oversimply, is that minority domination is inevitable. Because minority domination is inevitable, democracy is impossible. To assert that democracy is desirable, or that it is the best possible kind of government, or that we should strive to attain it are propositions all utterly irrelevant to human possibilities. To be sure, statements like these may be useful to rulers because they serve as myths that help to disguise the reality of domination and ensure the compliance of the dominated. But these noble sentiments do not and cannot alter the fundamental empirical fact that minorities always rule. If minorities always rule, then obviously majorities never rule. And if majorities can never rule, then democracy cannot exist. In practice, then, what we call democracy is nothing more than a facade for minority domination.

In one form or another some such view is and probably always has been rather widely held, though often perhaps in a guise less stark than the simple summary statement I just offered. Variants have been advanced by Marx, Lenin, Mosca, Pareto, Michels, and Gramsci, among many others.[2]

However, we need to distinguish theories of minority domination from other accounts of polyarchy that give great weight to the impairment of democracy, political equality, and freedom caused by inequalities in political resources, strategic positions, and bargaining advantages, both overt and implicit. Interpretations of the significance of inequalities in polyarchies range from Panglossian optimism to apocalyptic visions to deep pessimism:

1. Inequalities are so trivial they scarcely need correction; or if they do, they can rather easily be removed.

2. (a) Inequalities seriously diminish the democratic process in polyarchies. (b) Even so, polyarchy is significantly more democratic and much more desirable than alternatives lacking one or more major institutions of polyarchy. (c) Nonetheless, these inequalities can be significantly reduced (if not entirely eliminated); doing so would considerly improve the democratic quality of polyarchy; and the appropriate changes should therefore be undertaken.

3. (a) and (b) as above. But (c) the inequalities cannot be reduced (at least without intolerable costs to other values, and in some cases not at all), and hence represent an essentially irremediable aspect of the best attainable system in a highly defective world.

4. (a) The effects of inequalities are so preponderant as (b) to allow only trivial aspects of the democratic process to exist in polyarchies. (c) However, inequalities can be removed and "real democracy" can be created by a process of complete revolutionary transformation. (d) Until this revolutionary transformation is finally achieved, all societies will be ruled by a dominant minority.

5. (a) and (b) as in 4. But (c) the inequalities and their effects are irremovable. (d) Thus all societies will always be ruled by a dominant minority.

My summaries of course do no more than identify a few bands of a more variegated spectrum. The Panglossian view of (1) scarcely deserves our attention. The examination of the limits and possibilities of democracy undertaken in this book might be seen as in about the same band of the spectrum as (2), though some of the limits are, as we have seen, irremediable. Ironically, the authoritarian systems that have so far been the invariable result of Leninist revolutions or regimes have in effect turned the apocalyptic vision of the fourth perspective into another variant of the bleakly pessimistic ruling class theories of the fifth persuasion.

What we shall be concerned with in this chapter are ruling class theories of the fourth and fifth kinds.

Though theories of minority domination are radically different in important ways (some of which I shall take up in a moment) they concur in asserting that in polyarchies or even "democracies" (except for the "true democracies" of the apocalypse), a privileged minority dominates the rest. I am going to assume that the writers I have just mentioned adequately represent the main similarities and differences in leading theories of minority domination.[3]

The most influential exponent of such a theory is Marx, who portrays all history as domination by a minority exploitive class over exploited majorities. And so history must go on repeating itself, until the ultimate triumph of the proletariat at last brings exploitation and domination to an end. Mosca, Pareto, and Michels seek to undercut Marx with theories of domination that purport to be much more objective and scientific, and infinitely less romantic and utopian. Because domination by a ruling class is inevitable, they argue in effect, it is utterly futile to hope that minority dominance can ever be brought to an end, whether by Marx's *deus ex machina*, the proletariat, or any other class, group, or person. Both Lenin and Gramsci follow Marx in holding that even where the outward forms of "democracy" exist, under capitalism the bourgeoisie dominates the working classes; but Lenin and Gramsci differ profoundly in their understanding of how that domination is achieved. Where Lenin stresses coercion, Gramsci, like Mosca, emphasizes the hegemony of ideas and culture.

In order to grasp the challenge to democratic ideas posed by theories of minority domination, I shall first provide an overall summary that blurs the distinctions among them, and then a more detailed exposition that reveals some important differences.

## WHY AND HOW MINORITIES RULE

Theories of minority domination are persuasive because, as Mosca points out, they seem to fit closely with human experience. They appear to be supported not only by a vast array of historical evidence but also by the great amount of evidence that is casually cast up to us as we engage in our daily actions and observe the events around us. Can anyone who is active in organizational life fail to notice how often, even in ostensibly democratic organizations, it is the few who make the decisions and the many who do little more than go along?

If majorities really are governed by minorities, we might ask, why is this so? Although the writers above give special emphasis to different factors, I think they would all agree on the crucial importance of the relatively enduring (though ultimately impermanent) structures and institutions—social, economic, political—that strongly shape choices and opportunities for large numbers of people over a comparatively long time. To take an extreme case, in a country ruled by the military, no matter how meritocratic or egalitarian recruitment and promotions may be, only a few can enter into the ruling group. The top of a pyramid has only a limited space; and by definition all theories of minority domination interpret the world as made up of structures of power in which the top is considerably smaller than the bottom. Probably all the writers mentioned would also agree that in the last two centuries the structures and institutions of capitalism, markets, and bourgeois society have been enormously important in determining patterns of domination.

It is structures like these that also influence the specific composition of the ruling class: what sorts of persons are likely to enter into it, what sorts are not. For it is *within* these structures, and in considerable measure because of them, that individuals and aggregates of individuals—classes—achieve their domination. Personal qualities may of course facilitate a person's gaining and maintaining a dominant position within the limits set by the structures. Like Niccolò Machiavelli before them, Mosca, Pareto, and Michels call attention to the usefulness to leaders of cunning, shrewdness, drive, ambition, intelligence, clearheadedness, and on occasion ruthlessness. Marx mentions how in some circumstances "a man without fortune but possessing energy, solidity, ability, and business acumen may become a capitalist" (Marx [1894] 1967, 3:600). Mosca, Pareto, and Michels also stress certain qualities among the ruled that incline them to accept, even yearn for, domination. With Pareto it is the greater frequency among the ruled of habits, beliefs, and predispositions that favor order, risk-avoidance, obedience, conformity, and acceptance of nonrational myths.[4] With Michels it is the mass's need for leadership, their political gratitude, their veneration of their leaders, and so on (Michels 1962, 85ff., 92ff.). In addition, and depending on the requirements of the institutions and structures of a given historical period, superior specialized knowledge and skills of certain kinds can be helpful or even necessary.

Some of the personal advantages that enable a few persons to gain entry into the governing class may, like intelligence, be partly innate, but personal advantages depend also on resources and endowments that are socially determined. Resources and endowments are allocated by inheritance, social class, luck, and achievement. Yet in whatever way they may have been acquired, education, wealth, knowledge, information, status, and other resources expand a person's opportunities for entry into the ruling class.

Once again, however, to the extent that the advantages conveyed by personal qualities, resources, and endowments enhance opportunities for those fortunate enough to possess them, they do so only *within* the limits set by the major institutions and structures. As Pareto remarks, "Ruling classes, like other social groups, perform both logical and non-logical actions, and the chief element in what happens is in fact the order, or system, not the conscious will of individuals" (Pareto [1916] 1935, 1576 [para. 2254]).

As to the means the ruling minority employs to secure and maintain its domination, all give some weight to both force and persuasion. But theorists of minority domination differ greatly in the relative importance they assign these factors, and it is to these and other differences among them that we must now turn.

## WHO RULES WHOM, HOW, AND WHY?

Although advocates of minority domination theories purport to provide accounts that are strictly objective and "scientific," their theories serve markedly different, indeed sharply conflicting, ideologies and political aims. Lenin and Gramsci were, of course, followers of Marx, though both men greatly altered the master's theories. For all three, the version of minority domination they presented was, in its general implications for political action, instrumental to their ideological ends. Mosca, Pareto, and Michels were strongly anti-Marxist; they responded to Marxism by posing an alternative that if accepted would destroy its credibility and thus weaken it as a political force.

We may surmise that partly because of these diverging ideological purposes the idea of minority domination is not a set of more or less consistent theories but a heterogeneous collection of mutually inconsistent theories.

One minor though troublesome inconsistency is in terms and concepts. Marx referred to the bourgeoisie or capitalist class as a ruling class. Mosca used the term "ruling class" (*classe dirigente*) as synonymous with political class (*classe politica*) (for example, 1939, 50). Pareto's favored term seems to be "governing class" (*classe governante*) (for example, *Trattato* 1923, paras. 2033–34). However, his governing class is also the dominant class (*classe dominante*) and *the* elite (distinguished from the innumerable elites that are defined by their superiority in a particular matter, whether athletic skill, art, riches, or whatever).[5] In later social theory, most conspicuously perhaps in the United States, *the* elite of Pareto became the *political* elite or the *power* elite; or, with quite different implications, it was transformed into the political *elites* (cf. Sartori 1961, 94ff.; Treves 1961, passim).[6] The inclusive term I adopt here is *dominant minority*.

Of more importance than these hardly trivial differences in terms and concepts, theories of minority domination differ in describing the composition of the dominant minority. In modern capitalist societies, the dominant minority in all the theories under consideration would definitely include businessmen and major owners of large economic enterprises. But the theorists differ greatly in the relative importance they assign to politicians, government leaders, bureaucracies, intellectuals, and military and police forces, or other leaders. To Pareto, for example, modern popular government is in reality a plutocracy of speculators and others who profit through and from political life (1935, 4:1566ff.). But his plutocracy is not so much government by businessmen as it is government by spoliator-politicians who use government to their own personal advantage. On Jon Elster's reading, Marx was compelled by events to change his views about the extent to which the bourgeoisie directly ran the government of the state. Though capitalists were the ruling class, they did not necessarily do the governing themselves. Before 1850, Marx adhered to the position of *The Communist Manifesto* that "the executive of the modern State is but a committee for managing the affairs of the whole bourgeoisie." The state served the interests of the capitalist class because it was a direct extension of the will of that class. After 1850, however, he could no longer sustain this view, for it was now apparent to him that in England, France, and Germany those who directly governed the state were not businessmen but "the coalized Aristocracy of England," Bonaparte in France, and in Germany the landed aristocracy, the official bureaucracy, and the monarch. He therefore sought to preserve his theory of capitalist domination by holding that the bourgeoisie collectively decided to "abstain from political power," as long as its interests were protected (Elster 1985, 411–22).

Specifying the composition of the dominant minority is of course essential to any possibility of an empirical verification or disproof of a theory of minority domination. I shall come back to this point in a moment. But differences in the composition of the dominant minority will also have crucially different theoretical and practical consequences. If the dominant minority is a homogeneous class with essentially similar interests, and if in addition the interests of that class are fundamentally in conflict with the interests of the dominated class or classes, then electoral and party competition among members of the dominant minority will be nonexistent or trivial, while serious political competition between representatives of the dominant minority and of the dominated majority presumably will not exist (for reasons the theory will have to provide). If, however, the dominant minority is a heterogeneous collection of groups, and if the interests of these groups sometimes diverge, then political competition may in some circumstances induce leaders to seek support among the majority by advancing their interests. This possibility, as we shall see later, has far-reaching implications.

As we have seen, theories of minority domination also differ in their implications for the possibility that domination may be brought to an end, and thus in their consequences for human hopes and action. Though advocates of minority domination theories tend to lean strongly on notions of historical determinism, to explore what they assume or imply about human autonomy, freedom, free will, and determinism is too large a task to undertake here and not strictly necessary to my purpose. More to the point is whether minority domination is an inescapable feature of human life (beyond the stage of hunter-gatherer societies, at any rate) or might be eliminated. On this point Marx and his followers are highly optimistic— to the point, indeed, of outright utopianism. Because of the forces, relations, and modes of production,[7] in capitalism, as in all previous societies, minority domination has been inescapable. But it is equally inevitable that capitalism will be superseded by communism. Under communism, domination in all its forms— political and economic—will cease, and human beings will at last enjoy full freedom. So runs the Marxist scenario.

To Mosca, Pareto, and Michels, on the other hand, once humankind moved beyond the Stone Age to more complex civilizations, minority domination became an inherent feature of human society. Mosca and Pareto insist with almost tiresome repetition on this inescapable law of human society. Although the forms of minority domination may change, and even if some forms are "better" than others (which was Mosca's increasing conviction as he witnessed fascism in Italy), minority domination in one form or another is inevitable.

Unlike Mosca, Michels came to support Italian fascism; but in his famous *Political Parties* published a decade before Mussolini's March on Rome[8] his tone is sometimes more tragic than cynical. After asserting that the "sociological phenomena" he has described "would seem to prove beyond dispute that society cannot exist without a 'dominant' or 'political' class, and that the ruling class . . . constitutes the only factor of sufficiently durable efficacy in the history of human development," he strikes the tragic note: "Thus the majority of human beings, in a condition of eternal tutelage, are predestined by tragic necessity to submit to the dominion of a small minority, and must be content to constitute the pedestal of an oligarchy" (Michels 1962, 354). His "final considerations" are these:

> The democratic currents of history resemble successive waves. They break ever on the same shoal. They are ever renewed. This enduring spectacle is simultaneously encouraging and depressing. When democracies have gained a certain stage of development, they undergo a gradual transformation, adopting the aristocratic spirit, and in many cases also the aristocratic forms, against which at the outset they struggled so fiercely. Now new accusers arise to denounce the traitors; after an era of glorious combats and of inglorious power, they end by fusing with the old dominant class; whereupon once more they are in their turn attacked by fresh opponents who appeal to the name of democracy. It is probable that this cruel game will continue without end.

## CRITIQUE

Theories of minority domination are, as I see them, a distorted reflection of an important truth about human life. Significant inequalities in power have been a universal feature of human relationships throughout recorded history; they exist today in all democratic systems; they may be inescapable in organizations with more than several dozen members. The condition of equality portrayed in Locke's state of nature, as well as in anthropological reconstructions of life among the small hunter-gatherer groups in which humankind lived until about ten thousand years ago, has not been duplicated in historical societies. No matter whether that equality ever existed widely or is little more than a fable told by philosophers and anthropologists; it has long since escaped us, perhaps irrevocably. The upshot is that even in democratic countries citizens are far from equal in their political resources and in their influence over the policies and conduct of the government of the state (not to mention the governments of other important organizations). To the extent that citizens in a polyarchy engage in political affairs on markedly unequal terms—if indeed they choose to engage in them at all—then polyarchy falls short of the criteria of the democratic process.

Theories of minority domination might be interpreted, then, as saying that political inequality exists to an important degree in all human associations (except perhaps for very small groups under special conditions), including all historical "democracies" and all now existing polyarchies. But if this were the main message of these theories, they would be indistinguishable from most other social theory and description, and except as additional testimony to the pervasiveness and inevitability of inequality they would hold no special interest for us. It seems obvious to me, however, that theories of minority domination are intended to say much more than this. Their authors appear to be saying that even a satisfactory approximation of democracy is, in one variant of the theory, flatly impossible; or, in another variant, would be possible only under conditions that have hitherto not existed in all of recorded history and may be well out of reach of human efforts in the foreseeable future. A satisfactory approximation of democracy is, then, either unattainable or requires unique conditions that have never been achieved. Meanwhile, these theories contend, in "democratic" and nondemocratic systems alike minority domination is the inevitable lot of mankind.

### Can Theories of Minority Domination Be Verified or Disproved?

For several reasons it may not be possible, unfortunately, either to verify or disprove theories of domination, at least in a way that approaches reasonable standards of rigor. To begin with, the theories are presented at such a high level of generality that it is hard to determine what evidence could be brought to bear that would conclusively verify or disprove the central hypothesis of minority domination. Each of these theories could probably be "saved" from conclusive disproof in the face of any evidence likely to be available. I want to come back to the question of evidence in a moment; but meanwhile it is worth noting that many, perhaps most, social theories are highly resistant to rigorous verification or disproof. If, nonetheless, we want to arrive at judgments about their validity, as many of us do, we must usually make our judgments on the basis of rather inconclusive and certainly highly debatable "tests." Thus an advocate's commitment to a high-level theory is very likely to be far stronger than a rational decision would warrant. In this respect, then, theories of minority domination are not unique.

If a high-level theory is also conceptually ambiguous, however, judging its validity becomes an even more formidable task. It is fair to say that conceptual clarity and precision are not among the virtues of theories of minority domination. Their conceptual ambiguity is partly but not wholly a consequence of an unsolved problem in social theory: how to specify the meaning of concepts, and apply the concepts to experience, in the family of related terms that includes power, influence, control, domination, hegemony, coercion, and so on. Concepts like these have proved to be notoriously difficult both to interpret and to employ rigorously in empirical work.[9]

A particularly troublesome concept or set of concepts involve notions like *potential* or latent power as against *manifest* power (for example, Mokken and Stokman 1976, 39ff.), *having* as against *exercising* power and influence (Oppenheim 1981, 20ff.), authority derived from the *anticipated reactions* of others

(Friedrich 1937, 16–18), and the like. It is characteristic of courtiers, for example, that they try to anticipate the wishes of their superiors.

Whether or not the murder of Thomas Becket was ever actually ordered by Henry II, the knights who murdered him undoubtedly believed they were acting according to the wishes of the monarch. A relation like that between Henry and his knights is common. An experienced member of Congress, for example, does not always need overt pressures in order to work for government actions favorable to constituency interests. The control of a dominant minority would doubtless include an important quota of anticipated reactions, as we can see most clearly in countries where the military forces are important political actors. Although military officers often take over a government and rule directly, they sometimes yield nominal control to civilians. The civilian officials, however, are strictly limited by their constant awareness that the military would replace them if they should adopt policies contrary to the wishes of military leaders. These forbidden policies need not be confined to military matters; they might also extend (as they often have in Latin America) to redistributive measures like land reform, taxation, and other social and economic matters. As an empirical matter, a dominant military establishment rarely permits genuinely free elections, free expression, and opposition parties and thus can rather easily be seen to lack the institutional requirements of polyarchy. But this is not always so. If the main institutions of polyarchy appear to exist in a country, but in fact the military controls the governmental agenda by means of the anticipated reactions of civilian heads, then of course final control of the agenda lies not with the demos but with the military, who might truly be called the dominant minority in the country.[10] Unfortunately, however, the concept of anticipated reactions is not readily interpretable; to observe its operation is often difficult or impossible; and assertions about its operation are therefore hard to verify or disprove.[11]

A drastic limit on the rigor of concepts like power and influence is also set by the unhappy fact that no satisfactory quantitative measure of power or influence has yet been devised. Consequently the distribution of power in actual systems can be described only in qualitative terms. If as I have suggested inequality of power is a feature of all social systems, how can we judge whether inequality is greater in one than in another, and by how much? How are we to compare different "degrees" or "amounts" of inequality? When does mere inequality pass the threshold to coercion or domination? If our task were to compare the distribution of income or wealth in different systems, we could often use acceptable quantitative indicators. But since even reasonably satisfactory quantitative indicators do not exist for power and influence, in practice we must rely on qualitative descriptions that are inherently highly inexact.

But after allowing for a certain amount of unavoidable ambiguity, theories of minority domination seem to me unnecessarily and excessively vague. I shall come back to this problem shortly. The point I want to make now is that because of their high level of generality and their conceptual indeterminacy they probably cannot be either verified or disproved. As a result, our judgments about their validity probably depend mainly on how they fit with our prior views about the world. Once we adopt or reject a theory of minority domination, our view may easily serve as a filter for our perceptions; thereafter, the familiar psychological process of selective perception ensures that the incoming stream of evidence constantly enhances the validity of the view we have chosen.

If it is true that because of their high level of generality and their conceptual ambiguities, theories of minority domination cannot be disproved, critics face an impossible task. But why should this impossible task be placed on the critics? It is reasonable to insist that the advocates provide us with considerably more in the way of validation than they have done so far. Although it is too much to expect that these—or probably any other—important social theories could ever be verified in a way that would satisfy all their critics, it is possible to sketch out what a convincing validation might reasonably require. Advocates of a theory of minority domination are obliged to provide satisfactory answers to at least these questions: What does minority domination mean? What distinguishes it from other forms or degrees of inequality in power? Who dominates whom? By what means is domination achieved? Over what matters?

### Coercion, Persuasion, Indoctrination

As to the means of domination, the advocates tend to agree, as I said earlier, that minorities rule by both coercion and persuasion. Persuasion includes not only inducements (including corruption) but also influence over beliefs or, if you like, indoctrination. As I also pointed out, different theorists give greater weight to one or the other. Although the early Marx and Lenin seem to have believed that the ruling class dominates primarily by coercion, this view became increasingly implausible with the fuller development of the institutions of polyarchy and the enfranchisement of workers. As a consequence, later Marxists began to give great weight to the importance of social indoctrination in producing a "false consciousness" among the workers. In the extreme case, coercion became unnecessary. While elections might be formally fair and free, workers had been so thoroughly brainwashed by bourgeois ideologues that they were unable to understand how their interests would be served by social ownership and control of the means of production. Thus domination had become more indirect, less obvious, and less detectable.

Probably no Marxist went further than Gramsci in replacing coercion with the hegemony of culture and beliefs. In strongly emphasizing these more remote means of domination, Gramsci was undoubtedly influenced by the work of his predecessor (and contemporary), Mosca.[12] Mosca had argued forcefully that every ruling class finds a "political formula" that justifies its domination. While the content of the political formula varies according to the needs of a particular ruling class—some, for example, draw on religious beliefs and the supernatural, others on ostensibly rational beliefs like democracy—all serve the same purpose: to gain the acquiescence of the masses in the domination of the rulers and, even more, their willing consent and support. The political formula is not, however, a mere instrument of mass deception created by the rulers and imposed on the masses. It meets deep and universal human needs, felt by the rulers as well as the ruled, for rulership that can be accepted by its subjects not only because of its superior material and intellectual forces but also because rulers and ruled alike believe it to be justified on moral grounds (Mosca 1923, 70–73, 75ff.; Mosca 1925, 36–37). Because of the political formula, rulers usually do govern with the "consent" of the governed.

Like Mosca, Pareto, and Michels, Gramsci contended that a ruling class could not long maintain its domination by force or even by direct inducements like corruption. Minority domination requires an intellectual and cultural hegemony of certain ideas and beliefs that are widely shared in a society—in a capitalist society by workers as well as the middle classes. Held fast in the cultural grip of the hegemonic belief system, even workers support a system of domination that violates their long-run interests. Thus cultural hegemony cements an alliance among classes, a *blocco storico*, with a common ideology and a common culture (Pellicani 1976, 17). In creating and maintaining cultural hegemony, Gramsci pointed out, intellectuals necessarily play a crucial role.

It follows from Gramsci's analysis that workers could gain power only by throwing off the invisible chains of the beliefs and values that tie them to capitalism. To do so they would need their own worldview, their own cultural hegemony, a system of beliefs that would appeal not only to the workers and to the poor and oppressed generally but also to the potential allies of the workers among the middle classes. However, workers are not themselves equipped to create their own hegemonic culture. That is, as it has always been, the task of intellectuals. By this critical move, Gramsci thrusts the intellectuals—the creators, interpreters, and purveyors of ideas and beliefs—onto the stage as important actors in the historical drama.[13]

## Rivalry, Competition, and the Costs of Ruling

It is characteristic of theories of domination that they give little weight to the importance of organized competition as an instrument by which nonelites may influence the conduct of political elites. This is not to say that they overlook the rivalry and competition for personal advancement so characteristic of political elites in all systems. On the contrary, both Mosca and Pareto strongly emphasize that not only do some persons make their way into the ruling class through skill and guile but rivalry for place is a constant preoccupation within the ruling class itself. In the second part which he added to his 1923 edition of the *Elementi*, Mosca (who upon looking fascism full in the face was now more favorable to liberal representative government than ever before) recognized that mass suffrage and party competition will induce a section of the ruling class to direct its appeals to the masses (411–12). But he dismissed these appeals as demagoguery, persisted in referring to the "monopoly" of power enjoyed by the ruling class, and thus neglected to follow through on his insight. Even Pareto, who as an economist insisted that competition would inevitably force firms to adapt their products to the preferences of consumers, failed as a sociologist to apply a similar notion to the party competition he acknowledged occurred in the electoral marketplace (for example, 1935, vol. 4, para. 2262, 1593ff.).

Yet as later theorists were to argue, competition for votes among political parties intent on winning elections is analagous to competition among firms in a market. In both cases if barriers are low to the formation of new firms or parties, then monopoly domination becomes impossible to sustain—a conclusion that rulers in one-party authoritarian political systems understand perfectly. If oppositions are granted the right to form political parties, if the parties are entitled to participate in elections, if the elections are fair and free, and if the highest offices in the government of the state are held by those who win elections, then competition among political elites makes it likely that the policies of the government will respond in time to the preferences of a majority of voters.

From the perspective of later political science, then, Michels committed an elementary mistake in generalizing from political parties to the government of a polyarchal system. His generalizations were derived from the study of a single organization, the German Social Democratic party. His famous "iron law of oligarchy" explicitly referred to political parties:

> Reduced to its most concise expression, the fundamental sociological law of political parties (the term "political" being here used in its most comprehensive significance) may be formulated in the following terms: "It is organization which gives birth to the dominion of the elected over the electors, of the mandataries over the mandators, of the delegates over the delegators. Who says organization says oligarchy." (1962, 365)

But even if we grant that political parties are oligarchical, *it does not follow that competing political parties necessarily produce an oligarchical political system.* Business firms are among the most "oligarchical" organizations in modern societies; but as I pointed out, Michels's mentor, Pareto, writing as an economist, would never have said that these competing oligarchies produced monopolistic control over consumers and the market. Not even Marx, who saw business firms as despotic organizations, made such an elementary mistake. Quite the contrary: It was competition that *prevented* monopoly. If Michels had strictly limited his conclusions to political parties, his case would have been far stronger. But as the quotations given earlier show clearly, Michels went on to draw the unwarranted conclusion that democracy is impossible in a *political system* because it was, he believed from his study of one party, impossible in a particular *element of the system.* Had he been writing today it is inconceivable that he would have moved so casually from his observation of oligarchy in a political party to the conclusion that oligarchy is inescapable in a political system in which the political parties are highly competitive.

Michels's elementary mistake reminds us that for the most part the theorists of minority domination discussed here had little or no experience with systems of competitive parties in countries with a broad suffrage or, certainly, with systematic analysis of competitive party systems. Marx, for example, did not live long enough to witness the operation of "mass democracy" in Britain; and Lenin never really experienced it (even in exile in Switzerland). Pareto, Mosca, Michels, and Gramsci witnessed only its beginnings.

Nonetheless, we cannot conclude that greater experience with polyarchy and party competition would have compelled them to abandon their theories of minority domination. They could still have saved their theories by arguing that the dominant elites continue to rule, not by directly controlling the state but by shaping the preferences of the voters and thus indirectly controlling the results of elections.

## Links in the Chain of Control between Rulers and Ruled

Thus as *direct* domination over the government of the state became more difficult for a single minority to achieve in polyarchies with a broad suffrage, and thus became correspondingly more implausible as an account of privilege and domination, theorists turned to explanations that depend on the use of *indirect* means of domination. In these accounts, the chain of control[14] from the actions of the prime movers, the rulers, to the compliant and supportive actions of the ruled becomes longer; it is less easily observed; it relies less on manifest control and more on potential power and anticipated reactions; and consequently it is more difficult to verify or disprove. To my knowledge, no theory or account contending that minority domination is a standard characteristic of countries governed by polyarchy has yet provided the evidence needed to verify the existence of such a chain of control.

If we assume without dispute that a particular account has adequately specified the composition of the dominant minority, it might then describe the path of the minority's control over the dominated majority in several different ways. In the following, for example, the paths run from more direct to less direct domination by the ruling elite. (All the paths may include greater or lesser mixtures of control by means of anticipated reactions.)

1. The dominant minority directly controls the specific decisions and policies of the government of the state.
2. It directly determines what matters are or are not placed on the government's decisionmaking agenda. For example, it exercises a veto over some matters that would otherwise have been placed on the agenda.
3. It sets the boundary between the spheres of governmental and nongovernmental activity (by controlling 1 and 2).
4. It creates and maintains prevailing beliefs about 1, 2, and 3.
5. It creates and maintains beliefs about the legitimacy, desirability, or acceptability of major political, social, and economic structures.
6. It does not *create* but does *maintain* beliefs about 1, 2, 3, and the structures of 5.
7. Although it neither creates nor maintains beliefs about 1, 2, 3, and the structures of 5, it nonetheless occupies its privileged position *because of* these beliefs.

With respect to the first six paths of domination, an account might also assert that the scope of control by the dominant minority is one of the following:

(a.1). It attempts to control all (or almost all) matters in 1–6. Or (a.2), it attempts to control only those matters of the greatest importance to it. [What is of greatest importance may mean either (b.1) what members of the dominant majority believe to be so or (b.2) what an observer judges by other criteria to be most important to it.]

(c.1). The dominant minority possesses exclusive control. Or (c.2), its control is shared with individuals and groups not specified as members of the dominant minority.

In order for minority domination to exist, the minority would have to be successful in overcoming any significant opposition to its rule. However, an account might furnish a number of different descriptions of the opposition to minority domination. To simplify the possibilities rather drastically,

(d.1). The opponents are a "significant" threat to minority domination and act overtly to oppose the minority.

(d.2). Opposition is significant but acts covertly.

(d.3). Opposition is not significant.

The possible combinations are of course absurdly large (formally 486). Yet the distinctions are hardly trivial: Accounts proposing different combinations (or subsets of combinations) could have profoundly different implications for the possibilities and limits of democracy. Consider two very different possibilities.

1. A minority directly and indirectly controls all matters on the agenda of government decision. Its control is exclusive. Because of its effective creation and maintenance of beliefs favorable to it, it encounters only negligible opposition. Thus its control and its interests are essentially uncontested "nonissues."

2. A minority generally succeeds in securing policies it considers favorable to its most essential interests. It does so both by directly influencing governmental decisions and by indirectly influencing beliefs. However, it does encounter significant opposition and it rarely is able to succeed except in coalition with other groups. Moreover, on matters that do not deeply affect its most essential interests its influence is much weaker, its allies fewer, its opponents much stronger, and its failure to control outcomes more common. On many matters, in fact, the minority makes little or no effort, directly or indirectly, to influence policies. What is more, elected officials compete vigorously for office. As a result other minorities are also "dominant" (in the same sense) on matters they regard as most important: farmers, say, on farm subsidies, older persons on old-age pensions and medical care, environmentalists on air and water pollution, military heads on defense expenditures . . .

Clearly the first constitutes minority domination, the minority is surely a "ruling class," and because it governs the state democracy is nonexistent. But does the second constitute minority domination? Certainly not in the same sense. And while it hardly corresponds with many ideal descriptions of majority rule democracy, the democratic component in this system of minorities rule is by no means unimportant.

My point here is not to propose an account that would adequately describe any particular polyarchy, much less polyarchies as a class of political systems. My point is simply that none of the theories of minority domination I have described—nor, so far as I know, any others—adequately specify the details of the chain of control they propose or provide the evidence necessary to a satisfactory showing that the chain of dominance they assert or imply actually exists.

## The Problem of Evidence

The evidence provided by theorists of minority domination is broad and loose.[15] Pareto and Mosca provide sweeping historical interpretations. Michels's evidence consists almost entirely of his study of a single political party. Perhaps because Gramsci advanced his theory of cultural hegemony under the limitations of prison life and censorship, perhaps also because systematic inquiry was uncongenial to him, he is long on insight and hypothesis and short on systematic evidence.

◆

Theories of dominance seem to me unable to sustain the assertion that in all polyarchies, or even in such a plausible candidate as the United States, a ruling minority dominates directly or indirectly the government of the state.

These theories do testify to the extent and pervasiveness of inequality. We hardly need their testimony, however, to convince us that political inequalities exist in polyarchies, or that these inequalities violate democratic criteria, or that their persistence poses a serious problem for democratic theory and practice.

By asserting the existence of a dominant minority, these theories divert us from a realistic assessment of the true limits and potentialities of democracy in the modern world. Either they offer ill-founded hope for an apocalyptic revolutionary transformation that will lead us into the promised land of perfect freedom, self-realization, and full acceptance of the equal worth of all human beings; or else they offer us no hope at all and counsel us, directly or by implication, to give up the ancient vision of a society in which the citizens, possessing all the resources and institutions necessary to democracy, govern themselves as free and equal citizens.

# Chapter 20

✦✦✦✦✦✦✦✦✦

# Pluralism, Polyarchy, and the Common Good

Earlier (in chapters 12 and 13) we considered whether and how the democratic process might be prevented from harming the fundamental rights and interests of some persons subject to collective decisions, particularly minorities who could be outvoted by majorities. To avoid harm is to do good; but we usually understand doing good to require something beyond avoiding harm. So also to achieve the common good of a group: To serve the interests and goods the members share with one another may often demand more of the members than their not acting harmfully toward one another.

A strong tradition in political life is that among the members of any proper polity there exists a common good, which it is the function and obligation of rulers to bring about. Yet how to interpret the obligation of rulers to seek the common good, whether in a democratic or nondemocratic system, poses formidable problems. These problems have always defied simple, straightforward, compelling, and at the same time rationally justifiable solutions. They have been compounded by the skeptical analysis of modern critics who find little meaning in the notion of a common good and further compounded in modern democratic countries by such a diversity of groups, associations, and interests that we are entitled to wonder whether any *common* good exists among the citizens of a country, and even if it does, how it may be discovered and acted on.

Some of the difficulties in the notion of a common good are revealed in the course of a dialogue between a traditionalist, a modernist, and a pluralist.

## THE IDEA OF A COMMON GOOD

MODERNIST: You've often expressed the view that in a proper democratic system citizens would aim to achieve the common good in all their collective decisions.

TRADITIONALIST: Certainly. I'm hardly alone in saying so. After all, that belief has been dominant in Western political thought from its recorded beginnings. I think it is also central to Confucianism, which continues to be an important influence in the ideas of both leaders and ordinary people throughout much of Asia. To the extent that I understand Hindu and Buddhist thought, though they are far less explicitly political than Confucianism they also seem to adopt an assumption of this kind. I would guess that most people everywhere believe that truly good rulers would strive for the common good, even if many people have little hope that their actual rulers will do so. In short, I can't think offhand of another proposition about political life that has been endorsed by so many people over so many centuries.

MODERNIST: So the idea isn't restricted to democratic systems?

TRADITIONALIST: Obviously not. But from a general belief of this kind it follows that in a democracy the demos, and in a representative democracy the people and their representatives, should seek to bring about the common good.[1]

PLURALIST: May I intervene? If we assume that in a democracy "the people" and their representatives ought to govern in behalf of the common good, and yet "the people" govern themselves in a variety of relatively autonomous associations, then *which* people should govern themselves on *what* matters, and toward the common good of *what public* should they aim?

MODERNIST: Hold on! You pluralists seem to be addicted to disorder. If we start with your question we'll surely be plunged immediately into a most disorderly discussion. Won't you permit me to raise my questions first?

PLURALIST: Sorry. I only wanted to make sure that my question is on our agenda. Please do go ahead.

## PRELIMINARIES

TRADITIONALIST: At the risk of offending our friend Pluralist, but also in the interests of intellectual order, may I suggest that we start by assuming we're dealing with a small, unitary system? Its citizens, let's assume, are members of a state, a polis, a sovereign and independent political society. Thus citizens are members of only one political association (in conventional usage, the state) and have no competing loyalties or obligations to any other political association, such as a political party, an organized pressure group, the government of a smaller, more parochial political unit, or the government of a larger, more inclusive unit, and so on.

PLURALIST: I'd meant to remain silent but I really must object. Do you mean to assume that no smaller associations exist, like the family, groups of friends, economic entities, and so on? If so, you're no longer talking about a human society.

TRADITIONALIST: No, I agree that would be an absurd assumption. Smaller groups like those you mention do of course exist. But the point is that they do not as such participate in political life. Let's assume also that our simple political system is governed directly by its demos through the democratic process. What I'm proposing as a feasible ideal is that in their collective decisions the citizens of our small state aim toward achieving the common good, that is, the good of all. We would therefore say that the citizens possess the quality of civic virtue.

MODERNIST: In proposing that ideal aren't you making, at least implicitly, two kinds of claims? The first is normative: You're prescribing the common good as the goal toward which citizens *should* aspire in public affairs.

TRADITIONALIST: That is so, obviously.

MODERNIST: The second is an empirical claim as to feasiblity: Since you want the ideal to be relevant to human life, you must believe that under certain attainable conditions people can be expected to behave virtuously. Presumably therefore you could provide us with some evidence in behalf of your empirical claim. What might that be, by the way?

TRADITIONALIST: I could offer historical examples, perhaps classical Athens or the Italian city-state republics.

MODERNIST: I have to say that in my view the validity of both your claims is highly dubious.

TRADITIONALIST: I'm not surprised. And I wouldn't be surprised if you're eager to tell us why.

## THE COMMON GOOD AS A NORMATIVE IDEAL

MODERNIST: I should rather say willing, not eager, since I come not as an enemy to the idea of the public good but rather as a friend . . .

TRADITIONALIST: Like Antony to Caesar?

MODERNIST: . . . seeking enlightenment, and if possible, reassurance.

TRADITIONALIST: Which I hope to provide.

### Philosophical Difficulties

MODERNIST: I share your hope. But I do foresee grave difficulties. As a prescription for civic virtue, the idea of the common good seems to me to suffer from three major kinds of problems. First are the philosophical difficulties, ontological and epistemological, that have plagued all attempts over the past century to justify any specific interpretation. What *is* the common good? How are we to *know* what it is? Since these have been discussed so often, I don't intend to take them up here.[2] Yet we can't simply brush them to one side as if they were a minor inconvenience. The philosophical obstacles stand squarely in the way of all efforts to assert any interpretation of the public good.

TRADITIONALIST: A most lamentable aspect of our modern plight.

MODERNIST: I can sympathize with your lament. The lack of a consensus on the meaning of the public good—and even on whether such a thing exists—creates genuine difficulties for public life. But regrets and lamentations won't make the obstacles go away.

TRADITIONALIST: So what have you to offer instead?

MODERNIST: Instead of your regrets and lamentations over the absence of a condition that has probably never historically existed anyway, we should take it as axiomatic that unless and until the philosophical problems are overcome, and there are no convincing reasons for thinking they will be, the existence and nature of the common good must necessarily be a highly controversial issue, not merely among philosophers and social theorists but in political life as well. Every description of a *feasible* political ideal must begin the assumption that conflict over the common good is an inevitable part of normal political life.

TRADITIONALIST: What you propose certainly flies in the face of a lengthy tradition to the contrary. I have in mind particularly, of course, the Aristotelian tradition, which saw political conflict as an evil that could and should be eliminated from public life.[3]

MODERNIST: I'm aware of that. But in this respect the tradition you speak of is mistaken. What's more, some of the most repressive regimes mankind has known have resulted from rulers believing that political conflict is an unnecessary evil that can and should be stamped out. The alternative view, which I subscribe to, is that not only is conflict inescapable but under some conditions it can be a source of learning and enlightenment.[4]

TRADITIONALIST: I admit that conflict over the common good and other matters is a typical characteristic, perhaps a nearly universal characteristic, of political societies. I deny that it is inevitable or desirable.

PLURALIST: Since you two seem to have reached a standoff, why not let Modernist proceed?

## That Prescriptions are Too Limited or Too General

MODERNIST: My second objection is that even if we ignore the philosophical difficulties I just alluded to, every attempt I've seen to prescribe the common good is either too limited to be generally acceptable or too general to be very relevant and helpful.

TRADITIONALIST: What do you mean by "too limited" and "too general"?

MODERNIST: What I mean by "too limited" can be illustrated by the work of writers who want to provide criteria or rules that are specific enough to bear directly on constitutional requirements or on public policies. Their rules invariably prove to be unacceptable in many important instances: The rules may work in some cases but they can lead to appalling results in others. As a good example, take John Rawls's renowned principles of justice. As his numerous critics have shown, under some by no means improbable conditions, the rules lead to morally objectionable outcomes and even absurdities (cf., for example, Rae 1975a; Rae 1979; Fishkin 1983, 14–15, 154ff.).

More often, however, prescriptions of the common good are excessively general. If a writer takes seriously the notion that the common good is the common good of *all*, then it is exceedingly difficult to specify much that arguably would meet this highly exacting test, except for highly abstract and very general qualities. How would an advocate like you, for instance, describe the common good?

TRADITIONALIST: I hold to the traditional view that the common good consists of some specific objectives that unequivocally promote the well-being of, literally, everyone.

PLURALIST (interrupting): "Literally everyone" means everyone in the world, doesn't it? Do you really mean that?

TRADITIONALIST: Of course not! By everyone I mean everyone in the particular polis or state.

PLURALIST: I put you on notice that I can't go along with your definition of everyone. It's morally arbitrary. But I'll hold off for the moment.

MODERNIST: And what are your "specific objectives that unequivocally promote the well-being of, literally, everyone"?

PLURALIST: "In the particular polis or state," that is.

TRADITIONALIST: Well, they definitely include peace, order, prosperity, justice, and community.[5]

MODERNIST: Just what I expected. Your description leaves the content of "peace, order, prosperity, justice, and community" entirely unspecified. Unfortunately, these praiseworthy general goals provide little help in making collective decisions. What's worse, if one of these ends conflicts with another, as is not uncommon, they provide no help at all. Finally, if the common good literally means *everyone* (everyone, that is, who is a member of the particular polity), then it is by no means obvious that peace, order, prosperity, justice, and community are always a good for *everyone* included in the polity.

TRADITIONALIST: If those objectives were not in the good of everyone in a polity, then I'd say that particular polity would necessarily be an inferior one. The essence of a good polity is precisely that the good of one member does not conflict with the good of another.

MODERNIST: You confirm my point. In order to justify goals that would literally be in the good of *every* person in a polity, you have just limited the possibility of a common good only to polities in which the good of one member never conflicts with the good of another. In effect, the common good exists in polities in which . . . a common good exists. But if you require perfect harmony in order for a common good to exist, then it seems to me that your conception of the common good is irrelevant to most political systems that have ever existed—probably, in fact, to all real-world political systems.

TRADITIONALIST: I concede that I have laid down a very stringent requirement. Ideals often do pose stringent requirements.

MODERNIST: But they should also be relevant to human possibilities. If, on the other hand, you were simply to gloss over the stringency of "all," as if "all" meant 99 percent or 85 percent or two-thirds or anything less than 100 percent, then a claim that any particular value is indeed in the common good fails to meet your traditional requirement, and you'll have to redefine the common good so that it no longer includes everyone. But if the common good does not mean everyone, then who is to be left out, and on what grounds can you justify their being left out?

PLURALIST: Now you're straying into my territory. Why should "everyone" mean only members of one particular polity? Shouldn't the good of nonmembers, outsiders who are seriously affected by the collective decisions of the polity, also be counted? If not, why not?

## Reasonable Criteria Conflict with One Another

MODERNIST: If you could restrain yourself just a bit longer, Pluralist, I'd like to mention the third difficulty I find in the notion of the common good. Even if, once again, we put the philosophical problems to one side, entirely reasonable criteria can lead to conflicting prescriptions for collective decisions. A moment ago I said that the goals Traditionalist mentioned—peace, order, prosperity, justice, and community—could conflict; conflicts would require tricky judgments about priorities and trade-offs, which the goals themselves don't reveal. But the problem is even deeper. To illustrate it, I want to use an argument set out by James Fishkin (1987). You said, Traditionalist, that the objectives you named promote the well-being of everyone. Would you say then that a policy that promotes more general well-being is better than one that promotes less?

TRADITIONALIST: Obviously yes.

MODERNIST: And would you also agree that a policy that promotes the well-being of more persons is better than a policy that promotes the well-being of fewer persons?

TRADITIONALIST: Again, obviously yes.

MODERNIST: Would you say, as some writers have, that other things being equal a policy that improves the lot of those who are worse off is better than one that doesn't, though it may better the lot of those who are already better off?

TRADITIONALIST: That seems less self-evident to me, but it does sound like a rather reasonable judgment.

MODERNIST: But improving the lot of the worse off could mean at least two things. It could mean improving the *relative* standing of the worse off, or it could mean raising "the *absolute* standing of the *least* well-off stratum" (Fishkin 1987, 10; see also Bonner 1986, 35ff.).

TRADITIONALIST: I'm not sure I see the difference.

MODERNIST: Well, suppose a system has three income groups. I'll call them strata. The average annual income of people in stratum A is $100,000, in B $20,000, and in C $2,000. A policy that allotted the same average income to each stratum would certainly improve the *relative* standing of the worse off, would it not? But a policy that increased the incomes of the lowest stratum to, say, $5,000 would raise their *absolute* standing.

TRADITIONALIST: Yes, that seems clear.

MODERNIST: So we have four reasonable criteria we might use to judge whether a policy is in the common good, do we not?

TRADITIONALIST: So it would seem.

MODERNIST: We could say, then, that a policy is in the common good if (1) it maximizes the total welfare, (2) betters the welfare of the largest number, (3) improves the relative standing of the worse off, or (4) raises the absolute standing of the worse off?

TRADITIONALIST: The first two taken together are simply the old utilitarian idea of "the greatest good of the greatest number," aren't they? The third and fourth are not so much utilitarian as Kantian in derivation.

MODERNIST: However that may be, what Fishkin shows is that these four principles are inconsistent. Under certain not unlikely conditions, no policy can simultaneously satisfy all four criteria. What's more, if we were to insist that a policy need meet only three of the four to satisfy our idea of the common good, even this requirement, as Fishkin shows, could lead to decision cycles exactly like the well-known voting cycles: According to one set of three criteria, policy B would be better than policy A; according to a second set, policy C would be better than B; by a third, policy D would be better than C; by a fourth, policy E would be better than D—but by the first set, A would be better than E, and so on indefinitely (Fishkin 1987, 13, 14).

TRADITIONALIST: But might it not be that on further reflection we could find a way of conceiving of the common good that would be superior to all four of the criteria Fishkin employs in his demonstration?

MODERNIST: My point is that no one has been able to produce a concept of the common good that isn't either too general to serve as a relevant guide to collective decisions or else is appropriately specific but would lead to unacceptable policies. I can't help feeling that a vast amount of academic discussion of the public good is carried on by philosophically inclined scholars who are never required to apply their ideas rigorously to collective decisions.

## THE COMMON GOOD AS AN HISTORICAL PHENOMENON

MODERNIST: The upshot is that even if citizens wanted to aim toward the common good, the broad interpretations wouldn't help them much to find the target, while if they tried to employ the more specific rules and principles they'd sometimes hit the wrong target. This bears on my second concern. I said earlier that the traditional idea of the common good makes an implicit empirical claim: that under some humanly attainable conditions, we can reasonably expect that as they participate in public life citizens—most citizens, anyway—will aim to achieve the common good. One way of justifying such a claim would be to point to historical instances in which most citizens have done so. I believe you suggested some.

TRADITIONALIST: I'm inclined to think that the bulk of Athenian citizens in the fifth century generally aimed at the common good.

MODERNIST: But we really don't have anything like adequate historical evidence to support your belief, do we? On the evidence available, one might reasonably make that inference, I suppose; but it would be just as reasonable to infer that Athenians often voted according to their individual or group interests. A. H. M. Jones, an historian highly sympathetic to Athenian democracy, concludes that in matters of war and peace, rich and poor citizens tended to vote according to their divergent economic interests.[6]

PLURALIST: And did the citizens aim at the good of those who were excluded from political life, particularly women and slaves? If they did, surely it was only in the sense that they conveniently rationalized the subjection of women and the existence of slavery as necessary to the common good. But if the common good is merely a phrase used to conceal a defense of particularistic interests, then wouldn't political life be better off without it?

MODERNIST: I believe you also suggested there might be other instances of citizens dedicated to the public good.

TRADITIONALIST: Yes, I had in mind the Republic of Venice and perhaps other republics of medieval and Renaissance Italy.

PLURALIST: But those republics were packed with conflict![7] And Venice, which was more tranquil than the other republics, was after all ruled by an extremely small aristocracy. Even if we were to assume for purposes of the argument that the rulers generally aimed at the common good, the Venetian experience wouldn't speak to the question of civic virtue in a democratic system with an inclusive demos. If you're not careful, your argument will turn out to be a justification for rule by the enlightened few who possess the requisite wisdom and virtue!

MODERNIST: Traditionalist, aren't you confusing prescription with description? As we all know, what we often refer to as the Aristotelian tradition and its companion, the republican tradition, do of course insist that civic virtue must be a central quality of a good polity. Aristotle well knew the difference between the ideal polis and the actual polis. Yet scholars who sympathetically portray the Aristotelian and republican traditions, and contrast them favorably with what they regard as modern departures from them, rarely provide us with descriptions of actual political life. What J. G. A. Pocock and others call "civic humanism" was an ideal. It most definitely was not a description of the realities of political life in Greece, Rome, or the Italian republics. In Italy the disjunction between ideal and reality was enormous: Machiavelli testifies to that. What I'm wondering, Traditionalist, is whether you may not have assumed, without quite being aware of having done so, that what the civic humanists prescribed as an ideal wasn't also a fair description of actual political life in the Italian republics.

PLURALIST: Like assuming that "government of the people, by the people, for the people" really describes American politics.

MODERNIST: In considering historical claims about civic virtue and the common good, it seems to me that we need to distinguish between three different possibilities. First, an historical claim may be reducible to nothing more than this: At some times and places philosophers, theologians, and perhaps political leaders as well tended to believe that civic virtue was a desirable and, under certain conditions, attainable characteristic of a good political order. Second, however, one might claim that in the times and places in which this view was intellectually dominant, it also characterized the *beliefs* of all those, or most of those, who actually participated in public affairs. Finally, one might claim that in these times and places, most people in public life did indeed *act* virtuously, in the sense that their public activities were predominantly influenced by a concern for the common good. What I am saying, and I believe Pluralist agrees, is that recent writings on civic virtue, civic humanism, and the Aristotelian and republican traditions at most establish the first claim. They don't demonstrate, and as I read them don't try to demonstrate, the validity of the second and third claims, which are left completely up in the air.

PLURALIST: In order to evaluate the third kind of claim, I'd suggest a further distinction. In theory, every citizen might *intend* to support the public good or in Modernist's language might *aim* at what he or she believes is the common good. Yet citizens might disagree as to what they conceive the common good to be. In fact, I'd hazard the guess that aiming at the public good is more common in political life than cynical observers assume; people just don't agree on what it is. So we can distinguish four possibilities, which are shown in this little table:

|                        |     | Do citizens |           |
|------------------------|-----|-------------|-----------|
|                        |     | Agree?      | Disagree? |
| Do citizens aim at the | Yes | 1           | 2         |
| common good?           | No  | 3           | 4         |

Citizens can: (1) aim at the common good and agree as to what it is; (2) aim at the common good but disagree as to what it is; (3) agree on the common good but not intend to achieve it; (4) not intend to achieve it and disagree as to what it would be.

TRADITIONALIST: Your third possibility seems to me self-contradictory.

PLURALIST: Not necessarily. For example, citizens might agree that the common good consists of nothing more than the aggregated self-interest of every citizen, and every citizen might seek only his or own interests. Nothing self-contradictory about that. I can also imagine everyone agreeing that objective X would be in the common good, and some citizens saying: "But Y is in *my* interest, and that's the policy I support." Hardly virtuous, but certainly not self-contradictory, is it?

TRADITIONALIST: A neat table, I grant you. But what is the point of it?

PLURALIST: The point is that an empirical assertion about the historical existence or future possibility of virtuous citizens in a democratic or republican order would have to specify precisely whether what is being asserted is (1), (2), or (3).

TRADITIONALIST: The first, I assume.

PLURALIST: But that implies perfect consensus and thus absolutely no political conflict, doesn't it? Even if we allow for a close approximation rather than perfect consensus, I don't see adequate evidence to support the claim that the first state of affairs has ever existed in any historical system, except maybe for a very brief period of time.

TRADITIONALIST: But political conflicts may have been over means rather than ends.

MODERNIST: Wasn't that exactly the point I tried to make earlier? Even if you assume that consensus on general ends exists in some times and places, that wouldn't necessarily eliminate political conflict over what constitutes the good of all in specific instances, would it? And such conflicts could be quite intense, couldn't they?

## PLURALISM AND THE COMMON GOOD

PLURALIST: This may be an appropriate time for me to express my concerns. At the beginning of our discussion we agreed to accept Traditionalist's preliminary assumption that we were dealing with a comparatively small and unitary polity—something like an idealized polis. I can readily imagine how in a small democracy, and even more so one with a restricted demos, a citizen might feel confident that he could easily perceive the common good, the good of all, the good of the polis. I'm not suggesting that the philosophical problems would vanish, but only that they might recede in salience. Both the existence of a common good—or goods—and the possibility that most citizens would want to achieve the common good might seem entirely plausible, even self-evident. But we don't live in a world of small unitary republics. If the notion of citizen virtue and the common good are to be relevant to the modern world, we have to situate them in the context of very large-scale democratic systems, that is, in the context of polyarchy and the pluralism that accompanies it. Wouldn't you agree, Traditionalist?

TRADITIONALIST: Within limits. I might draw the conclusion that polyarchy and pluralism are inherently inferior to the polis, and we should therefore do what we can to restore the polis. You give me all the more reason to prefer the past and reject the present as the model for the future.

PLURALIST: Nonetheless, you do agree, do you not, that the transformation from democracy in the city-state to democracy in the nation-state has greatly altered the conditions under which civic virtue and the common good might exist?

TRADITIONALIST: Yes, though I'm not sure what *you* see as the consequences of that transformation.

PLURALIST: The consequences were beautifully suggested by Rousseau in his essay on *Political Economy* when he said:

> All political societies are composed of other, smaller societies of different types, each of which has its interests and maxims . . . The will of these particular societies always has two relations: for the members of the association , it is a general will; for the large society, it is a private will, which is very often found to be upright in the first respect and vicious in the latter. (1978, 212–13)

Here Rousseau presents a contradiction for which there appears to be no solution: it's Rousseau's antinomy, if you like. I've often thought that this passage undoes in advance the whole project of the *Social Contract*. For Rousseau's antinomy precisely directs our attention to the problem of large-scale pluralist systems, to which the idea of democracy was about to be transferred. The small scale and rather homogeneous kind of republic presupposed in the *Social Contract* was rapidly becoming a relic of past history. To take one interesting historical relic, San Marino is not exactly typical of the world we live in, is it?

TRADITIONALIST: But the world of giant states won't last forever. Who knows? The future of the democratic idea may lie with a world of San Marinos. In any case, what's your point?

PLURALIST: I hope you'll allow me to come at it indirectly. I'd like us to engage in an imaginary reconstruction of history—one totally implausible, I hasten to add. Let's take ourselves back to classical Athens and imagine—hold your breath!—that in addition to the males who at that time were full citizens, the demos also included women and long-time resident foreigners. And, historically preposterous as the assumption is, let's also imagine that slavery had been abolished, all the new freedmen (and women) worked as wage earners on farms, in households, and elsewhere, and they, too, were citizens: The proletariat had been enfranchised.

TRADITIONALIST: You're right about one thing: These imaginings are totally implausible and historically preposterous.

PLURALIST: Agreed. But now I want you to try to imagine this heterogeneous body of Athenian citizens trying to achieve their common good. How much more difficult it would have become! So too would have been the task of providing a rationally grounded and compelling demonstration of what the good of *all* would consist of. Suppose, for example, that the freedmen demanded compensation for what was now generally understood to have been a long-standing injustice. If you'll allow me a demotic expression, the Athenians would have a real donnybrook, wouldn't they?

TRADITIONALIST: Possibly.

MODERNIST: Unquestionably.

PLURALIST: Now I want to take one more step into a world that never was. Imagine that instead of the weak and transitory schemes of confederation that developed later, Athens joined with all the other city-states populated by Greeks and formed a Greek nation incorporated in a single state, governed according to the democratic process. Wouldn't we expect that the problem of determining what constituted the public good of all Greeks would now be enormously more difficult? Wouldn't we also expect great disagreement and severe political conflict among Greeks? Might not Athenians tend to seek what they believed was in the interests of Athenians, Corinthians in the interests of Corinthians, Spartans of Spartans, and so on? Might not the new proletarians believe, however, that the highest common good was improving the miserable conditions they had in common with other proletarians all over Greece?

TRADITIONALIST: All you've done is to transform classical Greece into a modern nation-state—one with some resemblance to Greece today, perhaps, but none at all to classical Greece. I can't see that your flight of imagination takes us anywhere.

MODERNIST: I think Pluralist has shown rather dramatically that we can't engage in an intelligible discussion of the common good and the possibility of virtuous citizens if we assume, either explicitly or implicitly, that what might be intuitively plausible to citizens in your small unitary city-state still makes sense if what we have in mind is a modern polyarchy characterized by enormous scale and considerable social pluralism.

PLURALIST: My flight of imagination, as Traditionalist called it, was originally stimulated by Rousseau's antinomy. Consider now the perplexities of a virtuous Athenian in the new polity. To his surprise and dismay he learns that what he had hitherto regarded as virtuous conduct, conduct for which he was highly esteemed by his fellow citizens, is no longer virtuous. He had loved Athens. Throughout his mature life he had devoted himself to its independence and security. In the assembly, in the Agora, wherever discussions and actions bearing on Athenian public life took place, he had always tried to promote the well-being of all Athenians. But what had hitherto been virtuous, he is instructed, is now vicious. Now, he is told, he must seek the good not just of Athenians but of all Greeks. Why so, he inquires? Because, he is told, we are one people. But I am an Athenian! he says. I do not share enough in common with these other Greeks—the Spartans least of all—to feel obliged to promote their good. And by the way, he goes on, why only Greeks? If I am obliged to consider the well-being of Spartans, why not the well-being of the barbarians on our borders—or our perennial enemies the Persians?

MODERNIST: A Stoic might have responded that he *was* so obliged.

PLURALIST: Such a response reveals how elusive the boundaries of the common good are. And that's the point I'd like to elaborate.

TRADITIONALIST: Please, no more historical monstrosities.

## The Public Good of Which Public?

PLURALIST: For the time being, I promise you I'll confine myself to the historical present. Rousseau's antinomy suggests two questions we face in modern democratic countries. *Whose* good? *How* can it be advanced? The first poses a moral problem, the second a political problem.

Consider the first question. Whose good, the good of what aggregate of persons, ought to be taken into account in democratic decisions? By "taken into account" I mean that the good of each of the relevant persons is weighed equally. When we speak of the common good, or the general welfare, or distributive justice, whose good do we have in mind? The common good of specifically what set of persons? The general welfare of whom? Distributive justice among whom? If it is sometimes true, as Rousseau argues, that achieving the common good of one set of persons (or maximizing their welfare, or securing distributive justice among them) may damage the common good of another set of persons, should the good of one aggregate of persons take priority over the good of the other aggregate? If so, which group, and on what justifiable grounds?

MODERNIST: Are you seriously proposing that we try to answer those questions here?

PLURALIST: No. It's my impression, though, that most philosophically inclined writers who discuss the public good fail to specify what collectivity, aggregate, or community they have in mind—the domain of the common good, you might say. Or they take some implicit answer for granted. Or if they refer to the domain at all, they refer to a vague and unbounded entity like "society" or perhaps "the society." But they don't specify any boundaries to "the society."

TRADITIONALIST: Are you contending that we must never allow ourselves to think and speak at that level of abstraction?

PLURALIST: No, I admit that sometimes discussion can be fruitful at that abstract level. But not for the problem we're discussing right now. We can't possibly reach an answer to my first question if we stick with high-level abstractions.

TRADITIONALIST: Actually, the Aristotelian and republican traditions were pretty specific. They assumed that the public in question was composed of persons who shared citizenship in a particular state. So the relevant community—your terms aggregate and collectivity repel me—would consist of all the persons living in a particular state.

PLURALIST: To escape the vagueness of the term "state," and since our concern is with modern democratic countries, your answer could be interpreted as meaning that the domain of the public good would be all the citizens of a particular country, could it not?

TRADITIONALIST: That seems reasonable.

PLURALIST: But it isn't reasonable. If by citizens you mean persons with full rights of citizenship, including rights of political participation—full citizens— your solution is morally arbitrary. It's morally arbitrary to exclude persons who aren't full citizens, but whose good or well-being is directly affected by the decisions of the government of a country.

TRADITIONALIST: What excluded groups do you have in mind?

PLURALIST: Two are obvious. One consists of persons living within a democratic country and subject to its laws, like children, foreign workers, other foreigners, even illegal aliens, and so on. I see no acceptable grounds for saying that the good of these persons—children, for example—should not be counted equal to the good of adults who are full citizens.

TRADITIONALIST: Nor do I. What I originally said was that the relevant community would be all the persons living within a given state. You promptly narrowed it to full citizens, which I had not. I would count as relevant, and to be taken equally into account, the good of every person living within a country or subject directly to its laws.

PLURALIST: I appreciate your clarification. But that solution won't do, either. It fails to take into account a second important group: persons not living within the country or subject to its decisions. On what grounds can we reasonably say, for example, that in judging American foreign and military policies during the Vietnam war, the good of the Vietnamese should have been regarded as irrelevant? Or that in appraising American policies in Central America the good of the people of that region needn't be considered?

MODERNIST: Permit me to make two observations. First, no governments take the interests of foreigners equally into account, if they take them into account at all. Your moral judgment would apply to any government, wouldn't it—democratic and nondemocratic? A government doesn't escape moral judgment simply because it is nondemocratic, though there may be precious little most people can do about it.

PLURALIST: I agree. But here we're concerned with democratic governments, aren't we?

MODERNIST: Second, it looks as if you're moving toward universalistic criteria: The domain of the common good is nothing less than all human beings—the world community, some people would say. But in that case aren't you pushing the argument back up the ladder to an excessively high level of abstraction? I'm going to be mighty disappointed if we conclude that the domain of the common good must be either the parochial community of the little city-state at one extreme or a hopelessly impractical worldwide Kantian universalism at the other. Surely there must be something in between.

PLURALIST: A reasonable range in between would be all persons who are *affected* by a decision. Very few political decisions literally affect all human beings.

MODERNIST: A decision to launch a nuclear war might be one.

PLURALIST: And those who made such a decision should therefore consider its consequences for all human beings.

MODERNIST: At least with decisions like that we can specify the domain: all human beings. But for other decisions, determining the domain would generally be impossible. If you mean your solution literally, it's a counsel of perfection: a nonsolution, really. Democratic decisionmakers would be obligated to take into account minuscule effects they couldn't possibly know about. And if you don't mean it literally, you would need to draw a justifiable boundary around your domain.

PLURALIST: I don't know any entirely satisfactory solution to the problem you pose. I doubt whether there is one. However, I would offer two additional criteria for bounding the domain of the common good. First, it would be reasonable to employ a minimum threshold principle and exclude those on whom the effects are negligible. Suppose we say, then, that the relevant aggregate is all persons who are likely to be significantly affected by a decision?

MODERNIST: How do you determine the threshold of "significant" effects?

PLURALIST: I think no general answer is possible. It would require a judgment in each instance. But notice that the domain may include persons not yet born. Notice, too, that the set of persons affected by one decision may be different from the set affected by another decision; consequently the specific domain of the public good may vary a great deal, depending on the matter to be decided.

MODERNIST: I can't imagine how any political system could live up to the moral demands you make of it.

### Can Pluralism and Polyarchy Achieve the Common Good?

PLURALIST: That's of course the other main problem: How is it politically possible to achieve the common good or at least approximate it? Monistic theories of democracy, like that of Rousseau in the *Social Contract*, tended to adopt two assumptions as to how the general good could be achieved. First, effects on persons outside the state could be ignored. Second, under certain conditions the citizens could be counted on to act to bring about "their common preservation and the general welfare" (1978, bk. 4, chap. 1). But neither of these judgments is warranted.

As to the first, it's simply preposterous to say that the domain of the common good stops at the boundaries of a state, no matter how much the governmental decisions of that state harm the people outside it.[8]

TRADITIONALIST: It's just as unreasonable to ask that Rousseau solve a problem for which no one has ever come up with a feasible solution.

PLURALIST: The fact is, he did leave it unsolved. Putting that intractable problem to one side, however, the other assumption is also unjustified. Presumably the domain of the common good includes all those within the state who are excluded from full citizenship. But since they are excluded from participating in political life, the advancement of their well-being will depend on the virtue—indeed the altruism—of those who are entitled to participate, that is, the citizens. Perhaps it's not too much to hope that in political life people will act from motives of enlightened self-interest, which I hasten to add includes a concern for the benefits of community life. And it's not unrealistic to expect people to act altruistically toward those to whom they're deeply and intimately attached by bonds of love and affection. But surely it's too much to expect people to be steadily altruistic in political life.

MODERNIST: On that matter, I must say Rousseau seems inconsistent. On the one hand, he evidently assumed that in a good republic the citizens could comprise a very small proportion of the inhabitants. I'm thinking of his praise for Venice and Geneva as veritable models for a good republic. In both cities the full citizens were a minority, in Venice an extraordinarily small minority. On the other hand, to expect that these citizens would weigh the good of noncitizens equally with their own appears to contradict Rousseau's view of the motives for civic virtue. I don't believe he thought that citizens would seek the common good from purely altruistic motives. Their desire for the common good depended instead on a happy coincidence of enlightened egoism and the welfare of all.[9]

PLURALIST: And that in turn presupposes a body of citizens so homogeneous that the interests of all tend to coincide or whose interests are complementary at least, rather than conflicting.

TRADITIONALIST: But we don't need to accept Rousseau's seeming indifference to the question of inclusion. Suppose we put aside for the moment the effects on persons outside the boundaries of a democratic state. Let's now assume an inclusive democracy where every adult is a full citizen. Couldn't we then conclude that the good of all persons within the state would be adequately taken into account? As for children, might we not reasonably assume that their interests would be adequately cared for by adults, either directly as paternalistic authorities responsible for the welfare of children or indirectly through such laws as the adult citizens wish to enact for the protection of children?

PLURALIST: Your amendments might furnish a solution that would be sufficient in a small monistic polity. But when democratic ideas were extended to the nation-state, it was soon observed that many citizens no longer counted on equal citizenship alone to protect their interests, and rightly so. As Tocqueville pointed out, to protect and advance their interests Americans had by 1832 already formed themselves into associations of enormous variety. Pluralist democracy—or more accurately, a pluralist white male polyarchy—had already arrived in the United States. Indeed, while in very small and rather homogeneous democratic systems citizenship alone might have ensured equal consideration, Tocqueville's observations encouraged the view that in large democratic systems on the scale of a country, ensuring that the good of each was equally considered required associations. It seemed plausible that if associations were relatively easy to form, and if virtually all citizens possessed adequate resources for participating in them, then even in enormously large countries the interests of all citizens would be adequately taken into account in government decisions. Not only voluntary associations but also local democratic governments, which might be thought of as a special kind of association, would help to ensure that the interests of all citizens would be given appropriate consideration.

MODERNIST: Always?

PLURALIST: I'm about to get to some of the difficulties. But first I would like you to notice that in the perspective I've just described, the public good is not necessarily a monolithic goal that can or should be realized by a single, sovereign government. Though this might sometimes be so, probably more frequently "the public" will consist of many different publics, each of which may have a somewhat different good or set of interests. This of course is exactly what Rousseau feared; his antinomy was also his nightmare. Yet despite Rousseau, in a democratic order on the large scale of a country, associational pluralism, combined with a good deal of decentralization of decisions to local governments, would help to ensure that the interests of citizens in the different publics would be given more or less equal consideration. In that sense, the public good would be achieved in a pluralist democracy.

MODERNIST: A remarkably optimistic assessment, I'd say.

PLURALIST: Yes, it was. To head you both off at the pass, I'm going to admit that this seemingly happy solution suffers from at least three grave defects. First, it doesn't solve the problem of how the interests of persons outside a state or country may be taken into account. It might be said that the interests of these persons can be protected only by the citizens themselves. Insofar as citizens believe that the interests of persons outside their country are relevant to decisions about policies, then these moral judgments may enter into political discussion and decisions. This possibility is not entirely farfetched. For example, American critics of their government's policies in the Vietnam war often stressed the harsh effects of American military actions on Vietnamese civilians; and domestic critics of American policies in Central America mainly emphasized the adverse consequences for the people of that region. Yet it would be foolish to contend that the moral sentiments of the full citizens are a sufficient guarantee that the interests of persons outside a country will be adequately taken into account in political decisions.

MODERNIST: Indeed, to assume so would contradict one of the basic justifications for the democratic process: that, as John Stuart Mill put it, "each is the only safe guardian of his own rights and interests"—a proposition that he regarded as "one of those elementary maxims of prudence which every person capable of conducting his own affairs implicitly acts upon wherever he himself is interested."[10]

PLURALIST: Even if we conclude that policies will almost surely fail to take the interests of foreigners adequately into account, this defect isn't peculiar to a pluralist democracy or, for that matter, to a democratic state. It's a problem for all political orders, democratic and nondemocratic alike. Since this defect isn't related to pluralism as such, now that I've identified it as an unsolved problem for any kind of political system, may I proceed?

TRADITIONALIST: Please do. I must say, though, that by comparison monistic democracy is looking better and better to me.

PLURALIST: I'm giving you a portrait warts and all. Your idealized monistic democracy has not only had the warts removed; it's undergone an extensive beautifying face-lift.

MODERNIST: Less polemics and more reason, if you please.

PLURALIST: Well, to get on with the blemishes, a second defect in the solution I just sketched out has to do with persons *within* a country, who on our assumptions are full citizens if they're adults. But suppose that some citizens are organized in associations and some are not? In that case—surely not uncommon in democratic countries—the interests of the organized will almost certainly be taken more fully · into account than the interests of the unorganized. Sometimes, in fact, the interests of the unorganized will be almost entirely neglected in political decisions.

MODERNIST: But surely all polyarchies aren't identical in that respect, are they?

PLURALIST: No, they aren't, and it's extremely important to understand that democratic countries do vary a great deal in their constellations of organizational pluralism. For example, in some countries, such as Sweden and Norway, the major associations of economic groups—business, unions, farmers, consumers— are both highly inclusive and rather centralized. In these systems of corporate pluralism, nearly everyone belongs to one of the organizations involved in national bargaining. In sharp contrast, in other countries, such as Britain and the United States, the economic organizations are not very inclusive and are rather decentralized, so that bargains may be struck at the expense of the unorganized. But even where the economic organizations are highly inclusive, they don't ordinarily speak for noneconomic interests, and most citizens do have other interests than merely economic ones. Even highly inclusive systems of national bargaining don't ensure that in matters outside the purvey of national negotiations the interests of different citizens will be weighed at all equally. On those matters, differences in organizational resources will make for differences in influence on decisions.

TRADITIONALIST: Why don't you extend the principle of inclusion to organizations? Just as a similar defect in monistic democracy could be remedied by including all adults in the demos, the right remedy for a pluralist democracy might be to make sure that every citizen has more or less equal access to organizations.

PLURALIST: What's going on here? When I point out defects in pluralism, you jump to its defense. However, I don't fully trust your conversion. Anyway, one problem with your solution is that even if *everyone* were organized and thus no important interests were unrepresented in democratic decisions, it wouldn't necessarily follow that the good of every citizen would be taken equally into account.

TRADITIONALIST: Why not?

PLURALIST: Are we changing sides? The idea of pluralist democracy poses a fundamental question that advocates of monistic democracy, like you, can avoid. Should we seek political equality among individual *citizens* or equal influence on crucial decisions among *organizations*? The principle of equal consideration of interests refers to persons, not organizations. So also does the principle of equality in voting. If an association with five hundred members had the same influence on collective decisions as an association with fifty thousand, equality in voting would be nullified. Unless the number of citizens were the same in all associations, then equal influence among associations would necessarily produce inequality of influence among citizens. Yet the number of citizens is never the same in all associations.

MODERNIST: Would you escape the dilemma if the basis of representation in the legislature were functional groups rather than territorial units? The Guild Socialists once played about with proposals like that.

PLURALIST: The Guild Socialists of the 1920s—like G. D. H. Cole, for example—were premature pluralists of the Left at a time when monistic visions of a centralized socialist economic and political order were dominant. Unfortunately, however, they and other proponents of functional representation have never succeeded in escaping the dilemma. Either a "parliament of industry" composed of economic associations would violate the principle of voting equality among citizens, which the advocates of functional representation were unable to justify; or else equality of citizens' votes would somehow be maintained; yet that would seem to require that the weight of an association in the parliament be directly proportional to the number of persons who are counted as members. But in that case, I find it hard to see why functional representation would be significantly superior to territorial representation. Different, perhaps, but clearly superior? No. In fact, the systems of corporate pluralism—or democratic corporatism, if you prefer—that have evolved in the Scandinavian countries pose the problem in stark relief. There, a significant degree of control over crucial economic decisions, which in conventional democratic theory should remain with the citizens' representatives in parliament and cabinet, has plainly been transferred to a kind of nonelected parliament of industry—a functional legislature, if you like—consisting of the heads of the peak associations. In the prophetic words of Stein Rokkan written some years ago in a description of Norway, "Numerical democracy and corporate pluralism: votes count but resources decide" (Rokkan 1965, 105).

TRADITIONALIST: I really am beginning to wonder how you can possibly continue to think that pluralist democracy is superior to monistic democracy!

PLURALIST: I know how tempting it is to think that we might solve the problems of pluralism by eliminating organizational pluralism and thus restoring the ideals, institutions, and practices of monistic democracy. But if we wish to preserve governments on the scale of the nation-state or country, that is a temptation we should resist. To destroy pluralism would require an authoritarian regime that would devote extraordinary coercion to that end. A monistic system is an ideal appropriate to authoritarianism; it cannot be an ideal for democrats. For better or worse, a modern democrat must also be a pluralist.

◆

The discussion between Traditionalist, Modernist, and Pluralist breaks off, leaving us with three questions. First, in determining the common good, *whose* good ought to be taken into account? The answer, it should now be evident, is that in a collective decision the good of all persons significantly affected by the decision should be taken into account. Clearly, however, to apply that answer in practice is enormously complicated by the existence of pluralism *within* democratic countries, the existence of pluralism *among* democratic countries, and the existence of persons outside a democratic country who are seriously affected by decisions taken within the country.

Second, *how* can the common good best be determined in collective decisions? Pluralism also compounds the difficulties of finding a satisfactory solution to this question. While we have concluded that the democratic process is best for arriving at binding collective decisions, a large political society (a country, to be more concrete) includes different associations and political units or types of units, each of which may lay a competing and conflicting claim that *it* is a proper democratic unit, and perhaps the *only* proper democratic unit, for making collective decisions on the matter in question. How then are we to determine which unit or type of unit is proper for making these decisions? We reached a part of the answer in chapter 14, and I shall return briefly to that answer in the next chapter.

Third, a question to which an answer has proved highly elusive: *What* is the substantive content of the common good? Once again, the search for an answer is complicated by the pluralism of modern democratic countries, where diversity sometimes appears to reduce common interests almost to the vanishing point or, Modernist might argue, to it. I want to show in the next chapter why in my view this answer, though tempting, is mistaken.

# Chapter 21

◆◆◆◆◆◆◆◆◆

# The Common Good as Process and Substance

The discussion between Traditionalist, Modernist, and Pluralist in the last chapter compels us to consider possible solutions. If, as Pluralist contends and I believe, associational pluralism is inevitable in democracy on the scale of a country; if it is also necessary to and desirable in large-scale democracy; and if, nonetheless, it is unable to ensure that public decisions will generally achieve the good of all, can its defects be remedied, if not eliminated?

## RETURN TO A LOST TRADITION[1]

Traditionalist implies that the solution is to recover an earlier conception of civic virtue and the common good, notably one embodied in an Aristotelian tradition and also in what some writers have called the republican tradition.[2]

In this spirit it is sometimes suggested, but more often implied, that once upon a time there was somewhere a Golden Age of civic virtue, where public life was largely governed by a general dedication to the common good. But (it is further suggested) belief in a common good receded, even died out, and was replaced by beliefs in egoism, radical moral relativism, positivism and other conceptions hostile to a belief in a common good.

When and where the Golden Age existed, and when and where it came to an end, are questions marked by ambiguity and disagreement. In Alisdair MacIntyre's view the Aristotelian tradition endured in Europe for "eighteen or nineteen hundred years after Aristotle" when "the modern world came systematically to repudiate the classical view of human nature—and with it the end of a great deal that had been central to morality" (1984, 165). Pocock prolongs the tradition even further. Although he traces the origins of modern republican ideas to Aristotle and the Aristotelian tradition of the Middle Ages, in his interpretation these ideas underwent a crucial crystallization into the civic humanism of Florence," which in turn "forms a significant part of the legacy to subsequent European and American political perception" (1975, 84). To Gordon Wood, "The sacrifice of individual interests to the greater good of the whole formed the essence of republicanism and comprehended for Americans the idealistic goal of their Revolution . . . This republican ideology both presumed and helped shape the Americans' conception of the way their society and politics should be structured and operated" (1969, 54).

The conclusion we are sometimes expected to draw is that we must reject modernity and return to the Aristotelian or republican beliefs of the Golden Age. Although that conclusion is often merely implicit, MacIntyre makes it explicit: "Modern systematic politics, whether liberal, conservative, radical or socialist, simply has to be rejected from a standpoint that owes genuine allegiance to the tradition of the virtues; for modern politics itself expresses in its institutional forms a systematic rejection of that tradition" (255).

Yet though these and other scholars invite us to return to older traditions of political virtue and the common good, they fail to provide us with a scintilla of evidence that modern political life in democratic countries is less moral and decent, or that persons involved in public life are less committed to serving the public good, than was the case during the many centuries when the traditions they describe dominated intellectual life. What they provide—and valuable as their accounts are, *all* they provide—are descriptions of certain aspects of the moral and philosophical *views* of a comparatively small number of relatively prominent notables, insofar at least as these views were recorded. But they do not demonstrate, or attempt to demonstrate, that during any of the times when these views were prevalent among elites, political life even remotely approximated the ideal embodied in the "tradition," much less came close to its exalted requirements. Indeed, none of the writers I have named even claims that political life was ever greatly influenced by the ideal. Wood and MacIntyre explicitly repudiate such a claim.[3]

And for very good reason. After all, the subject of Machiavelli's *Prince* was the political life of Italy as Machiavelli knew it in his own time. The confrontation of political ideals with political reality was shocking to his contemporaries. By some accounts it was a shock from which the Aristotelian tradition never fully recovered.

If lamentations for the decline or disappearance of the Aristotelian and republican traditions are interpreted strictly within the limits of the evidence provided by scholars, what is being lamented is the decline or disappearance of certain *views* about virtue and the common good that at some times and places were more commonly expressed among certain elites than has been true (it is argued) during the last century or so. But unless these views produced a higher standard of conduct in public affairs than has recently existed, need we so greatly lament their disappearance? Is it not altogether possible that restoring a political ideology so poorly integrated with political actualities would do more harm by obscuring reality than it would do good by stimulating civic virtue? If we today are less shocked by *The Prince* than Machiavelli's contemporaries, it is not because political life is worse in modern democratic countries than it was in the Italian city-states—arguably it is far more decent and public spirited—but because, accustomed as we are to distinguishing political life in ideal states from political life in actual states, we are less prone to draw a veil of idealization over the politics of everyday life.

## RETURN TO THE SMALL COMMUNITY

How the lost traditions of Aristotelianism or republicanism are to be recovered, together with "community" and communitarian values, is obscure. Exhortation by scholars hardly constitutes a solution. Yet I am aware of no plausible proposal.

One suggestion is to restore the small community. This is evidently MacIntyre's solution. He draws on the analogy between our modern period and "the epoch in which the Roman empire declined into the Dark Ages" when rather than "shoring up the Roman *imperium*" what

> men and women of good will . . . set themselves to achieve instead—often not recognizing fully what they were doing—was the construction of new forms of community within which the moral life could be sustained so that both morality and civility might survive the coming ages of barbarism and darkness. If my account of our moral condition is correct, we ought also to conclude that for some time now we too have reached that turning point. What matters at this stage is the construction of local forms of community within which civility and the intellectual and moral life can be sustained through the new dark ages which are already upon us. (263)

But what these new forms of community might be, and how they are to come about, he does not reveal.[4]

Building a secure place for smaller communities amid the tempest of modernity and postmodernity is an appealing vision. It is one that I share (cf. Dahl 1967). But as a solution to the problem of the common good this vision suffers from two grave difficulties. First, in the modern world the most elementary conditions for a good life cannot be supplied by political units small enough to be homogeneous and consensual; yet units large enough to provide at least some of these conditions are almost certain to be too large to be homogeneous and consensual. If because of a community's small size, consideration of the common good of its members is necessarily restricted to trivial questions, the issues of this chapter will not be confronted; they will only be evaded. Yet a political community large enough for its political life to be vital to its citizens is likely also to be so large as to include within it a variety of associations and—precisely as Rousseau feared—its citizens will hold conflicting views about what constitutes the common good and the policies that will best achieve it.[5]

Second, even if most people in democratic countries were to live in smaller, democratic, more homogeneous, and more consensual communities, all the problems associated with the idea of the common good that were discussed earlier in this chapter would still have to be faced in the larger political society within which these communities existed. For reasons explored in chapters 15 and 16, the transformations resulting from the shift of democracy to the vastly enlarged scale of the national state are not likely to be reversed. In a world populated as densely as ours, one made interdependent by communications, travel, technology, economic life, common threats to our environment, and the standing danger of nuclear destruction, it is preposterous to assume that political life can be carried on exclusively in small, autonomous communities. To maintain the small community itself, and its virtues, will necessarily require the support and protection of larger, even gigantic, political systems. Many of the most crucial questions bearing on human welfare will necessarily be on the agendas of political systems far bigger and more inclusive than the small community itself. And for these larger systems the questions with which we started will still remain: Whose good ought to be taken into account in democratic decisions? And how if at all can the common good of these persons be attained by democratic procedures?

However valuable the construction of small communities might be, it will not solve the fundamental problems in the idea of the common good.

## CHANGING ECONOMIC STRUCTURES

Might not the diversity and conflicts of interests so characteristic of democratic political orders be reduced by fundamental changes in the economic order—if, say, economic enterprises were publicly or socially owned?

This view, though common, particularly among socialists, also seems to me mistaken. A shift from "private" to "social" or "public" ownership need not necessarily reduce the number and autonomy of organizations in a country—even of economic enterprises, much less other kinds. The relevant question is not whether enterprises are privately or socially owned but whether and to what extent economic decisions are decentralized, that is, on the amount of autonomy permitted to enterprises. This appears to be theoretically independent of forms of ownership, hence of "capitalism" and "socialism" as such. A privately owned economy may, but need not be highly decentralized; a socialist economy may be highly centralized, but, as the example of Yugoslavia shows, need not be.

It might be said, however, that a transformation from a privately to a socially or publicly owned economy would necessarily eliminate or anyway vastly reduce the conflicts of interest inherent in capitalism. Because citizens had more interests in common, and fewer in conflict, they would find it easier to converge around a public or common good. Thus the two problems we have been concerned with in this chapter might be solved, at least with respect to the people within a country. While I think this argument has merit, I also believe that it often leads to illusory expectations about the extent to which a socialist order would reduce political and economic conflicts and achieve social harmony. For one thing, by no means all conflicts are economic. Often, indeed, the most intractable conflicts are non-economic: matters of religion, race, nationality, ethnic rivalries, language, regional loyalties, and so on. Or they have their origins in ideological perspectives,

*environment*

ethical principles, and ways of perceiving, thinking about, and acting in and upon the world. In addition, in a decentralized economic order, whether socially owned or not, interests are likely to attach themselves to a particular enterprise or economic sector rather than to some abstract notion of a general good. Yugoslavia now furnishes abundant evidence for both of these propositions. Indeed, it may not be wildly off the mark to say that in no democratic country in the world, with the exception of India, is the public more fragmented than in Yugoslavia today. If we needed a laboratory demonstration of how little social ownership of the means of production can contribute, by itself, to the integration of diversity into unity, Yugoslavia provides a decisive case.     *Bosnia*

## ABANDONING THE QUEST: SOCIAL AND CULTURAL RELATIVISM

As both Modernist and Pluralist contend, in a pluralistic country with even a moderately complex society, that is, in any modern democratic country, it is difficult to specify "the common good" precisely enough to guide collective decisions. All three terms—"the," "common," and "good"—are problematical, to say the least.

One alternative is to abandon the effort to discover a *common* good, or a set of common goods, for all the people over the entire scope and domain of collective decisions and to search instead for the good of people within various spheres of collective decision. In *Spheres of Justice* (1983), Michael Walzer proposes just such a solution. To be sure, the problem he addresses is not "the common good" as such but distributive justice. However, since virtually every account of the common good specifies justice as one of the most crucial of the common goods, his argument speaks directly to the issues discussed in this chapter. Distributive justice, as Walzer points out, has to do with the distribution of goods to people. Community life makes possible a variety of goods that are distributed, in some fashion, to the members of the community: among others, security, welfare, money, commodities, work, leisure, education, and political power. The distribution of these goods is therefore subject to moral claims in behalf of distributive justice (6, 63ff.).

Several aspects of Walzer's argument are particularly relevant to the problems of this chapter. First, goods like those just mentioned, he contends, constitute different spheres of distributive justice. What would be appropriate criteria for distributing a social good in one sphere, such as money, would be inappropriate in another, such as political power. Hence general, overarching principles of distribution across all spheres are largely devoid of meaning. Indeed, no single standard exists against which all distributions should be measured. But there are appropriate standards for "every social good and every distributive sphere in every particular society" (10).

Second, the standards appropriate to a particular sphere are wholly derived from the "social meanings" that exist among the people concerned. "Distributive criteria and arrangements are intrinsic not to the good-in-itself but to the social good. If we understand what it is, what it means to those for whom it is a good, we understand how, by whom, and for what reason it ought to be distributed. All distributions are just or unjust relative to the social meanings of the goods at stake" (9). Thus there can be no rational appeal to some "higher" form of justification for principles of distribution, such as reason, social contract, nature, natural law, intuition, or process. The highest court of appeal is social meaning. "Justice is rooted in the distinct understandings of places, honors, jobs, things of all sorts, that constitute a shared way of life. To override those understandings is (always) to act unjustly" (314). — *than nature is unjust.*

Third, it follows that justice (and to that extent the common good) is culturally relative. It is specific not only to its particular sphere, such as money or power, but to the time, place, historical experiences, and culture of a particular group of human beings. "Every substantive account of distributive justice is a local account" (314). Walzer does not shrink from the consequences of his cultural relativism. From his perspective, even the traditional Indian caste system and the privileges it gave to the Brahmins would be just if "the understandings governing village life were really shared" (313).[6]

Fourth, Walzer provides an answer to the crucial question: *Whose* attributions of social meaning are (or should be) decisive? To what specific group of persons should we look for the social understandings that define justice? Walzer's response is "the political community." The political community

> is not, to be sure, a self-contained distributive world: only the world is a self-contained distributive world . . . Nevertheless, the political community is probably the closest we can come to a world of common meanings. Language, history, and culture come together (come more closely together here than anywhere else) to produce a collective consciousness. (28)

By political community he means more concretely "cities, countries, and states that have, over long periods of time, shaped their own internal life" (30).

It is in this rather loose notion of political community that, in my view, we find one of several deficiencies in Walzer's argument. As we have seen in chapter 14, what constitutes a proper "political community" for democratic purposes is itself a highly problematic question. Although Walzer shows us how different principles of justice are appropriate for different social goods, he fails to give much consideration to the possibility that a larger political community (to use his expression) may consist of smaller political communities; the good of a smaller community and the good of the larger community, as Rousseau rightly asserted, may not be identical; and the good of one smaller community need not be identical with the good of another. Yet just as different goods justify different principles of distribution, so different political communities, associated in a more inclusive political community, also justify different specific conceptions of the common good.

A second difficulty results from the extreme relativity of social meanings among different groups within a large political community, such as a country, and the conflicts these different meanings often engender. Take justice. If justice within a particular sphere means different things to different members of a "political community," how should these conflicts be resolved? Although he accepts the prospect that conflicts will occur, his solution is unclear. Are they to be settled by majority rule? If so, a majority of what unit? And why *that* unit?

Consider a specific instance. If it is always unjust to override the shared understandings of the members of a political community (312–14), then was it unjust for U.S. federal officials to override the social meanings of "justice" among whites in the South in the 1960s and 1970s? I am certain that Walzer would say that justice required the overriding of the meaning of justice among white southerners. But I am uncertain as to how he could do so without imperiling the premise of his argument: that justice is to be found, and can only be found, in social meanings. He would no doubt contend that the practices of the American South constituted an exclusion of blacks from membership in the political society of the South and thus of the United States. But surely that exclusion was "just" according to the "social meaning" of membership among most white southerners. What entitles the social meaning of justice among some Americans to prevail over the social meaning among other Americans? Relativism may be satisfactory for describing justice, but can it be satisfactory for prescribing justice?

Finally, then, it is the lack of much attention to *process* that seems to me a major omission in Walzer's argument. Before turning to that omission, however, I want to reemphasize the relevance of his argument to the problem of this chapter.

In his detailed account of the meaning of justice in the various spheres he distinguishes, he furnishes powerful testimony in support of the proposition that universal *substantive* principles of justice (and thus the common good) suffer from the dilemma mentioned earlier by our Modernist. Either such principles are vacuous, or nearly so, because they are too general to offer much guidance for distributing different types of goods, much less distributing goods in specific cases; or else if they are specific enough to provide guidance, they are inappropriate for some kinds of goods and all the more so for specific cases.

While general principles of distributive justice and common good need not be completely irrelevant, they cannot contribute much as constitutional (or constitutive) principles for a political order, particularly a large and complex order. At most they can serve as points of departure in the discussions about justice, the general good, and public policy that take place among members of a political order. Civic dialogue is not a discussion among professional philosophers attentive to the fine points of an abstract and tightly reasoned argument. In civic discussion, precise principles from which conclusions may be rigorously drawn are far less important than the normative orientations embedded in the culture, which may be local and parochial, national, or transnational. These normative orientations themselves are usually rather open-ended. While they may influence the course and substance of discussion they by no means fully determine its outcome.

The search for rationally justified moral criteria for determining justice or the general good, which has been so ardently pursued by so many moral philosophers, is likely to remain, for the most part, an intellectual exercise performed by and for a small group of intellectuals, mainly professional philosophers. To be sure, the results of that search may marginally influence normative orientations in the civic culture by giving some support to rough-and-ready axioms like "Act so as to achieve the greatest good of the greatest number" or "Act so as to care for the interests of the worse off before caring for the interests of the better off." But even such rough-and-ready axioms as these serve in political life as no more than very general orientations, often with rather uncertain implications. Consequently, interpreting the axioms and orientations and applying them in particular spheres and cases is not likely to bear much resemblance to the discourse of professional philosophers. Civic discussion is more likely to be a loosely bounded process of conversation and controversy among political elites, activists, and citizens.

Should we therefore abandon the quest for the philosophical perfection of *substantive principles* of the common good and look instead to the practical perfection of *processes* for achieving it?

## THE COMMON GOOD AS BOTH SUBSTANCE AND PROCESS

The last chapter left us with three central questions: (1) In determining the common good, *whose* good ought to be taken into account? (2) *How* can it best be determined in collective decisions? (3) *What*, substantively speaking, is the common good?

As to the first I argued that in a collective decision the good of all persons significantly affected by the decision should be taken into account.

But this theoretical imperative does not give much help in answering the second and third questions. As we have seen throughout this and the preceding chapter, pluralism compounds the difficulties of finding a satisfactory solution to the second question because, among other things, it requires us to consider how we are to determine which unit (or type of unit) is proper for making democratic decisions. However, we have already anticipated at least part of the answer, which comes, I think, in several parts. The unit ought to govern itself by the democratic process. The unit ought also to be justifiable as a relatively autonomous democratic unit, in the sense that it satisfies the criteria for a democratic unit set out in chapter 14.[7] Finally, it ought to include all adult persons whose interests are significantly affected, or if that is not feasible, the maximum number who can feasibly be included. The last clause generates new questions, of course, but strictly theoretical answers to these are impossible. What they require instead are practical judgments sensitive to the particularities of time and place.

As to the third question, it should now be evident that it seems to me misguided to search for the good exclusively in the *outcomes* of collective decisions and ignore the good that pertains to the arrangements by which they are reached.

It is true that the values or interests that many persons share—their common good—might sometimes include, at one extreme, values associated with rather specific objects, activities, and relations that they enjoy or appreciate through consumption, use, interaction, and the like. But the more concrete these are, the more likely it is that people will disagree about their specific value. Indeed, at the most specific level we are inclined to speak of "tastes," on which people notoriously disagree, rather than "values," on which we may reasonably hope for some measure of agreement. Thus everyone, or nearly everyone, values food to some extent, but we do not all agree on our tastes in food. Nor, generally speaking, is it necessary for community life that we do agree. So too, while we may place a high value on having access to opportunities to act in certain ways—to make choices, for example—and we may also agree that it is essential to preserve these opportunities, we need not agree on our specific choices. The opportunity to disagree about specific choices is the very reason for valuing the arrangements that make this opportunity possible. In the same way, we might all agree with Traditionalist that in order to promote the well-being of everyone (or as even Modernist might concede, nearly everyone) we need peace, order, prosperity, justice, and community. But as Modernist rightly pointed out, if trade-offs are necessary, as they generally are, we are likely to disagree about the acceptability of different trade-offs.

Our common good, then—the good and interests we share with others—rarely consists of specific objects, activities, and relations; ordinarily it consists of the practices, arrangements, institutions, and processes that, in Traditionalist's terms again, promote the well-being of ourselves and others—not, to be sure, of "everyone" but of enough persons to make the practices, arrangements, etc. acceptable and perhaps even cherished.

Although I doubt whether it would be possible to specify fully what these arrangements should be, the central argument of this book has been an attempt to specify some of its essential elements. These would include, to begin with, the general features of the democratic process indicated in chapter 8. One of these, the criterion of enlightened understanding, is particularly relevant to the quest on which we are engaged. In presenting it I said I did not know how to formulate the criterion except in words rich in meaning and correspondingly ambiguous. I did, however, suggest this formulation: In order to express his or her preferences accurately,

*each citizen ought to have adequate and equal opportunities for discovering and validating (within the time permitted by the need for a decision) the choice on the matter to be decided that would best serve the citizen's interests.*

In chapter 13 I expanded somewhat on the meaning of enlightened understanding by proposing:

*A person's good or interest is whatever that person would choose with the fullest attainable understanding of the experience resulting from that choice and its most relevant alternatives.*

The criterion of enlightened understanding, I suggested, could now be interpreted to mean that persons who understand their interests in the sense just given possess an enlightened understanding of their interests.

Following this line of thought, I now propose that an essential element in the meaning of the common good among the members of a group is what the members would choose if they possessed the fullest attainable understanding of the experience that would result from their choice and its most relevant alternatives. Because enlightened understanding is required, I would propose to incorporate opportunities to acquire enlightened understanding as essential also to the meaning of the common good. Still further, the rights and opportunities of the democratic process are elements of the common good. Even more broadly, because the institutions of polyarchy are necessary in order to employ the democratic process on a large scale, in a unit as large as a country all the institutions of polyarchy should also be counted as elements of the common good.

# PART SIX

◆◆◆◆◆◆◆

# TOWARD A THIRD
# TRANSFORMATION

# Chapter 22

◆◆◆◆◆◆◆◆◆

# Democracy in
# Tomorrow's World

The vision of the democratic process that has guided the argument of this book stretches human possibilities to their limits and perhaps beyond. It is a vision of a political system in which the members regard one another as political equals, are collectively sovereign, and possess all the capacities, resources, and institutions they need in order to govern themselves.

The democratic process, I have argued, is superior in at least three ways to other feasible ways by which people might be governed. First, it promotes freedom as no feasible alternative can: freedom in the form of individual and collective self-determination, in the degree of moral autonomy it encourages and allows, and in a broad range of other and more particular freedoms that are inherent in the democratic process, or are necessary prerequisites for its existence, or exist because people who support the idea and practice of the democratic process are, as a plain historical fact, also inclined to give generous support to other freedoms as well. Second, the democratic process promotes human development, not least in the capacity for exercising self-determination, moral autonomy, and responsibility for one's choices. Finally, it is the surest way (if by no means a perfect one) by which human beings can protect and advance the interests and goods they share with others.

Insofar as the idea and practice of democracy are justified by the values of freedom, human development, and the protection and advancement of shared human interests, the idea and practice of democracy also presuppose three kinds of equality: the intrinsic moral equality of all persons; the equality expressed by the presumption that adult persons are entitled to personal autonomy in determining what is best for themselves; and, following from these, political equality among citizens, as this is defined by the criteria for the democratic process.

The close association between democracy and certain kinds of equality leads to a powerful moral conclusion: If freedom, self-development, and the advancement of shared interests are good ends, and if persons are intrinsically equal in their moral worth, then opportunities for attaining these goods should be distributed equally to all persons. Considered from this perspective, the democratic process becomes nothing less than a requirement of distributive justice. The democratic process is justified not only by its own end-values, then, but also as a necessary means to distributive justice.

But the democratic process does not, and cannot, exist as a disembodied entity detached from historical conditions and historically conditioned human beings. Its possibilities and its limits are highly dependent on existing and emergent social structures and consciousness. Yet because the democratic vision is so daring in its promise, it forever invites us to look beyond, and to break through, the existing limits of structures and consciousness. The first democratic transformation broke through the previous limits of traditional government by the few, whether in the form of monarchy, aristocracy, oligarchy or tyranny, and created new structures and beliefs that supported government by the many in democratic or republican city-states. Two millennia later the second democratic transformation broke through the limits of all previous structures and beliefs by deliberately applying the idea of democracy to the large domain of the national state. As a result the institutions of polyarchy superseded older institutions and beliefs that supported city-state republicanism or the centralized monarchies and the remnants of feudalism.

Is a third transformation of democratic limits and possibilities now on the horizon? The history of democratic development offers us encouragement, but it also posts a warning. For the story of democracy is as much a record of failures as of successes: of failures to transcend existing limits, of momentary breakthroughs followed by massive defeats, and sometimes of utopian ambitions followed by disillusionment and despair. Measured against its exacting ideal, the imperfections of any actual democracy are so obvious and so enormous that the palpable discrepancy between ideal and reality constantly stimulates unbounded hopes that the ideal may somehow be made real. But feasible solutions often prove elusive, and those who so easily construct an ideal democracy in their imaginations soon discover that it is far harder, or even impossible, to construct that ideal in the real world.

With these warnings in mind, I want to consider three possible changes that might produce a third democratic transformation.

1. Changes in the *conditions* for polyarchy in different countries might bring about a change in the number of polyarchies. At one extreme, polyarchy might shrink to a few countries where the conditions are exceptionally favorable; at the other it might expand to include countries that contain most of the world's population.
2. Changes in the *scale* of political life might once again profoundly alter the limits and possibilities of the democratic process.
3. Changes in *structures and consciousness* might help to make political life more democratic in some countries now governed by polyarchy. A more democratic

society might result, for example, from a far greater equalization of political resources and capacities among citizens or from an extension of the democratic process to important institutions previously governed by a nondemocratic process.

I shall consider the first two possibilities in this chapter and the third in the next.

## THE PROSPECTS FOR DEMOCRACY IN NONDEMOCRATIC COUNTRIES

Though the strength of democratic ideas and practices has waxed and waned historically, until the twentieth century democratic states had existed, when they existed at all, only in a few places in the world, for a few centuries at a time, and with citizen bodies that invariably excluded all women and some, often many, men. The twentieth century, particularly during the second half, has witnessed four important changes in the world setting of democracy. The most problematic from a democratic perspective is still in process: The scale of crucial decisions has expanded beyond the nation-state to transnational systems of influence and power. The significance of this change for the limits and possibilities of democracy will be taken up in the next section. Let me now briefly call attention to the others.

One of these, as I mentioned in the introduction, is the nearly universal effort by rulers in the late twentieth century, including rulers in nondemocratic regimes, to exploit the idea of "rule by the people" in order to provide legitimacy to their rule. Never in recorded history have state leaders appealed so widely to democratic ideas to legitimate their rule, even if only to justify an authoritarian government as necessary to a future transition to true or purified democracy. Another change is the extent to which democratic countries with modern dynamic pluralist societies provide the rest of the world with images—if not exactly models—of a relatively desirable though perhaps distant future. That polyarchy and MDP societies have grown more attractive around the world is attributable not only to their own achievements but to the failures of the main alternatives: authoritarian regimes and centrally directed economies. A final change worth mentioning is the enormous direct influence and power that countries with polyarchal governments and MDP societies have come to wield in the world over economic activities, military and security affairs, popular and elite culture, and many other matters. Because of the influence these countries exert, the support they give to the development of democracy in nondemocratic countries has become potentially more important than it has ever been before. But so too is the negative influence of their indifference or opposition.

### The Futures of Polyarchy

One can construct several plausible futures for polyarchy in the world. An optimistic scenario would foretell its steady long-run expansion, as the political institutions of more and more nondemocratic countries are transformed into polyarchy. A pessimistic scenario would envision a long-run decline, as the conditions for polyarchy become more unfavorable, particularly among countries that have only recently gained, or regained, polyarchy. Another possiblity is that countries on the margin will oscillate between polyarchy and nondemocratic regimes (cf. Huntington 1984). Yet another: While some countries with nondemocratic regimes will become polyarchies, some recent polyarchies will be replaced by nondemocratic regimes; thus for the foreseeable future the number of polyarchies will hover around a limit that is already fairly close at hand.

Let us reflect briefly on the possibility that the upward trend in the number of polyarchies over the past century will continue more or less indefinitely. Presumably the trend would continue because conditions favorable to polyarchy would grow stronger in more and more countries. As a result, in many countries hitherto governed by nonpolyarchal regimes the institutions of polyarchy would not only emerge but would be consolidated into stable systems of polyarchy.

As I suggested in chapter 18, the most favorable conditions for stable polyarchy are five: leaders do not employ the major instruments for violent coercion, notably the police and the military, to gain and maintain their power; a modern, dynamic, organizationally pluralist society exists; the conflictive potentialities of subcultural pluralism are maintained at tolerable levels; among the people of a country, particularly its political active stratum, a political culture and a system of beliefs exists that is favorable to the idea of democracy and the institutions of polyarchy; and the effects of foreign influence or control are either negligible or positively favorable.

Suppose we scan the world searching for countries where these five conditions are all relatively strong but a nondemocratic regime exists? The number of such countries looks to me to be much too small to warrant the heady optimism of the first scenario.

What about the second? Reversing the upward curve of the twentieth century, will polyarchal democracy enter into a long-run decline? In reaching a tentative answer, we need to distinguish two different circumstances for the breakdown of polyarchy: breakdown in "old" or "mature" polyarchies, that is, in countries where the institutions have existed for a generation or more; and breakdown in "new" polyarchies, that is, in countries where polyarchy has existed for less than a generation.

A renowned argument by Tocqueville in *Democracy in America* can be read as a conjecture that given enough time for the forces of equality to work their effects, democratic systems will tend to be self-destructive because of the necessary connection between equality and democracy on the one hand and the long-term consequences of equality on the other.[1] The breakdown of democratic institutions and their supersession by authoritarian regimes in Italy, Germany, Austria, and Spain from 1923 to 1936 seemed to many observers to validate Tocqueville's conjecture. As I remarked in chapter 17, after decades of expansion the breakdown of polyarchy in these countries appeared to foreshadow a continuing decline in the prospects for democracy in the world. As we saw, however, that reversal was only temporary. Since the 1940s the number of polyarchies has greatly increased.

When we examine the record of democratic breakdown in this century a striking fact emerges: In countries where the institutions of polyarchy have existed for as long as twenty years or more, the breakdown of democracy and its replacement by an authoritarian regime is extraordinarily rare.[2] In several countries, of course, stable polyarchy has been replaced by a nondemocratic regime imposed by a foreign military force, as in Belgium, Denmark, Holland, and Norway in World War II. But no sooner was the outside military force removed from these countries than polyarchy was restored.

The other side of the coin, obviously, is that democratic breakdown characteristically occurs in new polyarchies, that is, in countries that have experienced less than twenty years with democratic institutions. In most such countries democratic habits and practices have had quite shallow roots. It is hardly surprising, particularly if we take into account all the other acutely unfavorable conditions, that throughout Africa parliamentary systems that had replaced colonial rule were with few exceptions rapidly replaced by military dictatorships and personal autocracies. But even in Europe and Latin America, many countries in which democracy gave way to dictatorship had failed to develop a deeply rooted democratic culture. For example, in Germany in 1933 a democratic government had only recently replaced a nondemocratic system, indeed an authoritarian regime of a traditional kind. In some countries where democratic breakdowns occurred, political oppositions outside the closed circle of an oligarchy had only recently gained political rights. In others, like Italy from 1923 to 1925 and Chile in 1973, less than a generation had passed since the suffrage had been extended to most males. In several, such as Argentina in 1930 and Colombia in 1949, not only did democratic institutions suffer from the fragility of recent implantation, but the regime that broke down was at best only a partly democratized traditional oligarchy. In most of these countries, moreover, a substantial proportion of the leadership and, so far as one can tell, the general population were hostile to political equality, democratic ideas, and democratic institutions.

The conclusion I draw from this *tour d'horizon* is that probably neither the optimistic nor the pessimistic scenario is likely to prove correct. Short of a major catastrophe such as a deep and prolonged economic collapse or a nuclear war, polyarchy will continue in the large core of countries where democratic institutions have existed for a generation or more. At the margins of this core of stable democracies, transformations of both kinds are likely to occur. In some countries governed by nondemocratic regimes, the conditions that favor polyarchy will grow stronger, and as a result, polyarchy may be inaugurated. In a few such countries, polyarchy may even be consolidated and stabilized, thus adding to the core of stable polyarchies. Conversely, in some countries unfavorable conditions may well undermine newly inaugurated democratic governments.

If this scenario proves to be roughly correct, then the core of stable democracies will continue to retain enormous influence in the world; in most countries, whether governed by democratic or nondemocratic regimes, leaders will continue to invoke "rule by the people" as a foundation for their legitimacy; but a great many countries will be governed by nondemocratic regimes.

### Thinking about Nondemocracy

Though I have paid a good deal of attention to guardianship and its claims, in effect I have divided the universe of possibilities into democracy and non-democracy. While I have discussed many of the complexities in the idea and practice of democracy, I have for the most part deliberately ignored the equally complex constellations of nondemocratic systems. Yet if democrats are destined to live in a world populated by both democracies and nondemocracies, how and what are they to think about nondemocratic regimes?

A responsible answer to this important question would require a book of its own, and I shall make no attempt to provide it in this one. Nonetheless, I do want to suggest several points that seem to me directly relevant to the purposes of this book.

It is tempting to impose upon the moral and empirical complexities of the world a false Manichean orderliness. For a democrat the temptation is to divide the world neatly into democracies, which are by assumption good, and nondemocracies, which are by assumption bad. But such a Manichean division is morally inadequate, empirically misleading, and politically inept.

It is empirically misleading (and therefore morally inadequate and likely to lead to inept policies) because even if we were to appraise countries only by democratic criteria, we would discover that countries below a reasonable threshold for full polyarchy are of extraordinary variety. At one extreme, in some countries below the threshold the political institutions are nearly as democratic as in countries above the threshold; at the other extreme are countries in which all the institutions of polyarchal democracy are absent.

Yet even democratic criteria oversimplify the task of appraisal. In appraising a nondemocratic regime, we need to make judgments about the *dynamics of change*, and particularly the *direction* and *rate* of change. A near polyarchy that is swiftly sliding deeper into repression is not equivalent to a near polyarchy that is moving steadily toward full polyarchy. Even highly repressive regimes are not morally and empirically equivalent if their dynamics of change are radically different. In appraising nondemocratic regimes we also need to remember that historically the pace of democratization has typically been slow—in the case of nation-states extending over several centuries. Hence we need to take into account the fact that nondemocratic regimes may vary enormously in the extent to which important *pre*democratic institutions exist or might be encouraged: literacy, education, human rights, a fair and independent judiciary, organizational autonomy and pluralism, dispersion of wealth and income, and so on. We cannot reasonably rule out the possibility, for example, that in a country ruled by a traditional oligarchy whose monopoly of coercive violence makes peaceful change impossible, the changes brought about by a revolutionary nondemocratic regime may prepare the ground for the eventual appearance of a democratic system.

When I reflect on the conditions favoring polyarchy I am driven to the conclusion that the capacity of democratic countries to transform nondemocratic regimes into stable polyarchies is very limited in the short run. Successful intervention requires an unusual conjunction of favorable conditions, like those that Germany, Austria, and Japan presented to the Allies after World War II.

Yet democratic countries could make a difference in the long run, I think, if they steadily pursued a policy of supporting changes in the direction of democracy and discouraging changes away from it. If the United States had steadily followed such a policy in Latin America throughout the twentieth century, I believe that democratic institutions would have become more deeply implanted, at an earlier time, in more Latin American countries than historically has been true. But the United States did not follow such a policy. On the contrary, more often than not its direct and indirect intervention weakened the development of democratic institutions in Latin America.

Even if the the United States and other democratic countries were to pursue policies more favorable to the evolution of democracy in nondemocratic countries, however, changes in the essential conditions would be slow. Political and military leaders long accustomed to using force to gain their political ends are unlikely to sacrifice their superior political resources on the altar of democracy. The transformation of social and economic structures is also slow. If we have learned anything from foreign economic assistance it is that the development of a modern, dynamic, pluralistic society requires more than foreign aid; it depends on prior conditions, including cultural factors, that are themselves not particularly well understood. Nor can a democratic belief system and culture develop over a season. Likewise the roots of subcultural conflicts are usually too deep to be eradicated by outside intervention.

It would be wise for citizens in democratic countries to recognize, then, that throughout the foreseeable future many if not most countries in the world will not be democratic. The enormous variety of regimes in nondemocratic countries require discriminating empirical and moral appraisals and a firm rejection of Manichean dualism. The capacity of democratic countries to bring democracy about in other countries will remain rather limited. Yet democratic countries could aid in the democratization of nondemocratic countries by steadily pursuing policies over many years that focus on changes in the underlying conditions that support stable polyarchy.

## CHANGES IN THE SCALE OF POLITICAL LIFE

The limits and possibilities of the first democratic transformation were determined by the structures and consciousness of the city-states of Greece, Rome (even when the republic broke out of the boundaries of the city), and medieval and Renaissance Italy, which in turn were profoundly influenced by the small scale of the city-state. The small city with its limited demos offered theoretical possibilities for direct participation—possibilities not always taken—that were eliminated by the larger scale of the nation-state. In addition, civic virtue was a plausible ideal, even if it was not usually acted out in political life. The common good, it was plausible to believe, could be known to citizens, and a common civic culture could successfuly cultivate in citizens the aspiration to achieve the common good.

The second transformation simultaneously contracted and expanded the limits of democracy. Given the enlarged scale of the political order in the nation-state, direct forms of participation had to be greatly displaced by representation. Direct participation by the demos in national lawmaking by discussions and voting in face-to-face assemblies was no longer possible, even if in some countries citizens could participate directly in the government of small local units. Yet while democratic possibilities contracted along one dimension, they expanded along another. Representation broke all theoretical barriers to the scale of a democratic unit. The rule of law could now cover an entire country, an impossibility under the old city-state ideal. A uniform body of legal rights could now be extended to an entire nation. To that extent violent conflict among the numerous small independent localities, the chronic disease of city-states, was replaced by a common and enforceable legal system.

The nation-state also incorporated a much greater diversity of groups and interests, which, it was discovered, could somehow live together peacefully. Moreover, as Rousseau feared and as Tocqueville later sympathetically observed, democracy in the nation-state not only tolerated but stimulated the formation of relatively autonomous associations of all kinds: political, social, economic, cultural. Older visions of monistic democracy clashed with pluralist reality. Political conflict was plainly unavoidable. As a consequence, conflict rather than consensus gradually came to be understood as a normal and (within ill-defined limits) even healthy characteristic of political life.

As a further consequence of the attempt to apply the democratic process to the large scale of the nation-state, political practices and institutions evolved, such as political parties, that were unknown to the city-states. A new type of political order appeared in the world: polyarchy. The institutions that distinguished polyarchy from other political orders also required systems of political and civil rights far more comprehensive than any that had heretofore existed or that exist contemporaneously in nondemocratic regimes. Therefore even while the second transformation drastically reduced the opportunities for direct political participation in the decisions of the national government, and virtually eliminated prospects that all citizens might be committed to a harmonious vision of the common good, it prodigiously increased the number of people who lived within a common legal and constitutional system and enjoyed a comprehensive body of equal rights. While the first transformation had transferred the right to govern from the few to the many, "the many" were in actual fact rather few while those who were excluded were in actual fact rather many. By contrast, after the second transformation was completed in democratic countries (with no little struggle), equal rights of citizenship had been extended to virtually all adults.

Are we now in the midst of another dramatic increase in the scale of decision-making? And may not this change prove to be as important for democracy as the change in scale from city-state to national state?

The boundaries of a country, even a country as large as the United States, are now much smaller than the boundaries of the decisions that significantly affect the fundamental interests of its citizens. A country's economic life, physical environment, national security, and survival are highly, and probably increasingly, dependent on actors and actions that are outside the country's boundaries and not directly subject to its government. Thus the members of the demos cannot employ their national government, and much less their local governments, to exercise direct control over external actors whose decisions bear critically on their lives. The result is something like the second transformation writ large on a world scale. Just as the rise of the national state reduced the capacity of local residents to exercise control over matters of vital importance to them by means of their local governments, so the proliferation of transnational activities and decisions reduces the capacity of the citizens of a country to exercise control over matters vitally important to them by means of their national government. To that extent, the governments of countries are becoming local governments.

## The Myth of the Autonomous Democratic State

How then does this new change of scale transform the limits and possibilities of democracy?

The answer requires one to judge whether the trend is reversible—reversible, that is, without costs that too many people will be unwilling to accept. While it would be a mistake to interpret the trend as uniform and inevitable with respect to all matters, in my judgment for the foreseeable future transnational forces will continue to erode national autonomy with respect to the matters I just mentioned. One may of course disagree with that judgment—I make no effort to defend it here—and dismiss the problem as of no great importance. But if it is correct, it means that the demos of a country, like the demos of the earlier city-state, will suffer a considerable reduction in its capacity to control decisions on matters of importance to it.

To put this change in proper perspective, however, we need to remember that the autonomy of the city-state and the sovereignty of the national state were always less fact than fiction. International conflicts, rivalries, alliances, and wars have eternally demonstrated how much the autonomy of all states, democratic and nondemocratic, has been radically incomplete. Not just conflict but also trade, commerce, and finance have always spilled over state boundaries. Democratic states, therefore, have never been able to act autonomously, in disregard of the actions of outside forces over which they had little or no control. Athens itself was more than a city-state; it ruled an empire, depended heavily on external trade, engaged frequently in international conflict, and repeatedly sought help from allies. Rome was only briefly a true city-state, even though the republic never fully adapted its city-state institutions to its ever expanding scale. So too with national states, particularly in Europe. Even the autonomy of the United States, though protected by oceans, has been from the beginning reduced by wars and the danger of war, international finance (both as borrower and lender), and trade.

Moreover, whereas the relative autonomy of democratic states has varied prodigiously, the quality of democracy in a country does not appear to depend directly
on the extent of its autonomy. While judgments as to the "quality of democracy" in
different countries are debatable, the smaller European democracies may serve as
a useful illustration. In general, the smaller an advanced country is, the more the
economic well-being of its citizens is dependent on foreign trade; in addition,
smaller countries tend to be more vulnerable to invasion and more dependent on
allies. Yet even though more of their control over key matters has been pre-empted
by international actors, many of the smaller European democracies display a
vigorous and self-confident political life. Indeed, the very consciousness of vulnerability and dependence appears to have stimulated the greater use of government action to protect people in smaller democracies from the potentially harmful
effects of international forces they cannot control (cf. Cameron 1978).

### Adaptive Strategies

These reflections suggest several ways by which the democratic idea might
be adapted to the new change in scale. The most obvious is to duplicate the second
transformation on a larger scale: from democracy in the national state to democracy in the transnational state. However, the historical analogy is too imperfect to
allow that facile conclusion. For in the countries where polyarchy emerged, the
structures and consciousness of nationhood were already rather fully developed,
but transnational political structures and consciousness are likely to remain weak
in the foreseeable future. Only the European Community shows much sign of
harboring a supranational growth gene. There the incipient institutions of a "democratic" transnational political community are faintly visible. A sort of transnational
polyarchy might gradually come into existence. Though its citizen body would be
massively larger than that of the United States, the central Community government
might not be much more remote from its citizens than the American national
government is from Americans. There, then, democratic ideas and practices might
gradually assume a comparable importance.

Except for the European Community, however, the prospects for even moderately "democratic" governments of transnational political associations look to be
quite poor. Even if transnational political systems are greatly strengthened, for a
long time to come decisions are likely to made by delegates appointed by national
governments. Thus the link between the delegates and the demos will remain
weak; and the democratic process will be even more attenuated than in existing
polyarchies. With respect to decisions on crucial international affairs, then, the
danger is that the third transformation will lead not to an extension of the democratic idea beyond the nation-state but to the victory in that domain of de facto
guardianship.

This emerging possibility means that in order to maintain the vitality of the
democratic process, democratic institutions within countries would need to be
improved. For one thing, stronger democratic institutions would provide whatever
democratic control may be possible over the authority delegated to transnational

decisionmakers. Democratic controls would help to prevent delegation from becoming alienation. Stronger democratic institutions would also help to provide a healthy democratic political life within the large sphere of relative autonomy that democratic countries will still possess. Here the experience of the smaller European democracies is encouraging. Just as they maintained a vigorous and self-confident political life in the very process of adapting to their international vulnerability and dependence, so in the future all democratic countries will be challenged to discover ways of maintaining and strengthening the democratic process as they adapt to transnational forces. In this way, while freedom and control might be lost on one front, they could yet be gained on others.

Finally, democratic life in smaller communities below the level of the nation-state could be enhanced. The larger scale of decisions need not lead inevitably to a widening sense of powerlessness provided citizens can exercise significant control over decisions on the smaller scale of matters important in their daily lives: education, public health, town and city planning, the supply and quality of the local public sector, from streets and lighting to parks and playgrounds, and the like.

# Chapter 23

◆◆◆◆◆◆◆◆◆

# Sketches for an
# Advanced Democratic Country

If we could design a society that, within feasible human limits, would facilitate the maximal achievement of democracy and its values—that is, an advanced democratic society—what would it look like? This is a question of breathtaking enormity, and I can do no more here than sketch out a few possibilities.

We can reasonably start with several conclusions from previous arguments. The first, a judgment about feasibility, is no more than the conclusion of the previous section. A world consisting only of very small and highly autonomous political units is out of the question. Countries requiring large-scale governments are bound to exist. It is desirable that they be democratic. Therefore we cannot design a feasible democratic society without large-scale governments. And as we have seen, scale has important consequences for the limits and possibilities of democracy.

My second conclusion, a moral judgment, is that, within the limits of feasibility, in an advanced democratic country citizens would possess the political resources they would require in order to participate in political life pretty much as equals.

To many people this proposition will seem so extravagant in its implications that they will wish to dismiss it as absurd. We may need to remind ourselves, therefore, why political equality is so important. In my view, neither political equality nor the democratic process is justified as intrinsically good. Rather, they are justified as the most reliable means for protecting and advancing the good and interests of all the persons subject to collective decisions. To repeat, among the fundamental goods served by the democratic process and political equality are freedom, not least the freedom of self-determination; self-development; and the protection and advancement of other shared interests. Political equality is not, then, an end we can obtain only at the expense of freedom and self-development; it is instead an essential means to a just distribution of freedom and to fair opportunities for self-development.

*322*

So while my explicit concern is with political equality, my implicit and real concern is with freedom, human development, and human worth.

What we seek, then, is a design for a large-scale society of political equals, the citizens of a country. But how can the citizens of a country possibly be political equals?

At one extreme, we might try to imagine a country in which the social and economic structures, without regulation by the state, automatically distribute to all citizens the resources they need in order to participate in collective decisions as political equals. Thus the social structures spontaneously bring about such an equality of resources that political equality is inescapable. But such a self-regulating egalitarian order has never existed in historical times (though it may have been approximated by some small preliterate societies), and try as hard as I may I can discover no way by which it could be made to exist in the foreseeable future.

These reflections lead me to a third conclusion, about public policies: an advanced democratic country would deliberately regulate its social, economic, and political structures so as to achieve political equality.

With this conclusion in mind, we might now try to imagine a country in which the social and economic structures are so finely regulated by the state that all political resources are distributed equally to all citizens (though exactly what "equally" means, I immediately realize, is highly problematic). But try as hard as I may I cannot see how such a completely regulated egalitarian order could exist. For I cannot see how a country with a large and moderately complex society so fully regulated by the state would actually maintain political equality. I do not believe that citizens could successfully prevent the officials of the state, particularly the top leaders, from using their extraordinary regulatory power to increase their own power and privileges. What began in the name of political equality would then end as political inequality and state oppression. (The consequences for efficiency, growth, creativity, and productivity would no doubt also be disastrous.)

Considerations like these lead me to a fourth conclusion: Because of constraints set by reality and trade-offs among various values, the optimum feasible attainment of the goal of political equality in an advanced democratic country would still leave significant inequalities among citizens in their political resources, capacities, and opportunities.

The fourth conclusion immediately leads me to a fifth: Because it is easier to discover ways of reducing inequality than ways of achieving perfect equality (whatever that might mean), an advanced democratic country would focus on the reduction of the remediable causes of gross political inequalities.

What then are the remediable causes of political inequalities? While I cannot attempt anything like an adequate answer here, it is useful to consider three universal causes of political inequalities (and therefore inequalities in freedom, opportunities for personal development, and the advancement and protection of valid interests). These are: differences in resources and opportunities for employing violent coercion; in economic positions, resources, and opportunities; and in knowledge, information, and cognitive skills. In chapter 17 I discussed ways of remedying the first. Incomplete as that discussion may be I shall say no more about the problem and shall focus instead on the other two. For I conclude—and this is my sixth conclusion—that an advanced democratic country would actively seek to reduce great inequalities in the capacities and opportunities for citizens to partici-pate effectively in political life that are caused to an important degree by the distribution of economic resources, positions, and opportunities and by the dis-tribution of knowledge, information, and cognitive skills.

## REFLECTIONS ON THE ECONOMIC ORDER
## OF AN ADVANCED DEMOCRATIC COUNTRY

The solution to the problem of the distribution of economic resources, positions, and opportunities, it might be objected, is right under our noses. Isn't a modern, dynamic, pluralist (MDP) society essentially a democratic society?

As we saw in chapter 18, it is true that an MDP society favors the institutions of polyarchy and to that extent favors democracy. But while the dynamics of an MDP society produce some of the conditions necessary for polyarchy, for reasons I shall turn to in a moment they do not spontaneously produce the conditions necessary for the further democratization of polyarchy.

In the kind of MDP society associated with polyarchal democracy, the govern-ments of the economic enterprises are for the most part chosen (at least nominally) by, and are legally responsible to, the owners; and the owners are for the most part private persons or collectivities outside the firm. Characteristically, too, the pro-ductive activity of the enterprise is oriented to markets. While this kind of econom-ic order is often called "capitalism," Charles E. Lindblom more accurately calls it a market-oriented private enterprise system (1977, 107ff.). In any case, the category includes an extraordinary variety: from nineteenth-century, laissez faire, early industrial systems to twentieth-century, highly regulated, social welfare, late or postindustrial systems. Even late twentieth-century "welfare state" orders vary all the way from the Scandinavian systems, which are redistributive, heavily taxed, comprehensive in their social security, and neocorporatist in their collective bar-gaining arrangements, to the faintly redistributive, moderately taxed, limited so-cial security, weak collective bargaining systems of the United States and Japan.

It would be a mistake, therefore, to conclude that the economic order of demo-cratic countries with MDP societies poses identical problems for democratization or requires identical solutions. Nonetheless, it is possible to suggest some common elements of a satisfactory solution.

### Conflicting Theoretical Perspectives

Let me begin with what amounts to my seventh conclusion: In an advanced democratic country the economic order would be understood as instrumental not merely to the production and distribution of goods and services but to a much larger range of values, including democratic values. The economic order would be seen as intended to serve not merely consumers but human beings in all the activities to which an economic order may contribute. This conclusion may seem too obvious to need saying. Yet it runs directly counter to more than a century of intellectual history in Europe and the English-speaking countries, where the theoretical perspective that has largely dominated thinking about the economy has diverged sharply from the theoretical perspective presented in this book. At the risk of simplification verging on caricature, in broad strokes let me sketch the diverging viewpoints.

The theoretical vision of democracy focuses on men as citizens—more lately, men and women as citizens. By contrast, the standard theoretical interpretion of the economy so rigorously extolled in classical and neoclassical economics focuses on men and women as producers and consumers of goods and services. To be sure, the democratic perspective cannot ignore the elementary fact that citizens are also producers and consumers; and implicitly or explicitly the standard economic perspective recognizes that producers and consumers exist in a political system of some kind, ideally perhaps as citizens in a democratic order. Yet each perspective gives central emphasis to the one aspect rather than the other.

The citizen exists within a definitely and often narrowly bounded political system—a city-state or in modern times a nation-state. The state is, or at least once was thought to be, a hard-edged system; your specific liberties, equalities, and obligations depend on your being inside or outside the system. Producers and consumers exist in a more indefinite, almost unbounded economic system that may in principle cover the globe. The citizen is expected to feel and generally does feel attached to the others living within the particular state, to a historically specific, unique aggregation of human beings, to their mores and cherished practices, their common past, their hoped-for future. These attachments may be reasoned and rational in part, but their strength also comes from nonrational, primordial bonds and beliefs. The producer/consumer is—in the theoretical imagination, if not in actuality—a supremely rational computer forever calculating and comparing precise increments of gain and loss at the margin and acting always to maximize net utilities. Loyalty may be of interest to historians, sociologists, advertisers, and ordinary human beings everywhere, but in the standard theoretical perspective of capitalism it is not a characteristic of rational economic actors.

In the democratic vision, opportunities to exercise power over the state, or more concretely over the decisions of the government of the state, are, or at any rate ought to be, distributed equally among all citizens. That citizens ought to be political equals is, as we have seen, a crucial axiom in the moral perspective of democracy. In the standard economic interpretation of a competitive, market-oriented, free enterprise economy, relations of power and authority do not exist. Their place is entirely taken by exchanges and contracts freely entered into by rational actors. Therefore neoclassical economists saw no need for such impalpable, ambiguous, and seemingly unmeasurable phenomena as power and authority. Nor in the standard version is an equality of economic resources, which might help to facilitate political equality among citizens, and thus democracy, and thereby the liberties associated with democracy, necessarily a desirable goal, much less a likely outcome of market decisions.

In the democratic vision, political equality must be maintained by a definite set of legal and constitutional arrangements, supported by general opinion and enforced if need be by law, that effectively guarantee each citizen certain rights, opportunities, and obligations necessary, and if fully achieved, perhaps even sufficient to ensure political equality among citizens. In the classical and neoclassical vision of the economic order, a state somehow lays down and enforces rules governing contracts, property, and collusion that are necessary to the function of markets. But why and whether political leaders will undertake the tasks assigned to them in the standard version, and whether and how much they will or should tamper with the distribution of wealth and income resulting from market forces, are questions that, strictly speaking, the standard theory is not expected to answer, nor can it.

In the democratic vision, the freedom achieved by a democratic order is above all the freedom of self-determination in making collective and binding decisions: the self-determination of citizens entitled to participate as political equals in making the laws and rules under which they will live together as citizens. As I have already said, it follows that a democratic society would, among other things, manage to alllocate its resources so as to optimize political equality, and thus the primary freedom of collective self-determination by means of the democratic process, as well as the liberties necessary to that process.

In the standard economic view, the freedom achieved by the economic order is above all the primary freedom of choice in the marketplace: the freedom of consumers to choose among goods and services, of businessmen to compete with others in offering commodities and services and in acquiring the resources to produce them, of workers—the rational alter ego of the rational consumer—to contract with employers to engage in labor in exchange for wages and thus to acquire the resources necessary to perform their functions as consumers. If the standard theory is neutral as to political equality, which it neither endorses nor excludes, it does assume the existence of one important variety of equality: All economic actors, whether consumers or producers, are equally rational (that is, perfectly so) and they are all equally free to accept or reject the offers and contracts available to them. But what "equally free" means is by no means fully specified.

Thus are the first small seeds of discord between democracy and capitalism scattered by the winds of doctrine. What consumers are free to spend depends on their income, and incomes are not likely to be, almost certainly will not be, distributed equally. But if income, wealth, and economic position are also political resources, and if they are distributed unequally, then how can citizens be political equals? And if citizens cannot be political equals, how is democracy to exist? Conversely, if democracy is to exist and citizens are to be political equals, then will democracy not require something other than a market-oriented, private enterprise economy, or at the very least a pretty drastic modification of it?

## The Governments of Economic Enterprises

Enthusiastic democrats have sometimes insisted that in a truly democratic society all associations would be democratic. This view seems to me mistaken. Certainly the justification for the democratic process presented in this book (chapters 6–9) does not compel us to conclude that every association should be governed democratically. Whether an association ought to be governed democratically depends on the applicability of certain assumptions (see chapter 8). If these assumptions do not hold for an association, we cannot reasonably argue—at least on the basis of *these* assumptions—that the association ought to be governed democratically. Conversely, however, if we judge that the assumptions are applicable, then we *are* obliged to conclude that the association ought to be governed by the democratic process. In effect, if the assumptions hold, then the members of the association are entitled to claim the democratic process as a matter of right.

For this reason citizens in an advanced democratic country would think it important to give careful attention to this question: What associations, other than the state, ought to be governed by the democratic process, and what need not be, or perhaps even should not be? In an advanced democratic country with an MDP society, the most obvious candidate for consideration would be business firms, or speaking more broadly, economic enterprises. For typically in all MDP societies these organizations are not only immensely important in the everyday lives of most citizens, but they stand out starkly because of their nondemocratic governments. Their internal governments are in fact systems of guardianship at best and despotism at worst. Yet in democratic countries where guardianship (and even more, despotism) is widely and properly viewed as unjustified in governing the state, guardianship, which sometimes degenerates into despotism, seems to be the preferred form for governing economic enterprises. At the very least, the contrast ought to invite thoughtful public consideration. By and large, however, the belief that firms are best governed by nondemocratic systems goes pretty much unchallenged in democratic countries.

Why should citizens in an advanced democratic country be concerned with the internal governments of firms? We might better ask: How could they possibly not be? Work is central to the lives of most people. For most people, it occupies more time than any other activity. Work affects—often decisively—their income, consumption, savings, status, friendships, leisure, health, security, family life, old age, self-esteem, sense of fulfillment and well-being, personal freedom, self-determination, self-development, and innumerable other crucial interests and values. Of all the relations of authority, control, and power in which people are routinely involved, none are as salient, persistent, and important in the daily lives of most persons as those they are subject to at work. What governments have such immense consequences for daily life as the government of the workplace? Where could despotism work its effects more insidiously?

How then should firms, enterprises, corporations be governed internally? I say *internally* because I intend to assume without argument that economic enterprises would be subject to some control by the government—or rather the governments—of the state. Even in an economy in which firms are predominantly privately owned and market oriented, the government of the state would regulate some of the actions of private firms, as it does in all democratic countries. If a democratic country were ever to construct a socialist economy, obviously government regulation of firms would still be required. To achieve both democratic values and tolerable efficiency would require most firms—whatever their ownership—to possess considerable autonomy and to orient their activities toward the market. In short, the only general form of a socialist economic order consistent with democracy and efficiency would be a relatively decentralized system of market socialism (cf., among others, Nove 1983, Selucký 1979). Under market socialism, as under capitalism, the firms would have to be regulated by the government of the state. Under either system, the degree and kinds of regulation required would be a matter of considerable political and scholarly controversy and would, I assume, vary greatly over time in any given country and from one democratic country to another. Important as these issues are, and though they unquestionably have some bearing on democratic theory and practice, I cannot undertake to discuss them here.

### Is the Democratic Process Justified in Economic Enterprises?

I have no doubt that many people will immediately reject the idea of extending the democratic process to business firms as foolish and unrealistic. It may therefore be helpful to recall that not long ago most people took it as a matter of self-evident good sense that the idea of applying the democratic process to the government of the nation-state was foolish and unrealistic. This foolish and unrealistic idea was rejected on the one hand by antidemocratic elites throughout the world who thought it obvious that wisdom and realism required some form of guardianship; and on the other by many advocates of democracy, a tiny minority at best, who contended that democracy on such a large scale was, as had been well known to all right thinking people for several thousand years, flatly impossible.

Consider for a moment the principal objections to democracy considered in this book. Some critics—anarchists—reject democracy in governing the state on the ground that since there is no need for a state, there is no need for a democratic government of the state. Historically the much more formidable critics of democracy, the advocates of guardianship, readily grant the need for a government of the state but deny that ordinary people have a *right* to govern the state. Ordinary people surely cannot have a right to govern, these critics contend, for they are not *qualified* to govern. From this perspective, if any group were endowed with a right to govern it would be that minority of persons who are best qualified to govern the state because they alone possess the requisite wisdom and virtue. As we saw, certain important critics of democracy have also contended that ordinary people are flatly *unable* to govern, for in their view, despite constitutional forms, political rhetoric, and prevailing ideology, the government of the state will inevitably rest with a dominant minority, an oligarchy, a ruling class, or a ruling elite.

These arguments, as I have tried to show in earlier chapters, are by no means inconsequential. Yet for reasons I have set forth I believe them to be mistaken. What is more, as I have pointed out, in this century the idea of democracy as a necessary element of legitimate governent has won a clean sweep over these and other competitors. But the triumph of the idea of democracy has not brought about the triumph of the process of democracy. As the modern embodiment of the idea, polyarchy requires certain conditions; and as I suggested in the last chapter in many countries—most, in fact—these conditions are absent or too weak to support the institutions of polyarchy.

Objections to the idea of extending democracy to the governments of economic enterprises are surprisingly (or perhaps not so surprisingly?) parallel to the objections to the idea of applying democracy to the governments of states. To begin with, some critics contend that there is no need for a democratic government in a business firm because there is no government in a business firm. In the standard economic interpretation, for example, the internal government of economic enterprises is essentially an irrelevant topic, since no "government," no set of officials endowed with power and authority, can be said to exist within a firm: Power and authority simply dissolve into contracts and exchanges freely, voluntarily, and rationally entered into by employers and workers. But if an economic enterprise is understood, as I believe it must be, to require relations of power and authority that constitute a government of the persons who participate in the productive activities of the enterprise, then we are entitled to ask—indeed we are obliged to ask—how that government should be constituted.

Conceding the need for a government, some critics insist that no one has a *right* to govern a firm except its owners. These critics argue that the only way in which the idea of democracy could rightly be applied to private enterprises, if indeed it could be applied to them at all, would be in the form of "stockholder democracy." This argument seems to me defective in several respects. For one thing, "stockholder democracy" is an oxymoron, since allocating votes by shares would violate a fundamental criterion of the democratic process, voting equality among citizens. Democracy requires that the votes of each *citizen* be counted equally, a requirement that cannot be satisfied by counting the vote of each *share of stock* equally. In order for stockholders to govern their firms by a process that could correctly be described as democratic, it would be necessary for each stockholder to have an equal vote. Few advocates of "stockholder democracy" seriously propose that solution.

But even if they did, the solution would be badly flawed because the conditions for the democratic process almost never exist among stockholders, particularly in large firms. The democratic process in a large firm would require something like the institutions of polyarchy; in a small firm it would require something like the institutions of the democratic city-state. But these institutions do not exist, nor do the conditions that would support them. There is no reason to expect them to exist, since few persons buy shares in order to participate in the governing of firms: They buy shares in order to participate in the earnings of firms.

Even if one were to accept the dubious premise that the right to govern firms (internally) must be lodged exclusively with the owners, it would not follow that the proper solution is "stockholder democracy" in the usual sense. For the democratic process in the governments of economic enterprises could be brought about by transferring ownership to the employees in a form that provides each such person—no longer an employee but an owner-worker—with one share, entitling the owner-worker to one and only one vote.[1]

Finally, the argument from a general right to property to the proposition that modern economic enterprises ought to be controlled by private owners is jam-packed with non sequiturs. To take only one, to say that people are entitled to the fruits of their labor is not to say that investors are entitled to govern the firms in which they invest.[2]

Still other critics insist, however, that even if the people who work in a firm can make a reasonable claim to a right to participate in governing it, they are not *qualified* to do so. Perhaps they possess the right, this argument might run, but they would be foolish to exercise it. Better that they forgo their right and let those who are better qualified run the firm. We hear in these arguments all the familiar defenses for guardianship, and we should approach them with the skepticism that case warrants.

Just as the question of competence is central and perhaps decisive in judging the relative desirability of democracy and guardianship in the government of the state, so it is the central issue, I believe, in judging whether it would be desirable to democratize economic enterprises. For unless the Strong Principle of Equality applies among the members of an enterprise, we cannot conclude that they are entitled to govern themselves by the democratic process. As we have seen throughout this book, the choice of democracy over guardianship rests heavily on the Strong Principle. To accept it is to take a long and crucial step toward the democratic process; to reject it is to turn toward guardianship. Because of the overwhelming weight of existing institutions and ideologies, probably most people, including many thoughtful people, will find it hard to believe that employees are qualified to govern the enterprises in which they work. Applying the Strong Principle to the workplace will seem dubious. The case for guardianship will no doubt seem much stronger.

As with the state, the question is complex, and I cannot hope to resolve it satisfactorily here. However, let me suggest several reasons why the case for guardianship is much weaker than seems to be commonly believed.

To begin with, we need to recall that the Strong Principle of Equality does not require that citizens be competent with respect to all matters, for they can delegate decisions about some matters to others. Except in exceedingly small firms, employees would find it sensible to delegate some decisions. In larger firms, they would no doubt delegate a good deal of their authority to an elected board, which in the typical case would probably be granted the authority to select and remove executives.

We also need to keep in mind that in MDP societies the firm is not the idealized efficiency-maximizing enterprise of ideal theory. It is the privately owned corporation, in which nominal sovereignty rests with stockholders who ordinarily face almost insuperable difficulties in contesting a managerial decision, including their utter dependence on management for information about decisions. One of the hallmarks of polyarchy, an effective right of opposition, does not exist in business firms.

If the question were merely whether employees are as qualified on the whole to run their firms as the stockholders, the answer is, I think, that they are a good deal more qualified. But of course, as we have seen, the stockholders do not run the firms they own. "Stockholder democracy" is not only a contradiction in terms; government of firms by the shareholders is a myth. Though managers may run firms for the benefit of the shareholders (at least in part and some of the time) control over key decisions is typically in the hands not of the stockholders but of the management.

Thus the relevant judgment is whether the employees of firms would be as competent in choosing managers, to whom in larger firms they would delegate a good deal of their authority, as are the shareholders, or, more realistically, the managers themselves, who select their peers and successors by co-optation. Although the growing body of recent evidence seems to me positive, citizens in an advanced democratic country might reasonably decide to answer this and other questions about the democratization of firms by proceeding experimentally.

What the best solution would prove to be for all economic enterprises or for every democratic country, I cannot say.[3] But it seems to me undeniable that in an advanced democratic country citizens would place the question of governing economic enterprises high on their agenda of important issues. To justify the introduction of the democratic process in governing economic enterprises, they would not have to conclude that democratically run firms would function better by economic standards than conventional firms. If democratically run firms were as good by economic standards, then taken all around they would be superior to conventional firms. For the scales would be tipped by the added values of the democratic process.

One might concede all this and yet deny that democracy is possible in economic enterprises. Just as some critics of the idea of democracy in the government of the state insist that minority domination is inevitable, no matter the constitutional forms, so some critics contend that the idea of democratizing economic enterprises is a chimera, since firms are inherently so unsuitable for democracy that minority domination is inevitable. Though that argument cannot be lightly dismissed, it becomes less convincing as we probe beneath its surface plausibility.

With enterprises as with the state, democratization requires favorable conditions, conditions that do not arise spontaneously, inevitably, or "naturally." Favorable conditions must be created. Just as democracy in the government of the state has failed to develop in many countries, or has developed and then collapsed, so, though to an even greater degree, the economies of MDP societies are the graveyard of uncounted attempts to democratize the workplace. What these innumerable failures demonstrate is that without appropriate systems of internal and external support, attempts to introduce the democratic process in the government of firms are likely to fail. Like democratic countries, democratic firms would require a properly democratic constitution, effectively enforced, guaranteeing such basic rights as freedom of speech. In addition, the successful democratization of enterprises would require other support systems. These would include adequate sources of credit, extensive training programs, particularly for managers, and organizations for assisting in the development of new products and the founding of new enterprises. The absence of these supports has greatly contributed to the failures of many earlier attempt to introduce democracy in the workplace.[4]

Finally, just as in the government of the state, the idea of democratically governed enterprises stimulates excessive expectations. Both advocates and opponents of democratization, whether in the state or elsewhere, typically overstate its likely effects. Nonetheless, the disappointment of exaggerated hopes for the democratic government of states does not justify the conclusion that the consequences have been unimportant. So too it would be a mistake to underestimate the importance of authoritarian institutions in the daily lives of working people and the consequences of introducing a more democratic system in the governing of economic enterprises. To be sure, in governing firms as in governing states the universal tendency toward minority domination in human organizations would work its effects. Yet it is reasonable to expect that democratic structures in governing the workplace would satisfy the criteria of the democratic process about as well as democratic structures in governing the state. Just as we support the democratic process in the government of the state despite substantial imperfections in the process, so the citizens of an advanced democratic society would support the democratic process in the government of economic enterprises despite the imperfections that surely would exist in practice.

## DEMOCRACY, MINORITY DOMINATION, AND THE MODERN GUARDIANS

Citizens in an advanced democratic country might thus bring about a more democratic alternative to the undemocratic governments of their economic enterprises. But they would face an even more daunting problem in the government of the state.

Inequality among citizens is a persistent and serious problem in all democratic countries. Inequalities in their political resources, in their strategic positions, and in their overt and implicit bargaining power are sufficiently great even in democratic orders to lend considerable plausibility to theories of minority domination. Yet for reasons discussed in chapter 19 these theories are unsatisfactory both as empirical descriptions and as guides to action. Nonetheless, because of the persistence and seriousness of political inequality, the ancient vision of a political order in which citizens participate in political life on essentially equal terms still remains far from realization.

An adequate account of the inequalities among citizens in their opportunities and capacities for influencing the government of the state is far beyond the scope of this book. From ancient times to the present day, however, virtually all thoughtful advocates of democratic and republican government have strongly emphasized how democracy is threatened by inequalities in economic resources. It was an axiom of classical republican theory, for example, that power and property tend to coincide; and therefore to ensure the wide distribution of power necessary to a republic, property must necessarily be widely distributed.

The consequences of the economic order for the distribution of resources, strategic positions, and bargaining strength, and hence for political equality, provides an additional reason for concern over the ownership and government of economic enterprises. For the prevailing systems of ownership and control result in substantial inequalities not only in wealth and income but in the host of other values attached to work, job, ownership, wealth, and income. But because few problems have been given more attention by advocates of democracy, and because of the obvious impact of economic arrangements on political life, I am simply going to assume that an advanced democratic country would place high on its agenda the problem of how best to achieve an economic order that would strengthen the democratic process.

Difficult as that problem is, I want to turn instead to a problem that seems to me even more formidable. For I am inclined to think that the long-run prospects for democracy are more seriously endangered by inequalities in resources, strategic positions, and bargaining strength that are derived not from wealth or economic position but from special knowledge. Perhaps it is not altogether surprising that the danger I see springs from a source that provided Plato with his hopes for guardianship: intellectuals.

I use the terms "intellectuals," "the intellectual stratum or class," and so on—modern terms unknown to Plato[5]—in the meaning given by Edward Shils: "Intellectuals are the aggregate of persons in any society who employ in their communication and expression, with relatively higher frequency than most other members of their society, symbols of general scope and abstract reference, concerning man, society, nature, and the cosmos" (1968, 399).

In chapter 18 we observed how theories of minority domination that give greater weight to persuasion than outright coercion attribute decisive importance to intellectuals. In these theories, intellectuals provide the systematic ideas that rationalize the legitimacy of the ruling class (and the counterclaims of their opponents), create and diffuse ideologies, develop the prevailing "political formula" of a society (Mosca), and give form and content to the "cultural hegemony" of the ruling class (Gramsci). While theories of minority domination seem to me unsatisfactory, I do not believe they are mistaken in attributing to intellectuals considerable influence on political life. And for reasons I shall explain shortly, the influence of intellectuals—or rather of a special subset of the intellectual stratum—has greatly increased in the last half of this century and will probably increase even more in the future.

Because intellectuals rely on persuasion rather than command or coercion and the effects of their persuasion are often indirect, delayed, and difficult to observe, their influence in public life, while easy to detect in a general way, is not easy to verify in a systematic way. Moreover, intellectuals seem loath to give to their own influence the same severe and critical scrutiny they so readily give to that of others. I believe nonetheless that a contemporary observer would find strong evidence for the importance of intellectuals in shaping attitudes, beliefs, and values. Through their influence over educational institutions and the media, the content of the public's agenda and its sense of priorities, the policies and programs supplied to governments and oppositions, the ideas that are thought to be intellectually respectable and need to be taken seriously, whether in support of or opposition to the status quo, and in many other ways, intellectuals play a preeminent role in modern democratic countries. To take only one example, in the United States the relative importance that viewers of television news broadcasts assign to a public issue is strongly influenced by the amount of attention the news commentators themselves give to that particular issue (Iyengar and Kinder 1987).

In assessing the influence of intellectuals it is important not to be misled by notions of a homogeneous "class" with common "class interests." While throughout history and in virtually every society the intellectual stratum has worked mainly in the service of civil and ecclesiastical authorities, in recent centuries a significant part of the stratum has come to consist of intellectuals who are distant or alienated from these authorities and who play a role not as supporters but as critics and opponents.[6] Thus intellectuals in the modern world have tended to espouse diverse and often conflicting views on most matters, including public policies. To this extent they are remote indeed from forming a "class" dedicated to promoting their own "class interests."

To be sure, like businessmen intellectuals do tend to share, though weakly, certain advantages that they generally try to protect and advance; in this sense, they do have some common interests. In modern democratic countries, intellectuals, particularly those in the upper part of the stratum, are—like businessmen—among the most privileged members of society. Ordinarily they are not only relatively secure economically, but many of them possess a degree of professional independence and autonomy that is unmatched by people in other social roles. Naturally when their privileges are threatened, intellectuals fight vigorously to protect them. Yet these common group interests do not bear very directly on public policies.

Consequently it is not the influence of the intellectual stratum in general that concerns me here. It is the influence of a particular subset of intellectuals who are essential to the intelligent functioning of modern political systems (democratic or not)—those who are particularly concerned with public policy and actively engaged in influencing governmental decisions, not only directly but also indirectly through their influence on public and elite opinion. In democratic countries, these public policy intellectuals are to be found in public bureaucracies, executive offices, legislatures, political parties, universities, research institutions, the media, lobbying organizations, advisory groups, business firms, labor unions, law firms, and many other places. Typically the leading specialists in a particular area—arms control, say, or health care, or environmental regulation—know or are known to one another even in a large country like the United States and all the more so in smaller countries. But the boundaries that mark off a group of specialists in a particular policy area tend to be somewhat uncertain. Today the groups often transcend national boundaries.

For lack of standard terms I am going to call these intellectuals public policy specialists (or policy specialists, for short); the aggregate of specialists in a particular area of policy constitutes a public policy elite (a foreign policy elite, for example); the aggregate of different public policy elites might be termed the public policy elites.[7]

Though these are convenient and appropriate terms, it would be a mistake to read too much into them. As with intellectuals generally, I do not mean to suggest that the public policy elites are a "ruling class" with common "class interests," which by persuasion or coercion imposes policies beneficial to its "class interests" on a majority of their countrymen. Like intellectuals generally, policy elites are a diverse lot.[8] The common interests of the members of a policy elite, and even more of the policy elites as an aggregate, are for the most part too weak to enter in any important way into their evaluations of alternative policies. It is a fact of great bearing on democratic prospects that members of a policy elite do tend to advocate different and often conflicting policies.

Their role in public policy decisions would hardly be a matter of profound concern to citizens in an advanced democratic country if it were not for the increasing complexity of public policies. For complexity threatens to cut the policy elites loose from effective control by the demos. The result could be—and to some extent already is—a kind of quasi guardianship of the policy elites. Like Plato's philosophers, this is not a role that members of the policy elites necessarily seek. Yet even if they may be unwilling and unwitting guardians, the complexity of modern policies and policymaking often thrusts that role upon them.

## Complexity and the Democratic Process

To describe the consequences of complexity for the democratic process I am going to employ the excessively simple and yet useful dichotomy of ends and means. Decisions on public policies may be conveniently thought of as consisting of decisions (implicit or explicit) about the ends the policy is intended to serve and the means chosen for attaining those ends. In the simplest version of a democratic system, where the sovereign demos directly makes all important policy decisions, it simultaneously decides on both ends and means. The closest approximations to such a simple democracy have been, of course, the systems of assembly democracy. While we ought not to underestimate the difficulty citizens must sometimes have faced in making these decisions, we also need to keep in mind that decisionmaking in the citizen assemblies was a part-time activity and dealt with a very limited agenda. Naturally the assemblies delegated some administrative tasks, usually to ordinary citizens who served as part-time officials or held office for only a brief period. Thus while the demos implicitly or explictly decided on both the ends and the critical means in its choices of laws and policies, it did delegate to officials some authority to implement the policies; but it kept delegated authority within highly restricted limits. We can reasonably characterize these policymaking systems, then, as both simple and direct.

With the application of the democratic idea to the government of nation-states, the simple and direct policymaking systems of the assembly democracies were replaced by the more differentiated institutions of polyarchy. However, it was still possible to interpret polyarchy as a system in which policy decisions were made by the demos and its elected representatives and where, as before, certain limited administrative tasks were delegated to officials. The policymaking of early polyarchy—let me call it Polyarchy I—could thus be described as simple but indirect.

The development of MDP societies and the expanding internationalization of society, however, brought about the adoption of increasingly complex policies. Not only did policies within a particular issue-area grow more complex, but the increase in the sheer number of policies, as governments expanded the scope of their concerns, was itself a source of complexity. The management of this growing complexity in policies led in turn to greater complexity in the policymaking process. Just as the extension of the democratic idea to the scale of the nation-state required a radical adaptation and innovation in political institutions—the creation of polyarchy—so new institutions were now required in polyarchies to meet the demands of complexity in policy and policymaking. Thus in yet another respect modern democracy created institutions and practices so profoundly different from assembly democracy that one might wonder whether the same term, "democracy," could properly be applied to both. In the United States, for example, Congress early on developed powerful committees whose members not only drafted legislation but often became experts in their policy areas. From World War II onward the staffs of these committees, and the office staffs of senators and representatives as well, added a further layer of policy specialists. Meanwhile in all democratic countries specialists proliferated in the ministries, departments, and other executive and administrative organizations. The mobilization of specialized intelligence in the service of modern democratic government—let me call it Polyarchy II—was a heroic and generally speaking successful attempt to adapt democracy to the daunting complexity of public policies.

Yet it was still possible to interpret Polyarchy II as meeting the ancient goal of rule by the people. Although the democratic process could no longer be carried out in the simple and direct way of assembly democracy, its requirements could be satisfied by *a process of successive approximation*. By means of electoral decisions the demos would simultaneously determine the general ends of policy and set some broad limits on acceptable means. Typically, too, the citizens would narrow these limits further by their activities between elections—lobbying, for example.

Within these limits on ends and means set by the demos, which were sometimes broad and sometimes narrow, elected representatives would adopt laws and policies. Within the limits of these laws and policies, the executive and administrative agencies would still more narrowly define the means. And so the process of successive approximation continued on down to the clerk who finally carried out the activity.

In a confounding of the ancient categories, Polyarchy II could be interpreted as grafting the expertness of guardians to the popular sovereignty of the demos.

## Democracy or Guardianship?

But what if important policies are now so complex that ordinary citizens no longer understand what will best serve their interests? Has the democratic idea become a vision of a political order that is impossible in the complex universe in which we seem destined to live?

If so, then guardianship might replace democracy, not in symbols or even beliefs, perhaps, but in practice. We could no longer properly interpret Polyarchy II as a grafting of the expertness of guardianship to the popular sovereignty of the demos. We might have to interpret it instead as the grafting of the symbols of democracy to the de facto guardianship of the policy elites. Even then, we would be wrong to describe it as a system of minority domination of the kind envisioned by the theorists described in chapter 18. For the "rulers" would be a highly heterogeneous aggregate of relatively autonomous groups whose primary source of influence would be their specialized knowledge. We might want to call them quasi guardians—quasi rather than true guardians, because they would not possess the moral and epistemological justification that Plato and others have claimed for true guardianship. In chapter 5 I argued that this justification is deeply defective. Yet all the defects in the idea of guardianship described in chapter 5 would apply with even greater force to our quasi guardians.

Let me recapitulate that critique as it applies to our potential quasi guardians. Decisions about public matters—whether nuclear weapons, poverty, social security, health, or other issues like those I mentioned earlier—require (implicitly or explicitly) judgments both moral and instrumental. These decisions are not and cannot be strictly about ends, but neither are they nor can they be decisions strictly about means. No intellectually defensible claim can be made that policy elites (actual or putative) possess superior moral knowledge or more specifically superior knowledge of what constitutes the public good. Indeed, we have some reason for thinking that specialization, which is the very ground for the influence of policy elites, may itself impair their capacity for moral judgment. Likewise, precisely because the knowledge of the policy elites is specialized, their expert knowledge ordinarily provides too narrow a base for the instrumental judgments that an intelligent policy would require.

In addition, public policy decisions, particularly about complex matters, are virtually always made behind a thick veil of uncertainty. They invariably require judgments about alternatives the outcomes of which are highly uncertain. The

probabilities of the various outcomes, in a strict sense, are almost always unknown. Informed guesses substitute at best for statistical probabilities. Even when
the probabilities can be more or less estimated, judgments are required about the
acceptability of risks. Policy judgments also invariably require judgments about
trade-offs among values or policy goals. On all these questions, we have scant
reason for trusting ourselves to policy elites.

Finally, we should not overestimate the virtue of policy elites. Throughout the
world policy elites are famous for the ease with which they advance their own
narrow bureaucratic, institutional, organizational, or group interests in the name
of the public good. The freer they are from public scrutiny and public judgment, it
seems, the more likely they are to be corrupted—not necessarily in a venal way—
by the familiar temptations of power.

Although adopting quasi guardianship as a solution might draw the final curtain
on the democratic vision, it would not inaugurate rule by true guardians who
possess the wisdom and virtue necessary to political knowledge.

## Citizenship in Polyarchy III

Could an advanced democratic country prevent the drift toward government
by de facto quasi guardians? To do so it would have to focus attention on the
weakest link in the chain of successive approximations. That link is the demos
itself. If the democratic process is not firmly anchored in the judgments of the
demos, then the system will continue to drift toward quasi guardianship. If the
anchor holds, the drift will stop.

The problem arises because of the gap between the knowledge of the policy
elites and the knowledge of ordinary citizens. To suggest that the gap might be
sufficiently reduced to enable the process of successive approximation to proceed
fruitfully will no doubt strike many people as utopian. But I think important
possibilities are yet to be explored. Just as Polyarchy I resulted from the creation of
new institutions necessary in order to adapt democracy to the nation-state, and
Polyarchy II resulted from the addition of new institutions in order to adapt
democracy to the growing need for the mobilization of specialized knowledge to
the solution of public problems, so Polyarchy III would result from the need to
narrow the growing gap that separates policy elites from the demos.

Let me suggest several elements of a possible solution.

It is now technically possible:

- to ensure that information about the political agenda, appropriate in level and
  form, and accurately reflecting the best knowledge available, is easily and
  universally accessible to all citizens,
- to create easily available and universally accessible opportunities to all citizens,
- to influence the subjects on which the information above is available,
- and to participate in a relevant way in political discussions.

What makes these technically possible is telecommunications. By means of telecommunications virtually every citizen could have information about public issues almost immediately accessible in a form (print, debates, dramatization, animated cartoons, for example) and at a level (from expert to novice, for example) appropriate to the particular citizen. Telecommunications can also provide every citizen with opportunities to place questions on this agenda of public issue information. Interactive systems of telecommunication make it possible for citizens to participate in discussions with experts, policymakers, and fellow citizens.[9]

It is important to keep in mind, however, that the function of these technical innovations is not merely to facilitate participation, as some advocates of participatory democracy have proposed. Citizens cannot overcome the limits in their political understanding simply by engaging in discussions with one another; and while technology would enable them to follow a discussion by voting directly on issues, voting without adequate understanding would not ensure that the policies adopted would protect or advance their interests.

The technical problems can be easily solved. The evolving technology is bound to be used somehow, for good or ill. It can be used to damage democratic values and the democratic process, or it can be used to promote them. Without a conscious and deliberate effort to use the new technology of telecommunications in behalf of democracy, it may well be used in ways harmful to democracy.

Solving the technical problems is only a part of the solution and the easiest part at that. How would an advanced democratic society ensure that the information so readily accessible to citizens was the best available? I have said that the new technology could be used to harm the democratic process. Might not the policy elites exploit the technology of interactive communications to manipulate the public to serve their own goals? Will that new technology not be a standing invitation to the policy elites to consolidate their position into the quasi guardianship it offers hope of preventing?

The prospects for democracy hinge on the diversity of views among policy specialists and the relative weakness of their common interests as a "class." While the most appropriate design of the institutions by which their knowledge can be made readily accessible to citizens will probably vary from one advanced democratic country to another, a solution in the United States might be built out of the pluralism and autonomy of the numerous professional, scientific, and scholarly associations.[10]

The effectiveness of the process of successive approximation does not require that every citizen should be informed and active on every major issue. Such a requirement would be just as impossible to fulfill in Polyarchy III as it is in Polyarchy II. What is required instead is a critical mass of well-informed citizens large enough and active enough to anchor the process, an "attentive public," as Gabriel Almond put it many years ago (1950, 139, 228, 233). No doubt advocates of participatory democracy will fault my solution as inadequate. Yet desirable as I think an informed and broadly participating demos would be, I believe that under the conditions of extreme complexity in public policy which Polyarchy II faces and which Polyarchy III will have to cope with, such a goal exceeds human possibilities. Happily, however, if I am wrong then the attentive public would expand to include the entire demos.

But what is to ensure that an attentive public is also representative of the broader public, the demos? An attentive public smaller than the demos—and ordinarily it would be very much smaller—would not necessarily be representative. If, however, one of the attentive publics was clearly not only highly informed but also representative, its existence and views would demonstrate for all to see the divergences, if any, between its judgment—the informed judgment of the demos itself—and the prevailing judgments not only of the policy elites but also of the other attentive publics.

An attentive public that represents the informed judgment of the demos itself? The idea seems self-contradictory. Yet it need not be. Suppose an advanced democratic country were to create a "minipopulus" consisting of perhaps a thousand citizens randomly selected out of the entire demos. Its task would be to deliberate, for a year perhaps, on an issue and then to announce its choices. The members of a minipopulus could "meet" by telecommunications. One minipopulus could decide on the agenda of issues, while another might concern itself with a major issue. Thus one minipopulus could exist for each major issue on the agenda. A minipopulus could exist at any level of government—national, state, or local. It could be attended—again by telecommunications—by an advisory committee of scholars and specialists and by an administrative staff. It could hold hearings, commission research, and engage in debate and discussion.

I see the institution of the minipopulus in Polyarchy III not as a substitute for legislative bodies but as a complement. It would supplement, not replace, the institutions of Polyarchy I and Polyarchy II. What weight, it might be asked, would the judgments of a minipopulus have?

The judgment of a minipopulus would "represent" the judgment of the demos. Its verdict would be the verdict of the demos itself, if the demos were able to take advantage of the best available knowledge to decide what policies were most likely to achieve the ends it sought. The judgments of the minipopulus would thus derive their authority from the legitimacy of democracy.

In these ways, and citizens in an advanced democratic country would discover others, the democratic process could be adapted once again to a world that little resembles the world in which democratic ideas and practices first came to life.

Whatever form it takes, the democracy of our successors will not and cannot be the democracy of our predecessors. Nor should it be. For the limits and possibilities of democracy in a world we can already dimly foresee are certain to be radically unlike the limits and possibilities of democracy in any previous time or place. We can be confident that in the future as in the past the exacting requirements of the democratic process will not be fully met and many of the theoretical and practical problems in the democratic proces explored here will not be completely solved.

Yet the vision of people governing themselves as political equals, and possessing all the resources and institutions necessary to do so, will I believe remain a compelling if always demanding guide in the search for a society in which people may live together in peace, respect each other's intrinsic equality, and jointly seek the best possible life.

# Notes
✦✦✦✦✦

## INTRODUCTION

1. Earlier, in the seventh and sixth centuries, the demos appears to have had an even more restrictive meaning (Fine 1983, 108; Sealey 1976, 91–92).

## CHAPTER ONE: THE FIRST TRANSFORMATION

1. "It is curious that in the abundant literature produced in the greatest democracy in Greece there survives no statement of democratic political theory. All the Athenian political philosophers and publicists whose works we possess were in various degrees oligarchic in sympathy" (Jones 1969, 41).
2. The assumptions and problems of this alternative, which, following Plato, I call guardianship, are assessed in chapter 2.
3. For this and the next section I have drawn on Agard 1965, Alford 1985, American School of Classical Studies 1960, Aristotle 1952, Connor 1971, Fine 1983, Finley 1973a, Finley 1973b, Finley 1980, Finley 1983, Larsen 1966, Montgomery 1983, Sealey 1976, Ste. Croix 1981, and Thucydides 1951.
4. Although the number is not known with certainty, most historians concur with Fine that "Athens in its prime, before the outbreak of the Peloponnesian War in 431, had some 40,000 to 50,000 adult male citizens. . . . The majority of Greek states, however, contained anywhere from about 2,000 to 10,000 adult male citizens. Greek political theorists considered 5,000 to 10,000 to be the ideal number. In such a state, ideally, every citizen could at least recognize by sight every other citizen" (1983, 51).
5. As on many other questions, hard evidence on the exact nature of the governments of the leagues or confederacies appears to be lacking. An interpretation sympathetic to the hypothesis that incipient forms of federalism did exist in classical Greece is Larsen (1966). However, the earlier systems (the Peloponnesian League, circa 510–365 B.C., the Boetian Confederacy, 447–386 B.C., and the Chalcidic Confederacy, 432–? B.C.) were composed of oligarchies. Moreover, as Larsen observes,

Representative government, after its promising start in early Greece, received a setback in the fourth and third centuries. Instead, direct government with primary assemblies was adopted also in federal states. (66)

Something . . . happened to check the natural development toward representative government. This seems in part to have been the wide adoption of the theory of democratic government with its glorification of primary assemblies and of the collective judgment of the masses. In the second place, it seems to have been discovered by statesmen who wished virtually to subject the rest of the confederacy to the capital [of the confederacy] that a primary assembly meeting in the capital was an excellent instrument for that purpose. The development may also have been influenced by the fact that some of the new organizations were created in opposition to Sparta, the traditional champion of oligarchy, and so naturally adopted a democratic organization, and, by that time, a democratic organization meant a primary assembly. (46)

6. "Virtually every citizen would serve as a magistrate, about half would sit on the council, and of those who sat on the council better than seventy percent (roughly 365 out of 500) would serve as president of Athens for a day (the presidency—before 380 a position of some importance, after that largely ceremonial—rotated daily among council members)" (Alford 1985, 9).

7. "The Greeks and Romans invented politics, and, as everyone knows, they also invented political history, or rather history as the history of war and politics. But what everyone knows is imprecise: historians in antiquity wrote the history of policy, which is not the same thing as politics; they wrote primarily about foreign policy, concerning themselves with the *mechanics* of policy-making (apart from speeches in Senate or Assembly) only in moments of acute conflict turning into civil war" (Finley 1983, 54). See also Finley's comments on the lack of historical evidence concerning politics and constitutional change in cities other than Athens (1983, 103). Even so crucial a question as the population of Athens has long been a subject of dispute, with widely varying estimates. The range of estimates of the slave population is extraordinary (see particularly Gomme 1933).

8. A notable example is the influence of George Grote's twelve-volume *History of Greece* (1846–56) on nineteenth-century liberal thought in Britain and elsewhere (Turner 1981, 213–34).

9. On one interpretation, "Loyalty to the city was, of course expected. But the literature of the age is surprisingly silent about what we would call patriotic obligation, and surprisingly inexplicit about the priority of the city's claims over those of the friend or relative. The contrast between Athenian and modern politics is a sharp one, so much so that one recent student of Greek ethics could describe the commonest Greek attitude toward the problem in these terms: 'The city's claims *may* override others in times of stress; but where the city's interests are not threatened, or seem irrelevant to the case in hand, there is nothing in these standards to prevent the *agathos polites* (good citizen) from attempting to thwart the laws of the city on behalf of his family and friends, with whom he has closer ties'" (Connor 1971, 48).

10. "By 415 the rivalry between Nicias and Alcibiades was the chief personal issue in Athens, and early in the year an ostracism was held to choose between the two men. But a few days before the vote was to be taken Alcibiades approached Nicias and suggested that they should combine their forces against a third man, Hyperbolus. This was done and Hyperbolus was ostracized. The incident reveals much about the political struggles of Athens. Nicias and Alcibiades each commanded a personal following, whose votes

were determined neither by issues nor by political principle but by the wishes of leaders. Such a following need not have been very large, but it was cohesive and impressive enough to sway the outcome in the assembly decisively, even though the procedure for ostracism was secret voting" (Sealey 1976, 353). Ostracism was thereafter abandoned (Fine 1983, 490).

11. This is partly an inference, by no means conclusive, from the fact that a quorum for a vote on ostracism and for certain other matters was 6,000, during a period when the number of Greek citizens was probably somewhere between 35,000 and 50,000. A highly prejudiced source, the oligarchs of 411, also "declared to the democrats of Samos 'that owing to military service and business overseas more than 5,000 Athenians had never yet assembled to debate any question however important'" (Jones 1969, 109). Finley concludes, "The best analysis of the evidence, some of it archeological, suggests that attendance ran to 6,000 in the fifth century, to substantially more in the fourth" (1983, 73). Fine conjectures that "the Athenians may often have had recourse to ostracisms which never were mentioned in the sources, because, the quorum of 6,000 votes not having been obtained, they remained abortive." He concludes that "in the last half of the fifth century, at least, it is probable that several thousand were on hand for most meetings" (1983, 240, 408). As with so many other questions, in the end the evidence on political participation is inconclusive: As Finley puts it, "Our guessing-games are an academic exercise" (1983, 75).

12. Connor conjectures that in the later fifth century a new pattern emerged which "deemphasizes the power of the friendship groups and stresses the mass allegiance which skillful and eloquent leaders can win. It focuses precisely on those segments of the citizenry which had least influence in the first pattern" (Connor 1971, 135).

13. The term *demagogos* by which they were sometimes known was initially descriptive (leader of the people) rather than pejorative. A leader-orator was also known as "protector of the demos" (*prostates tou demou*) (cf. Connor 1971, 108–10). For an assessment of Demosthenes' role and influence, see Montgomery 1983.

14. "Fundamental to the *polis*, Greek or Roman . . . was the deep conviction that membership in the *polis* (which we may call citizenship) was inextricably bound up with the possession of land, the obligation of military service, and religion" (Finley 1980, 89).

15. "In all Greek states, as far as we know, only a decision of the sovereign body could confer citizenship upon a freed slave, as upon anyone else who was not born a citizen; and such decisions were uncommon" (Ste. Croix 1981, 174).

16. In his celebrated essay comparing ancient and modern liberty (1819), Benjamin Constant described "ancient liberty" in these terms and in contrasting it with "modern liberty" emphasized the modern notion of a rightful sphere of personal autonomy and independence from government (cf. Holmes 1984, 31ff.). Here I have given somewhat more emphasis to the contrast between the particularism of claims to membership in ancient Greece and the strong tendency to universalize claims in modern conceptions of equality and freedom.

17. "There were no theoretical limits to the power of the state, no activity, no sphere of human behaviour, in which the state could not legitimately intervene provided the decision was properly taken for any reason that was held to be valid by the Assembly. . . . The Athenian state did from time to time pass laws abridging the freedom of speech. . . . If they did not do so more often, that was because they did not choose to, or did not think to, and not because they acknowledged rights or a private sphere beyond the reach of the state" (Finley 1972, 78).

## CHAPTER 2: TOWARD THE SECOND TRANSFORMATION

1. The origins, development, and diffusion of the republican tradition are set out in Pocock (1975). Radical Whig doctrines of republicanism in eighteenth-century Britain and the United States are described in Wood (1969). For my brief account here I have drawn freely on both.

2. Even if distance had not been a factor, the sheer number of male citizens eligible to attend—some two to four hundred thousand in the third and second centuries B.C. (Cowell 1962, 61)—would have made attendance at an assembly something less than a significant exercise in citizenship. Although discussion and voting in the most important type of assembly, the *comitia tributa*, took place separately among the thirty-five tribes, the average tribe would have had some five to ten thousand members, with enormous variations around the mean.

3. See, for example, his comments in the *Second Treatise*, paras. 140, 151, 157, 192.

4. The only significant medieval exception was the Swiss Confederation, which began with an alliance of three small and isolated communities for defensive purposes in 1291 and was completed as a league of thirteen cantons in 1513. Six of the cantons, including the original three, were direct democracies where sovereignty resided in an annual assembly of all free citizens. In the others, although sovereignty nominally resided with the whole body of free citizens, legislation was in the hands of largely aristocratic or oligarchic legislatures. The Diet of the Confederation consisted of representatives of the thirteen cantons (Codding 1961, 21–26).

5. Nothing reveals this more clearly than the single sentence in John Stuart Mill's *Considerations on Representative Government* with which he dismisses the two-thousand-year-old assumption in his conclusion to a chapter entitled "The Ideally Best Form of Government." Having concluded that "the only government which can fully satisfy all the exigencies of the social state is one *in which the whole people participate*," he adds his final sentence almost as if it were an afterthought: "But since all cannot, in a community exceeding a single small town, participate personally in any but very minor portions of the public business, it follows that *the ideal type of a perfect government must be representative*" (Mill 1958, 55; italics added).

6. I deliberately avoid discussing here a number of tricky empirical questions, e.g., how widely and deeply a belief of this kind must prevail among the members of an association, the relative importance of leaders and ordinary members, and so on. Moreover, a widespread belief in the Strong Principle might not be strictly necessary or even always sufficient; my assumption is, however, that wide belief in the principle greatly increases the probability that an association will be governed democratically. The empirical questions arise because at this point I take the perspective of the members as determinative. If the perspective were shifted, the nature of the argument would change. For example, an outsider might judge the Strong Principle to be valid among the members of an association even if the members did not. The outsider might then assert that the members *should* adhere to the principle and its consequences. At an even more abstract level one might simply show that *if* the principle is assumed to be valid, *then* certain consequences logically follow. Obviously it is this last perspective, which is taken in chapter 5, that implicitly underlies the logic of the others.

7. In *Industrial Democracy* (1920), Sidney and Beatrice Webb described how "in the local trade clubs of the eighteenth century democracy appeared in its simplest form" and how "dimly and almost unconsciously . . . after a whole century of experiment"

the conclusion "forced itself upon the most advanced trades" that none of the contrivances of direct democracy, such as rotation in office, were satisfactory, and that representative government was necessary (3, 36, and chaps. 1, 2).

8. "As in the order of grace all believers are equal, so in the order of nature all men are equal, so the state should be composed of men all equally privileged. The premise was the lesson taught by the sects; the conclusion was the inference drawn in politics by the Levellers and in economics by the Diggers" (Woodhouse 1938, 69.) The Levellers strongly emphasized the need for consent. As John Lilburne put it in 1646, no one was entitled "to rule, govern, or reign over any sort of men in the world without their free consent" (Woodhouse 1938, 317). One sixteenth-century writer in the mainstream of the republican tradition who, in contrast to the Levellers, was familiar with the great political philosophers from the Greeks to Machiavelli was James Harrington. However, Harrington admired Charles I, did not participate actively in political life during the Puritan Revolution, and did not publish his first and most important work, *The Commonwealth of Oceana* until 1656 (cf. Blitzer 1960).

## CHAPTER 3: ANARCHISM

1. For a variety of approaches to and critiques of the political theory of anarchism, see Pennock and Chapman 1978. The volume contains an extensive bibliography (341–65).

2. Anarchists are more likely to speak of "overthrowing the government" than "the state." The "government" of an association might be defined as consisting of the offices, roles, and organizations that make and enforce the rules. The government of a state, then, may enforce the rules by coercion, if need be. Of course the term "state" can be and has been defined in many different ways, and in some of these coercion is played down or eliminated as a defining characteristic, as it tends to be in idealist conceptions. But to eliminate coercion in the definition of the word "state" would do nothing to eliminate it in the real world, where certain associations would continue to exist, as they have through recorded history, that regularly employ coercion to enforce their rules. Whether or not these are called "states" is irrelevant to the anarchist argument: The point is that *these* are the associations the anarchist believes ought to and can be replaced by voluntary associations. Hence to reject the usage of "state" employed here would simply be a trivial and essentially irrelevant response to the anarchist argument.

3. The summary consists almost in its entirety of verbatim extracts from Wolff, though I have generally changed Wolff's consistent use of "man" or "men" to a gender-neutral or inclusive expression.

4. Although the historical relationship between domination and the origins of states are largely unknown, some theorists have conjectured that states often may have originated in domination.

5. In a second edition (1976), Wolff added a reply to a critique by Jeffrey H. Reiman. By then, Wolff had evidently changed his views about anarchism: "My present views are rather different, though I am not now able to articulate them clearly or defend them adequately" (90 *n* 1). However, though our critiques overlap somewhat, in what follows I have not tried to recapitulate Rieman's analysis nor the numerous other critiques to which Wolff's argument has been subject. I should like to say, however, that in my view, by presenting his original argument Wolff performed an important service to political philosophy.

6. Wolff recognizes the objection and attempts to deal with it as follows:

> It might be argued that even this limiting case is not genuine, since each man is obeying himself, and hence is not submitting to a legitimate authority. However, . . . the authority to which each citizen submits is not that of himself simply, but that of the entire community taken collectively. The laws are issued in the name of the sovereign, which is to say the total population of the community. The power which enforces the law *should there be any citizen who, having voted for a law, now resists its application to himself* is the power of all, *gathered together into the police power of the state.* . . . The voice of duty now speaks with the authority of law. Each man, in a manner of speaking, *encounters his better self in the form of the state, for its dictates are simply the laws which he has, after due deliberation, willed to be enacted* (23, italics added).

To speak of the citizen encountering "his better self in the form of the state" looks to be the kind of mystification of the state that Wolff's whole essay is intended to rebut. And if "its dictates are simply the laws which he has, after due deliberation, willed to be enacted," then may not any citizen, after due deliberation, now choose—responsibly and in the full exercise of moral autonomy—to disobey a law to which he or she had earlier consented? But in that case, why is "the police power of the state" entitled to override the moral autonomy of the citizen if it was not entitled to do so in passing the law in the first place?

7. Rather surprisingly, he adds: "Indeed, we may wonder whether, in a complex world of technical expertise, it is ever reasonable *not* to do so!" (15).

8. As is well known, some writers, notably Hobbes, have so feared the conditions of life in a "state of nature" that they regarded *any* state as preferable to no state. But even Hobbes agreed that unless the state provided greater protection than the state of nature, one would have no obligation to obey it. And obviously to justify a state one does not need to adopt Hobbes's assumption as to the extreme consequences of living without a state.

9. Some writers who support both democracy and a moral right to disobey would restrict the right more narrowly than I would. For a fuller discussion than I can provide here of the issues involved in disobeying a law, see Pennock and Chapman 1970.

## CHAPTER 4: GUARDIANSHIP

1. A minority of scholars argue that Plato really intended to show the impossibility of a regime like that described in *The Republic.* It is true that on close textual analysis Plato's argument is more ambiguous and complex than it appears to be on the surface. Here I assume one plausible interpretation and make no claim that it is the only reasonable interpretation.

2. I use the term here to include all forms of rule in which leaders exercise a very high degree of unilateral control over nonleaders: "Two pragmatic but not precise tests can be used to distinguish a hierarchical organization. Non-leaders cannot peacefully displace leaders after explicit or implicit voting; and leaders substantially decide when, in what conditions, and with whom consultation takes place" (Dahl and Lindblom [1953] 1976, 227).

3. On John Stuart Mill, see particularly Thompson 1976.

4. Conceivably, democrats might not entirely agree among themselves on a somewhat different issue: Should persons who may not *now* be qualified nonetheless be admitted to full citizenship if it can be foreseen that participation may be necessary or sufficient

for them to become qualified within some reasonable time? Depending on how democrats answer this question, they might also disagree on another. Suppose that members of some well-defined group are not now qualified, but *no other persons* can be safely counted on to protect their interests. What is the best solution? In his *Considerations on Representative Government* (1861), J. S. Mill implicitly acknowledged this dilemma but never quite confronted it. He chose instead to contend that qualifications must take precedence over the benefits of participation. Many contemporary democrats would find his solution unacceptable.

5. These are essentially J. S. Mill's criteria. See the excellent discussion in Thompson (1976, 54ff.).
6. Lenin appears to have held such a view, as did George Lukács. Many military regimes, particularly in Latin America, have justified their rule as transitional; thus in Chile after 1973, the Pinochet regime claimed that it would serve to create the conditions necessary to a restoration of democratic government.

## CHAPTER 5: A CRITIQUE OF GUARDIANSHIP

1. In his critique of Plato, MacIntyre emphasizes the need to distinguish betweem the two propositions (1966, 49).
2. The relevant passage in *The Republic* follows on Socrates' asking Adeimantus whether among some citizens there was knowledge "about the city as a whole," to which Adeimantus replies:

> It is the knowledge of guardianship, he said, and it resides in those rulers whom just now we named the complete guardians. . . . Do you think, I asked, that the metal-workers or these true guardians are the more numerous in our city? – The metal-workers, he said, by far. Of all those who are called by a certain name because they have some knowledge, the guardians would be the least numerous? – They are by far the fewest. Then a whole city which is established according to nature would be wise because of the smallest group or part of itself, the commanding or ruling group. *This group seems to be the smallest by nature* and to it belongs a share in the knowledge which, alone of them all, must be called wisdom (*Plato's Republic*, Grube trans., 428d, e, p. 94; italics added).

3. Certain aspects of quantum physics have caused some scientists to question the standard assumption that the experimental findings are, or can be, independent of the experimental design in all cases. But unlike moral philosophers, quantum physicists agree, or converge toward agreement, on the laws of physics. Thus even in these extreme cases, and certainly in all others, quantum physics retains its intersubjective validity.
4. Some advocates of guardianship might make a self-validating move at this point by asserting that those who disagree with them thereby prove themselves to be unqualified to judge the validity of their claim to rule. Backed up by the force of the state, this move can effectively put down critics. Backed up only by the force of reason, however, a move of this kind fails to win credibility.
5. Studies have shown that in a great many fields the forecasts of experts are no better, or in some cases only slightly better, than the forecasts of laymen. One scholar, himself an expert on problems of long-range forecasting, concludes from the examination of a large number of systematic studies of the reliability of expert predictions in a great variety of fields: "Overall, the evidence suggests there is little benefit from expertise.

And because improved accuracy shows up only in large samples, claims of accuracy by a single expert would seem to be of no practical value. Surprisingly, I could find *no* studies that showed an important advantage for expertise" (J. Scott Armstrong, 1980), "The Seer-Sucker Theory: The Value of Experts in Forecasting," *Technology Review* (83:21). Unfortunately, the inability of experts to make reliable forecasts does not seem to reduce their confidence, or the willingness of nonexperts to treat their predictions with undeserved respect.

6. John C. Kemeny, himself a mathematician, after chairing a presidential commission on the famous breakdown of the nuclear power station at Three Mile Island, observed:

> In the course of our commission's work, we again and again ran into cases where emotions influenced the judgments of even very distinguished scientists. . . . I kept running into scientists whose beliefs border on the religious and even occasionally on the fanatical. . . . These people distort their own scientific judgments and hurt their reputations by stating things with assurance that they know, deep down, could only be assigned small probabilities. They become advocates instead of unbiased advisors. This is incompatible with the fundamental nature of science, and it creates an atmosphere in which there is a serious mistrust of experts: even when the hard evidence is overwhelming, if the issue is sufficiently emotional you can always get an expert to dispute it and thereby help throw all of science into national disrepute. (Kemeny 1980, "Saving American Democracy: The Lessons of Three Mile Island," *Technology Review* 83:70).

For criticism directly related to nuclear weapons, see Michael Walzer, "Deterrence and Democracy," *New Republic* (July 2, 1984), 16–21.

7. Para. 577d, p. 225. The organic metaphor is explicit in para. 462b,c,d,e, pp. 123–24, and implicit in many passages, including the famous functional definition of justice as "to do one's own job," analogous to each part of an organism performing its own function (para. 433, 434, pp. 97–98).

8. I take this definition from Lukes (1977, 180) who provides a succinct and powerful critique.

9. As James Grier Miller puts it, "A man with a head is something much more than a man's body plus his separate head" (1978, 44).

10. Though some recent writers who employ an organic metaphor would agree, their language leaves me uncertain. Thus Roberto Unger (1975) attributes to liberalism a principle of individualism that involves the twin errors of methodological individualism and neglect of "the group . . . as a source of values in its own right." He contrasts individualism with its polar opposite: "the principle of collectivism, exemplified by organicist conceptions of the group." "These conceptions," he continues, "view the group as an entity with independent existence irreducible to the lives of its members, with group values that stand apart from the individual and subjective ends of its membership, even with its own 'personality'" (1975 [1984], 82). What he means by the last half of this sentence is unclear to me. Later, as his alternative to liberalism Unger offers "The Theory of Organic Groups" (236–95). I find nothing in that theory incompatible with the human-centered ground for collective decisions. While I conclude that he rejects "organicist conceptions of the group," I cannot find any specific statement to that effect.

11. In discussing this problem, writers often speak of "aggregating" individual interests. I prefer the word "composing" at this point in order to avoid any implication that the best solution is simply to add up votes and adopt the choice indicated by the largest number of votes.

12. The example and quotation above are from Kahneman and Tversky (1983a, 39; See also 1983b, 293–315).

13. As G.M.A. Grube notes, in the famous sentence above and elsewhere in *The Republic*, "Plato does not mean that the world should be ruled by pale metaphysicians from the remoteness of their studies; he is maintaining that a stateman needs to be a thinker, a lover of truth, beauty, and the Good, with a highly developed sense of values" (ibid., *n.* 13, 133).

## CHAPTER 6: JUSTIFICATIONS

1. Forty years earlier the Levellers had already insisted that natural equality implied the need for consent. Cf. Richard Overton and John Lilburne in 1646 in Woodhouse 1938, 69, 317.

2. "For really I think that the poorest he that is in England hath a life to live, as the greatest he; and therefore truly, sir, I think it's clear, that every man that is to live under a government ought first by his owen consent to put himself under that government." Major William Rainborough in the Putney Debates, 29 October 1647 (Woodhouse 1938, 53).

3. In Rawls's view, justice is owed to all "moral persons," but not all human beings qualify as moral persons (1971, 505).

4. Richard Flathman finds the doctrine of the "equal intrinsic value of human personality" of Frankena and Vlastos adequate "only if the various manifestations of value are self-regarding in significance or if there is a harmony between them such that all can be served equally well. . . . But moral and political questions arise primarily where other-regarding behavior and conflicts of needs, interests, and demands are present" (Flathman 1967, 58). Though Rawls rejects equal intrinsic worth as a ground for his theory of justice, his solution to the problem of caring for the interests of persons who lack the necessary features of "moral personality"—a badly retarded child, for example—requires paternalistic authorities to act on their behalf. "Paternalistic decisions are to be guided by the individual's own settled preferences and interests insofar as they are not irrational, or failing knowledge of these, by the theory of primary goods" (Rawls 1971, 249). But why should the interests of persons without moral personality be protected? Rawls's answer seems to be that it would be imprudent in practice to withold justice to those who lack the capacity for moral personality, for "the risk to just institutions would be too great" (506). He does not defend these dubious practical judgments, and one cannot but wonder whether he has not smuggled in the idea of equal intrinsic worth through the back door.

5. The exact source from which Mill drew Bentham's remark is not altogether clear. Cf. F. Rosen 1983, 211–20, and 223–28. I am indebted to Jane Mansbridge for calling my attention to this difficulty.

6. The "first principle of the utilitarian scheme, of perfect impartiality between persons . . . may be more correctly described as supposing that equal amounts of happiness are equally desirable, whether felt by the same or by different persons" (Mill [1863] 1962, 319 *n.* 2).

7. In the *Mahabharata*, an epic source for traditional Hinduism, people come into the world inherently unequal because of differences in the relative purity or evil they have picked up through actions in their previous lives. Thus past actions and their consequences explain the origins of the castes (Somjee 1967, 187).

8. For an explicit principle of neutrality, see Ackerman 1980, 11.

9. The relation between the democratic process and political rights is discussed in chapter 12.

10. Thus Patrick Riley (1978) criticizes Robert Paul Wolff (1976) for turning "'autonomy' into a substantive moral duty, into 'the primary obligation of man,'" whereas "autonomy . . . for Kant is a necessary point of view . . . the hypothetical condition of being able to conceive *any* duties" (294–95). A closely related dispute is whether moral autonomy can ever be forfeited or alienated (Kuflik 1984).

11. Although Kant was no doubt the most influential exponent of the idea of moral autonomy "as the supreme principle of morality," one does not need to accept Kant's view that an autonomous will would necessarily adopt the categorical imperative as "the sole principle of ethics" (Kant 1964, 108) in order to respect moral autonomy. Kant himself was greatly influenced by Rousseau's argument in the *Social Contract*, which depends entirely on the assumption that no regime that fails to respect man's moral autonomy can be legitimate. Rousseau's own justification for moral autonomy occurs during his discussion of slavery and is remarkably brief: "To renounce one's freedom is to renounce one's status as a man, the rights of humanity and even its duties. . . . Such a renunciation is incompatible with the nature of man, and taking away all his freedom of will is taking away all morality from his actions" (1978, bk. 1, chap. 4, p. 50).

12. In describing the effects of Dachau on himself and all others associated with it, Primo Levi concludes that guards as well as inmates simply ceased to be human, and it is permissible to interpret him as saying that they ceased to be human because they became incapable of moral autonomy. Yet hardly had the camp personnel left in advance of the arrival of Russian troops than human qualities began to reemerge. (Levi 1976)

13. Mill illustrates the first proposition and fills in the second by implication in contending that the exclusion of "the working classes . . . from all direct participation in the government" left them without adequate means of protecting their interests.

14. It should be noted that Plamenatz (1973) was explicitly directing his argument toward the economic model of democracy developed by Anthony Downs (1957) and the description, explanation, and justification for democracy by Dahl and Lindblom (1953). As will be seen, the thrust of my argument here is in some respects closer to Plamenatz than to the quasi-utilitarian justification in Dahl and Lindblom (1953).

15. Possibly Plamenatz (1973) would have agreed with this statement. In describing what would be required "if democracy is to be genuine," he appears to set out conditions intended to ensure that a majority of citizens can induce the government to do what they most want it to do and to avoid doing what they most want it not to do (cf. 186–92).

## CHAPTER 7: PERSONAL AUTONOMY

1. One might hold the first sentence to be wrong and the second correct. Thus an anarchist might contend that *no one* is qualified to make binding collective decisions. But for reasons set out in chapter 3 we can I believe reject that argument.

2. For a different treatment but one consistent, I believe, with the one here, cf. Barry 1965, 173ff.

3. The question of delegation is considered in more detail in the next chapter.

4. The problem highly complex questions pose for the presumption is considered below in chapter 22.
5. As may be seen, for example, in both Kant and Rawls. Presumably because "ought implies can" and to understand the moral imperative requires the use of reason, for Kant the duty to *obey* the categorical imperative appears to extend to all persons capable of reason, or rational beings. But the persons *toward* whom all rational beings are obligated to apply the categorical imperative appear to include all humanity. That Kant does not always sharply distinguish between the two suggests that "rational beings" would comprise most of (adult) humanity. As we saw in the law chapter, Rawls refers to "moral persons," and almost all adult persons, he implies, are moral persons.

## CHAPTER 8: A THEORY OF THE DEMOCRATIC PROCESS

1. The term *demokratia* came into usage in Athens around the middle of the fifth century B.C. It may have replaced older expressions involving *iso* or "equal," as in *isonomia* or equality before the law. The word *demokratia* may have been coined by critics of the Athenian constitution; if so, it was meant to have an unfavorable connotation. Earlier, in the seventh and sixth centuries, the *demos* may not have included the mass of the people. However, after the mid-fifth century, *demokratia* seems to have been used largely with the meaning attached to it ever since, as "rule by the people" (Sealey 1976, 159, 301; Fine 1983, 108, 208–09).
2. Expressions like "acting" are meant to include not acting in certain ways.
3. As I indicated earlier, "policies" specify a *means* to an intended *end, purpose, good, or interest*. Cf. the discussion above, ch. 7, p. 99.
4. It may need saying that the perspective I use at this point is that of a hypothetical concerned observer trying to reach normative judgments. The hypothetical observer might be a putative member of the association but need not be. Presumably the engaged reader is such a hypothetical observer. Although the normative judgments expressed here carry implications for the empirical conditions that would be required in order for a democratic process to exist, or that would facilitate its existence, at this point I largely ignore these empirical requirements. I discuss these requirements for large systems, such as nation-states, in chapter 17.
5. In this respect the criterion comes closer than might first appear to meeting Rousseau's insistence in the *Social Contract* that sovereignty is inalienable (1978, bk. 2, chap. 1, p. 59). Rousseau would allow a sovereign people to grant executive power to (1) itself or a majority ('democracy'), (2) a minority ('aristocracy'), or (3) a single person ('monarchy'). What the people may not do is alienate its sovereignty, its power to make laws. Although 'democracy' in sense (1) is impractical, in his view all three forms of delegating executive power are equally legitimate because, and as long as, the people does not alienate any of its sovereignty. Cf. particularly bk. 2, chaps. 1, 6, pp. 46–47, and bk. 3, chap. 6, pp. 87–91.

## CHAPTER 9: THE PROBLEM OF INCLUSION

1. The whole discussion occurs in less than three pages.
2. I do not mean to suggest that Locke and Rousseau or later writers presented similar views on democracy. For example, Locke permitted the delegation and even the

indefinite alienation by the demos of the power to make laws (*Second Treatise*, chap. 10, chap. 19, para. 343). Rousseau did not. However, because their differences are not directly relevant to the argument of this section, I ignore them here.

3. The phrases are from Locke's *Second Treatise*, chap. 8, "Of the Beginning of Political Societies," paras. 95–7 and passim.

4. For example: "Since no man has any natural authority over his fellow man, and since force produces no right, there remains only conventions as the basis of all legal authority among men. . . . Even if everyone could alienate himself, he could not alienate his children. They are born men and free" (bk. 1, chap. 4, p. 49). "Each individual, contracting with himself so to speak . . . Indeed, each individual can, as a man, have a private will contrary to or differing from the general will he has as a citizen" (bk. 1, chap. 7, pp. 54, 55).

5. In Venice, the number of noblemen, who alone had rights to participate in the government, were from 1 to 2 percent of the population of the city. If the mainland is included, they were around one-tenth of 1 percent. In 1797 there were 1090 noblemen, 137,000 residents of the city, and 2.2 million people on the mainland. The number of noblemen was never larger than about 2,000 (Davis 1962, table 1, 58).

   In Geneva the percentage, though not as tiny, was small. Of the five orders subject to the laws, only males in the two top orders participated in making laws: "at the top, the 'citizens,' who had the legal right to hold office, and of whom Rousseau was one; next, the 'burghers,' who had the right to vote but not to hold office." Together the citizens and burghers were "some 1500 in number" in a population of 25,000. Moreover, the top offices were monopolized by a few families (Palmer 1959, 36). R. R. Palmer remarks that "Rousseau himself, in all the study he made of Geneva politics at Neuchatel, showed no interest in the Natives. The Natives, however, [were] three-quarters of the population who were not Burghers" (137).

6. For example, *Second Treatise*. chap. 8, para. 93.

7. See his discussion on the status of women in "conjugal society" (chap. 8, paras. 78–84). "It seems highly improbable that Locke was thinking in terms of extending those rights to women" (Kendall 1941, 121).

8. For example, *Considerations on Representative Government* (Mill 1958, 42, 55, 131). A much fuller exposition of Mill's ideas about the conflict between "the principle of participation" and "the principle of competence," which draws on a wide variety of Mill's work, can be found in an excellent study by Dennis F. Thompson (1976).

9. For examples, see Peter Bachrach's comments on "classical democratic theory" and its contrasts with "elitist theory" (1967, 2–9). Carole Pateman presents Rousseau and John Stuart Mill as "two examples of 'classical' democratic theorists, whose theories provide us with the basic postulates of a theory of participatory democracy" (1970, 21).

10. Douglas Rae has commented that children may be thought of as having a lifetime bundle of rights, some of which they become eligible for as they mature. Locke seems to make a similar point in the paragraphs cited above. By contrast, for excluded adults "the bonds of . . . subjection" never "quite drop off, and leave a man at his own free disposal."

11. Suppose I were able to demonstrate that I had carefully studied the issues, parties, candidates, and the like. My exclusion would seem less justified. Still, a French citizen might say, "You will hardly be in France long enough to justify your inclusion. Your coming here is voluntary. By coming you acknowledge your willingness to obey our

laws. You will have left the country before the election will affect any changes in existing laws. Consequently you will not bear any responsibility for your choices. Therefore you are, in that respect, *morally* unqualified to participate in this election." This seems to me a powerful rebuttal to my claim. However, the force of the objection derives mainly from the fact that I may not be subject to the laws my participation might have helped to bring about. To that extent, I am not a member in the sense defined, and consequently I *ought* to be excluded under the assumption that binding decisions should be made only by members.

## CHAPTER 10: MAJORITY RULE AND THE DEMOCRATIC PROCESS

1. Following common usage I use "majority rule" as shorthand for the principle of majority rule.
2. Writers who support "majority rule" do not necessarily mean majority rule in the strong sense above. In the *Social Contract* Rousseau wrote:

   Except for this primitive [i.e. original] contract, the vote of the majority always obligates all the others. . . . But between unanimity and a tie there are several qualified majorities, at any of which the proportion can be established, according to the condition and needs of the body politic.

   Two general maxims can serve to regulate these ratios. One, that the more important and serious the deliberations, the closer the winning opinion should be to unanimity. The other, that the more speed the business at hand requires, the smaller the prescribed difference in the division of opinions should be. In deliberations that must be finished on the spot, a majority of a single vote should suffice. The first of these maxims appears more suited to laws; the second, to business matters. However that may be, it is a combination of the two that establishes the proper ratio of the deciding majority. (bk. 4, chap. 3, p. 111).

3. A rigorous demonstration of the argument is provided by Douglas Rae (1969). Although Rae does not refer to self-determination, his argument begins with the "value assumption" that a citizen ("Ego", in his terminology) "wishes to optimize the correspondence between his schedule of values and the list of policies which are imposed." He also assumes that the association (in his model, a committee) "will deal with a succession of policy proposals, and is free to impose or reject each;" "this list of proposals (agenda) is unknown at the time the decision-rule is chosen;" and consequently "so are the preferences of the members on each proposal." His model shows that "majority rule is as good (i.e., optimal) as any alternative decision-rule." Moreover, he points out, "*majority-rule is the one decision-rule which precludes the possibility that more people will be outvoted by less people*" (41, 44, 52, italics in original).
4. Rae acknowledges that a person might entertain "a *positional* (as opposed to substantive) *preference*, which leads him to think bad actions . . . are worse than bad inactions. . . . This might be so, for example, if he were a 'conservative' in Samuel Huntington's sense of that term." (1969, 52). The reference is to Huntington's description of conservativism as a "positional ideology" involving "articulate, systematic, theoretical resistance to change" (Huntington 1957, 461).
5. Or in Black's description "a mathematician, philosopher, economist, and social scientist" (Black 1963, 159). Black provides a clear and orderly exposition of Condorcet's argument in a modern notation (164–80).
6. These and other probabilities "that the judgement taken by the $h$ members is right" can be readily calculated from the formula provided by Black, $v^{h-k}/v^{h-k} + e^{h-k}$, where

$h+k$ members are reaching a decision, $v$ (for *vérité*) and $e$ (for *erreur*) are each member's probability of being right and wrong respectively, and $v+e=1$ (1963, 164–65).

7. For an example of this argument, see Barry 1979, 176ff.

8. In this section and the next I have closely followed Kramer (1977, 264ff.). Kramer notes that even with two alternatives

> Some minor potential ambiguities should be noted and disposed of. One concerns the possibility of ties: here, we shall suppose (following normal practice) that there is a presiding officer who can vote to break ties, but not to create them, thus making a tied vote impossible. Another concerns the question of how to treat individuals who are indifferent between the two alternatives, and how abstentions are counted. We shall assume . . . that all voters have (strict) preferences for all alternatives (i.e., that there are no ties in any voter's preference ranking), and that they never abstain; hence no such ambiguities can arise. (295, *n* 1)

9. A philosopher, Alfred F. MacKay (1980), has undertaken an extensive and rigorous exploration of the reasonableness of the conditions. Depending on what one counts as a condition, the number is either four or five. In the first edition of *Social Choice and Individual Values* (1951) Arrow laid down five conditions, which in the second edition (1963) he reduced to four. MacKay focuses on four, while other writers often cite five (e.g., Frolick and Oppenheimer 1978, 19–23; Bonner 1986, 59–63).

10. The problem of the unit is taken up in chapter 14.

11. Theories of minority domination are discussed in chapter 19.

12. As will be seen in the next chapter.

## CHAPTER 11: IS THERE A BETTER ALTERNATIVE?

1. For a critique of unanimity requirements, see Rae 1975.

2. Caplin and Nalebuff (1987). Their assumptions are: (1) Individuals vote for the proposal closest (in Euclidean distance) to their most preferred point. When preferences can be arrayed on one dimension, this assumption implies the condition of "single-peakedness" emphasized by Black (1963); but unlike Black their more general assumption does not require preferences to be located along only one dimension. (2) Voters' preferences must be "concave," which presupposes "a degree of social consensus" and excludes polarization.

3. "To the extent that the outcomes of social choice are ambiguous, they render liberal democracy just as incoherent as populist democracy. If it is impossible to interpret the outcomes of elections in a reasoned way, officials removed from office under election system P might not have been removed under process Q and so on. How then can we interpret the removal of officials as an expression of dissatisfaction with their performance? How can we expect officials to take account of such ambiguous signals in deciding how to behave" (Coleman and Ferejohn 1986, 21).

4. Coleman and Ferejohn (1986) describe work showing that the alternatives less vulnerable to voting cycles "may turn out to be quite nicely connected to the distribution of preferences" and conclude: "Though we are concerned by the implications of instability theorems, we think it premature to see these results as establishing the arbitrariness of collective decision making. Rather, these results demonstrate the importance of gaining a fuller understanding of the likely performance of democratic institutions" (23–25).

5. However, they do not seem to yield up faith in judicial review entirely. "While we cannot fully explicate the rationale here, we do point out that judicial review, as developed in the seventeenth and eighteenth centuries, did render property rights more secure" (Coleman and Ferejohn 1986, 26). One cannot help wondering what seventeenth- and eighteenth-century political systems they had in mind and whether, in these systems, property rights were not rendered "more secure" by far more than "judicial review," including, among other things, a suffrage restricted to property owners.

6. For a more extended critique of some of the critics of majority rule discussed here, see Shapiro 1989.

7. The countries are Australia, Austria, Belgium, Canada, Denmark, Finland, France, West Germany, Iceland, Ireland, Israel, Italy, Japan, Luxembourg, the Netherlands, New Zealand, Norway, Sweden, Switzerland, the United Kingdom, and the United States. In some of his tables he counts the French Fourth and Fifth Republics as two systems. Because of voting restrictions two countries were not full polyarchies throughout this period. Switzerland was a male polyarchy until 1971. In the United States, blacks were largely prevented from voting in the southern states until after the passage of the civil rights acts of 1964 and 1965.

8. Though as indicated in footnote 7, because of suffrage restrictions the United States and Switzerland fell short of the requirements of full polyarchy during the first part of this period.

9. Today, however, the Westminster model is most nearly represented by the political institutions of New Zealand (Lijphart 1984, 16ff.).

10. The Westminster model contains nine "majoritarian elements": concentration of executive power: one-party and bare majority cabinets; fusion of power between executive and parliament and cabinet dominance; "asymmetric bicameralism," or near unicameralism; a two-party system; party disagreements mainly along the one dimension of socioeconomic policies; plurality systems of election; unitary and centralized government; an unwritten constitution with parliamentary sovereignty; and exclusively representative rather than direct democracy (e.g., absence of referenda). The consensus model contains "eight majority-restraining elements": executive power sharing; grand coalitions; formal and informal separation of powers; balanced bicameralism and minority representation in the second chamber; a multiparty system; disagreements among the parties along two or more dimensions, such as language and religion; a proportional representation electoral system; territorial and nonterritorial federalism and decentralization; a written constitution and minority veto (Lijphart 1984, 6–36).

11. Only two of the six countries Lijphart classifies as strictly majoritarian (see below, table 11.9) have such electoral systems; the other four have adopted proportional representation.

12. Among other reasons, because a third party may gain enough votes to keep either of the major parties from winning a majority of votes; yet even though it lacks a majority of votes, the largest party may nonetheless gain a majority of seats and thus become the "majority party" in parliament. In Britain, in all nineteen elections from 1922 to 1987 neither of the two major parties *ever* gained a majority of votes. In 1983, for example, Conservatives won 42.4 percent of the vote and gained 61 percent of the seats. (Cf. Heath, Jowel, and Curtice 1985, table 1.1, p. 2, table 1.2, p. 3.) In effect majority rule in the House of Commons rests on a minority of voters.

13. The exceptions are Ireland and Austria.

14. A discussion of consociationalism as a solution for the problem of acute subcultural pluralism in some countries will be found in chapter 18 below.

## CHAPTER 13: PROCESS VERSUS PROCESS

1. If I understand him correctly, this is essentially the position of Botwinick (1984), who in turn draws on Wittgenstein, particularly his *Investigations*.
2. For a similar treatment see Rawls's discussion of "The Definition of Good for Plans of Life" and "Deliberative Rationality" (1971, 407–24). Rawls likens his notion of deliberative rationality to a view of Sidgwick's, who "characterizes a person's future good on the whole as what he would now desire and seek if the consequences of all the various courses of conduct open to him were, at the present point of time, accurately foreseen by him and adequately realized in imagination" (416–17).
3. Connolly's definition of "interest" does lay down this more severe counterfactual requirement: "Policy x is more in A's interest than policy y if A, were he to experience the results of both x and y, would choose x as the result he would rather have for himself" (1974, 272). Though I prefer my somewhat looser formulation, in practice both definitions are intended to require a counterfactual thought experiment that for any given judge would probably lead to about the same conclusion.
4. For an analysis of some implications of political equality for voting schemes, see Still 1981 and Grofman 1981.
5. To account for the near unanimity of belief on this point among American lawyers would require an exercise in the sociology of knowledge. A part of the explanation is the parochialism of the American profession of law, resulting both from law school training and legal practice. In addition, judicial review greatly increases the power of certain lawyers, and indirectly of the legal profession, over the shaping of the American constitutional and political system and its public policies. Thus the power of judicial review nicely serves the corporate interests of the legal profession. In fairness, however, I must add that the extraordinary powers of the American judiciary to decide substantive issues have also been regularly attacked by distinguished legal scholars (see, e.g., Berger 1977; Ely 1980). Finally, it is striking how much attitudes toward the power of the Court during any given period depend on whether the Court's decisions fit the ideological perspective of the observer. When the Supreme Court steadily struck down New Deal legislation from 1933 to 1937, liberals attacked its power, conservatives defended it. Later, the extraordinary policy reach of the Warren Court was greatly praised by a generation of liberals and progressives, some of whom invited it to go even further; conversely, of course, conservatives interpreted its actions as a usurpation of power. As the Reagan Court took shape, another shift began that, like earlier ones, reflected ideological agreement or disagreement more than a neutral view of the Court's proper role.
6. Of the six federal systems among the stable polyarchies, five have constitutional review: Australia, Austria, Canada, Germany, and the United States. As noted, Switzerland allows the federal courts to review only cantonal legislation for constitutionality. Lijphart calls Belgium "semifederal." It does not provide for judicial review, along with Israel, New Zealand, the United Kingdom, Finland, Luxembourg, and the Netherlands. Among unitary systems, some provision for judicial review is made in Denmark, France (Fifth Republic), Iceland, Ireland, Italy, Sweden, Japan, and Norway (Lijphart 1984, table 10.3, 181, table 11.2, p. 193).
7. In *The New American Dilemma* (1984) Jennifer Hochschild contends that popular control and incremental policies have failed and must fail to bring about racial desegregation in the public schools. She also shows, however, that nearly three decades

of judicial intervention following the famous 1954 Supreme Court decision declaring public school segregation unconstitutional (*Brown v. Board of Education of Topeka, Kansas*) failed to bring about racially integrated schools. Indeed, in the Northeast racial segregation actually increased between 1968 and 1980 (30–34). Although her solution to this "New American Dilemma" is scanty in details, she would support greater coercion by elites, presumably by judges as well as elected officials. "If whites cannot bring themselves to give up the advantages that America's racial and class practices give them, they must permit elites to make that choice for them" (203). "Liberal democracy has always relied on elites to save it from itself" (204). But she does not explain how elites who are responsive to popular controls (including judges) would be able to bring about desegregation in the absence of strongly supportive attitudes among a majority of whites. The evidence and argument of her book clearly demonstrate, in fact, that they will not do so. See also Wildavsky (1986).

8. The two major delaying actions by the U.S. Supreme Court are highly instructive. A congressional act requiring employers to compensate longshoremen and harbor workers injured on the job was invalidated by the Supreme Court in 1920, revised and reenacted by Congress in 1922, again struck down by the Court in 1924, passed again in 1927, and finally upheld by the Court in 1932 after an interval of twelve years. The history of child labor legislation is even more egregious. In 1916, Congress passed legislation outlawing child labor, which in 1918 the Court held unconstitutional by a vote of five to four. The Congress immediately passed new legislation based on a different source of its authority (taxation rather than regulation of interstate commerce), which the Court declared unconstitutional in 1922. Two years later Congress voted to amend the Constitution; the proposed amendment, however, failed to gain the support of the necessary three-fourths of the state legislatures, although all the available evidence indicates that the amendment was supported by a large majority of the population. In 1938, new legislation was passed, which the Court finally endorsed as constitutional in 1941—a full quarter-century after the initial legislation. It would be hard to imagine a more palpable abuse of the Court's power to delay.

9. Ely (1980) argues that the U.S. Supreme Court should confine itself to correcting the failures of representation and should avoid deciding substantive issues.

## CHAPTER 14: WHEN IS A PEOPLE ENTITLED TO IT?

1. The problem is therefore sometimes called the boundary problem (cf. Whelan 1983).
2. I do not propose to define the term "state" rigorously. To do so would produce more questions than answers. It is enough, I hope, to say that I mean here, as in chapter 3, to refer to an association that to a high degree effectively and exclusively controls the employment of coercion among a collection of persons. In the standard view, territoriality is essential to a state, and on this view my saying "territorial state" would be redundant. But I see no need to preclude using the term for associations that do not occupy a specific and exclusive territory but possess the other distinguishing characteristics of a state.
3. In the Dutch system as described by Daalder (1966) and Lijphart (1975) control over many important matters was granted to the four main societal groups, which were not distinctly territorial.
4. And what happens to the general will? In *Essay on Political Economy* (1755), Rousseau wrote: "All political societies are composed of other, smaller societies of different

types, each of which has its interests and maxims. . . . The will of these particular societies always has two relations: for the members of the association, it is a general will; for the large society, it is a private will, which is very often found to be upright in the first respect and vicious in the latter." So which ought to be allowed to prevail? Rousseau never developed a satisfactory solution to this problem.

5. The error attributed here to James was originally in my *Federalism* (1983). I am indebted to David Braybooke for his correction (Braybrooke 1983).

6. In "Federalism and the Democratic Process" (1983; for full citation, see appendix to this volume) I concluded, like Jean-Jacques in the dialogues, that beyond employing, as general guides, what I have called here the Principle of Equal Consideration of Interests and the Presumption of Personal Autonomy, little of a general nature could be said. Later reflection and discussion, which led to the conclusion that follows, convinced me that my earlier view was in some respects mistaken.

## CHAPTER 15: THE SECOND DEMOCRATIC TRANSFORMATION

1. "Nation" is intended in its meaning as "a territorial division containing a body of people of one or more nationalities and usually characterized by relatively large size and independent status." Because a standard definition of "nation-state" as "a form of political organization under which a relatively homogeneous people inhabits a sovereign state; *esp*: a state containing one as opposed to several nationalities" is too restrictive for my purposes, I prefer instead the term "national state." Country of course refers to "a political state or nation or its territory." (The definitions are from *Webster's Seventh New Collegiate Dictionary* 1965.) Despite these differences in meaning, the referent is essentially the same entity, and I therefore use the three terms interchangeably.

2. On the authority of James Madison in *Federalist* nos. 10 and 14 and John Adams in *A Defense of the Constitutions of Government of the United States of America* it is sometimes asserted by Americans that the term "democracy" referred historically to "direct" systems in which, as in Athens, the citizen assembly was sovereign, whereas the term "republic" referred to representative systems. But there is little warrant for this belief. For example, the Italian city-states of the Middle Ages and the early Renaissance were often referred to as republics—and like Venice so designated themselves—though they did not possess representative governments in the later sense. Following this tradition both Montesquieu and Rousseau defined republics as states in which the citizen assembly was sovereign; and they distinguished democratic republics from aristocratic republics and monarchies by the relative proportion of rulers to subjects. Thus a democracy was also a particular kind of republic. Cf. Montesquieu [1748] 1961, vol. 1, bk. 2, chaps. 1 and 2, 11–12; and Rousseau [1762] 1978, bk. 3, chaps. 3 and 4, 83–87.) From his examination of newspapers and other sources, Willi Paul Adams shows conclusively that during the American Revolutionary era the terms were used without any clear distinction (1980, 99–117). From his investigation Robert W. Shoemaker agrees that "the terms were used in a variety of ways. Often, for example, they were used synonymously." However, he concludes that "representation was much more often associated with republicanism than with democracy, and thus serves as a legitimate criterion to distinguish the two" (1966), 83, 89). Since he does not convincingly demonstrate relative frequencies, and given the fact that the terms were often used synonymously, his conclusion seems to me unwarranted.

3. Alan Ware has called my attention to the fact that while the goal of the democratic elements in Britain in 1831–32 was to extend the franchise, the actual result was a smaller electorate.
4. Cf. the discussion of the Levellers in ch. 2, supra, p. 29.
5. Together with such terms as modern democracy, modern representative democracy, democratic countries, and so on. The term "polyarchy" is intended to emphasize the distinctiveness of its institutions. The origin of the term is briefly discussed in Dahl (1984, 227–28, 289, *nn* 4–6; for full citation see appendix to this volume.).
6. On the term "pluralism," see Dahl (1984, 231–32, 239–40 *nn* 7–13).

## CHAPTER 17: HOW POLYARCHY DEVELOPED

1. For much of the data in this chapter I have drawn on research by Michael Coppedge and Wolfgang Reinicke (1988).
2. In the United States, though popular votes quickly became decisive in the election of the president, for the first nine elections presidential electors were chosen by the legislature in about half the states, and U.S. senators were not popularly elected until 1913. Although these indirect elections probably satisfied the requirements of polyarchy, beyond some point indirect elections would so attenuate popular control that a system would drop below the threshold of polyarchy.
3. Although cabinet responsibility to parliament was not made a part of the written constitution until 1953, the practice dates to 1901 "when the King accepted he had to take the majority in the Folketing into consideration when appointing the government. Since this so-called 'Change of system' the principle of Government responsibility to the Folketing—the house elected by the broadest suffrage—has been an efficient norm in Danish politics, even if the Kings at first had some difficulties to identify themselves with their new and more restricted role" (Svensson 1987, 22).
4. In the United States, before 1900 four Rocky Mountain states—Wyoming, Idaho, Colorado, and Utah—had extended the suffrage to women in presidential elections by means of state constitutional referenda (cf. McDonagh and Price 1986, 417).
5. The number of relevant studies has become enormous. I mention here a few that greatly broadened the range of systematic comparative studies. A major turning point was the publication in 1965 of *The Civic Culture* by Gabriel A. Almond and Sidney Verba (Boston: Little, Brown), for which the primary data were attitudes and opinions gained from sample surveys of citizens in the United States, Britain, West Germany, Italy, and Mexico. A second comparative work that broke new ground was *The Breakdown of Democratic Regimes*, edited by Juan J. Linz and Alfred Stepan (Baltimore: Johns Hopkins University Press, 1978), which contains essays on eleven European and Latin American countries. In 1986 comparative studies of the next phase—redemocratization—were provided in Guillermo O'Donnell, Philippe C. Schmitter, and Laurence Whitehead, eds., *Transitions from Authoritarian Rule* (Baltimore: Johns Hopkins University Press, 1986). Still forthcoming are the studies inaugurated in 1985 by Larry Diamond, Seymour Martin Lipset, and Juan Linz, who supervised a comparative study of experiences with democracy in twenty-eight developing countries in Asia, Africa, and Latin America. Specialists were invited to write case studies modeled on a common analytic framework. For a description see Diamond, Lipset, and Linz, 1986. Although the project had not been completed at the time of writing this book, the editors kindly made drafts of a number of the studies available to me.

6. In an analogous scheme, Leonardo Morlino (1980, 94) uses eight pairs of transitions between four types of regime—traditional, authoritarian, totalitarian, and democratic—to classify the experiences of eight European countries.

7. It is important to distinguish the stability of a polyarchal system or regime, meaning the uninterrupted persistence of polyarchal institutions, from constitutional stability (e.g., France maintained system stability despite the constitutional shift from the Fourth to the Fifth Republic) and from the instability of cabinets, party coalitions, policies, etc. Because of the dual meaning of "government," the term "unstable government," which usually refers to cabinet turnover, might be misinterpreted as meaning that the polyarchal system is unstable. Presumably for a democrat, the stability of a democratic system is a good thing, but this does not imply that stability in the other senses is necessarily desirable.

## CHAPTER 18: WHY POLYARCHY DEVELOPED

1. In this section I use terms like "democracy" and "popular government" in a loose generic sense to include both modern polyarchies and earlier democracies and republics.

2. Judging from evidence furnished by a vase and certain poems, Fine concludes that by the middle of the sixth century "hoplite tactics had been adopted in many parts of the Greek world. This phenomenon weakened the almost total control over all aspects of the state which the aristocrats had enjoyed, for these new fighting men could not be denied some participation in government. The granting of more privileges, however, affected only a comparatively small part of the population . . . for it is certain that the small peasants, artisans, and laborers could not have afforded to buy the necessary equipment to serve as hoplites" (Fine 1983, 59). Sealey writes that from "recent study of vases . . . the several items of hoplite equpment were adopted piecemeal; none of them is attested before 750, but all of them appeared by 700. However, at first they were used separately . . . the full hoplite panoply is first shown on a vase ca. 675" (1976, 30). For his comments on the social effects of hoplite tactics, see p. 57.

3. Fine speculates that in the seventh and sixth centuries the term *demos* "may have had a much more restricted meaning, including only that new element of the population which was trying to gain political recognition—namely the emerging hoplites" (1983, 108).

4. "It was only in the Roman period . . . that the last remaining vestiges of democracy were gradually stamped out of the Greek cities" (Ste. Croix 1981, 306–07).

5. "However, there were differences. . . . In the first place, the regularity, scale, duration, and geographical spread of Roman campaigning were incomparable with Greek practice, and the differences were steadily magnified. . . . Secondly, the Roman citizen-militia was totally integrated into the hierarchical structure of society, as the Athenian was not" (Finley 1983, 129).

6. "With national armies raised by conscription and supported by the whole people, one could do what was not possible with mercenary forces maintained by the prince for strictly dynastic purposes. They could be more ruthlessly expended in campaigning, because new levies would bring forward ample replacements" (Brodie 1959, 31).

7. The proportions are calculated from Series A 1–3, p. 7, and Series Y 763–75, p. 736 (U.S. Census Bureau 1961).

8. In Britain the police forces were historically under local control. The 1964 Police Act together with other legislation greatly reduced local control and created a more nation-wide, though not highly centralized, structure. No national police force exists in the United States or New Zealand. In Canada the Royal Canadian Mounted Police is a federal system. Australia has a small police force restricted to federal duties, while the various states maintain their own police forces (*Encyclopedia Britannica* 1970, 18:154).

9. "The same men wore both hat and helmet. . . . Military officers and civilian leaders came from aristocratic backgrounds, they were imbued with similar values, and they maintained familial bonds through blood and marriage" (Nordlinger 1977, 11).

10. For a comprehensive theoretical and comparative analysis of military intervention in politics, see S. E. Finer, *The Man on Horseback: The Role of the Military in Politics*, 2d ed. (Boulder: Westview Press).

11. I make no attempt here to distinguish among power, influence, authority, and control. Solely for convenience, through the rest of this discussion I mainly use the term power.

12. Vanhanen (1984) strongly emphasizes the first: "*Democracy will emerge under conditions where power resources have become so widely distributed that no group is any longer able to suppress its competitors or to maintain its hegemony*" (18). However, he assigns no independence to the second factor and appears to believe that it is simply a product of the first.

13. A leading exception illustrates the point. The de facto exclusion of southern blacks from effective citizenship in the United States was greatly facilitated by the relatively distinguishable features of race associated with caste.

14. "Democracies first emerged in countries where land ownership was widely distributed and literacy was nearly universal but where the . . . Urban Population and NAP {non-agricultural population} were still relatively low" (Vanhanen 1984, 126). In his comparative study of the emergence of democracy in 119 states, 1850–1979, Vanhanen finds that the percentage of family farms is a useful explanatory variable. However, as an MDP society develops and the proportion of the population in agriculture declines, family farms can no longer account for the dispersion of power. For the contemporary period, therefore, Vanhanen weights family farms by the percentage of the population in agriculture and the percentage that agriculture contributes to GNP (1985, no page no.). Stephens (1987) shows that among thirteen West European countries (including Finland and Austria-Hungary) in seven where the dominant pattern of landholding as of 1900 was one of small holdings, democratic institutions, which had already been established by 1919, survived the interwar period, while in one (Finland) a "partial eclipse of democracy" took place. Of the five countries in which the pattern was one of large landholdings in 1900, only in Britain did democracy survive while in Austria-Hungary, Spain, Italy, and Germany authoritarian regimes were established. (fig. 1, no page no.)

15. In my discussion of subcultures in *Polyarchy* (see appendix) I excluded party-ideological subcultures. I now think I was mistaken, since democracy has broken down in countries where party-ideological subcultures were important, as in Chile in 1973.

16. Although drawn from the early 1960s, the data in *Polyarchy* (105–14) reveal a strong relation. Cf. table 7.1, 111.

17. These countries are among the lowest in ethnic and linguistic fractionalization. High percentages of the population are nominally of the same general religious group, i.e.,

Protestant, Catholic, or Muslim. These general religious groupings may of course contain internal splits. Cf. Taylor and Hudson 1972, tables 4.15, 4.16, 4.17, 271–81.

18. The term "consociational" was introduced by Arend Lijphart in the late 1960s (Lijphart 1975). Although he did not use it initially in his account of "the politics of accommodation" in the Netherlands, he later employed it in the second edition to characterize democratic systems like that of the Netherlands (1975, 209). He derived the term from Johannes Althusius's concept of *consociatio* in his *Politica Methodice Digesta* (1603) (Lijphart 1977, 1). He points out, however, that "the first modern author to use the term 'consociational'" was David Apter, who applied it to Nigeria (161–62). The reference is to Apter 1961, 24–25. Although "consociational polyarchy" would be more consistent with the usage of terms in this book, consociational democracy has become standard, and I follow that usage here.

19. The detailed patterns of subcultural cleavages in these countries are described in Lijphart 1975, 16–58; Lijphart 1977, 71–74, 92–94; Lorwin 1966, 147–187; Lorwin 1974, 33–69, 179–206; Daalder 1966, 188–236; Daalder 1974, 107–124; Engelmann 1966, 260–83; Nordlinger 1972; Steiner 1974, 120–46, 167–85, 409–26, and passim. Criticisms of Lijphart's analysis of Dutch politics are in Daalder 1987.

20. In Austria,

> The end of the Great Coalition thus did not mean a return to the strained interelite relationships of the First Republic. In fact, the degree of psychological distance between the leaders of the two camps that existed then can hardly be imagined today. The changes in the political culture of the top elite clearly softened the anticipated shock of the return to one-party government.
>
> The group in each lager most resistant to changes in the relations with the opposing lager seems to be located within the echelon of activists and functionaries, linking the top leaders with the mass of followers. (Steiner 1972, 174)

The changes in the Netherlands are described in Daalder 1987.

21. The estimate in Dix (1967, 362) is for the period 1948–64.

22. These cases are briefly described by Lijphart (1977, 134–41, 147–64). However, in his view Nigeria "hardly fits the narrower definition of consociational democracy at all" (162). On Lebanon see also Hudson 1985.

23. The experience of Austria and Colombia suggests some qualifications. In the Austrian Second Republic the third political subculture of the First Republic (the Nationalist lager) has declined. While Steiner describes a continuing Nationalist lager in the Second Republic (1972, 146), it is clearly of much less importance culturally and politically than the other two. The People's party and the Socialists have gained more than 80 percent of the vote, and sometimes more than 90 percent, in all the National Assembly elections (Steiner 1972, table II, 430). Based on the assumption that "coalition in a two-party system imposes severe strains and probably tends to an unstable solution," in 1966 in *Political Oppositions in Western Democracies* I concluded that it was doubtful "whether, given these strains, the arrangement in Colombia will run the full 16 years" (337). As it turned out, however, the arrangements did endure until the end of that period, though the government failed to overcome a small but intractable guerrilla movement.

24. Juan Linz has given particular emphasis to the role of political leaders in breakdowns and successful transitions (cf. Linz and Stepan 1978).

25. In the 1980s the GNP per capita of the Soviet Union and most other Eastern European countries had reached levels well above those of the European democracies in the

1920s and probably higher than that of what was then the wealthiest democratic country, the United States, in 1929. Although the comparisons are tricky, U.S. GNP per capita in 1929 can be estimated at $5795 in 1982 prices (U.S. Bureau of the Census 1986, table 698, "Gross National Product," p. 416; table 2, "Population," p. 8, table 766, "Gross National Product Implicit Price Deflators 1919 to 1985," p. 456). Estimates for 1983 for the Warsaw Pact countries are $6273, for the USSR $6784, and for East Germany $7427 (Sward 1986, table 1, *n* 2).

26. Stephens and Stephens (1987) concur with a comment by Lewis (1968, 107–08) that in responding to "the West Indian movement for self-government and representative institutions . . . Colonial Office policy, in practice, was to grant minuscule reforms at the last moment . . . seeking every way to delay the inevitable; and . . . progress, in any case, was the result of the militant progressive forces in each colony, extracted from London through protest and agitation." They remark further that "progress towards democracy and independence was far from automatic and unilinear. . . . Internal pressures had to be credible enough to elicit concessions, but not threatening enough to provoke defensive reactions and regress" (15–16).

27. For accounts of American intervention and its effects see LaFeber 1984, Trudeau and Schoultz 1986, 25–28, Gilbert 1986, 88–89.

## CHAPTER 19: IS MINORITY DOMINATION INEVITABLE?

1. Mosca regarded this general "law" as one of his major contributions to political science, though he freely acknowledged his predecessors, mainly Machiavelli, Saint-Simon, and Compte (Mosca [1923] 1939, 329ff.). He had first presented it in *Teorica dei Governi e Governo parlamentare* published in 1884, and had repeated it in the first edition of the *Elementi di Scienza Politica* (Turin 1896). The quotation here is from part I of the second edition of *Elementi*, which reproduces the first edition unchanged. Pareto's failure to recognize Mosca's primacy in the theory of a ruling class gave Mosca great umbrage. For details of "his famous running feud with Pareto" see Meisel 1958, 170. Meisel also provides an excellent and extensive account and critique of Mosca's theory, which I have found very useful.

2. For earlier antecedents and contemporary versions see Pennati 1961a, chap. 3; Pennati 1961b, 3ff.; and Bobbio 1961, 54ff.

3. The relevant theories and descriptions asserting minority domination are vast in number and highly varied in content. Arguably the ones I choose to emphasize here are an inadequate selection. Thus though I include Gramsci I do not discuss later neo-Marxist analyses nor post-Michels conservative and rightist advocates of a theory of minority domination (e.g., Burnham, 1943). A recent symposium on Mosca indicates how widely diffused his and related ideas have become (Albertoni 1982). However, I believe that the arguments of other writers on minority domination are adequately dealt with in the discussion that follows.

4. This is my rather free interpretation of his "Class II residues."

5. Pareto further qualified his concept of the governing class by remarking that "the governing class is not a homogeneous class. It too has a government—a smaller, choicer class (or else a leader, or a committee)—that effectively and practically exercises control" (1935, 4:1575).

6. In Italian political science and journalism the terms *classe dirigente, classe politica,*

and *classe governante* have passed into common usage since 1945, somewhat purged of their undemocratic implications. According to Bobbio (1961, 56) the distinctions originated with Guido Dorso, whose posthumously published unfinished essay defines *la classe governante* to include both *la classe dirigente*, composed of political, economic, intellectual and other elites, and *la classe politica*, which actually directs the government and includes not only the leaders in office but also the heads of the opposition. It is my impression, however, that these distinctions are by no means consistently maintained.

7. I have deliberately used the three terms in order to avoid the tangled question of the primacy of the first with respect to the others. For an exhaustive discussion see Elster, 1985, chap. 5, 241ff.

8. This work was published in German in 1911, in Italian in 1912, and in an English translation in 1915. The English translation, republished in 1962, is used here.

9. A vast literature is devoted to clarifying the meaning of concepts related to power, distinguishing among different terms and concepts (such as power, influence, authority, etc.), designing suitable measures and research methods, and investigating and describing power relations in certain settings. But consensus on these matters still remains low among scholars. Some of the diversity and problems can be seen in the collection of essays edited by Barry (1976). Cf. also Oppenheim 1981, chaps. 2–4, 10–81.

10. After thirty-one years of military rule in Guatemala following the overthrow of Jacobo Guzmán Arbenz in 1954, the military allowed elections to be held in 1985. Observers generally described the elections as fair and free, the main institutions of polyarchy were reestablished, and the elected government was widely pronounced "democratic." However, the president avoided direct challenges to the military by, for example, not prosecuting military officers involved in political killings (Kinzer 1986, 32ff.). A similar situation of an elected civilian government conducting itself so as to avoid military takeover also prevailed in Honduras, where the weakness of the government was further compounded by the influence of the U.S. government (cf. Shepherd 1986).

11. One conceptual difficulty has to do with the accuracy of the attributions. Suppose B acts according to what he assumes A's desires to be. But suppose B mistakenly attributes intentions or wishes to A that A does not in fact have, or B expects potential rewards or punishments from A that A in fact will not or cannot supply. Perhaps Henry II did not wish Becket dead after all. In the extreme case, B may be wildly irrational, even deranged. Are we to say that Henry VIII dominates B because B believes he hears voices instructing him, as a loyal subject, to obey the wishes of Henry VIII?

12. Though clearly Gramsci was influenced by Mosca's *Elementi di scienza politica*, he never acknowledged the fact (Pellicani 1976, 12). It would probably have been impolitic to admit an intellectual debt so great to so prominent an enemy of Marxism. His debt to Croce, on the other hand, was equally great or greater but more openly indicated. "As for all Italian intellectuals of that generation, his philosophical teacher *par excellence* was Benedetto Croce. . . . In later years Gramsci became increasingly critical toward Croce, as the latter became more and more anti-Marxist" (Kolakowski 1978, 3:222).

13. In the final chapter I shall return to the importance of intellectuals or more accurately the strata in postmodern societies that specialize in the acquisition and distribution of knowledge and information. The power of intellectuals in postmodern society tends to

be greatly underestimated by intellectuals themselves. As Mosca might say, they create political formulas that serve their purposes by disguising their own influence.

14. A disputed question is whether what I have called the "chain of control" can also be interpreted in every instance as a chain of *causation*. Thus Oppenheim contends that *having* power, as distinguished from *exercizing* power, does not necessarily entail causation (1981, 31ff.).

15. An exception is C. Wright Mills's *The Power Elite* (1956) and other studies of the origins and background of top officials and executives in business, government, and the military. What these studies characteristically fail to do, however, is to provide much evidence on the chain of control from these elites to the outcomes—e.g., beliefs, agendas, or government decisions—over which they presumably dominate. The disproportion between evidence on backgrounds and evidence bearing on the chain of control is striking.

## CHAPTER 20: PLURALISM, POLYARCHY, AND THE COMMON GOOD

1. In discussions about the common good, "good," "interest," "welfare," and other terms, modified by "common," "general," "public," etc., are often used synonymously. Bruce Douglass (1980) has argued, convincingly I think, that because of differences in historical meanings, the usual meaning of the term "the public interest" is not equivalent to "the common good," and he proposes to recast it in order to make it equivalent. Barry has interpreted and distinguished a number of the combinations of the terms above (1965). To reduce confusion I do not use the term "interest" in this chapter. However, I do use "common good" and "public good" interchangeably.

2. For previous discussions in this book, see especially chs. 5, 11, and 12 above.

3. Whether the traditional interpretation is actually a misinterpretation of Aristotle's work is a source of controversy. The traditional view is provided by MacIntyre. "As with Plato, [Aristotle's] belief is one aspect of an hostility to and denial of conflict either within the life of the individual good man or in that of the good city. Both Plato and Aristotle treat conflict as an evil and Aristotle treats it as an eliminable evil. The virtues are all in harmony with each other and the harmony of individual character is reproduced in the harmony of the state" (MacIntyre 1981, 157). Yack contends that "Only an extremely selective reading of the *Politics* could support the claim" by MacIntyre, which however "epitomizes a widespread understanding of Aristotle's concept of political community" (Yack 1985, 92).

4. MacIntyre, whose account of the virtues draws heavily on Aristotle, writes:

> The absence of this view of the centrality of opposition and conflict in human life conceals from Aristotle also one important source of human learning about and one important milieu of human practices of the virtues. The great Australian philosopher John Anderson urged us 'not to ask of a social institution: "What end or purpose does it serve?" but rather, "Of what conflicts is it the scene?"' . . . For it was Anderson's insight- a Sophoclean insight—that it is through conflict and sometimes only through conflict that we learn what our ends and purposes are. (1981, 163–64)

5. Thus Bruce Douglass interprets "the common good in traditional formulations" as consisting of "a number of specific objectives designed to promote general human well-being—such as peace, order, prosperity, justice, and community. . . . The benefits in question were to be common in the sense that they pertained to all members of

society. There was no equivocation or uncertainty about whose good was at issue. The common good meant *everyone*" (1980, 104).

6. At the other end of scale [sic] there was a broad distinction of outlook between the propertied classes and the poor. Aristotle thought that he could discern this distinction throughout political history, and he is not likely to have been entirely wrong. In domestic affairs it is difficult to trace it. . . . The distinction can be most clearly discerned in foreign policy—which of course involved finance. On a number of occasions we are told that the propertied classes favored peace or appeasement, while the poor were more bellicose. . . . But this merely means that people tended to vote according to their economic interests. The rich disliked paying war tax and serving frequently as trierarchs, farmers feared their land would be ravaged and they themselves called up for military service. The poor on the other hand had less to lose, and might hope for land allotments abroad in case of success, besides being more keenly interested in the defense of the democratic regime, which they rightly felt was threatened by the predominance of Sparta and Macedon. (Jones, 1969, 131–132)

Though highly sympathetic with Greek democracy in the fifth and fourth centuries, in his monumental work on *The Class Struggle in the Ancient Greek World* Ste. Croix interprets political life as essentially a muted struggle between a relatively rich propertied class and the majority of citizens, who were small peasants, artisans, shopkeepers, and others without much property of their own (1981, 114ff., 285–93, and passim). See also Finley 1983, 101ff.

7. See, for example, Hale 1977, 43–75; Hyde 1973, 48–64, 104–23, 168–71; Martines 1979, 45–71, 148–61; Pullan 1972, 116–62.

8. In fact, in his *Political Economy* Rousseau clearly identified the problem; but his solution is murky and he did not return to it in the *Social Contract*. In a passage just before the one quoted above, p. 289, he reminds us that the "general will, which always tends toward the preservation and welfare of the whole and of each part, and which is the source of the laws, is—for all the members of the State in relation to themselves and to it—the rule of what is just and unjust." But he quickly goes on to say:

It is important to note that this rule of justice, infallible in relation to all citizens, can be defective with foreigners. And the reason for this is evident. Then the will of the State, although general in relation to its members, is so no longer in relation to other States and their members, but becomes for them a private and individual will that has its rule of justice in the law of nature, which fits in equally well with the principles established. For then the large town of the world becomes the body politic, of which the law of nature is always the general will and the various States and peoples are merely individual members" (1978, 212).

9. Cf. bk. 2, chap. 4, of the *Social Contract* where he writes: "The engagements that bind us to the social body are obligatory only because they are mutual, and their nature is that in fulfilling them one cannot work for someone else without also working for oneself. Why is the general will always right and why do all constantly want the happiness of each, if not because there is no one who does not apply this word *each* to himself, and does not think of himself as he votes for all?" (1978, 62). This passage is taken over without change from the *Geneva Manuscript* (1978, 62).

Cf. also *Social Contract*, bk. 1, chap. 7, where he writes: "As soon as this multitude is thus united in a body, one cannot harm one of the members without attacking the body, and it is even less possible to harm the body without the members feeling the effects. Thus duty and interest equally obligate the two contracting parties to mutual assistance, and the same men should seek to combine in this double relationship all of the advantages that are dependent on it." (55)

10. Mill 1958, 44. It would be consistent with Mill's political views to amend his phrasing to make it apply explicitly to women as well as men.

## CHAPTER 21: COMMON GOOD AS PROCESS AND SUBSTANCE

1. In writing this section I have benefited from an unpublished paper by Ian Shapiro, "Notes on the republican ideal in American politics, history and political theory" (1987).

2. For the Aristotelian tradition of virtue, see especially MacIntyre 1984; however, it is important to keep in mind that in MacIntyre's account, in Homeric society, Athens, and Aristotle, the good life and the good citizen are distinguished not by *virtue* in the singular but by *virtues* in the plural: honor, justice, courage, restraint, among others. (On the virtues at Athens, for example, see 135ff.) On the republican tradition, cf. the discussion in ch. 2, supra, and citations there to the work of Wood and Pocock.

3. Wood directly continues the passage I have just quoted on p. 300 by describing the republican ideology as

   a vision so divorced from the realities of American society, so contrary to the previous century of American experience, that it alone was enough to make the Revolution one of the great Utopian movements of American history. By 1776 the Revolution came to represent a final attempt, perhaps—given the nature of American society—even a desperate attempt by many Americans to realize the traditional Commonwealth ideal of a corporate society, in which the common good would be the only objective of government. (*Loc. cit.*).

   MacIntyre rejects the supposition that agreement among the Athenians on their ideal of the good man and good citizen led to agreement on the common good, "for moral disagreement in the fifth and fourth centuries does not only arise because one set of virtues is counterposed to another. It is also and perhaps more importantly because rival conceptions of one and the same virtue coexist that conflict is engendered. The nature of . . . justice . . . is the subject of just such disagreement" (1984, 133–34).

   Neither in *The Machiavellian Moment* nor elsewhere, so far as I am aware, does Pocock claim that political life in Florence, England, or America ever actually lived up to the ideal of the *vivere civile*.

4. In fairness, it should be said that, as he comments in a generous postscript to the second edition, *After Virtue* "ought to be read as a work still in progress" (MacIntyre 1984, 278). And possibly MacIntyre believes it is not the philosopher's task to provide a feasible program for achieving the good society.

5. I have offered elsewhere the estimate of 50,000–200,000 as about the size of a political community small enough in the United States to make effective citizenship possible and large enough to retain authority over a fairly broad agenda of important questions: education, housing, traffic, health, planning, development, and the like (Dahl 1967). Although that figure is somewhat arbitrary, the smaller a community, the more that decisions on these and other matters will be controlled by the decisions of larger and more inclusive units.

6. However, Walzer appears to have reservations about actual practice, particularly with respect to the untouchables (1983, 151*n*). Perhaps the understandings are not really shared, and lower caste members are angry and indignant. "If that were so, then it would be important to seek out the principles that shaped their indignation. These principles, too, must have their part in village justice" (314).

7. The domain and scope of the unit can be clearly identified; the people in the domain of the unit strongly desire political autonomy with respect to matters within its scope; they strongly desire to govern themselves by the democratic process; the scope is within justifiable limits; the interests of persons in the unit are strongly affected by decisions within that scope; consensus among persons whose interests are significantly affected is higher than it would be with any other feasible boundaries; measured by relevant criteria, the gains must outweigh the costs.

## CHAPTER 22: DEMOCRACY IN TOMORROW'S WORLD

1. Cf. particularly 2:378–81, in Tocqueville [1840] 1961. For a fuller exposition see Dahl 1984, chap. 1, 7–51. The following paragraphs are adapted from 36ff. For a full citation see appendix.
2. The only case known to me is Uruguay, and it is worth noting that democracy was restored in Uruguay more rapidly than in its neighbors, Argentina, Brazil, and Chile.

## CHAPTER 23: SKETCHES FOR AN ADVANCED DEMOCRATIC COUNTRY

1. It would also be possible to transfer ownership of an enterprise to a cooperative that owns the enterprise collectively and in which each worker is entitled to one vote but not to a marketable share. This is the solution that was adopted in the highly successful worker-owned and -controlled enterprises of Mondragon, Spain (cf. Thomas and Logan 1982). Elsewhere I have offered reasons why this form of ownership seems to me preferable both to individually owned shares and various forms of collective ownership (Dahl 1984).
2. For other difficulties and non sequiturs, see Dahl 1984, chap. 2.
3. For some particulars of a solution that seems to me appropriate for many firms in the United States, see Dahl, 1984, chaps. 3, 4.
4. An important part of the explanation for the success of the Mondragon cooperatives is the existence of effective support systems of precisely these kinds. For descriptions see Thomas and Logan 1982, chaps. 3, 4; Ellerman 1982.
5. The editors of the Oxford English Dictionary evidently found only one use in English before the nineteenth century in a meaning close to the modern concept. Cf. the definition of "intellectual," no. 4.
6. As Shils remarks, a "more general feeling of distance from authority has been engendered and has become one of the strongest of the secondary traditions of the intellectuals. It happened first in the West and then, in the present century, in Africa and Asia among intellectuals who have come under the influence of Western traditions" (1968, 407).
7. The internal diversity of this category was indicated by Almond in a classic work on foreign policy and public opinion, where he distinguished various types of policy elites in the United States:

1. The *political elites* which include the publicly elected, high appointive, as well as the party leaders. The official political elite, of course, is subdivided according to its position in the policy-making process (i.e., legislative, executive, judicial) and according to the policy matter with which it is charged (e.g., in the foreign policy field, the Department of State and the foreign affairs committees of the House and Senate). 2. The *administrative* or *bureaucratic elites* . . . 3.

The *interest elites* which include the representatives of the vast number of private, policy-oriented associations. . . . Here too . . . we may distinguish between the *elected* or *political interest elites* and the *bureaucratic staffs*. . . . 4. Finally, there are the *communications elites*, the most obvious representatives of which are the owners, controllers, and active participants of the mass media. . . . Perhaps the most effective opinion leaders are the vast number of vocational, community, and institutional 'notables', known as trusted men and women . . . with personal followings. (1950, 139–41)

8. Almond remarks of one subset of the public policy elites, the communications elites, "Any simple description of the structure of communications necessarily does violence to its variety and complexity" (1950, 139–41).
9. For some descriptions and analysis of experiences with telecommunications in a number of American states and communities, cf. Arterton et al. 1984. Although these attempts were all at a simple level of technology, they reveal the enormous possibilities of existing and more advanced levels. See also Abramson, Arterton, and Orren 1988.
10. A brief sketch of a solution along these lines will be found in Dahl 1984, 82–85.

# APPENDIX
◆◆◆◆◆◆◆◆

Previously published works of my own that I have freely drawn on for parts of chapters in this book are:

Chapter 18: *Polyarchy: Participation and Opposition*. New Haven: Yale University Press, 1971.

Chapters 7, 8, 9: "Procedural Democracy," in *Philosophy, Politics and Society*, ed. Peter Laslett and James Fishkin. New Haven: Yale University Press, 1979.

Chapters 12 and 13: "The Moscow Discourse: Fundamental Rights in a Democratic Order," *Government and Opposition* 15 (Winter 1980): 3–30.

Chapters 20 and 21: *Dilemma of Pluralist Democracy: Autonomy versus Control*. New Haven: Yale University Press, 1982.

Chapter 14: "Federalism and the Democratic Process," *Nomos* 25, *Liberal Democracy* (1983).

Chapter 15: "Polyarchy, Pluralism, and Scale," *Scandinavian Political Studies* 7, no. 4 (1984): 225–40 (Rokkan Memorial Lecture, Bergen, May 16, 1984).

Chapters 12, 22, and 23: *A Preface to Economic Democracy*. Berkeley: University of California Press, 1985.

Chapters 4, 5, and 23: *Controlling Nuclear Weapons: Democracy versus Guardianship*. Syracuse: Syracuse University Press, 1985.

Chapter 23: Introduction to *Democracy, Liberty, and Equality*. Oslo: Norwegian Universities Press, 1986.

Chapter 20: "Dilemmas of Pluralist Democracy: The Public Good of Which Public?" in *Individual Liberty and Democratic Decision-Making*, ed. Peter Koslowski. Tübingen: J. C. B. Mohr, 1987.

# BIBLIOGRAPHY
◆◆◆◆◆◆◆◆◆◆◆◆◆

Abramson, Jeffrey B.; Arterton, F. Christopher; and Orren, Gary R. 1988. *The Electronic Commonwealth: The Impact of New Media Technologies on Democratic Politics*. New York: Basic Books.

Ackerman, Bruce A. 1980. *Social Justice and the Liberal State*. New Haven: Yale University Press.

Adams, John. 1850–56. *Defence of the Constitutions of Government of the United States of America*. In Charles F. Adams, ed., *The Works of John Adams*. Boston: Little, Brown.

Adams, Willi Paul. 1980. *The First American Constitutions: Republican Ideology and the Making of the State Constitutions in the Revolutionary Era*. Trans. Rita Kimber and Robert Kimber. Chapel Hill: University of North Carolina Press.

Agard, Walter R. 1965. *What Democracy Meant to the Greeks*. Madison: University of Wisconsin Press.

Albertoni, Ettore A., ed. 1982. *Studies in the Political Thought of Gaetano Mosca: The Theory of the Ruling Class and Its Development Abroad*. Milan: Giuffrè editore.

Alford, C. Fred. 1985. "The 'Iron Law of Oligarchy' in the Athenian Polis." *Canadian Journal of Political Science* 18 (2): 295–312.

Almond, Gabriel A. 1950. *The American People and Foreign Policy*. New York: Harcourt Brace.

Almond, Gabriel A., and Verba, Sidney. 1965. *The Civic Culture*. Boston: Little, Brown.

American School of Classical Studies at Athens. 1960. *The Athenian Citizen*. Princeton: The American School of Classical Studies at Athens.

Andreski, Stanislav. 1968. *Military Organization and Society*. Berkeley: University of California Press.

Apter, David. 1961. *The Political Kingdom of Uganda*. Princeton: Princeton University Press.

Aristotle. 1952. *The Politics of Aristotle*. Trans. Ernest Barker. Oxford: Clarendon Press.

Arrow, Kenneth. 1968. *Social Choice and Individual Values*. 2d ed. New Haven: Yale University Press.

Arterton, F. Christopher; Lazarus, Edward H.; Griffen, John; and Andres, Monica C. 1984. *Telecommunication Technologies and Political Participation*. Washington: Roosevelt Center for American Policy Studies.

Bachrach, Peter. 1967. *The Theory of Democratic Elitism*. Boston: Little, Brown.

Barber, Benjamin. 1984. *Strong Democracy*. Berkeley: University of California Press.

Barry, Brian. 1965. *Political Argument*. London: Routledge and Kegan Paul.

————, ed. 1976. *Power and Political Theory: Some European Perspectives*. New York: John Wiley and Sons.

————. 1979. "Is Democracy Special?" In Peter Laslett and James W. Fishkin, eds., *Philosophy, Politics, and Society*, Fifth Series, 155–96. New Haven: Yale University Press.

Bautista Urbaneja, Diego. 1986. "El Sistema Político, o Cómo Funciona la Máquina de Procesar Decisiones." In Moises Nam and Ramón Piñango, eds. *El Caso de Venezuela: Una ilusión de armonaia*. Caracas: Ediciones IESA.

Benn, Stanley I. 1967. "Egalitarianism and the Equal Consideration of Interests." In J. R. Pennock and J. W. Chapman, eds. *Equality (Nomos IX)*, 61–78. New York: Atherton Press.

Berger, Raoul. 1977. *Government by Judiciary*. Cambridge: Harvard University Press.

Blachman, Morris J.; LeoGrande, William M.; and Sharpe, Kenneth, eds. *Confronting Revolution: Security Through Diplomacy in Central America*. New York: Pantheon.

Blachman, Morris, and Hellman, Ronald G. "Costa Rica," In Morris J. Blachman, William M. LeoGrande, and Kenneth Sharpe, eds. *Confronting Revolution: Security Through Diplomacy in Central America*, 156–82. New York: Pantheon.

Black, Duncan. 1963. *The Theory of Committees and Elections*. Cambridge: Cambridge University Press.

Blitzer, Charles. 1960. *An Immortal Commonwealth: The Political Thought of James Harrington*. New Haven: Yale University Press.

Bobbio, Norberto. 1961. "La teoria della classe politica negli scrittori democratici in Italia." In R. Treves, ed., *Le élites politiche*. Bari: Editori Laterza.

Bonner, John. 1986. *Introduction to the Theory of Social Choice*. Baltimore: Johns Hopkins University Press.

Botwinick, Aryeh. 1984. "Wittgenstein and the Possibility of an Objective Defense of Democratic Participation." Paper presented at meeting of Northeastern Political Science Association, Boston, November 15–17.

Bracken, Paul. 1983. *The Command and Control of Nuclear Forces*. New Haven: Yale University Press.

Braybrooke, David. 1983. "Can Democracy Be Combined with Federalism or with Liberalism?" In J. Roland Pennock and John W. Chapman, eds., *Liberal Democracy (Nomos XXV)*, 109–18. New York: New York University Press.

Brodie, Bernard. 1959. *Strategy in the Missile Age*. Princeton: Princeton University Press.

Burnham, James. 1943. *The Machiavellians*. New York: John Day.

Buzzi, A. R. 1967. *La Théorie Politique d'Antonio Gramsci*. Paris: Béatrice-Nauwelaerts.

Cameron, David. 1978. "The Expansion of the Public Economy: A Comparative Analysis." *American Political Science Review* 72 (4): 1243–61.

Caplin, Andrew, and Nalebuff, Barry. 1987. "On 64% Majority Rule." Mimeo.

Carter, April. 1978. "Anarchism and Violence." In J. Roland Pennock and John W. Chapman, eds., *Anarchism (Nomos XIX)*, 320–40. New York: New York University Press.

Codding, George Arthur, Jr. 1961. *The Federal Government of Switzerland*. Boston: Houghton Mifflin.

Coleman, Jules, and Ferejohn, John. 1986. "Democracy and Social Choice." *Ethics* 97 (1): 11–22.

Congressional Quarterly. 1979. *Presidential Elections Since 1789.* 2d ed. Washington: Congressional Quarterly.

Connolly, William. 1974. "On 'Interests' in Politics." In Ira Katznelson, Gordon Adams, Philip Brenner, and Alan Wolfe, eds., *The Politics and Society Reader.* New York: David McKay.

Connor, W. Robert. 1971. *The New Politicians of Fifth-Century Athens.* Princeton: Princeton University Press.

Coppedge, Michael, and Reinicke, Wolfgang. 1988a. "A Scale of Polyarchy." In Raymond D. Gastil, ed., *Freedom in the World: Political Rights and Civil Liberties, 1987–1988,* 101–25. Lanham, Md.: University Press of America.

———. 1988b. "A Measure of Polyarchy." Paper prepared for the Conference on Measuring Democracy, Hoover Institution, Stanford University, May 27–28.

Cowell, F. R. 1962. *Cicero and the Roman Republic.* Baltimore: Penguin Books.

Daalder, Hans. 1966. "The Netherlands: Opposition in a Segmented Society." In R. A. Dahl, ed., *Political Oppositions in Western Europe,* 188–326. New Haven: Yale University Press.

———. 1974. "The Consociational Democracy Theme." *World Politics* 26 (4): 604–21.

———. 1987. "The Dutch Party System: From Segmentation to Polarization—And Then?" In Hans Daalder, ed., *Party Systems in Denmark, Austria, Switzerland, The Netherlands, and Belgium.* London: Frances Pinter.

Dahl, Robert A., and Lindblom, Charles E. [1953] 1976. *Politics, Economics, and Welfare.* 2d ed. Chicago: University of Chicago Press.

———, ed. 1966. *Political Oppositions in Western Democracies.* New Haven: Yale University Press.

———. 1967. "The City in the Future of Democracy." *American Political Science Review* 61 (4): 953–70.

Davis, James C. 1962. *The Decline of the Venetian Nobility as a Ruling Class.* Baltimore: Johns Hopkins University Press.

Diamond, Larry; Lipset, Seymour Martin; and Linz, Juan. 1986. "Developing and Sustaining Democratic Government in the Third World." Paper prepared for delivery at the annual meeting of the American Political Science Association, Washington, D.C.

Dix, Robert. 1967. *Colombia: The Political Dimensions of Change.* New Haven: Yale University Press.

Douglass, Bruce. 1980. "The Common Good and the Public Interest." *Political Theory* 8 (1): 103–17.

Downs, Anthony. 1957. *An Economic Theory of Democracy.* New York: Harper and Brothers.

Dworkin, Ronald. 1978. *Taking Rights Seriously.* Cambridge: Harvard University Press.

Ellerman, David P. 1982. "The Socialization of Entrepreneurialism: The Empresarial Division of the Caja Jaboral Popular." Somerville, Mass.: Industrial Cooperative Association.

Elster, Jon. 1985. *Making Sense of Marx.* Cambridge: Cambridge University Press.

Ely, John Hart. 1980. *Democracy and Distrust.* Cambridge: Harvard University Press.

Encyclopaedia Britannica. 1970, s.v. "Military Service." Vol. 15, pp. 451b–454. Chicago: Encyclopaedia Britannica, Inc.

Engelmann, Frederick. 1966. "Austria: The Pooling of Oppositions." In R. A. Dahl, ed., *Political Oppositions in Western Europe*, 260–83. New Haven: Yale University Press.

Fine, John V. A. 1983. *The Ancient Greeks, A Critical History*. Cambridge: Harvard University Press.

Finer, S. E. 1988. *The Man On Horseback: The Role of the Military in Politics*. 2d ed. Boulder: Westview Press.

Finley, M. I. 1973a. *Democracy, Ancient and Modern*. New Brunswick: Rutgers University Press.

———. 1973b. *The Ancient Economy*. Berkeley: University of California Press.

———. 1980. *Ancient Slavery and Modern Ideology*. New York: Viking Press.

———. 1983. *Politics in the Ancient World*. Cambridge: Cambridge University Press.

Fishkin, James S. 1983. *Justice, Equal Opportunity, and the Family*. New Haven: Yale University Press.

———. 1984. *Beyond Subjective Morality*. New Haven: Yale University Press.

———. 1987. "Ideals Without an Ideal: Justice, Democracy and Liberty in Liberal Theory. In Peter Koslowski, ed., *Individual Liberty and Democratic Decision-making*, 7–30. Tübingen: J. C. B. Mohr.

———. 1988. "The Complexity of Simple Justice". *Ethics* 98 (3): 464–71.

Flathman, Richard E. 1967. "Equality and Generalization: A Formal Analysis." In J. R. Pennock and J. W. Chapman, eds., *Equality (Nomos IX)*, 38–60. New York: Atherton Press.

Fralin, Richard. 1978. *Rousseau and Representation*. New York: Columbia University Press.

Friedrich, Carl J. 1937. *Constitutional Government and Politics*. Boston: Ginn.

Frolick, N. J., and Oppenheimer, Ernest J. 1978. *Modern Political Economy*. Englewood Cliffs: Prentice-Hall.

Gilbert, Dennis. 1986. "Nicaragua." In Morris J. Blachman, William LeoGrande, and Kenneth Sharpe. *Confronting Revolution: Security Through Diplomacy in Central America*, 88–124. New York: Pantheon.

Glassman, Ronald M. 1986. *Democracy and Despotism in Primitive Societies*. Port Washington, N.Y.: Association Faculties Press.

Gomme, A. W. 1933. *The Population of Athens in the Fifth and Fourth Centuries* B.C. Oxford: Oxford University Press.

Grofman, Bernard. 1981. "Fair and Equal Representation." *Ethics* 91 (3): 477–85.

Habermas, Jurgen. 1973. *Theory and Practise*. Trans. John Viertel. Boston: Beacon Press.

———. 1979. *Communication and the Evolution of Society*. Trans. Thomas McCarthy. Boston: Beacon Press.

Hale, J. R. 1977. *Florence and the Medici*. New York: Thames and Hudson.

Hamilton, Alexander; Jay, John; and Madison, James. n.d. *The Federalist*. New York: Modern Library.

Heath, Anthony; Jowel, Roger; and Curtice, John. 1985. *How Britain Votes*. Oxford: Pergamon Press.

Hochschild, Jennifer. 1984. *The New American Dilemma: Liberal Democracy and School Desegregation*. New Haven: Yale University Press.

Holmes, Stephen. 1984. *Benjamin Constant and the Making of Modern Liberalism*. New Haven: Yale University Press.

Huntington, Samuel. 1957a. "Conservatism as an Ideology," *American Political Science Review* 51 (2): 454–73.

————. 1957b. *The Soldier and the State: The Theory and Politics of Civil–Military Relations*. Cambridge: Harvard University Press.

————. 1968. *Political Order in Changing Societies*. New Haven: Yale University Press.

————. 1984. "Will More Countries Become Democratic?" *Political Science Quarterly* 99 (2): 193–218.

Hyde, J. K. 1973. *Society and Politics in Medieval Italy: The Evolution of the Civil Life, 1000–1350*. New York: St. Martin's Press.

Iyengar, Shanto, and Kinder, Donald R. 1987. *News That Matters*. Chicago: University of Chicago Press.

Janowitz, Morris. 1978. *The Last Half-Century*. Chicago: University of Chicago Press.

Jenkyns, Richard. 1980. *The Victorians and Ancient Greece*. Cambridge: Harvard University Press.

Jones, A. H. M. 1969. *Athenian Democracy*. Oxford: Basil Blackwell.

Kant, Immanuel. 1964. *Groundwork of the Metaphysic of Morals*. Trans. H. J. Paton. New York: Harper and Row.

Karl, Terry Lynn. 1986. "Petroleum and Political Pacts: The Transition to Democracy in Latin America." In Guillermo O'Donnell, Philippe C. Schmitter, and Laurence Whitehead, eds., *Transitions from Authoritarian Rule*, 196–219. Baltimore: Johns Hopkins University Press.

Katznelson, Ira; Adams, Gordon; Brenner, Philip; and Wolfe, Alan, eds. 1974. *The Politics and Society Reader*. New York: David McKay.

Kendall, Wilmoore. 1941. *John Locke and the Doctrine of Majority Rule*. Urbana: University of Illinois Press.

Kinzer, Stephen. 1986. "Walking the Tightrope in Guatemala." *The New York Times Magazine* (November 9), 32ff.

Kolakowski, Leszek. 1978. *Main Currents of Marxism*. 3 vols. Trans. P. S. Falla. Oxford: Clarendon Press.

Kramer, Gerald. 1977. "Some Procedural Aspects of Majority Rule." In J. Roland Pennock and John W. Chapman, eds., *Due Process (Nomos XVIII)*, 264–95. New York: New York University Press.

Kuflik, Arthur. 1984. "The Inalienability of Autonomy." *Philosophy and Public Affairs* 13 (4): 271–98.

LaFeber, Walter. 1984. "The Burdens of the Past." In Robert S. Leiken, ed., *Central America: Anatomy of Conflict*, 49–68. New York: Pergamon Press.

Larsen, J. A. O. 1966. *Representative Government in Greek and Roman History*. Berkeley: University of California Press.

Laski, Harold. 1939. "The Obsolescence of Federalism." *New Republic* 98: 367–69.

Levi, Primo. 1976. *Se questo è un uomo*. Turin: Giulio Einaudi.

Levine, Daniel. 1973. *Conflict and Political Change in Venezuela*. Princeton: Princeton University Press.

Lewis, Gordon. 1968. *The Growth of the Modern West Indies*. New York: Modern Reader.

Lijphart, Arend. 1975. *The Politics of Accommodation*. 2d ed., rev. Berkeley: University of California Press.

————. 1977. *Democracy in Plural Societies*. New Haven: Yale University Press.

————. 1979. "Religious vs. Linguistic vs. Class Voting: The Crucial Experiment of Comparing Belgium, Canada, South Africa, and Switzerland." *American Political Science Review* 73 (2): 442–56.

————. 1984. *Democracies*. New Haven: Yale University Press.

Lindblom, Charles E. 1977. *Politics and Markets*. New York: Basic Books.

Linz, Juan, and Stepan, Alfred. 1978. *The Breakdown of Democratic Regimes*. Baltimore: Johns Hopkins University Press.

Locke, John. [1689/90] 1970. *Two Treatises of Government*. 2d ed., ed. Peter Laslett. Cambridge: Cambridge University Press.

Lorwin, Val. 1966. "Belgium: Religion, Class, and Language in National Politics." In R. A. Dahl, ed., *Political Oppositions in Western Europe*, 147–87. New Haven: Yale University Press.

Lukes, Steven. 1977. *Essays in Social Theory*. London: Macmillan Press.

MacIntyre, Alisdair. 1966. *A Short History of Ethics*. New York: Macmillan.

———. 1984. *After Virtue*. 2d ed. Notre Dame, Ind.: University of Notre Dame Press.

MacKay, Alfred F. 1980. *Arrow's Theorem: The Paradox*. New Haven: Yale University Press.

Maclean, Douglas, ed. 1986. *The Security Gamble: Deterrence Dilemmas in the Nuclear Age*. Towota, N.J.: Rowman and Allanheld.

Mansfield, Harvey C., Jr. 1968. "Modern and Medieval Representation." In J. R. Pennock and J. W. Chapman, eds., *Representation (Nomos X)*, 55–82. New York: Atherton Press.

Marshall, T. H. 1950. *Citizenship and Social Class*. London: Cambridge University Press.

Martines, Lauro. 1979. *Power and Imagination: City States in Renaissance Italy*. New York: Knopf.

Marx, Karl. [1894] 1967. *Capital, A Critique of Political Economy*. Vol. 3, *The Process of Capitalist Production as a Whole*. New York: International Publishers.

May, Kenneth. 1952. "A Set of Independent Necessary and Sufficient Conditions for Simple Majority Decision." *Econometrica* 10: 680–84.

McCarthy, Thomas. 1978. *The Critical Theory of Jurgen Habermas*. Cambridge: MIT Press.

McRae, Kenneth, ed. 1974a. *Consociational Democracy: Political Accommodation in Segmented Societies*. Toronto: McClelland and Stewart.

———. 1974b. "Consociationalism in the Canadian Political System." In Kenneth McRae, ed., *Consociational Democracy: Political Accommodation in Segmented Societies*, 238–61. Toronto: McClelland and Stewart.

McDonagh, Eileen L., and Price, H. Douglas. 1985. "Woman Suffrage in the Progressive Era: Patterns of Opposition and Support in Referenda Voting, 1910–1918." *American Political Science Review* 79 (2): 415–35.

Meisel, James H. 1958. *The Myth of the Ruling Class: Gaetano Mosca and the "Elite."* Ann Arbor: University of Michigan Press.

Michels, Robert. 1962. *Political Parties: A Sociological Study of the Oligarchical Tendencies of Modern Parties*. Trans. E. Paul and C. Paul; intro. S. M. Lipset. New York: Collier Books.

Mill, John Stuart. [1861] 1958. *Considerations on Representative Government*. Ed. C. V. Shields. Indianapolis: Bobbs-Merrill.

———. [1859] 1962a. *On Liberty*. In *John Stuart Mill, Utilitarianism and Other Writings*. New York: New American Library.

———. [1863] 1962b. *Utilitarianism*. In *John Stuart Mill, Utilitarianism and Other Writings*. New York: New American Library.

Miller, James Grier. 1978. *Living Systems*. New York: McGraw Hill.

Mills, C. Wright. 1956. *The Power Elite*. New York: Oxford University Press.

Mokkan, R. J., and Stokman, F. N. 1976. "Power and Influence as Political Phenomena."

In Brian Barry, ed., *Power and Political Theory: Some European Perspectives*, 33–54. New York: John Wiley.

Montesquieu, Charles-Louis de Secondat, Baron de. [1748] 1961. *De l'Esprit des lois*. 2 vols. Paris: Editions Garnier Frères.

Montgomery, Hugo. 1983. *The Way to Chaeronea: Foreign Policy, Decision-making and Political Influence in Demosthenes' Speeches*. Oslo: Universitetsforlaget.

Moon, J. Donald. 1987. "Thin Selves, Rich Lives." Paper prepared for the annual meeting of the American Political Science Association, August 27–31.

Morlino, Leonardo. 1980. *Come Cambiano i Regimi Politici*. Milan: Franco Angelo Editore.

Mosca, Gaetano. 1923. *Elementi di Scienza Politica*. 2d ed. Turin: Fratelli Bocca Editori.

———. 1925. *Teorica dei Governi e Governo Parlamentare*. Milan: Soc. An. Istituto Editoriale Scientifico.

Nagel, Thomas. 1979. *Mortal Questions*. Cambridge: Cambridge University Press.

Nelson, William N. 1980. *On Justifying Democracy*. London: Routledge and Kegan Paul.

Noel, S. J. R. 1974. "Consociational Democracy and Canadian Federalism." In Kenneth McRae, ed., *Consociational Democracy: Political Accommodation in Segmented Societies*, 262–68. Toronto: McClelland and Stewart.

Nordlinger, Eric. 1972. *Conflict Regulation in Divided Societies*. Cambridge: Center for International Affairs, Harvard University.

———. 1977. *Soldiers in Politics: Military Coups and Government*. Englewood Cliffs: Prentice-Hall.

Nove, Alec. 1983. *The Economics of Feasible Socialism*. London: George Allen and Unwin.

Nozick, Robert. 1974. *Anarchy, State, and Utopia*. New York: Basic Books.

O'Donnell, Guillermo. 1978. "Permanent Crisis and the Failure to Create a Democratic Regime: Argentina." In Juan Linz and Alfred Stepan, eds., *The Breakdown of Democratic Regimes*, part III, 138–77. Baltimore: Johns Hopkins University Press.

O'Donnell, Guillermo; Schmitter, Philippe C.; and Whitehead, Laurence, eds. *Transitions from Authoritarian Rule*. Baltimore: Johns Hopkins University Press.

Oppenheim, Felix. 1981. *Political Concepts*. Chicago: University of Chicago Press.

Ormsby, William. 1974. "The Province of Canada. The Emergence of Consociational Politics." In Kenneth McRae, ed. *Consociational Democracy: Political Accommodation in Segmented Societies*, 269–74. Toronto: McClelland and Stewart.

Oxford English Dictionary. 1971. *Compact Edition*. 2 vols. s.v. "Intellectual." New York: Oxford University Press.

Palmer, Robert R. 1959. *The Age of the Democratic Revolution: A Political History of Europe and America, 1760–1800*. Princeton: Princeton University Press.

Pareto, Vilfredo. 1926. *Les Systèmes Socialistes*. 2d ed. 2 vols. Paris: Marcel Giard.

———. 1935. *The Mind and Society*. 4 vols. Ed. Arthur Livingston; trans. Andrew Bongiorno and Arthur Livingston. New York: Harcourt Brace.

———. 1966. *Sociological Writings*. Selected and introduced by S. E. Finer; trans. Derick Mirfin. New York: Frederick A. Praeger.

Pateman, Carole. 1970. *Participation and Democratic Theory*. Cambridge: Cambridge University Press.

Pellicani, Luciano. 1976. *Gramsci e la questione communista*. Florence: Vallechi.

Pennati, Eugenio. 1961a. *Elementi di sociologia politica*. Milan: Edizioni di Comunità.

———. 1961b. "Le élites politiche nelle teoriche minoritarie." In R. Treves, ed., *Le élites politiche*. Bari: Editori Laterza.

Pennock, J. R., and Chapman, J. W., eds. 1967. *Equality (Nomos IX)*. New York: Atherton Press.

―――. 1968. *Representation (Nomos X)*. New York: Atherton Press.

―――. 1970. *Political and Legal Obligation (Nomos XII)*. New York: Atherton Press.

―――. 1977. *Due Process (Nomos XVIII)*. New York: New York University Press.

―――. 1978. *Anarchism (Nomos XIX)*. New York: New York University Press.

―――. 1983. *Liberal Democracy (Nomos XXV)*. New York: New York University Press.

Perlmutter, Amos. 1977. *The Military and Politics in Modern Times*. New Haven: Yale University Press.

Plamenatz, John. 1973. *Democracy and Illusion*. London: Longman.

Plato. 1937. *The Dialogues of Plato*. 2 vols. Trans. B. Jowett. New York: Random House.

―――. 1974. *Plato's Republic*. Trans. G. M. A. Grube. Indianapolis: Hacket.

Pocock, J. G. A. 1975. *The Machiavellian Moment*. Princeton: Princeton University Press.

Pullan, Brian. 1972. *A History of Early Renaissance Italy*. New York: St. Martin's Press.

Rae, Douglas. 1969. "Decision-Rules and Individual Values in Constitutional Choice." *American Political Science Review* 63 (1): 40–56.

―――. 1975a. "Maximin Justice and an Alternative Principle of General Advantage." *American Political Science Review* 69 (2): 630–47.

―――. 1975b. "The Limits of Consensual Decision." *American Political Science Review* 69 (4): 1270–94.

―――. 1979. "A Principle of Simple Justice." In Peter Laslett and James W. Fishkin, eds., *Philosophy, Politics, and Society*, Fifth Series, 134–54. New Haven: Yale University Press.

―――. 1981. *Equalities*. Cambridge: Harvard University Press.

Rawls, John. 1971. *A Theory of Justice*. Cambridge: Harvard University Press.

Riker, William, and Weingast, Barry R. 1986. "Constitutional Regulation of Legislative Choice: The Political Consequences of Judicial Deference to Legislatures." Stanford: Hoover Institution.

Riker, William. 1982. *Liberalism Against Populism*. San Francisco: W. H. Freeman.

Riley, Patrick. 1978. "On the 'Kantian' Foundations of Robert Paul Wolff's Anarchism." In J. Roland Pennock and John W. Chapman, eds., *Anarchism (Nomos XIX)*, 294–319. New York: New York University Press.

Rokkan, Stein. 1966. "Norway: Numerical Democracy and Corporate Pluralism." In R. A. Dahl, ed., *Political Oppositions in Western Europe*, 70–115. New Haven: Yale University Press.

Rosen, F. 1983. *Jeremy Bentham and Representative Democracy*. Oxford: Oxford University Press.

Rousseau, Jean-Jacques. [1762] 1978. *On the Social Contract, with Geneva Manuscript and Political Economy*. Ed. Roger D. Masters and Judith R. Masters. New York: St. Martin's Press.

Russett, Bruce M. 1984. "Ethical Dilemmas of Nuclear Deterrence." *International Security* 9: 36–54.

Sartori, Giovanni. 1961 "I significati del termine élite." In R. Treves, ed., *Le élites politiche*. Bari: Editore Laterza.

Sabine, George. 1964. *A History of Political Theory*. 3d ed. New York: Holt, Rinehart, and Winston.

Sánchez Vásquez, Adolfo. 1977. *The Philosophy of Praxis*. London: Merlin Press.

Sandel, Michael. 1982. *Liberalism and the Limits of Justice*. New York: Cambridge University Press.

Schumpeter, Joseph A. 1947. *Capitalism, Socialism and Democracy*. 2d ed. New York: Harper and Brothers.

Sealey, Raphael. 1976. *A History of the Greek City States ca. 700—338 B.C.* Berkeley: University of California Press.

Selucký, Radoslav. 1979. *Marxism, Socialism, Freedom*. New York: St. Martin's Press.

Shapiro, Ian. 1987. "Notes on the republican ideal in American politics, history and political theory." Manuscript.

———. 1989. "Three Fallacies Concerning Majorities, Minorities, and Democratic Politics." In John Chapman and Alan Wertheimer, eds., *Majorities and Minorities (Nomos XXXII)*. New York: New York University Press.

Shils, Edward. "Intellectuals." In *International Encyclopedia of Social Sciences*. 17 vols. 7:399–414. New York: Macmillan and the Free Press.

Simon, Herbert A. 1983. *Reason in Human Affairs*. Stanford: Stanford University Press.

Smith, Peter H. 1978. "The Breakdown of Democracy in Argentina, 1916–30." In Juan Linz and Alfred Stepan, eds., *The Breakdown of Democratic Regimes*, part III, 3–27. Baltimore: Johns Hopkins University Press.

Sniderman, Paul M. 1975. *Personality and Democratic Politics*. Berkeley: University of California Press.

Sola, Giorgi. 1982. "Elements for a Critical Reappraisal of the Works of Gaetano Mosca." In E. A. Albertoni, ed., *Studies in the Political Thought of Gaetano Mosca*. Milan: Giuffré editore.

Somjee, A. H. 1967. "Individuality and Equality in Hinduism." In J. R. Pennock and J. W. Chapman, eds., *Equality (Nomos IX)*, 177–92. New York: Atherton Press.

Spitz, Elaine. 1984. *Majority Rule*. Chatham, N.J.: Chatham House.

Ste. Croix, G. E. M. de. 1981. *The Class Struggle in the Ancient Greek World, from the Archaic Age to the Arab Conquests*. Ithaca: Cornell University Press.

Steiner, Jurg. 1974. *Amicable Agreement versus Majority Rule: Conflict Resolution in Switzerland*. Rev. ed. Chapel Hill: University of North Carolina Press.

Steiner, Kurt. 1972. *Politics in Austria*. Boston: Little, Brown.

Stepan, Alfred. 1971. *The Military in Politics: Changing Patterns in Brazil*. Princeton: Princeton University Press.

———. 1973. "The New Professionalism of Internal Warfare and Military Role Expansion." In Alfred Stepan, ed., *Authoritarian Brazil*, 47–65. New Haven: Yale University Press.

Stephens, Evelyne Huber, and Stephens, John. 1987. "Democracy and Authoritarianism in the Caribbean Basin." Prepared for delivery at the XII International Congress of the Caribbean Studies Association, Belize, May 26–29.

Still, Jonathan W. 1981. "Political Equality and Election Systems." *Ethics* 91 (3): 375–94.

Svensson, Palle. 1987. *The Development of Danish Polyarchy—or How Liberalization Also Preceded Inclusiveness in Denmark*. Aarhus: Institute of Political Science.

Sivard, Ruth Leger. 1986. *World Military and Social Expenditures*. 11th ed. Washington: World Priorities.

Taylor, Charles Lewis, and Hudson, Michael. 1972. *World Handbook of Political and Social Indicators*. New Haven: Yale University Press.

Taylor, Lily Ross. 1961. *Party Politics in the Age of Caesar*. Berkeley: University of California Press.

———. 1966. *Roman Voting Assemblies*. Ann Arbor: University of Michigan Press.

Thomas, H., and Logan, C. 1982. *Mondragon: An Economic Analysis*. London: Allen and Unwin.

Thompson, Dennis F. 1976. *John Stuart Mill and Representative Government*. Princeton: Princeton University Press.

Thucydides. 1951. *The Peloponnesian War*. Trans. John H. Finley, Jr. New York: Random House.

Tocqueville, Alexis de. 1961. *Democracy in America*. Vol. 1 (1835) and vol. 2 (1840). New York: Schocken Books.

Tracy, destutt de. 1811. *A Commentary and Review of Montesquieu's Spirit of Laws*. Philadelphia.

Treves, Renato, ed. 1961. *Le élites politiche*. Bari: Editori Laterza.

Trudeau, Robert, and Schoultz, Lars. 1986. "Guatemala." In Morris J. Blachman, William M. LeoGrande, and Kenneth Sharpe, eds.. *Confronting Revolution: Security Through Diplomacy in Central America*, 23–49. New York: Pantheon.

Turner, Frank M. 1981. *The Greek Heritage in Victorian Britain*. New Haven: Yale University Press.

Unger, Roberto Mangabeira. 1975. *Knowledge and Politics*. New York: Free Press.

U. S. Bureau of the Census. 1960. *Historical Statistics of the United States, Colonial Times to 1957*. Washington: U.S. Government Printing Office.

———. 1986. *Statistical Abstracts*.

Vanhanen, Tatu. 1984. *The Emergence of Democracy: A Comparative Study of 119 States, 1850–1979*. Helsinki: Finnish Society of Arts and Letters.

Walzer, Michael. 1983. *Spheres of Justice*. New York: Basic Books.

*Webster's Seventh New Collegiate Dictionary*. 1965.

Webb, Sidney, and Webb, Beatrice. 1920. *Industrial Democracy*. London: Longman, Green.

Whelan, Frederick G. 1983. "Prologue: Democratic Theory and the Boundary Problem." In J. Roland Pennock and John W. Chapman, eds., *Liberal Democracy (Nomos XXV)*, 13–48. New York: New York University Press.

Wildavsky, Aaron. 1986. "The New American Dilemma: Liberal Democracy and School Desegregation." *Constitutional Commentary* 3 (1): 161–73.

Wills, Garry. 1978. *Inventing America*. Garden City, N.Y.: Doubleday.

Wolff, Robert Paul. 1976. *In Defense of Anarchism, with a Reply to Jeffrey H. Reiman's* "In Defense of Political Philosophy." New York: Harper and Row.

Wood, Gordon S. 1969. *The Creation of the American Republic 1776–1787*. Chapel Hill: University of North Carolina Press.

Woodhouse, A. S. P. 1938. *Puritanism and Liberty*. Chicago: University of Chicago Press.

Yack, Bernard. 1985. "Community and Conflict in Aristotle's Political Philosophy." *The Review of Politics* 45:92–112.

# INDEX

Accountability, and polyarchy, 234–35
Adams, Willi Paul, 360n2
Administrative offices, citizen participation and, 15, 19, 20
Advanced democratic country, 322–41; capitalist versus democratic perspective and, 324–26; citizenship in, 338–41; economic order in, 324–32; internal governments of firms, 327–32; minipopulus in, 340; state government in, 332–41. *See also* Transnational political systems
Africa, 239
Agenda, control of: binding decisions and, 107; as criterion for democratic process, 112–14; federal systems and, 198–201; and majority rule, 146; minority domination and, 277, 278; transnational federalism and, 198
Aggression, 229–30
Agrarian society, 253–54
Almond, G. A., 339, 370n7–371n8
Anarchism: assumptions in, 39–41; conclusions of, 41–42; critique of, 43–47; empirical issues in, 44–45; objections to democracy from, 37–42, 50–51; voluntary associations in, 37, 38, 41; Wolff's defense of, 42–43
Anonymity, requirement of, 139, 141
Arbenz, Jacobo Guzmán, 366n10

Argentina, 262
Aristocracy: in republican tradition, 25–26; in Republic of Venice, 64, 99, 123
Aristotle, 141, 367n3; *The Politics*, 106; republican tradition and, 24, 25–26, 299–301; slavery and, 120
Arrow, Kenneth, 146
Assembly: in Greek polis, 16–17, 21; representative government and, 28–29
Associations, 327; autonomous, in nation-states, 318; democratic process and, 227, 228–29; interests of the unorganized and, 296–97; kinds of, and criterion for democratic process, 106–07, 130; necessity of, and public good, 295; types of, as democratic units, 193–94; voluntary, in anarchism, 37, 38, 41. *See also* Anarchism; Economic enterprises; Federalism
Athens. *See* Classical Greece
Attentive public, 339–40
Australia, 159, 216, 235
Austria, 364n23; decision rule in, 159; polyarchy in, 235; subcultural pluralism and, 256, 257, 258
Authoritarian regimes: growth of polyarchy and, 235, 239, 314–15; idea of democracy and, 233; justified as transitional, 349n6; language of democracy and, 2, 6